COMPUTER ANIMATION

COMPUTER ANIMATION

Neal Weinstock

Addison-Wesley Publishing Company, Inc.
Reading, Massachusetts • Menlo Park, California
Don Mills, Ontario • Wokingham, England • Amsterdam
Sydney • Singapore • Tokyo • Madrid • Bogotà
Santiago • San Juan

Credits for art in 4-color insert can be found on page 335.

Many of the designations used by manufacturers and sellers to distinguish their products are claimed as trademarks. Where those designations appear in this book and Addison-Wesley was aware of a trademark claim, the designations have been printed in initial caps (for example, VisiCalc) or all caps (for example, UNIX).

Library of Congress Cataloging-in-Publication Data

Weinstock, Neal.
Computer animation.

Bibliography: p.
Includes index.
1. Computer animation. I. Title.
TR897.5.W45 1986 778.5'347'0285 86-7895
ISBN 0-201-09438-X

Cover design by Steve Snider
Text design by Joyce C. Weston, Boston, MA
Set in 11 point Baskerville by Pine Tree Composition, Inc., Lewiston, ME

ABCDEFGHIJ-HA-89876
First printing, October 1986

Contents

Acknowledgments *xi*
Introduction *xiii*

1. Computer-Generated Imagery: An Introduction to the Technology **1**

1.1 Theory and Hardware *3*
1.2 Fractals *6*
1.3 Matching Computers and Television *9*
1.4 Raster Resolution *14*
1.5 Anti-Aliasing *16*
1.6 Raster Data Compression *18*
1.7 Frame Buffers and Windows *19*
1.8 Interacting with Technology *20*

2. Personal Computer Hardware for Graphics and Animation **23**

2.1 Resolution *24*
2.2 Aliasing *24*
2.3 Color Resolution *25*
2.4 Moving Simple Pictures is Easier Than Moving Complex Pictures *26*
2.5 Input Components *27*
The Keyboard *27*
Digitizing Tablets *27*
Light Pens *27*
Joy Sticks, Mice, Track Balls, Dials, etc. *28*
2.6 Image Digitization *29*
2.7 Memory and Processing Speed *29*

2.8 Output Components *30*
Monitors *30*
Video Recorders *30*
Film Recorders *31*
Plotters *33*
Videodisk *33*
2.9 Read Before You Buy; Program Before You Read *34*

3. Packaged Goods 35

3.1 From Pioneers to Consultants to Turnkey Systems *35*
3.2 Stage 2 *37*
3.3 Animation Programs *39*
3.4 Windows and Viewports *40*
3.5 Frame Buffers *41*
3.6 Stage 3 *42*

4. Programming Goals 46

4.1 Software Levels *46*
4.2 The Move to Higher-Level Languages *47*
4.3 The "Core" *47*
4.4 Comparing Languages and Operating Systems *48*
4.5 Beyond BASIC *50*
4.6 A Beginning Analysis of the Parts of a Graphics Program Package *50*
4.7 Logical Steps in the Graphics Creation Process *53*
4.8 Design Goals *59*
4.9 Production Planning *62*
4.10 Input Transformation *63*
4.11 Interactive Programming *65*

5. BASIC Graphics on the IBM PC 66

5.1 IBM BASIC Graphics Structure *67*
5.2 Hexadecimals *68*
5.3 Bit Mapping *70*
5.4 Coordinate Systems *72*
5.5 Basic BASIC Animation Graphics Vocabulary *74*
5.6 Point and Line to Plane *76*
5.7 The Hidden-Line Problem *79*
5.8 Relative Coordinates *80*
5.9 Circles *81*

5.10 PAINT *82*
5.11 WINDOW *83*
5.12 Viewports *85*
5.13 DRAW *87*
5.14 GET and PUT, BLOAD and BSAVE *88*
5.15 Computer-Assisted Animation Via the PC *89*

6. Programming Graphics and Animation in C, and Beginning the Palette Choice Program 90

6.1 Introduction to C *90*
6.2 Fundamentals *93*
6.3 Constants and Variables *95*
6.4 Program Looping and Recursive Functions *100*
6.5 **while, do,** Image Flipping, and Color Cycling *103*
6.6 **if, else,** Nested Statements . . . and a Color Palette Program Begins to Take Shape *106*
6.7 Compound Relational Operators *111*
6.8 **switch** *113*
6.9 Flags *115*
6.10 The Unexpected Input Bug *117*
6.11 Pointers *121*
6.12 Why Write This Program Providing Variable Palettes? *122*

7. C Functions, Structures, and Arrays 126

7.1 Developing Algorithms: Top-Down or Bottom-Up *126*
7.2 Functions *129*
7.3 Arrays *132*
7.4 A Parenthesis: Looking Forward to Addressing Memory Directly, and Knowing When to Do So *137*
7.5 Clearing the Screen, and a Quick Look at the Preprogrammer *139*
7.6 More on I/O *141*
7.7 Structures of Arrays of Arrays of Pointers to Memory Locations: The Basics of Commanding the Screen *143*
7.8 Dynamic Memory Allocation *146*
7.9 Operations on Bits *149*
7.10 A Parenthetical Note on Octals and Hexadecimals in C, and a Program for Converting Bases *153*
7.11 Accessing Bits Within Variables *158*
7.12 Bit Fields *160*

8. Implementing More Complex Algorithms 165

8.1 Finishing the Palette Program and Building a Paint Program *165*
8.2 Structuring a Graphics Library *168*
8.3 Building a Frame Buffer in RAM *172*
8.4 Macros to Redefine the Buffer Array *174*
8.5 Initializing the Buffer Array *175*
8.6 Beyond the Frame Buffer to the Paint *176*
8.7 Assigning Color to Pixels *177*
8.8 The Large Palette *180*
8.9 Color Cycling *184*
8.10 Filling in Outlines and Defining Images for Animation *185*
8.11 Analytic Geometry, Vector-Style Graphics, and 3D *186*
8.12 Image Transforms *188*
8.13 Windows and Viewports, Again *190*
8.14 In-betweening, and Calculating How Many Buffers You Can Afford *191*
8.15 Run-Length Encoding *194*
8.16 Vector Images Revisited *195*

9. Topics in the State of the Art 198

9.1 Catching Up with the Seventies *198*
9.2 Polygon Meshes *199*
9.3 Curved Surfaces *201*
9.4 Fractals *201*
9.5 Depth Cueing *202*
9.6 Hidden Surfaces *203*
9.7 Shaded, Reflected, and Textured Surfaces; Ray Tracing *207*

10. Interactivity 212

10.1 Where is Real-Time Now? *212*
10.2 Graphics-Making for Nonprogrammers *213*
10.3 ROM, More ROM, and Real-Time *216*
10.4 Pseudocode for a Video Game *217*
10.5 Videodisk *218*

11. Home-Made Motion Control 220

11.1 Why Motion Control, Not CGI? *220*
11.2 Getting Started *221*

12. Interviews With Leading Animation and Effects Designers 224

12.1 Clear Vision *224*
12.2 Alex Weil's and Charlie Levi's Charlex *225*
12.3 The Brothers Greenberg *228*
12.4 Robert Abel and Associates *231*
12.5 Bo Gehring and Associates *235*
12.6 Jim Lindner and His Fantastic Animation Machine *238*

13. The Market for PC-Generated Graphics 240

13.1 Corporate Video *241*
13.2 Nonmoving Graphics for Corporate Communications *242*
13.3 Advertising Design *242*
13.4 Publishing: Layout, Typography, and Illustration *243*
13.5 Industrial Design *243*
13.6 Architectural Design *244*
13.7 Simulated Learning Situations, Such as Flight Simulation *245*
13.8 Cartography *245*
13.9 Teletext and Videotex *246*
13.10 Making Software ''Friendlier'' *247*
13.11 Computer Games *247*
13.12 What Television and the Movies are Looking For *248*

14. Where's the Future? 250

14.1 Beyond Realism *250*
14.2 Interactivity *251*
14.3 What are the Cliches? *252*
14.4 The Future Audience *256*
14.5 Selling Our Children *257*
14.6 CGI As News, and As Part of the Game *258*
14.7 Imagining Animation *258*

Appendix A: Looking Backward 261

A.1 Before the Beginning *261*
A.2 The Comics *263*
A.3 Special Effects *264*
A.4 The Optical Printer *264*
A.5 The Divergence of Shorts and Features *267*
A.6 Winsor McCay's Achievement *268*
A.7 The Factory System Comes to Animation *270*

A.8 Cel Animation *271*
A.9 Rotoscope *272*
A.10 The Fleischers and Walt Disney *272*
A.11 Disney's Competitors *274*
A.12 Technical Innovations *275*
A.13 The Animation Stand *276*
A.14 Aesthetics of Hollywood Animation *277*
A.15 Special Effects in Live-Action Feature Films *278*
A.16 Television *281*
A.17 X-Rated Cartoons *282*
A.18 TV Commercials *283*
A.19 Video Effects *283*
A.20 The Experimentalists *284*
A.21 The Myth of Our Medium *286*

Appendix B: A Guide to the North American Animation Industry **289**

B.1 Animation Studios *289*
- California *290*
- New York Metropolitan Area (including New Jersey) *295*
- Midwest *300*
- South *302*
- West (Except CA, TX) *303*
- Canada *304*
- Northeast (Except NY Metro Area) *304*

B.2 Schools *306*
- Canada *307*
- California *307*
- Midwest *308*
- Northeast *309*
- South *310*
- West *310*

B.3 Vendors of Computer Animation Equipment *311*
- PC Graphics Hardware *311*
- PC Graphics Software *314*
- CAD *315*
- Large-Computer Graphics Systems *316*
- Broadcast and Film Equipment *317*

B.4 Industry Organizations *319*

Appendix C: Glossary **321**

Bibliography **331**

Index **335**

Acknowledgments

All that is bad in this book is mine; I owe what is good in it to many very helpful souls. First and invaluably, Ted Buswick has been as creative, sharp-eyed, and patient an editor and advocate as any book could have. Thanks, of course, to all suppliers of illustrations, including Augustin Alonzo, who did many of the book's line drawings; special thanks to Bo Gehring, Robert Greenberg, Richard Greenberg, Robert Abel, Charles Levi, Alex Weil, Jim Lindner, Maija Beeton and Suzanne Gavril for their contributions and for what they have taught me. David Hawthorne was responsible for introducing me to computer animation and for beginning this book's long germination as a series of stories for *Millimeter* Magazine. Many animators and hardware and software designers taught me about their craft, art, and industry, there are too many to thank here, but hopefully all of them will find their names spelled right in the Guide to the North American Animation Industry in Appendix B of this book.

Finally, Audrey Korelstein has been more inspirational, supportive, and patient than any writer has a right to expect of any mate. This book is for her, and would not have been possible without her.

Introduction

A revolution is quietly changing the making of animated motion pictures. Computers are being employed to assist animators in so many ways that what animators do is now often referred to as "computer animation." Concurrent home computer and home video revolutions have allowed many animators to experiment with these small machines, to ease the tedium of their art at far less expense than with the minicomputers and professional film and video equipment they have been used to. The change that is coming in animation is comparable to the change in documentary filmmaking in the early sixties with the advent of portable, inexpensive 16 millimeter equipment.

In the process of this big change, concepts and programs are being developed that allow the home-computer user to make animated films with little or no need for the techniques of traditional animation. The art of animation is being separated from much of its tedium and expense; it may just be on the verge of a popular explosion.

For people long involved in making animated films and video, this explosion can't come too soon. In recent years the industry has suffered shrinking pains similar to those of most other labor-intensive, factory-based systems. As magically artistic as the best of animation appears, the process of making images move has always involved many slightly changed but wholly redrawn pictures for each second of screen time. Vast armies of "inking and painting" workers were once employed in Hollywood, especially by Walt Disney, but also by the animation departments of Warner Bros., Metro-Goldwyn-Mayer, and various independent producers. In the 1960s, smaller producers such as Hanna-Barbera found success making animated films for children's television, but won contracts partly through lower costs based on less complex, cheaper work. By the 1970s, inking and painting was being shipped out to Japan and Hong Kong, and eventually, because of labor costs alone, a sizeable proportion of the Saturday morning cartoon schedule came from Japan. It wasn't just inked and painted there; it was wholly produced there. Quality, labor-intensive animation continued to be used for special effects and a few feature film titles, as well as for fewer and fewer television commercials. But animation seemed to be no career for the young.

No career, that is, unless one could foresee how concurrent developments in computer graphics and robotics, funded by the military and the space agency, would soon open new possibilities for movies. Most observers date the beginning of computer animation from Ivan Sutherland's 1962 interactive line drawing system, developed while he was a graduate student at MIT. Called "Sketchpad," its simple drawing capabilities can now be surpassed by anyone with a microcomputer and working knowledge of BASIC. At the time, however, the possibilities of the program and its interactive hardware spurred tremendous interest from the Pentagon and from the giant military equipment manufacturers; possibilities for computer-aided design (CAD) and flight simulation were not quite self-evident, but they developed quickly.

These early examples of computer-generated imagery (CGI) were "vector" or "wire-frame" graphics. Far fewer computations are needed to plot any two points and connect those points with a line than to plot each point along a line. Vector graphics take advantage of this, plot only end-points and connecting lines, and can be drawn and redrawn quickly. Vector images developed quickly through the 1960s and 1970s. Fully formed images were soon created by filling in vector outlines. At the University of Utah, Dr. Sutherland and others developed ways to describe objects as collections of polygonal edges and surfaces, and various ways to fill in their vector images with color. The Evans & Sutherland company was formed to take advantage of commercial applications; their methods for drawing three-dimensional vector and polygonal images quickly became, and remain, the most popular way to render solid objects by computer.

In the mid-seventies, in New York, Dr. Phillip Mittelman, a physicist, was growing MAGI, a company whose basic business had little to do with computer graphics. People there had written programs to calculate the paths of radioactive particles within any environment. Mittelman realized the software also could recreate the paths of light beams through any environment, and thus could be used to create any computer-simulated object from the point of view of the light source. "Ray tracing" is what this came to be called, and MAGI–Synthevision is what MAGI's animation graphics division came to be called. Under the initial direction of Bo Gehring, their work came to define much of the best of feature film and TV commercial work at the beginning of the eighties.

Ray tracing is not a modeling method; it is a method of lighting, or exposing to view, models built either out of combinations of polygons or in some other way. After the objects are built, rays of light are traced along their paths from an imaginary camera viewing the scene back toward whatever posited light source should be illuminating the scene. The objects in the picture are shown as the light rays bounce off or bend through them. This is a very slow and complex process, but it can produce dramatically realistic lighting. Ray tracing has enjoyed great popularity lately, as computing power has advanced and as animators have continued on their technological quest to wow the quickly jaded public with ever more realistic — or hyper-real — computer creations.

On another front, computers were called on to assist in the production of more traditional animation. In "cel" (for celluloid, the material on which animators most often draw) animation, several layers of transparencies depict various parts of a picture. These are held in precise registration on a multilevel table, with light shown through them either from underneath (bottom-lit) or from above (top-lit). A film camera looks down on the image on the table and shoots off, typically, two frames of each slightly different image. (Standard American film speed is 24 frames per second; film runs at 25 fps in countries with 50 Hz electrical systems, but 12 fps is quite sufficient for "persistence of vision," the phenomenon that allows us to perceive motion when viewing a series of quickly changed, unmoving images.) Combining the several layers of cels with standard Renaissance techniques of perspective allows for as much of a sense of three-dimensionality as the animator has the talent, patience, and budget to achieve.

Unfortunately, patience and budget have been the variables in shortest supply in recent years. The first computer-controlled animation stand, made by Oxberry (a long-time supplier of animation and special-effects hardware) in the early seventies harnessed the power of a minicomputer to remember and infinitely repeat the many slight changes in focal length, exposure, camera position, and image position that must be made for each shot of an animated film: twelve sets of changes for every second of screen time. The first application of robotics in filmmaking was born. As more powerful and cheaper computers allowed the computer-controlled animation stand to control more of the processes of animation, other companies — in particular Elicon, a hardware maker, and Robert Abel, a producer and director of TV commercials, feature film special effects and title sequences — turned the idea of Oxberry's stand on its side to create "motion control" tracks for photographing three-dimensional models frame by frame. Another special-effects device, the optical printer, also lent itself to computer control. By the middle of the 1980s, the computing power necessary to control these mechanical devices could be purchased for the price of a microcomputer.

So far, as fancy as the images get, we've described only computerized equipment that creates images which also could be created with nineteenth-century filmmaking technology, albeit with perhaps millions of hours of labor. In fact, most animated effects were pioneered from the early years of this century to the 1920s. Computers make these effects more efficient, more elegant, and more convincing, but the *structure* and *syntax* of modern computer animation has been determined very much by what was once possible with mechanical devices alone. The current generation of leading animators is well aware of this phenomenon as a creative gap between what computers may make technically feasible and what human minds can presently use these machines to imagine. It will be up to a generation that grows up intimately acquainted with generating graphic animation on microcomputers to create images that demonstrate a full understanding of the technology they use and that truly stretch that technology.

In other words, it was only with the rise of the generation of feature filmmakers led by Orson Welles, Roberto Rossellini, and later Federico Fellini, Jean-Luc Godard, and many others that motion-picture makers could make movies that understood the process of making movies — after a 50 to 75-year history of the medium. It will take a generation similarly raised on computer animation to take that form to the heights (or depths) of self-conscious art. One foreseeable avenue for development is already occurring in the hybridization of animation and audience interactivity. Video games seem to this author (among many others) to be a harbinger of new entertainment and information forms that will be as important to the next century as the movies and television have been to this one.

Both movies and video games, however, have most often given pleasure as unself-conscious art. Computer animation has given wide movie audiences a great deal of pleasure that, however technically sophisticated, has been most often seen by critics as dramatically meaningless. Yet there must be some meaning here that audiences are responding to, for audiences *are* responding. To anyone who would make animation that reaches its audience, it is important to understand how traditional animation has always done so, why audiences are currently drawn to the sort of computer animation they are drawn to, and what sort of hybrids of animation and other present and future computer technologies are possible.

Possible today. With a microcomputer. I hope in this volume to bring together the history and the technology that is right now evolving into the laps of microcomputer owners, and to point to some directions where we might take it all.

There will be a good deal of highly technical material presented here, but it is presented in the belief that artists must know their brushes and how to mix their paint. Many animation tools are on the market these days, but few of them ever allow users to understand what they are doing. If you don't understand why your paint simulation system does what it does, the pictures you make will reflect that lack of depth. A picture "painted" by computer can be either a tremendously expensive and inefficient way to simulate what real paints and canvas or paper do quite well (admittedly, adding the dimension of electronically storing and manipulating that image) or, with some understanding of the tools, a way to boldly go where paints and paper cannot.

This book will not demand much background in motion pictures beyond that provided by the average freely acquired lifetime in front of a television set, but there is a limit to the depth to which space will allow an examination of the history of film animation and both film and video special effects, or critical studies of these media. Please note the bibliography; there are many works without which this one would have been impossible, and a reading of which will impart far more meaning to my poor effort. It is supposed that the reader has some experience at the keyboard of a microcomputer and has one handy. It would be helpful if this is not the reader's first encounter with computer programming, but the sort of logical background provided by a knowledge of some BASIC, combined with an understanding of college-level algebra and geometry, ought to suffice. For less-technically grounded readers, a theoretical and historical understanding of the subject matter can be grasped while skipping the more technical chapters.

Finally, no other volume available today presents and collates as much information, about everyone in North America who is professionally involved in computer animation. There is a good deal more information that might be provided to students and industry participants. Please tell us what improvements you would suggest for future editions.

CHAPTER ONE

Computer-Generated Imagery: An Introduction to the Technology

Computer-generated imagery (CGI, or sometimes CIG) commonly refers to images built entirely in computer memory. Thus not every image created with the help of a computer is necessarily CGI — it may be mere computer-*assisted* imagery, a moniker not common enough for a generally accepted acronym, but common enough to be understood in the animation industry as meaning the use of a computer to speed otherwise standard animation. CGI images may be produced directly, by programming, or they may be created by manipulating the sundry devices that allow humans to communicate with their computers: digitizing tablets, light pens, track balls, mice, joy sticks, etc. Of course, much of the image content produced with these devices must already have been created by programming. Perhaps the original programming can be better described as producing latent images — images brought to a point of being almost produced.

Think of computer images as falling into several categories with many subdivisions. The two broadest classes of images, into one of which all computer-produced pictures fall, are

1. those that are inherently mathematical; these can be produced only by programming;
2. those with no wholly underlying mathematical basis.

The classic image of Mickey Mouse, for example, cannot be conveniently programmed, but must be assembled in its own arbitrary way from mathematical elements. The general outline of Mickey's head may be a perfect sphere, his ears may be mathematically defined filled-doughnut shapes, but something beyond algebra and geometry is needed to attach the ears to the head, shade them, and move them in a lifelike manner. Obviously, most computer animation falls into the second category. (To this observer, some of the most interesting work, aesthetically, pits second-category characters against a first-category landscape. Unfortunately, the Disney film *Tron,* which did this as well as could be done at the time, was so far from a commercial success that there have been no other large efforts since, so take my advice gingerly!)

Almost as obviously, somebody designing CGI on a system that has been programmed to accept input from light pen, joy stick, et al., has creative choices both made possible and limited by the system's operative programming. The programmer holds the key to creative CGI. Users who do not write their own programs may indeed produce creative and interesting work, but their work is really a partnership with the programmer. In certain respects, the user's imagination may take action only within the bounds of the programmer's imagination. Similarly, the programmer's imagination can work only within the bounds of the system designer's (who may or may not be the same person as the programmer), who in turn works within the bounds of the few sorts of systems for CGI thus far invented. These limits on the imagination of the next designer down the road are neither tight nor overt. For example, programmers always have managed to come up with ideas that hardware designers never imagined for their machines. Interactive graphics system users can similarly expand programmers' creations. However, given our long experience with this sort of thing, the ways in which they do so must be somewhat limited, and also predictable. Such prognostication will be attempted later in this volume.

The next two subsets of the main classes of CGI are two-dimensional (2D) and three-dimensional (3D) images. The differences between them are more than one-dimensional, oddly enough. Animators have built upon the strengths of each dimensionality, so that each has evolved in a different philosophical direction. Three-dimensional "solids modeling" is heavily geometrical, even if the end product is made of so many assemblages of mathematical building blocks that it has no obvious mathematical roots. Mickey Mouse could be built in 3D this way, but using the computing power necessary to build him in three full dimensions might limit the memory available to fully color him in, or to fully animate him. Compromises have been necessary in 3D imaging, so vector images, or line drawings, have been with us since the beginnings of computer graphics.

To define a straight line, you need to plot two points; for a curved line, a limited number of other points would be necessary. Plotting this limited number of points and then moving the objects so plotted involves far less memory than would be needed to move fully realized raster graphics (that is, images with all pixels in a typical, raster line-scanning cathode ray tube filled in). The classification system splits again, between vector and raster graphics, but this split overlays somewhat that between 3D and 2D; if you make another compromise and represent only two dimensions, then manipulating full raster images is easier. Thus, 3D images have tended toward vector graphics, which can be time-consumingly filled in and colored to present realistic objects; 2D images have tended toward raster graphics with programs to allow nonprogrammers to easily manipulate pseudobrushes and paint traditional animation on digitizing tablets or touch-sensitive screens.

Of course, progress makes things more complex. With more memory constantly becoming available, 3D graphics have recently begun to go raster, too.

1.1 Theory and Hardware

As may already be apparent, making a decision, say to go with either raster or vector graphics, is actually part of a system of compromises that involves assembling a set of choices. Not least among the variables that affect those choices are the hardware components that must make up a vector or raster, or 2D or 3D system. Three-dimensional vector graphics is the child of mathematical modeling. It has engendered, among other hardware that continues to be used for 2D and 3D raster graphics, two display devices now on the way to obsolescence but nonetheless worthy of mention here. The oldest, the direct view storage tube (DVST), displays vector images very quickly, with good brightness variation in monochrome, and with no image refresh needed. This means the screen never flickers, but it also means any image must be physically erased to be removed from the screen. Thus it is impossible to use a DVST for real-time animation. Micro users who find old DVSTs may put them to use by photographing off the screen and animating the film, as described later in this book.

The DVST was soon adapted to a refreshed video vector display that does not suffer from flicker because only that portion of the image that changes is completely redrawn. This continues to be the display system most commonly used in making 3D animation.

Ray tracing and polygonal modeling have already been introduced briefly. Both are strictly mathematical, but can be worked on with interactive tools after initial creation, to produce more-than-math images, too. Polygonal modeling, modeling of curved surfaces, and fractal modeling are the major ways of describing three-dimensional objects in CGI. Ray tracing is the best process yet devised to properly light those images once they are built. Any or all might be used for raster images, in full 3D color, or for vector graphics.

First came the "wire-frame" look: vector graphics in two dimensions and soon in three, and soon also in more than three dimensions, hard to visualize though that may be. In three-dimensional images, wire-frames (a purely analogous, descriptive image term) can be thought of as edges of polygons or as lines of sight. They can be monochromatic or colored, and either way (certainly even moreso in the former) take up far less computing power than a completely filled-in image, so they can be executed more complexly and faster than raster images. For more realistic images, though, somehow the lines must be filled in with planes of color. A common way to make full two or three-dimensional shapes by computer is to draw outlines first, then fill in defined areas: painting by numbers. This game plan can be standard operating procedure for both vector and raster graphics, as you'll see.

A defined area of a vector image could be filled in by one of two means: the planar surface could be filled with the defined color all at once, or it could be filled line by line, with parallel repetitions of any of the defining edge lines. The latter method is the easiest in terms of programming and cheapest in terms of memory, though it would take longer to implement with limited memory. It also may seem to violate the mathematical purity of defining edge lines; lines used to fill space are not lines that are purely the shortest distance between points. That any physical representation of a line must take up space in two dimensions is normally not of use to mathematicians, but to artists it is of common use; here computer graphics programming first crossed the line dividing science and art. That line was to get very muddy, from numerous crossings soon to come.

It is easier to program a line-by-line filling up of space than to fill a defined plane, because the code for line drawing already has been written. Little or no more memory need be taken up by this manner of filling planar space. Memory was at even more of a premium in the early days of CGI than now (and a defining condition of CGI is probably that memory will always be at a premium), with batch programming languages stretched to describe graphical phenomena for which they were ill suited, and of course, with much smaller and less versatile memories to hold the long, unwieldy codes. Advances in three-dimensional solids modeling in particular were constantly defined by advances in available memory. Filling two-dimensional planes that were part of 3D models involved the same choice of processes as plane-filling in 2D pictures; but with even less memory to go around, the only choice for filling in planes was line-by-line repetition.

Line-by-line filling-in is still done in some 3D graphic work where memory remains at a premium despite vastly expanded hardware technology and more efficient programs in more efficient languages. Though most micro users making animation will be limited to 2D work, they will be unable to resort to the vector graphic (or, by extension, line-by-line fill-in of vector images) alternative; micro systems are generally built for raster display, so micro compromises must usually take place within a raster framework.

There is almost always some compromise that needs to be made in terms of memory usage, but in most 3D work, and in practically all 2D work, filling-in has long been done by making planar images in the first place. Doing so entails using a different type of monitor than had previously been used for CGI.

That "different" monitor is the same sort that we are used to using for television display: a raster line scan that fills the whole screen surface. With monochromatic output of vector graphics, it is possible to use a different sort of display, one that only shows lines where they have been drawn by computer, and that traces those lines with a direct electron path from point to point, as opposed to the constant, horizontal, full-screen sweep of a raster scan pattern. A monochromatic vector display can easily have far higher line resolution than a color raster display. Thus vector graphics save display memory space, as well as internal memory for all sorts of complicated 3D forms and movements, at the price of displaying these images as monochrome wire-frames.

It is not very difficult to make a monochrome wire-frame drawing into a fully realized color image; it's just tedious. It is far less tedious, however, than traditional animation. How are colors achieved with a monochromatic display? The imaging system must be programmed to understand which area of an object would have how strong a shade of which primary visual colors. Three images actually would be produced for each final picture, one shaded for only green, one for blue, and one for red. The shaded areas for each would be filled in line by line (a vector monitor can only display such lines), either with lines farther apart for darker shades (the simplest, crudest, and least memory-intensive method), or with a variable intensity rating for defined picture elements or "pixels" on the screen. All three primitives would then be exposed onto the same frame of color film in a film recorder, the monochrome representing green light would be filtered green, the monochrome representing blue light would be filtered blue, and the monochrome representing red light would be filtered red.

Two fairly standard formats for CGI were developed at the end of the seventies. One involved 2D, full-color raster images and became known as ''paint systems.'' The other involved 3D, monochromatic wire-frames built of geometrical primitives cobbled together, which could be augmented by filling-in of planar surfaces and coloring, possibly done with ray-tracing techniques (tracing the path of light rays backward from the viewer's perspective to or through the object.) Obviously, these techniques did not allow for ''real-time'' animation, but as this book is being written, the frontier of animation graphics has moved on. Memory power and language power have advanced so far (with most code for professional work now being written in the flexible, machine-transportable C language, typically using a form of the Unix operating system) that animators can create 3D raster graphics images, building solid-model shapes that are easily filled with color.

To do so, polygonal modeling, curved-surface projections of quadratic equations, or any mathematical formula that can be used to form a geometric image comes in handy. One new field, fractal imaging, is particularly useful. Fractals were invented by Benoit Mandelbrot, who defined a fractal in a 1975 paper (in French) as ''a mathematical set or object whose form is extremely irregular and/or fragmented at all scales.''

1.2 Fractals

Fractals are a cross between geometry and sampling theory. In practice of making computer images, Mandelbrot's definition has been somewhat stretched, so that any polygon may be a fractal. In common usage, the word merely denotes an equal portion of a geometric sample that is infinitely divisible into equal portions. That is, unlike polygonal modeling, in which a large sphere may be combined with an arbitrarily smaller cone to make an ice cream cone, a fractal image of an ice cream cone must be built of many polygons equal in shape and size. It could be one large, ice-cream-cone-shaped fractal, or that fractal could be divided into many tiny ice-cream-cone shapes to form a complexly textured surface. The larger original fractal (the whole cone) would be defined as itself, divided into many selves, so the whole large outline would remain that of the ice cream cone. (This method of definition, "recursive" division, invokes philosophical notions of infinity. We will have many opportunities in the chapters ahead to use recursive functions, the theory of which has been used by mathematicians and philosophers to define unsolvable problems; for those inclined to pursue this, the Encyclopedia of Philosophy's listing — see Bibliography — is a good place to continue roving after learning how to program a recursive function.)

To those with a bit of chemistry, it must be apparent that fractals are a lot like crystals, except that they need not be symmetrical and may exist in less — or in more — than three dimensions. (Fractals in more than three dimensions go just a little beyond our scope here!)

Fractals may also be roughly and arbitrarily shaped forms. While the first computer pictures assembled from many fractals employed regularly shaped triangles (just to make computations easier), a fractal may also be shaped like a saw-toothed comb or a Coke bottle or an ice cream cone. But there's a lot more sense to using fractals with simpler shapes; the whole theoretical point of re-creating an image with fractals is to be able to split it up into, or build it up from, many copies of just one fractal shape. Simple shapes like similar triangles fit against each other easily. Saw-toothed combs would make a mad, impossible jigsaw puzzle.

The use of fractals to create original images goes somewhat beyond their meaning in sampling theory, thus our hazy slaughtering of Mandelbrot's definition. (Computer image-makers are less mathematicians than users of math, and of anything else that works. We cheat on mathematical theory with impunity, so long as we get the image we seek to make.) Images made of small fractals, whether 3D or 2D, most often appear to have more realistic surfaces than polygonal models, whether ray-traced or not. Fractals may be individually colored or shaded, making for varied textures. In fact, in a raster scan display system, each pixel or any combination of pixels may be used as a fractal. This variant of sampling theory becomes as important to making 3D raster graphics as any hardware, language, or operating system refinements, and perhaps more so.

A systematic review of sampling theory is beyond the scope of this volume, but is highly recommended for serious makers of computer graphics. To briefly suggest a couple of image-provoking concepts from this body of thought, it would be very germain to touch on the work of two mathematicians who influenced Mandelbrot's development of the fractal. Helge Von Koch in 1904 defined a snowflake, or triadic island, made from a constantly dividing equilateral triangle. This image, and images like it, are very handy for filling surface space in computer images.

Mandelbrot also advanced on the work of O. Richardson, who ran into a wonderfully fascinating problem in the 1930s while trying to measure the length of the coastline of Great Britain. With a compass divided to a small, arbitrarily defined setting, Richardson stepped it along a map of Britain, then multiplied the number of steps by the divider setting. He found that if he decreased the compass radius, the additional twists and turns of coastline he would be able to take in increased the length of the coast measured. The smaller the divider, the larger the length of the coast. The coastline of Great Britain proved to be infinite — the finer the resolution of the tool used to measure it, the longer it is. Or, in Richardson's terms, a plot of log step size versus log length yields a straight line (see Figure 1.1). Forty years later, Mandelbrot would demonstrate that this plot could be used to describe an object's fractal dimension. With all the talk of "high resolution" in this volume, and in the computer animation industry, one would do well to keep Richardson's work in mind.

Figure **1.1**
Resolution and the coast of Great Britain

1.3 Matching Computers and Television

Ever-higher-resolution raster monitors are a result of the demand created by 3D raster graphics makers. There are now reports of 8,000-by-8,000 raster monitors being used for output to 70-millimeter film. For anybody with less than the odd $200,000 to spend on hardware, however, the older 3D techniques maintain great relevance. On the microcomputer level, the hard reality of little available memory and slow processing speed make how-to instructions in this high end of the art something far beyond our range. For further reading on the state of the graphics art, the journals of the Association for Computing Machinery's Special Interest Group for Graphics (ACM SIGGRAPH; see Bibliography) are a good place to start; many theoretical and technical innovations in computer animation have been introduced in those pages and at the yearly SIGGRAPH meetings.

To speed up the operation of sending an image from computer memory to either a vector or raster display, and to maintain that image on screen, screen refresh buffers came into being. Especially for raster displays, the data rate required to sustain an image is very large in comparison to the data rate within the computer. Although refresh buffers have been used for years with vector displays, it has been the drive for full raster images that has really pushed buffer development. Refresh buffers are also sometimes known as "frame buffers," leading to some confusion. "Frame buffer" describes any memory store that can be loaded with a full image frame of information. This may be a refresh buffer, so that the display system can grab all the pictoral details available in it, or it may be a frame buffer not tied so tightly to the output/display system. Perhaps the words "refresh buffer" should describe the former and "frame store" the latter, but in practice many people call both frame buffers. In making your own computer images, as detailed in later chapters, you will have ample opportunity to work with each.

It is probably easiest to begin explaining how to send images from computer memory to display by considering the resolution obtainable from a standard NTSC (North American Television Standard) video monitor, the most common of raster displays. The NTSC raster contains 262.5 lines in a field and two fields in a frame. Fields alternate approximately every sixtieth of a second, to form thirty complete images per second. After subtracting information needed for a vertical blanking interval between frames (each frame being composed of two fields), 480 vertical points are needed every thirtieth of a second. These thirty images all have an aspect ratio of 4:3, with the horizontal being wider than the vertical; to maintain equal horizontal and vertical resolution, 640 horizontal points are needed. (In fact, horizontal resolution in NTSC is usually worse than vertical resolution, as will be explained below. But let's assume, for now, equal horizontal and vertical resolution as a goal, just in case images are to be transferred to film.) A video raster of 640 by 480 adds up to 307,200. If each of these is to be represented in memory by two bytes — nice to have for enough colors per pixel — and then fed into the display thirty times per second, 18.43 megabytes would need to be fed into the display every second. But not all of this information need be fed into the display; it can be assembled in a frame buffer in some sort of random access memory, then only a simplified finished product needs to be read into the display thirty times per second. This can be done by a refresh buffer, assigning perhaps just one bit to each of the frame buffer's two-byte images. Thus the refresh buffer would need to be constantly shuttling only some 1.15 megabytes every second, or 38.4 kilobytes in a one-sixtieth of a second sweep accomplished thirty times per second.

The first frame buffers to be used with NTSC video were videodisks, for instant replays and character information in sports programs on TV. A constantly spinning read/write disk could be read at 1.15 Mb/sec by the video display while simultaneously being written at a much slower speed. As the buffer gradually filled with picture information, the video display appeared to develop an image in the sequence in which pixels (picture elements) were loaded. Though many bits may be necessary to create the image in the frame buffer, and a representation rate of sixteen bits per pixel has become quite common in broadcasting and computer animation equipment (at least in the institutional and corporate price range), the goal in advancing refresh buffers is to figure out formulas to reduce the numbers of bits needed and increase the speed in which they are sampled. Sampling theory again.

The original color-TV encoding, standardized in the 1950s to be compatible with monochromatic receivers, is known as "composite" video. The full video signal is broken into composite parts of luminance (or brightness) and two "chrominance" (color) characteristics. One of the chrominance signals is approximately pure blue, chosen as the most often dominant color. The other is a subtractive combination of everything else in the visible spectrum. Together the two chrominance measurements for any signal measure what is left of a color when all possible white has been subtracted from it. The two chrominance measurements, commonly called U (blue) and V, can be plotted on a two-axis graph with the center point at zero, U being the horizontal axis and V the vertical (see Figure

1.2). The distance of any point from 0.0 represents its *saturation* — the strength of *U* and *V* relative to each other and both again relative to white. In other words, think of a Cartesian grid system with the *X* and *Y* axes being *U* and *V* and the numbers closest to the center point being largest in value instead of smallest, as usual. The farther from the center point, the more white mixes into the color; the closer to center, the stronger the color's saturation. The center point would represent black, with other hues represented by a point's relative distance from the *U* and *V* axes.

It may be obvious that an awful lot of color information must be represented in a very delicate way by this system. The graph in Figure 1.2 corresponds to the face of a vectorscope monitor, such as is in constant use in any professional video studio; the delicate task of rendering proper color often leads a video cameraperson to spend more time watching the "'scope" than the viewfinder. This may explain why TV productions often look worse than things shot on film: resolution differences alone aren't quite enough to suffice in explaining the difference.

In the frame buffer it is just as easy to break up colors into composites of *Y* (brightness), *U,* and *V,* as to break up colors into combinations of red, green, and blue, each representing a continuum of brightness levels. It does take at least sixteen bits of color information for each pixel, and

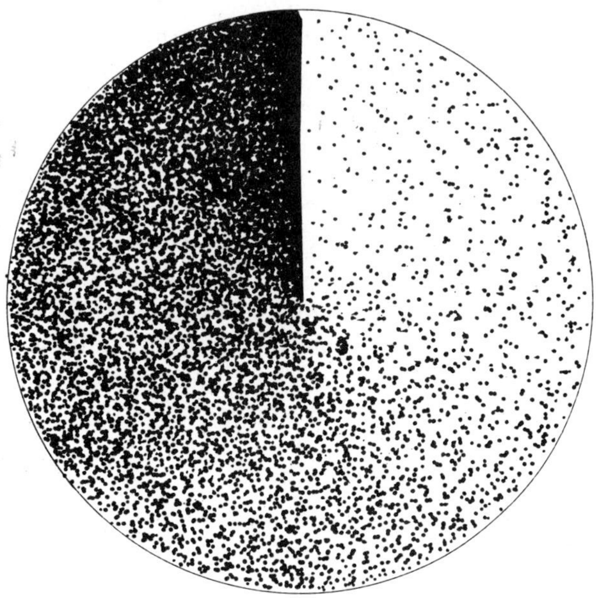

Figure **1.2** A simplified vectorscope face, measuring Y, U, and V

even 32 bits or more for accurate depiction of all the information in a composite signal, or for all the *Y*-type information that must be combined with a color breakdown into red, green, and blue. Realistic color and brightness take a lot of bits. Unrealistic but still somewhat acceptable color can be produced much more cheaply, and there is a market for it. This is why many makers of digital television effects systems and of standard PCs, as well as makers of devices oriented toward graphics, have opted for a different sort of color system that allows lower bit rates per pixel of display as long as not much luminance information is necessary.

The alternative is "component" television. The T.V. image can be broken into the three primary visual colors (red, green, and blue: hence the "RGB" monitor), with separate luminance and saturation information encoded for each. Even in this system there is much more information to encode for each screen pixel than simply, "make this dot green." You *can* get away with so little information, however, if image requirements are not rigorous. This is exactly what many personal computer color cards do — use as few bits per pixel as necessary to allow the average game-player or spreadsheet-user a splash of a little color. Thus the average color card is not really meant for the likes of us. In fact, with so much to describe in a high-quality image, even sixteen bits of information for each pixel have been used in different strategies with varying success. Some (more simple ones) of these will be detailed later on in this book. The most successful strategies allow bits per pixel to be dynamically allocated. That is, more bits are used when a lot of luminance information is needed, less when this variant of resolution (for such it is, as much a part of apparent resolution as the raw number of pixels making up an image) is less noticeable.

For the animator with limited color and brightness latitude to work with and limited total resolution, a sense of how these levels of image work together is critical to producing good pictures. For example, when zooming in on an image, certain types of subject matter may seem to be in sharper focus when brightness characteristics are emphasized in the mix of data making up a few pixels. At other times hue data may be more telling in an audience's sense of the image. Psychovisual experimentation seems to suggest that luminance is more important to viewers than chrominance characteristics, so TV standards makers back in the fifties used far more information to record luminance than to record color data. Of course, they were chiefly concerned with monochrome TV. Psychovisual research is a fascinating area, but experimentation in it seems still a realm more of artists than scientists.

Psychovisual sensations of image brightness have been subjected to more study than other components of sight. Brightness variance perception differs significantly from perception of color variation. The latter is seen to progress additively around the color spectrum, but brightness perception builds logarithmically, then slows logarithmically, in a sine-shaped curve that might be graphed rising from a starting point at 0.0 (Figure 1.3). The logarithmic perception of lighting variance was intuitively realized by the designers of the first photographic cameras, who spaced exposure f-stops to double or halve light entering the camera. Doubling was presumed to be the least significant difference detectable to the human eye, a quantization error attributable to insensitive chemical emulsions in early photographs. With more sensitive filmstocks (actually, more sensitive emulsions on glass, first, then gelatin film) it became apparent that no photochemical combination could react perfectly evenly to the whole range of possible brightness differences without a great deal of tinkering with the mix.

All of this necessary tinkering is what has by now allowed us a somewhat precise understanding of brightness perception. Film manufacturers and photographers have assembled vast data, over the years, from "gamma" tests of film "density." (Density of silver particles was once the sole determining factor in film's response to brightness. The *alpha* and *beta* measurements of the film were the frame's height and width; its density would be a *gamma* measurement.) This information is still collected, not just for new filmstocks, but for each new manufacturing run of the "same" filmstock; there are subtle differences in gamma ratings even in each new batch of what is supposed to be the same film.

Subtle logarithmic differences in brightness are what we want for a sense of reality in our images. Unfortunately, even where 256 or more colors may be displayable on a microcomputer terminal, brightness variation is usually more limited. If 256 additive levels of brightness are available, this translates to eight f-stops, or the range of a lens that goes from f.2 to f.22, quite satisfactory. High-quality video monitors have a

Figure **1.3** Brightness perception: Perceived marginal change (Y axis) versus actual change in brightness

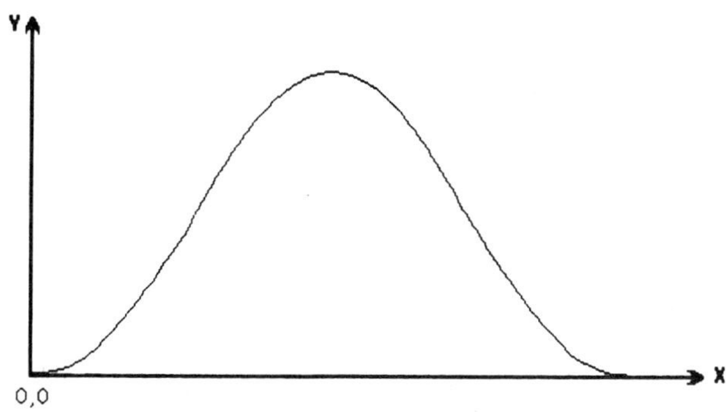

maximum brightness latitude of 30:1 — that is, six f-stops, equal to the range of a lens that goes from f.2 to f.11. This is very comfortable for micro animators outputting to video; a 30:1 range is not so demanding to program, if one's frame buffer and graphics card can handle it.

1.4 Raster Resolution

The way the frame buffer is matched to the video raster is of great importance, not least because different data ought to be emphasized for RGB and composite monitors. Also of importance are some vicissitudes of broadcasting television that shouldn't seem to affect us, but do very much. An optimal figure of 640 horizontal pixels has been mentioned for a TV-compatible image with identical vertical and horizontal resolution. Lower horizontal resolution, however, is not only tolerated by our current broadcast system, it is necessary in light of economic realities. Resolving distortions in broadcast cameras typically limit horizontal resolution to at most 600 lines, and often as few as 480. By the time a signal reaches a home receiver, the additional distortion from equipment down the signal chain limits horizontal resolution to about 430 lines. Many home receivers are limited to picking up and displaying some 300 lines. Home video cameras resolve at some 340 lines maximum, and VCRs at perhaps 250 lines, all of which adds up to far less horizontal than vertical resolution.

The resolution that many home computers with graphics cards are capable of may measure, say, 256 by 256. But this represents a different sort of compromise than a VCR resolving an image meant to be 640 by 525 (but effectively 480) at 250 horizontal and 525 (but effectively 480) vertical lines. For one, the computer's 256 by 256 pixels fills the very same 4:3-aspect-ratio screen as the video image. The horizontal dimension doesn't merely go fuzzy, as happens with a VCR's low horizontal resolution, it must be stretched to make a 4:3 aspect ratio out of a 1:1 aspect ratio. If images are made exclusively by and for such a system, no one will notice the difference, but if those images are fed out to video (and the problem is the same in any of the worldwide video standards, not just our own NTSC, but PAL and PAL M, common in most of the British Commonwealth and Western Europe, and SECAM, found chiefly in France, Scandinavia, eastern Europe, and the Soviet Union), they must be contracted in one direction or stretched in another.

Even when a computer's output looks better than standard video, its nonstandard aspect can cause problems. For example, most TV watchers are aware that television pixels are round dots. With even lower resolution available than TV is capable of, many microcomputer designers have long wanted to produce displays with rectangular pixels, which close up space better and — most of the time — give an illusion of higher resolution. The first microcomputer display to come out with rectangular pixels was the Apple Macintosh. People were indeed impressed with the Mac's graphics from the first moment they saw them, not least because of its rectangular pixels. But graphics makers who created images with the Mac, then output those to video, were in for a rude awakening: Pictures instantly deteriorated! If a final image is to be shown on video (as is most animation), it pays to produce it on a system that approximates video standards.

Square pixels do not look better than round ones in all cases, anyway. They look even worse than round ones when it comes to drawing diagonal lines — *even* worse because round pixels don't look very good either. The closer a line is to horizontal or vertical, while still being somewhat diagonal, the worse it tends to look in a raster system of limited resolution. Any diagonal line represented only by vertical and horizontal steps must, at some level of close examination, look jagged, or "aliased," a term from sampling theory. In a low-resolution raster, it is as if one always examines that vertically and horizontally stepped, imitation diagonal far too closely for comfort (see Figure 1.4). If Richardson's map of Britain doesn't come to mind here, go back and reread.

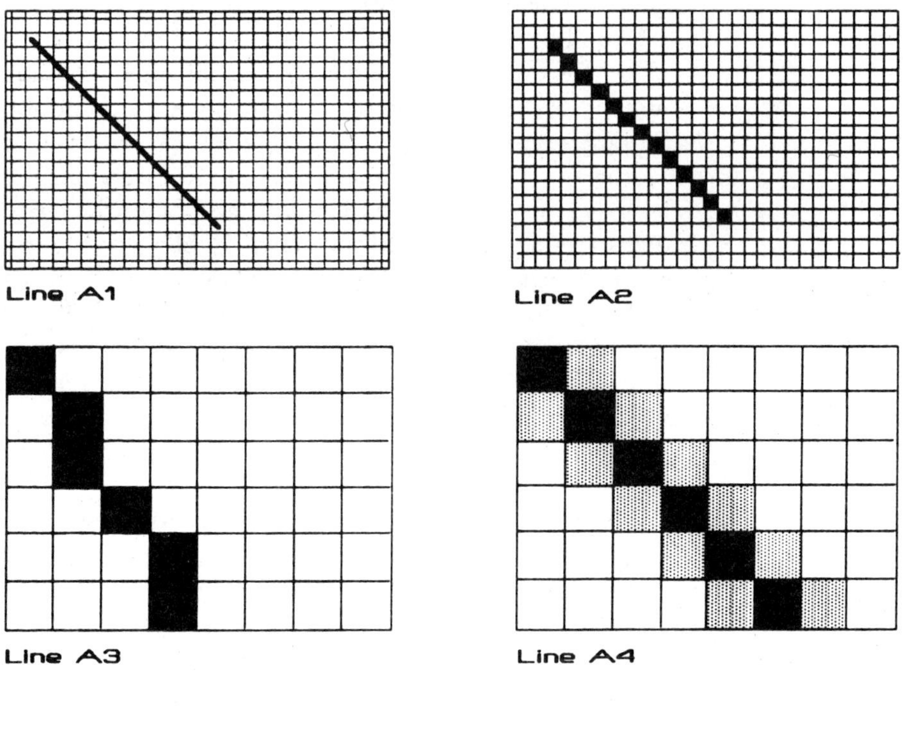

Figure **1.4** Lines represented by rasters

1.5 Anti-Aliasing

Here is the most pertinent drawback of raster scan to micro animators, especially as it is compared with vector scanning: You can draw a straight horizontal line, and have the computer remember it as such, but it won't come out looking that way without a lot of fixing up that most micro users can't afford. Micro users typically can't afford vector displays, either. (Not because these are so much harder to build, they are just less common, afford fewer economies of scale than standard TV-type CRTs, and thus cost more; raster scan is where the world is going anyway, jaggies and all!) Again, however, micro users programming in BASIC for monochromatic displays often have so little computing power at their disposal that their animation often amounts to no more than line drawing. How terrible to only be able to draw monochromatic lines, the perfect province of a vector display, and have to show them on a raster display full of jaggies!

The solutions to this problem involve investment in greater memory; a full video display monitor (still, raster scan is the only choice up to quite a high investment level) with higher resolution; a bit of supple programming that may even be done in BASIC; a good, quick refresh buffer (you knew we'd get back to frame buffers, didn't you?); and, most of all, lots of color and gray-tone choices in your color card. Put them all together, they spell *anti-aliasing.*

Anti-aliasing is a visual way to cheat sampling theory. There are correlates for anti-aliasing wherever an infinitely changing reality must be sampled by finite numbers, as in the measurement of the coast of Britain or in digital measurement of analog sounds, where dynamic compression is entirely analogous to visual anti-aliasing. Having a look at Figure 1.4, the problem with Line A_2 is that the slope of the "real" line it attempts to represent (Line A_1) falls somewhere between values that have all been assigned to the same columns of pixels. Thus, for several pixels above the horizontal, the line appears to be a vertical, then it suddenly shifts to the next vertical column, continues on, then stair-steps again. Try looking at this diagram from ten or more feet away, and Line A_2 may appear to be acceptably diagonal, a thicker but close approximation of A_1. Putting distance between the viewer and the diagram highlights another vagary of defining the word "resolution": When pixels appear to be smaller, for whatever reason, an image seems more realistic.

One way to solve the aliasing problem, then, would be to make the picture, and its pixels, smaller. Making the picture smaller while keeping the pixels the same size would make the problem worse, as in Line A_3.

Since the reason we have an aliasing problem is pixels too big for our diagonal, decreasing the picture size is no solution for us.

Look at Lines A_1 and A_2 again. The "real" line seems to divide pixels. If only there were some way to make a pixel part black and part white, we could more accurately represent the line. In fact, there is a way to do this: by making these pixels gray, like Line A_4. Looking at this line from up close, all its trickery shows; it doesn't appear to be much closer to a diagonal than Line A_2. Step back a few paces, though, and suddenly it looks very realistic. Not quite the real thing, but closer than any other alternative. Line A_4 is an example of *spatial filtering.*

Our eyes tend to pick out hard edges, which is what makes aliasing so objectionable. A spatially filtered line softens up the difference between color extremes, creating something of a blur. Very much related to the human eye's tendency to pick out every possible hard edge is its tendency to average and discard blurred information, to present itself with, in this case, a sharply defined straight line. With the blurred representation to go on, we guess easily at what is being represented, and think of the blur as that shape (a diagonal). With the stair-step to go on, our eyes accentuate the stairs. In nature, if one's vision is blurred, one gets used to subconsciously guessing at the true shape of things, and the shape of stairs can be very important!

Anti-aliasing has been called "cheating," because spatial filtering is just another name for making an analog of the digitally drawn line. In mathematical terms, what we've tried to do by representing this line with pixels too big for it is to truncate a transition, represented by a wave made of an infinite number of harmonics of the sampling frequency. Cutting off the number of harmonics taken into account to make that representation results in our distortion, because in the natural world those harmonics tend to blur off into the distance instead of cutting off quickly. Sampling theory shows that if, instead of cutting off the harmonic series at some arbitrary point, the whole frequency spectrum is averaged, observers are happier with the results. Sampling theory does not say *why* this is the case. Math has its limits.

It takes a fancier graphics system than most micro users can afford to include built-in, automatic anti-aliasing, a feature that, in its niftier forms, involves a function key and some swooping around one's diagonals with a light pen. But anybody with the right extra colors available can do ad hoc anti-aliasing. If you've got a badly aliased red line on a blue background, you'll need the right 50:50 purple to spatially filter it.

Finally, as you may have already guessed, spatial filtering is presently a tedious, frame-by-frame fix. In animation, the object that diagonal line represents may move in the very next frame, to a different diagonal or other position, against a different background, where a whole other aliasing problem exists. Say, for example, you've spatially filtered a bit of a red wheel purple, so it looks better against its blue background. In the next frame, the wheel rotates several degrees. As it moves, the purple section moves to an angle that presents no aliasing problems, and a different section of the wheel now does have aliasing problems. The original purple section must be recolored red, and a new section must be spatially filtered purple. This may need to be done for each frame. Then, say a few frames later, the wheel passes from its blue background to a green one; the proper color for spatial filtering would now be a shade of brown. As memory power increases, it will be possible to antialias moving pictures automatically. For now, this must be done frame by frame.

Tedium, yes, but the process does make for one incidental advantage in the final product. Painters have long known that colors reflect against one another. A red wheel seen against a green background is really a different, greenish red than the same red wheel seen against a blue background. At least spatial filtering allows the animator to reflect this reality simultaneously.

1.6 Raster Data Compression

The sad case of micro users with too little computing power available to do anything but vector drawings, yet having no choice but a low res' raster display, already has been bemoaned. Even with more computing power available and a better raster, vast amounts of data are necessary to draw complex pictures and, for animators, to change those pictures frequently. Thus most computer animators (and even many micro users) often work with far less than the memory they have available, because to make pictures that fully utilize their capabilities seems too tedious.

Data compression is a relatively new solution to this problem; pioneering work in the field has been done for the telecommunications industries. Now that multiplexed satellite, cable, and telephone-line transmission of video signals has become common, some of the compression techniques designed to cope with crowded raster signals have relevance for animators.

Every point on a raster system must be specified, whether the information to be written with that point seems to have relevance to one's picture or not. A raster must be built as a seamless, complete grid, with the computer and display knowing no difference between more or less important pixels. In most pictures, however, many points in series along a horizontal raster line will be identical. In the case of the micro animator who makes vector images which are later shown on a raster display, the pixels used to represent points not part of the vector drawing all have the same value. If the vector drawing is monochromatic, a great many fewer pixels used to represent those lines also have the same values. Instead of storing and transmitting all those individual pixel addresses, it is economical to map the picture in a different way than usual for raster scan.

Each mapped address can be a pair of numbers, one for the value of a pixel on a horizontal line, and the other for the number of following, adjacent pixels that have the same value. This is called *run length mapping,* as opposed to the standard way of mapping a raster with 1:1 correspondence. A problem with run length mapping is that if such a compressed signal is output to the display device, the display system must be able to decode it. And the process of decoding may be slower or faster, depending on how many changes there are from one pixel to the next. With a great many changes, run length mapping becomes a slower and more memory-intensive process than standard 1:1 pixel mapping.

If a picture has very few identical pixels that are adjacent to each other in a horizontal line, run length mapping doesn't accomplish very much, yet takes a lot of time and effort. There are other ways to compress pixel data, though. The most common is *difference mapping,* which takes us back to the earlier discussion of defining bits per pixel. I mentioned that 16 is now a common number of bits used to define a pixel, but let's say the next pixel along a horizontal differs from the first only in one or two — or eight — bits of its address. For example, it may have a different color value, but the same brightness. In difference mapping, only the bits that are different are denoted for each pixel.

There are many other ways to encode data, too; I can't begin to describe them all, but check the Bibliography for works on the subject.

1.7 Frame Buffers and Windows

Taking data from the map that exists in computer memory and remapping it someplace else, before it gets to the display, involves having that "someplace" to put it. Frame buffers provide someplace temporary to hold an image data map; they have been referred to often here because of their many uses, including as "frame stores." Generically, frame stores are places to store an image. "Windows" are another example of frame stores of great relevance to micro animators in particular, because windows are a very common concept in micro software design. Those pull-down menus and storage bins that most software seems to aspire to lately all involve windows, which is to say they use any number of frame buffers, viewed from a vantage within another buffer. Frame stores may be made of partitioned main memory, as is common in the programs just mentioned, or they may be built out of external memory components. Thus you can go to the frame store store (sorry about that) to buy a box labeled "frame store" that looks a great deal like a hard disk or a video-disk (because it is, with just a little bit of software installed).

Thinking of windows as little frame stores may instantly give the savvy animator some ideas as to how best to use them for our arcane purposes. Jot them down, if so inspired, to see how they compare with the ideas presented later in this book. This is mentioned with a fond hope that will continue right along through this volume, that the *concept of the technology to be explored should inspire the animation made with that technology.*

Enough sermon.

Packaged TV-effects devices typically employ simple frame stores. An incoming video signal is digitized, stored, and then acted upon by any number of preprogrammed operations. Self-programmed micro graphics systems typically build frame stores in RAM, as will be elucidated later.

1.8 Interacting with Technology

The ideal computer for animation is a quicker, more powerful beast than anybody has ever come up with. Ideal memory storage is deep enough to hold a whole feature film, yet flexible enough to instantly access any frame, any identifiable character, any pixel. Needless to say, nobody has come up with this yet, either. An ideal interface would be easy for computer-illiterates, yet powerful enough to recreate the contents of anybody's imagination. Probably this will never exist.

Ideals of the first two devices are being closed in on by reality, but as technology progresses the benefits of using a micro that has as much power as the most powerful mainframes of a few years ago is offset by still being unable to compete with the ever higher-quality images obtainable by users of larger systems. A solution I'll elaborate on elsewhere is for users to write code on micros and ship it out to a mainframe to run. This is growing increasingly common, but it has its limitations: writing code for a mainframe system must involve intimacy with the possibilities of that system. It's a lot easier to write code for big mainframe projects on a micro if you have constant access to that mainframe.

Raw processing speed and memory power aren't everything, though. Generally, computers have been designed for mathematical problem solving; using these systems to create images adds up to creating many problems just for their graphic representations, then smashing those representations together with no thought of solving the problems. Notions of unsolvable problems were mentioned already in this book, but graphics makers don't actually solve most of the mathematical problems they get involved in because the math is merely used as a tool to solve pictoral problems. The two sorts of problems — and their solutions — are rarely the same thing. Often it seems we are really using machines for functions other than what they have been created to perform.

For example, in most computer designs great effort has been put into making memory appear isotropic — that is, as unconnected with its physical residence as the human mind seems divorceable from the brain. There is often no way for casual users to know whether the data they access resides in RAM, chip ROM, floppy disk ROM, or someplace else. But we have been concerned for many pages now with addressing bits of data. How much more sense it would make, for raster graphics purposes, if computations could be made directly into individual frame buffers supporting known addresses in individual displays. We can do it, but it involves making graphics that run properly only on particular systems and are not easily transportable to other systems.

A computer designed from the ground up for graphics might have a whole different shape, with many screens tied into separate frame memories, all of which would be represented in consecutive frames on a random-access, read/write, large-scale memory. Images could be made a whole lot faster this way, often very interactively, in real time. Systems such as this are now being developed by a few of what will be called, in Chapter 3, Stage-1-type systems designers. They should eventually filter down to popular use in the next decade.

The sorts of computers we have now are really much better at making graphics *as an illustration of a problem,* and referenced to other, nongraphical data, than at making graphics for their own sake. These metagraphical uses of animated graphics are at the heart of computer animation's sibling relationship with industrial and architectural design (see Chapter 13). We can take some cues from the way data is used in these endeavors, and though we may wish for the golden era of devices such as described above, we can take advantage of the interactive uses that currently common system architecture provides. If graphics can be related to extraneous data such as wind stress information on the eightieth floor of a skyscraper, they also can be related to information more germain to telling an animated story. ''Want to know more about why the chicken in our cartoon just crossed the road?'' the screen may ask. When the user/audience answers affirmatively, another graphic may be called up to illustrate the famous punchline.

Imaginative use of whatever interactivity any given system allows is probably the key to what will make computer animation in the near future either sink or swim.

CHAPTER TWO

Personal Computer Hardware for Graphics and Animation

Just as CGI system users' imaginations only take action within the bounds of the programmer's imagination, so the programmer's imagination operates within the bounds of hardware. A few examples of input hardware were mentioned in the last chapter, in the context of their use with graphics systems that have already been programmed to produce complicated images. The same sort of input devices — the keyboard, always first, and then analog-style dials, switches, mice, track balls, joy sticks, and so forth — are all a programmer has to work with. One other most important input device enters the digital image: some sort of image capture system, usually composed of a video camera and a "genlocking" card that turns video input into digital data. (Strictly speaking, an image captured is not an image generated by computer, but an image captured is one that can be altered, replicated, animated, and generally used as raw material, just like a shape entered in coordinates via keyboard or drawn on a digitizing tablet.)

Output devices typically begin with the ubiquitous cathode ray tube. Film or video recorders of one sort or another are a distinct aid and perhaps a necessity, depending on the seriousness of the animator.

Some external form of frame buffer is also usually employed, serving as something of a traffic cop as information travels back and forth from input device to computer memory to image display. The term "frame buffer" is a rarity in the microcomputer world, but color graphics cards perform refresh buffering while other frame stores are built in RAM. A color and/or high-resolution graphics card is at least a very desirable addition to any microcomputer to be used for animation, if not an absolute necessity: depending again on how serious you are about animation. The same goes for genlocking.

Total available computer memory and CPU speed are certainly limiting factors to any animation design, and so is the memory contained in the frame buffer. The resolution capability of the display is a well-defined limit; less obvious is just how well this resolution corresponds to the resolution of the frame buffer and of the image that is resident in computer memory. The latter two limits are not strictly defined by how much memory power is resident in the hardware; memory can be apportioned to provide greater picture resolution, or it can be used to increase computational speed. Even working with a very powerful computer, some compromise is necessary. Working with a microcomputer, compromise is implicit in every move.

2.1 Resolution

The word *resolution* needs an awful lot of defining before we can go further. Usually, people speaking of resolution in terms of CGI are talking about the number of pixels that make up the image. Images made of fewer dots have lower resolution, of more pixels, higher resolution. Because computer images are usually made up of vertical columns and horizontal lines of pixels, in a picture of a rectangle one would not notice any resolution problems (unless the monitor's resolution were so low that any line looked fuzzy). A diagonal line, on the other hand, can be represented accurately only by a quite high-resolution picture; otherwise it looks more or less jagged, made as it is out of horizontal and vertical steps.

Let's come back to that parenthetical note about fuzzy monitor resolution. Monitors represent images of pixels. The original pixels exist in digital code. (This may call to mind grade-school definitions of what a point is, and how it may be represented by a dot from one's pencil.) One may speak of a monitor's resolution in pixels, if it has been formatted to represent a certain standard number of pixels, often done by building a mask into the cathode ray tube. But monitor resolution is also a function of the physical reality making up its picture — electron dots flowing across the screen, in the case of a CRT. Monitor resolution may grow fuzzy from long use without any diminution of the number of pixels represented.

2.2 Aliasing

In fact, a fuzzy picture may serve to *increase* apparent resolution! If a diagonal line looks jagged because its step pattern, or aliasing, is all too apparent, smudging the line, anti-aliasing, will make it more persuasively diagonal; it will appear to have higher resolution. Obviously, one doesn't want to smudge whole pictures to cure a few jagged lines. Anti-aliasing when and where a user wants it is a very helpful feature to be built into any graphics system, but it requires more sophisticated frame buffers than most microcomputer users can build out of available memory and more color choices than are usually available, for the same reasons (see Chapter 1's discussion of the subject).

If you do have sufficient colors to spare and find that a jagged line in your picture is particularly offensive, you can perform a sort of ad hoc anti-aliasing. Finding the average of the two colors on either side of the line, then using that combined color over a smudged line may not be supported by a magic wand in one's packaged graphics kit, but it is the essence of anti-aliasing. Yes, it is more available to those with programming knowledge than to users of packaged kits. That's life.

2.3 Color Resolution

Finally, color differences have much to do with human perceptions of resolution, even for line resolution that might seem to be independent of color. For example, a jagged line between two very different colors is far more plainly jagged than the same line between two colors that are close in hue, value, and/or intensity. In fact, if any of these three attributes of color is only slightly changed on either side of a jagged line, the line will seem less jagged than if there were a greater change. This is a correlate of anti-aliasing and a more subtle solution to the problem; using subtle color differences across lines, bad jaggies may never arise. *Color resolution* may thus be said to measure the amount of definable difference between possible colors.

Many "color" graphics monitors or cards represent only a few shades of three or four colors. Others may do sixteen colors, a common number lately. Some color graphics cards offer more color variation, but all must inevitably trade off in building more computing power into less space, by offering either more colors and less pixel resolution or more pixels and fewer colors. The maximum number of colors and pixels available in a graphics card for 16-bit personal computers at this writing is around 256 colors with pixel resolution of about 200 by 300. Many 32-bit, hard disk systems offer 32,000 colors and 400 by 600 pixels (roughly equal to an NTSC television picture). Since 32-bit micros are already common and hard disks are getting to be quite cheap, graphics cards with the color and pixel resolution of 32-bit dedicated graphics systems will become available at micro prices in the very near future.

Even in the present generation of 16-bit micros, a picture made up of 60,000 dots in 250 colors looks amazingly ''higher res'' than one made of 60,000 or even many more dots in any 16 colors. Subtle color change is what we expect of the world; if this is present in a picture, a harsh dot pattern can be overlooked by the viewer. For example, a Super 8 movie image has only about 60,000 dots, and few average viewers notice a great difference in image quality between Super 8 and a broadcast TV image made of 225,750 dots.

2.4 Moving Simple Pictures is Easier than Moving Complex Pictures

Yes, you can get a still picture with a Super 8 sort of resolution out of a micro at this writing, but to get a moving picture with such resolution requires a tremendous number of computations. To move a line with two defining points involves a short and quick *algorithm* (a step-by-step specification of the resolution to a problem). Moving a line with hundreds of defining points involves a much longer algorithm, and if those hundreds of points are in hundreds of colors, the problem multiplies in difficulty. So, now is about time to examine the difference between real-time animation — everyone's dream — and the real world.

Real-time animation means the movements you make happen, happen as you make them: no muss, fuss, or waiting. Longer than real time may imply a little finger drumming, a trip to the laundromat, or a wait overnight or longer. When working with a micro, extremely complicated animation can be programmed, and can take years to run! Thus, making CGI always involves trade-offs between apparent resolution and time. The resolution that counts is not the ultimate resolution of the hardware, but the resolution one can afford time to create and run.

If you can't produce a good-looking animated movie in real time on your computer monitor, how do you watch the animation? If you can create many seconds of your animation at a stretch, you can record it on home video and cut together shots. Even professional video editing cannot count on precise frame-to-frame cutting, so you'd only want to do this with relatively long sequences. Usually, images are output in small pieces, either to a film recorder or to one of the relatively new still-frame video recorders (costing in the ballpark of $20,000). A film recorder can be as simple and inexpensive an arrangement as a single-framing 16-mm or Super-8 camera aimed at the monitor. This may sound tacky, but it's basically what many pros have done for wide-screen science-fiction epics (using not 16-mm, but 65-mm film).

Many animators use micros to write code that they still never run on a micro; the micro is just a sophisticated, on-line version of a notebook, hooked into the mainframe or mini that will actually produce the CGI. Eventually, as your prowess grows, you may find this to be the most efficient way to make better and better pictures. In later chapters that review the industry, you'll get some idea as to how to proceed with this.

Compromise will decide which input, processing, storage, and output components you invest in. A lot more detail about the uses of each will help those decisions.

2.5 Input Components

The Keyboard

I've never met a personal computer that hasn't got a keyboard; it is almost always the principal input device. The problem with entering graphics exclusively via keyboard interface is visualization. It is very easy to make mistakes when programming the coordinates of an image that can't be seen as it is entered. With a fast refresh buffer and output system, the image that is being created can often be seen while it is being created; this also depends on the details of one's program. Many graphics programmers get around this problem by drawing out their images with a pencil on graph paper, then programming coordinates read off the paper — much as this may seem to defeat the whole point of computer graphics.

Digitizing Tablets

Conceptually, a digitizing tablet is a simple mechanization of the graph-paper-and-pencil method described above. The tablet is like erasable graph paper, with grid lines formed by wires beneath the board's plastic surface. These wires automatically record coordinates for any lines drawn across them, and thus speed-up interaction as they increase programming accuracy. Since no picture actually appears on the surface of the tablet, it becomes necessary to simultaneously watch the image one creates on a monitor, entailing a fair amount of programming.

Digitizing tablets work with either magnetic pens or light pens. The former allow for higher resolution and are usually included in quality graphics-tablet packages. Some light pens work without a digitizing tablet at all, but provide lower resolution than a light pen with tablet can.

Light Pens

Light pens are very commonly available for microcomputers; they are easy to manufacture and are thus usually inexpensive. Unfortunately, they are usually capable of creating only low-resolution images — a total of less than 100 by 200 pixels at maximum. A light pen may thus be useful as

1. an inexpensive way to allow many unsophisticated users to interact with an animation system that may have higher overall resolution than the light pen is capable of drawing;
2. a quick way to make changes in a graphic that has generally higher resolution, where the lower resolution of the light pen's additions will not be noticed easily;
3. a principal input device for low-resolution graphics systems based around the unaugmented graphics of most popular personal computers.

In other words, if you don't have or plan to get a high-res and/or color graphics card, a light pen may work fine as an input device.

Joy Sticks, Mice, Track Balls, Dials, etc.

All of these are simple directional switches that may help define line drawings, color combinations, or movement. They can be more or less successful, depending on what they are programmed to do. Many people find these devices particularly useful for defining color mixing and movement speed, because both of these phenomena are subjectively observed by human beings at other than constant numerical rates of change and dials, mice, et al. may be easily adjusted at other than constant rates of change.

What is meant by ''other rates of change''? Human movements begin slowly, speed up, then slow down as they end. To prove this, try watching the way someone lifts a glass or runs. Better yet, try filming or videotaping such movement, then precisely counting frames and dividing the movement at several points into the number of frames per second (30 for video, 24 for 16 or 35-mm film, 18 for Super 8 film). This will give you a good idea of how many frames a movement created by animation ought to take up.

Just as human movement begins slowly, speeds up, then slows down, so do other natural movements, and so do movements created as analogs based on ''natural'' human perception. Color blending is a perfect, and very pertinent, example. While mixing green and blue, for example, when does a color seem ''green,'' and when is it ''blue''? Other examples of this sort will come up throughout this volume; animation is a process not of mimicking reality, but of mimicking the perception of reality.

2.6 Image Digitization

A video camera can be connected to relatively simple circuitry that converts its signal to digital information. Such circuitry is typically fitted onto a card ready for a personal computer expansion slot. Many companies are currently in the business of selling image-digitizing cards for the IBM PC and compatibles, with resolution topping out at about 250 colors and 200 by 300 pixels. Many vendors of digitizing cards package them with inexpensive home video cameras and copy stands, though all of these items may be purchased separately, too.

Genlocking implies the ability to mix computer-generated information directly with incoming video. Some micros, such as Sony's SMC series, come with genlocking built in. It can also be purchased as a plug-in.

If you are genlocking with video, a standard television monitor (the higher the resolution, the better, of course) will serve best as your color monitor; what you see on video is, after all, what you get for an end product.

2.7 Memory and Processing Speed

The more the better. Besides the most sophisticated color graphics card and image-digitizing card your computer can support, you will want all the RAM it can support, too. If the computer has a 32-bit CPU instead of a 16-bit or 8-bit processor, so much the better. Though some specifics in this volume will be written from the point of view of using a 16-bit IBM PC, extremely little is irrelevant to users with more horsepower. Hard disk, of as many megabytes as you can afford, is advisable for permanent memory storage. Animation tends to use up as much storage space as is available.

As must be apparent by now, some sort of special frame-buffer memory is highly recommended. The simplest form of frame buffer will be constructed in RAM, as described in Chapter 8. Since the-more-memory-the-merrier holds true for frame buffering, too, animators with hefty budgets will opt for systems that offer an external box full of RAM for use as a frame buffer. Frame buffers are available either as stand-alone components (Ikonas has been a popular brand name in the animation industry; there are many others) or as parts of full systems put together by what the larger-than-personal computer industry knows as VARs (value-added resellers). VARs package various vendors' (perhaps their own) hardware, with their own proprietary software, into turnkey systems. A sample of these is discussed below.

2.8 Output Components

Monitors

You probably want a color monitor to display animation. You may also want to use a monochrome monitor, to display program lists and other instructions to the computer. Unfortunately, few micros will support both of these at the same time. The AT&T PC, equipped with color graphics card, is one exception that does very nicely at supporting both. Read on for a solution for other computers.

Video Recorders

The problem with recording your animation onto the average home video recorder is that your VCR was designed to record long ''takes'' (a take is what is recorded between any start and stop of the recorder). Animation generally comes out in very short takes and must be laboriously edited together. Editing on videotape is certainly possible, but requires two recorders (or rather one recorder and one player, but play-only video decks are uncommon these days, since economies of scale make recorders just as cheap if not cheaper). An edit controller is usually involved in the process, as well as a time-base corrector, time-code recorder, and other assorted hardware. All told, even a bare-bones half-inch ''home'' video editing suite can easily be a $5,000 proposition. You should be able to rent such a suite for $25 an hour in most large cities.

More importantly for an animator, editing video is not a terrifically accurate process. Even in professional systems, edits are predictable only to plus or minus two to eight frames (at 30 frames per second). Using home machines, frame loss may add up to a second or more for each cut. Animation must be planned accordingly, and this can be a large limiting factor to creativity.

A still-frame video recorder would be the answer to many animators' dreams. At the beginning of the eighties a small animation company called Lyon Lamb won an Academy Award for developing a computer controller for a VHS VCR that provided just that and cost a mere $23,000. More recently, Sony came up with the first one-inch Type C (long a broadcast standard) single-frame video recorder, the BVH-2500, which weighed in at the same professional price range. Prices for these sorts of devices are steadily dropping, however, and in the near future will surely offer a new frontier for inexpensive animation.

Film Recorders

Semantically speaking, any film camera is a film recorder, but there are devices that carry the label in a more specific sense. Meant to record from computer output, these machines have their roots in the first "flying spot scanners" developed in the early seventies to transfer video images to movie film. A flying spot scanner holds a single movie frame in the focal position while the shutter is opened to a projection-type CRT facing the camera's lens. The CRT is calibrated to emit one picture dot at a time, and the film is held in position until a full frame's image has been sequentially displayed. Then both film and video advance to the next frame.

In the computer world, the output half of this sort of device is generally known as a light-emitting plotter. The earliest of these relied on a film recorder's shutter being held open while the CRT's electron beam traced several points, making entire line images on each frame of film. This ought to strike a chord of remembrance from the description of a direct-view storage tube in Chapter 1; the only difference is whether the line is held, in unrefreshed form, by the CRT or by the film recorder.

Sophisticated computer film recorders work by timing long shutter exposures while electron beams from a precisely calibrated CRT are recorded, either on movie film or onto some still-picture format (typically 35-mm — inside most still-image film recorders is a compartment meant to hold one of the common Japanese still cameras). With a relatively uncomplicated automatic timing and advancing mechanism, such a film recorder can perform its time-consuming labors without human attendance.

This is an ideal situation. Home animators may normally expect to have to compromise at something less than the ideal. Using a 16-mm film camera with still-frame capability is a compromise in terms of convenience, certainly, but need not be one in terms of quality. The film such cameras use has resolution about equal to broadcast television (better in terms of light/dark latitude), which means it will not degrade in the slightest the image produced by your computer, certainly not if your system has very good resolution. Using such a camera entails aiming it at the monitor screen and filming straight off the tube. Film is easily and cheaply edited, especially in the short lengths involved in most animation. Total minimum materials cost of this method of recording will be under

$1,000 for the camera and editing accessories, and perhaps $5 per minute of finished color film.

There are a few problems in shooting film images off a CRT. Two types of distortions can creep in:

1. color distortion, caused by the differences between light balance on the CRT and that for which the film is balanced;
2. spatial distortion, caused by the curved front of the CRT.

Solutions to the latter problem seem easiest. With any CRT, one can plan animation for the flatter central area of the screen. Think of a template over the CRT screen that represents a smaller movie screen. Unfortunately, resolution is sacrificed by doing this — a smaller source picture will be blown up to the film's projection size. The "money" solution is to (a) buy a flatter, larger, best-possible-resolution CRT (a generation of video monitors began to come out in about 1984 that fits this bill, but most home computers come with cheaper, older monitor designs — buy wisely) or (b) buy a light-emitting plotter (for the wealthy, serious, or institutional buyer only).

A solution to the color problem involves more work, but less cost. As mentioned in Chapter 1, photographers and cinematographers have long been in the habit of shooting gamma, or exposure, tests of filmstocks before they use them. Color balance, often unreliable from filmstock to filmstock, is a prime reason to conduct such tests. The same films that amateur photographers take for granted at stated color temperature and ASA or DIN exposure-rating numbers actually do vary widely in response to many factors. The safest way to know what you will get is to test each consecutive batch of numbered stock. If shooting off either a color display or a monochrome display, with the image to be colored by filters in a few passes through the camera, test a wide variety of color filters at many exposure settings, with full notation, and use those that provide the best light balance. You don't have to buy all the filters to perform these tests (at about $10 each, they add up); filter manufacturers often provide sampler kits of gelatin (flexible, disposable) filters. Use the kits for the tests, then buy the filters you need.

If you record still-frame images off the computer monitor, it may be easier and result in higher quality to animate the images by traditional in-camera techniques, rather than produce full CGI. Limited computing power may thus be devoted to producing higher-resolution images. Pictures may be produced (and saved on disk) to represent, say, every sixth of a second of motion, and the film camera can fill in persistence of vision by dissolving between images. CGI purists may cavil, but if this technique produces the desired result, go for it. In the process of editing or printing the film, your CGI can be combined with other, traditional film special effects or with the computer-controlled effects discussed later in this volume.

Once a film of your animation is completed, either by animating film of still frames shot of CGI or by shooting moving film of already-animated CGI, it can be transferred to video for showing. This whole process actually can be easier, cheaper, and produce higher-quality images than recording CGI directly onto video. Such a production process mirrors on a small scale (but for the same reasons) the way most animation shown on broadcast television is made.

Plotters

Output printed on paper may be of some use for various computer-assisted animation schemes such as that described above, but not for true CGI. Why would someone want to make use of paper output in animation? One can imagine the special circumstance of an animator who happens to have access to a very-high-resolution plotter and a 16 or 35-mm film camera, and whose CRT output possibilities are much lower in quality. Instead of producing either full video or still-frame to be photographed and animated, the animator might output CGI onto paper, then shoot the images traditionally, on an animation stand. Though this scenario seems wasteful because of the relatively high expense and tedium of going through the paper stage, it may not be all that unlikely: students and workers in large corporations have to live with those tools they have access to, and may bend tools to purposes undreamed of by the tools' designers.

Videodisk

[In the interests of conformity, the Greek-based spelling "disk" has been used throughout this book. Though this is standard among computer users, video people have tended to adopt the Latin "disc," from the audio world. With no desire to discriminate against those whose primary port of entry to this volume is video, the word was Greek before it was Latin. On the other hand, audio discs existed before computer disks. The choice is arbitrary, but it must be made.]

Videodisk is just now coming into its own as an affordable read/write storage medium. At this writing, only Panasonic markets an affordable (under 3,000 1986 dollars) read/write, single-framing videodisk. This OMDR (optical memory disk recorder) uses an eight-inch disk and records with fairly low resolution (about 320 horizontal lines). Even now this is a several-years-old product, and very much improved versions are scheduled for quick introductions. By the time this book is in print, or soon thereafter, a $1,000 12-inch disk recorder with resolution equal to broadcast television may be a reality.

The implications of videodisk development for micro animators are tremendous. Here we have an easy tool that records far sharper images than a consumer VCR, that single frames, and that obviates the need to film off the CRT screen or do complicated video editing. Read-only 12-inch optical videodisk players have been widely available for years, so there is a ready network of machines on which to show work. Many of these machines have good interactive capabilities, too, making possible a new medium of interactive CGI movies, to pick up where video games left off. As soon as single-framing read/write videodisk is available, it's what all of us micro animators ought to be using.

2.9 Read Before You Buy; Program Before You Read

If you're just buying a CPU, it should go without saying to get the fastest one you can afford, with the most available RAM, as many ports as possible, and preferably with a large-capacity hard disk. Get a system that runs languages other than BASIC — especially C, since that's what most computer animators are using these days.

Finally, an understanding of the more technical matters discussed in this book will help you decide just what hardware you need. On the other hand, having the hardware on which to try out programming will help you understand the book better. If you already have a micro, and preferably one that runs C, you're well set to understand everything that follows. After reading, you'll be a whole lot readier to make any further investments.

CHAPTER THREE

Packaged Goods

3.1 From Pioneers to Consultants to Turnkey Systems

They come in all sizes and shapes. Graphics as a product category is today as unformed and many-formed as the whole personal computer industry was a decade ago. Basic directions, however, are fairly well set. Business graphics dominate the micro graphics field, as might be expected, but there are also many packages for varieties of computer-aided design (CAD). Then there are "paint" packages more specifically geared to making artistic pictures than business graphs, and there are various additional packages to provide limited animation for computer art, with the aid of a peripheral or two. Packages that combine painting capability with digitized camera input are quite common.

Anybody with the patience and energy to work their way through the programming chapters in this book will be able to devise their own software packages. If you don't feel like doing so, as much exposure to those chapters as you can bear (it really won't be all that hard, even for beginning programmers and artsy types) will allow you to buy commercially packaged systems more intelligently.

Although many of these "packages" are software only (and typically meant to be compatible with the IBM PC, Apple II, Macintosh, etc.), graphics applications don't lend themselves very readily to running on the same hardware that has been designed for running spreadsheets and word processing. So much hardware modification is necessary for worthwhile animation that the trend in animation (and other graphics) is toward complete hardware and software systems.

Here the micro arena mirrors developments in professional animation systems, which have tended to move in three stages for each new development:

1. The first few pioneers assemble their own systems out of available hardware and their own code.
2. Some of these pioneers sell their software and consult with a wide number of would-be competitors on how to assemble the hardware and operate it all.
3. For the real masses of the industry, turnkey systems of hardware and software come complete with one vendor's name and responsibility squarely assigned.

TV production facilities would here correspond on the professional level to the average hobbyist maker of micro animation.

Although Stage 1 must necessarily have come first in the business of animation, Stages 2 and 3 were and are coincident. In microcomputer animation, Stage 1 again came first, but now all three stages have been coincident and can be expected to remain so. Software-only packages are really Stage 2, but while we've seen some fascinating Stage-1-type work done with micros over the past ten years, software-only packages have not comprised nearly as creatively interesting a stage as the pros' Stage 2 custom software systems. People working with their own idiosyncratic (Stage 1) systems have been willing to wait hours for pictures, to interface with Super 8 film cameras in makeshift mechanical ways, and to perform various other miracles that software packagers could not expect of their average clients. Without buying more hardware, those average clients have not had much computing power available to fire the imaginations of the programmers of the packages.

Much of this is changing, now that ever better and cheaper memory moves us into a micro Stage 3. Through the beginning of the eighties, the fight between Commodore and Atari to see who would wrest control over the Amiga computer proved that both competitors knew the right graphics system probably would be the key to survival. The generation of micros beginning with Amiga, Mindset, etc. provides a much more inviting target for software writers, because such computers are already packages assembled to make good graphics.

In the first and second chapters my prejudice against packaged systems used by computer-illiterates was made known — too well known, probably — for there's another side to this situation. Character animation cannot possibly be entirely programmed by microcomputer, at least not yet; it must be drawn, or painted, or animated in the filming, too. Programming moving assemblages of polygons or polyhedrons is fine, if you've got loads of memory to work with. With a micro, memory is always a compromise, and if your goal as an animator is to make 2D painted cartoons — typical classic Disney product, for example — well, you can't program Mickey Mouse nearly so easily as you can draw him.

In many ways, insisting an artist know about programming is like insisting a programmer know about electrical engineering, or like insisting one must know the history of art before one begins to animate. The best and most serious probably do know, or eventually get to learn, the deep background of their craft. But without ever having come close to a computer before — or to an art studio — animators using some fine graphics packages can produce surprisingly high-quality pictures.

To review how these packages work, it is probably best to divide things up again into the three stages, and to add a fourth, a stage lately applicable as well to professional systems with extensive memory: additional software written for an already-assembled turnkey system.

Stage 1 is the unpackaged stage, and the stage about which this volume is going to spend most of its contents talking. That doesn't begin just yet, though.

3.2 Stage 2

For now, on to Stage 2 — software packages that come with hardware advice — which is to say almost all graphics software packages. Paint programs are by far the most common of these, and the least expensive. It's probably fair to say that most of these programs have been inspired more by the availability of particular hardware than by any creative programming leaps that really stretch the available hardware.

The first such paint program for micros, Steve Dompier's "Micro Illustrator" (for the Apple II) of 1983, did much to set this pace. It brought to the micro level memory-intensive features like pull-down menus filled with icons symbolizing various possibilities. This very graphic approach might seem time-consuming, wasteful, and unnecessary, both to programmers and to expert users of most standard applications software. Invariably, to beginners it seems exciting and helpful to have a great deal of graphic interaction, even for nongraphical processes — spreadsheets and word processing are the two major examples — but eventually, with memory always a compromised commodity, those graphic conveniences often add up to a slower or less versatile program. Programmers and experienced users therefore have a right to ask, about "user friendly" pull-down menus, icons, windows, et al., "What's the payoff after the thrill is gone?"

With graphics programs, the payoff is simply that all these snazzy effects *can* come cheaply, in terms of memory horsepower. The program must support frame buffering anyway, if it is to allow real-time paint interaction. If it is to have high pixel resolution for the drawings users make, it may as well use that resolution for icons, too. Windows may be structured to serve as handy pictures within pictures, or as menus. Not all paint programs are quite so versatile, but by the mid-1980s and beyond, prospective buyers ought to expect all of the above features to exact no noticeable speed or versatility trade-offs in a graphics program (even though such trade-offs remain common in programs for other applications).

As of 1986, paint programs tend to bunch themselves into two broad price/performance categories. At the lower level, little or no memory or graphics-card add-ons are necessary to run a paint program on a major brand microcomputer, but a color graphics card and some analog interaction device — mouse, tablet, or joy stick, typically — are certainly recommended. The add-ons enhance the programs' capabilities, but those capabilities are so limited by compromises that, for our purposes, they can hardly be said to function at all.

For about twice the price and up, software buyers can expect to chip in for the extra hardware peripherals and receive far more versatile programs. For example, expect to soon find a program for animation that works with a fairly high-resolution graphics card and utilizes most if not all of that card's color versatility. (You'll find it in this book, in Chapters 9 and 10.) "Windows" (subscreens, or frames within the frame) are a sign of a program that expects the user to have a large amount of usable memory installed, and are very helpful indeed for animation. To demonstrate, let's say you can use up to eight windows with a paint program and can transfer the contents of any window to any other. After drawing a basic picture, it can be copied into the other windows and changed slightly for each one. Presto — each could then be displayed for an eighth of a second, and a second of roughly animated movement is born. (Eight frames per second does not quite fool persistence of vision, but it comes close enough to be accepted by most viewers.)

Scrolling and color cycling are also *very* helpful for animation and can already be found in a few high-end paint programs for micros. Both are more illusions of animation than what is usually thought of as animation. Scrolling along a static picture, and shifting colors in a static picture, are movements so common to live-action films that they become necessary grammatical elements of film story-telling in animation, too. The former, in live action, is a pan or a tracking shot; the latter would occur whenever clouds move in a sky. Indeed, since viewers are used to these devices, they can be utilized far more extensively in animation sequences than in live-action shows without losing the sense of true animation. And scrolling and color cycling are much easier than true animation.

3.3 Animation Programs

High-end paint programs for micros segue into animation programs in terms of both cost and capabilities. Some of the simplest animation programs readily available are, like the low-end paint programs, compatible with monochrome displays or very-low-resolution/low-color-choice color displays, and with minimal memory. But these are becoming rarer. Most micro animation programs assume at least 320 kilobytes of available RAM and graphics cards capable of at least sixteen colors, and larger requirements are common. Most programs should allow users to manipulate a number of windows in various ways; expecting each of four to scroll and color cycle independently is not out of line for IBM PC, Macintosh, Mindset, or Amiga software.

There are a few basic structures that typical micro programs tend to use to achieve animation. Most commonly, programmers may make a few windows available for painting static images and allow users to designate one or a few objects within each image as a movable "sprite." The name derives from the days when computer games employed such low resolution that this was about the most favorable thing such moving characters could be called. These days, movable sprites may be pictures employing as many as hundreds of pixels and many colors — far more complex beings than the little bouncing balls or gremlins brought to mind by the term "sprite." These may be moved around the static (or sometimes scrollable) frame for a primitive sort of animation — "primitive" because it is usually not possible to make the sprite change form. (A full-fledged Mona Lisa sprite flying around her sitting room in forever three-quarter face may look more sophisticated than a gremlin doing the same, but is still not particularly realistic.)

If several designated sprites are available, the resulting animation can be made to look far more lifelike. Two or more may be used to represent one character; the more sprites are used, the more the arms, hands, legs, even facial characteristics of a character may be moved independently.

3.4 Windows and Viewports

Actually, a sprite is similar in code to a static little window, movable around the frame. (Building them will be discussed in Chapter 8.) The number of sprites a program gives users, and their possible complexity, are both something of a trade-off against the number and versatility of windows offered.

What should full-fledged animation programs offer in the way of windows that sophisticated paint programs don't? Being unconcerned with time, paint programs often don't make any particular efforts toward smooth and fast transition from one window to another. Often paint programs require the user to "pull down" the next window, which may be very user friendly for static picture painting — and also may conform exactly to standard operating procedure for integrated software packages — but which makes it impossible to animate by flipping quickly from one window to the next.

Even with systems that allow such quick changes from one window to another, the change is likely to be somewhat slow and jerky compared to professional animation. The most sophisticated of micro animation programs include "double buffering," to get that next image up on screen faster. Buffering and double buffering are discussed in the context of micros below, explained in a larger theoretical sense in Chapter 1, and fully explained technically in Chapter 8.

A very handy graphics feature from professional systems is becoming more widely incorporated in micros: use of the maximum resolution of the display as only a small "viewport" on a larger and possibly higher-resolution internal picture. As with many other computing processes, making graphics is very much a case of designers attempting to emulate philosophical visions of the way the mind works, and it has long been common to think of human vision as producing an internal picture in gray matter to correspond to the external "display" image of reality. Recreating an image by computer has been made into something of a reverse of this process. Just as we can never expect to be able to reproduce in physical reality a perfect high-resolution image of the mind's-eye view of some picture, why should the graphic display device be able to reproduce the whole of the interior image? Even if we have resolution of, say 400 by 600 pixels and sixteen colors, there is no reason that this cannot be used as a small view of a piece of an internal image resolving at 4,000 by 6,000 and 1,000 colors, as long as there is enough internal memory to hold this greater image.

This small view of the larger one can be thought of in one of two ways.

Either it can be a low-res version of the entire finer image, or it can be a full-resolution image of just a small piece of the larger picture. The most interesting animation programs have it both ways, by allowing users to zoom in on portions of the interior image or zoom out to the larger picture. Display resolution remains what it is (say 400 by 600 again) no matter what, but apparent resolution seems much better. More important for animation, a properly designed master picture can be zoomed and scrolled with a tremendous illusion of movement.

Regardless of how many windows the program allows one to keep stored (usually a quite limited number), if the program allows this sort of zooming in on a master frame, it allows many temporary viewports. These may not be permanently storable windows, but they may work very nicely with a frame-by-frame recording device (such as a still-frame Super 8 or 16 mm film camera). This latter sort of use has probably not been envisioned at all by most creators of micro programs with this capability, but exactly this sort of process has been commonly performed on a professional level for a few years.

3.5 Frame Buffers

Understanding the way frame buffers work also allows an exploitation of the capabilities of several commercially available micro animation programs that are meant to work in systems with frame buffer firmware (Amiga, Mindset, add-on cards for the IBM PC from AT&T, Number Nine Computer, Chorus Data Systems, and many others). Any buffered graphics system really is in the business of making at least three of each image presented. One is the original frame buffer inside the computer. Another is the display image that is created to correspond to that interior image. The third is that held in between, in the refresh buffer, which corresponds sometimes to the display, and sometimes to the interior image, thus speeding interchange between the two. Systems with "double buffering" involve four images on three levels, with dual refresh buffers shuttling a pair of in-betweens back and forth. In double-buffered systems one buffer always corresponds more to the interior image, another to the display image. (One may think of any permanently stored image, on disk, film, video, or paper, as yet another level of copy.) Just as obviously as double refresh buffers offer faster display interaction time, so three, four, or more frame buffers in RAM can be made and then juggled to feed that next, next, and next image into the (single or double) refresh buffer just as fast. Considering that really high-quality animation uses 12 frames per second, the contents of a frame buffer need to be thrown onto the display — and into memory — as quickly and as often as possible. Custom-built professional systems often employ many frame buffers on an ad hoc basis, however many may be needed for a specific job.

Unfortunately (or perhaps fortunately, for here is opportunity) there are not yet, at this writing, any micro-oriented programs to deal with multiple frame buffers. Micros with this sort of slick animation response tend to be Stage 3, turnkey systems. The next several chapters will show you how to build one of your own.

3.6 Stage 3

Videotex is as good a place as any to start looking at Stage 3, perhaps because, back when it was devised, it was the first turnkey high-level graphics system using micros in any way. As first and foremost a mass information system, though, videotex seems more like television, or like a large mainframe time-sharing system, than anything that fits within our three micro graphics stages. Where else this much-ballyhooed technology of the late seventies fits into the current world of micro users is still open to question.

In 1978 and 1979, AT&T and the Canadian Telidon system came up with a graphics standard for videotex, called the North American Presentation Level Protocol System (NAPLPS). Chunky-looking and slow-running by today's standards, NAPLPS graphics and animation software runs on mini or mainframe (AT&T runs it on their 3B Series) computers, and is communicated over telephone lines to small, dumb terminals or to micros that are programmed to act as dumb terminals. Running speed as well as graphic quality represent very tough compromises with minimum telephone-line data transmission rates. With a system that must be transmitted over the phone in real time, better graphics going in might only result in garble coming out.

Videotex was really meant to be a mainframe graphics system with output to any number of micros, but since the graphics standard was set relatively low for phone compatibility, it is also well within the capabilities of today's micros to originate graphics for NAPLPS. Since the originally envisioned commercial uses for videotex have not panned out in the U.S., several companies have tried to enhance and capitalize on the creative interaction that micro terminals can have with the graphics created by the host computer. (France and Britain have done more with their systems: their government monopolies have forced people to use videotex.) These have not had tremendous success, either. AT&T, with the largest investment in the technology, conceivably the most to gain by any success, and also the most ability to bear a large investment, has already bowed out of most if not all of its videotex activities. Large-scale public information would seem to require either much finer animation than videotex has been capable of (as in standard television cartoons), or no animation at all (as in various data banks).

It would be nice to be able to create graphics and animation on one's home computer with only a small monthly service charge for software and with graphic quality representative of the capabilities of a host mainframe. This sort of set-up could allow relatively easy creation of far better graphics than otherwise possible with a micro, and also provide a ready-made audience of other system subscribers for one's works. Instead of calling them other subscribers, let's call them coworkers, and we have a model for the modern animation workshop that is being realized in many places around the professional animation world. Many very creative animation programmers simply can't afford more than a micro; several very-high-tech computer animation businesses either have extra computer time available or need to take any business they can get to amortize the costs of their in-house monsters. This has created an increasingly common situation of animators using micros to communicate their creations to the mini or mainframe or supercomputer that will run them.

All of this has little to do with turnkey systems, except to show how the videotex key never quite turned. For users who do not want to learn to program (or at least not to learn to program rigorously), the solution is not to have many terminals connected to a distant mainframe, but to have one's own, very powerful, stand-alone personal computer set-up.

How would such a turnkey PC differ from a standard micro? Not in software alone, but the difference would be in providing many of the little extras we've been describing, bundled with software meant to make the most of them. A commonly offered sort of package includes a high-resolution/large-color-choice graphics card, a frame buffer (which may or may not be included on a card), a digitizing tablet and other analog input devices (mice, joy sticks, etc.), video input with genlock, video output, and of course, software to run it all. Listed in order, a high-res color monitor, hard disk, the PC itself, and recording devices such as still-frame video recorder are respectively less likely to be included in a package and more likely to be recommended for purchase from other vendors, for fairly obvious reasons.

This trend in equipment began in the late seventies with analog systems aimed at broadcast TV operations and price tags ranging up to

$200,000. By the beginning of the eighties the original systems, as well as their digital heirs, were known for their limited software and thus limited bag of oft-seen tricks, and a two-way reaction set in. First, twin quests for ever-better tricks and for ever-more-realistic animation both kept prices high and moved video effects performed with microcomputer-based turnkey systems into fairly close competition with truly high-resolution, custom-programmed minicomputer (Stage 1) systems. With programmers of the larger systems understandably loathe to share their valuable programs, and with most of such programs designed to work far more slowly than real time, the very-close-to-real-time turnkey systems have enjoyed great acceptance.

The tandem trend, though, is more interesting to our immediate desires as micro users. Turnkey systems quickly got a lot smaller and cheaper. Computer designers who cut their teeth on PCs began to look closely at the video effects systems made by the likes of Chyron, Dubner, MCI Quantel, and other suppliers to broadcasters, and to see that, with a couple of years of development, all of those systems' workings and more could be put on a few chips. Aside from the degree of demand and the resultant economies of production scale, there would be no reason these custom micro systems couldn't sell for little more than home computers.

Demand was the key, and though a few took a fling at the animation market, most of the next level of inexpensive turnkey micro graphics systems (priced generally from $20,000 to $40,000 in the years 1981 to 1984) came out aimed at the industrial design marketplace. The basic needs of a graphics system made for animation and one made for industrial design are not very different. In a design system, users will want to store and have access to miscellaneous nongraphic information, referenced to the graphic; there is also less need for delicate coloring. Some companies have shuttled their identities back and forth as they quarry customers.

The next generation began to come to market in 1983, with prices ranging from under $10,000 to over $30,000. These were aimed more squarely at artistic uses, but for corporate-communications or broadcast-television buyers. Most produce static graphics for slide shows; several systems specialize in typography and layout for the publishing industry, and many are for specialized heavy character use in TV (weather-map micros are a whole subindustry, with perhaps a dozen competitors at this writing). There are several turnkey systems that concentrate basically on animation, from companies like Cubicomp, DALIm, Chorus, Computer Graphics Lab (of the New York Institute of Technology), and Perspective Technologies.

The animation produced by these systems will not match the very-high-resolution systems often used in feature films and high-budget commercials, nor will they perform a bag of tricks in real time like the present high-end digital video animation devices exemplified by Chyron, MCI Quantel, et al. They will produce animation of at least standard television-quality resolution and color, all in two dimensions and some in three. Most do not do very much in real time, but an experienced user ought to be able to knock out anywhere from several seconds to a few minutes of animation per day, depending on the complexity of the work. Some of the lower-priced systems require a still-frame video or film recorder to do this, while those that make good use of large hard-disk capacity and frame-buffer memory can output many seconds at a time to a constantly running (and much cheaper) video recorder or film camera. Some of the 2D systems also promise to soon include anti-aliasing to smudge over "staircase" diagonal lines.

The creators of these systems are generally just computer animators who are a few years ahead of the readers of this book! They've taken their programming knowledge and love of animation, written software for the best small hardware they could find, and taken it to market. Some of this volume's readers will undoubtedly do the same.

Finally, yet another wave of turnkey systems started to come on stream in 1984, and promises to do the most to break the news about computer animation to the widest audience. A true micro Stage 3 is finally in full swing, beginning with the Motorola 68000-based systems like Amiga and Macintosh. These do not produce nearly the quality of animation of the better small vendors' large turnkey micros (many of which, interestingly enough, are based around the IBM PC XT or AT, with their relatively puny — compared to the 68000 — CPU), but with the vast marketing capabilities of their manufacturers, they comprise a very inviting target for software writers. Although they already come bundled with animation software, over time a variety of new software should produce some stunning graphics. The raw capabilities are certainly there, with Amiga, for example, offering better-than-TV resolution of 400 by 600 pixels in sixteen colors, with double buffering for quick screen movement and all sorts of built-in animation tricks.

As these computers demonstrate success in the wide micro marketplace, they ought to help bring down prices and popularize the better small turnkey systems that presently cost five to ten times as much. Exciting times are coming for home animators.

CHAPTER FOUR

Programming Goals

4.1 Software Levels

The evolution of software for computer graphics began with device-dependent packages supplied by hardware manufacturers. Hardware and software had to move hand in hand in early graphics systems (such as flight simulators), and for such purposes levels of software had to move hand in hand, too. To a user of a flight simulator — or of the average video game — the system must be entirely illusionary. To understand what I mean by levels of software, think of that later development, the turnkey graphics system. Such a system exists to create *final-product software* — animated movies, for example — and uses *enabling software* to do so. To break down software levels still further, think of an architectural CAD system, in which enabling software must be able to pull information from a *software data base* of details about building site, strength of structural elements, wind resistance, and so forth. Yet another software level is harder to exemplify with a particular sort of graphics system that makes most obvious use of it; just as there must be a structure of data to pull information from, so there must be a *graphical structure* to put it into. This comes to a five-level model for CGI devices:

1. hardware
2. application data base or data structure
3. graphics system
4. application program
5. metaprogram; user-made software.

We've already concerned ourselves quite a bit with the first level, hardware, and will address the fifth level in several chapters toward the end of this book. Levels 2, 3, and 4 are the three conceptual levels present in any application for the programming of graphics-enabling software.

4.2 The Move to Higher-Level Languages

In that first incarnation of custom-supplied, device-dependent software, Levels 2, 3, and 4 must seem to the user to be unified with the hardware level. To their programmer they are conceptually separate, but to a programmer of another graphics system they may as well be unitary. These early programs were written in machine and assembly language, "low-level" languages because they are not transportable to other computers. Programs in machine language are as much a part of the machine they are written for as any of its hardware. Assembly-language programs are only slightly more removed, and it takes a great deal of time and effort for any programmer other than the program's creator to get even any conceptual inspiration from an assembly-language program, much less adapt it to run in a different environment.

The first revolution in CGI was certainly to create any computer images, but the move to a high-level, transportable language for graphics was equally revolutionary. This second revolution is ongoing; in many cases the move is only now being made, and even where it was begun long ago, transportable code continues to evolve. At first, systems designers needed enough standardization to move from one generation of graphics device intended for one use to another intended for somewhat different use. Even at this stage, the future was apparent. Details of those three conceptual graphics levels needed to be codified so that, eventually, software written with one computer in mind could be run on another with only some few modifications in code. The process of standardization continues through books like this one and into off-the-shelf software of high graphics quality. It all began with that second-revolution move to programming in FORTRAN.

4.3 The "Core"

This began to happen about 1970, and within a few years it was apparent to programmers that some standardization on the graphics system level would be beneficial. In 1977, a committee of the ACM SIGGRAPH came up with a core graphics standard called the Graphical Kernel System (GKS), or more generally, the "core." It has been amended and refined a few times since, with the latest comprehensive definition now running to several hundred pages (and available from the ACM, see Bibliography). The GKS is not so much a precise enumeration of what the graphics structure level of software ought to be; rather, it is a conceptual, general standard (even in its hundreds of pages of definition!). It can accommodate software written in any language and graphics and animation of widely varying quality.

4.4 Comparing Languages and Operating Systems

The GKS has served as a sort of baseline definition of what the graphics system ought to be, similar to the way FORTRAN set a standard for what a machine-independent, portable language can be. The GKS has always been defined in terms of FORTRAN, as most computing standards are. Though FORTRAN is the first high-level language to be used for programming graphics, it is really not well suited to the task. Meant for batch processing on a relatively ancient generation of computers, it limits data types and flow in ways incompatible with optimal representation of images (the terms "data type" and "flow" of data will become clear to nonprogrammers in the next few chapters). Pictures are more complex structures than most numerical batches, or rather they *can* be if the programming language and the programmer's skill allow them to be so.

Programming in Pascal allowed significant steps forward, and some very interesting graphics programming has been done in that language. (The very helpful *Fundamentals of Interactive Computer Graphics,* by Foley and Van Dam, makes use of Pascal; see Bibliography for the complete listing.) Around the same time that advances in hardware capabilities and programming goals made FORTRAN seem obsolete to many programmers, however, C Language began to gain popularity and support in many computing applications. C seems quite similar to Pascal on first glance, but unique features such as bit operations and stackable structures and arrays (details on these in Chapters 7 and 8) make it more efficient for dealing with graphics, and with animation in particular. Many graphics programmers quickly took to C, most using Unix as operating system.

Unix and C had been developed together at Bell Labs in the early seventies; some ninety percent of the code in Unix is written in C. While C is not a standardized language and the different varieties of Unix are not the only operating systems being used with it, the benefits of using the combination of C and Unix are obvious enough that this has become the most common programming environment for advanced CGI at the present time.

C and Unix still are nowhere near the most often used language and operating system for *all* CGI. Because of the sheer volume of micro-made graphics, BASIC and MS-DOS (or PC-DOS) fill that description. Most micro graphics are unsophisticated stuff, but need not be. Programming in BASIC can be the best place to start to understand advanced CGI if you understand BASIC fairly well and have little or no knowledge of C, Pascal, or FORTRAN, or if you have access to a computer that will run BASIC but not to one that runs more advanced languages. Unfortunately, you'll only be able to go so far toward real-time animation and 3D images in BASIC, but the language itself presents no real limits to the resolution of the 2D images you can create, as long as you don't expect real-time movement. Most color PC displays limit your options even more. Animation graphics possibilities in BASIC look especially rosy for users of the relatively new BASIC compilers (such as QuickBASIC and TrueBASIC, compatible with the IBM PC BASIC interpreter). Quite uncynically, programming graphics in BASIC is a game of juggling limits; with a bit of practice, it's a fun game, and it can produce fine animation, too.

The real problem with programming in most versions of BASIC is the same whether you program graphics or any other application. In the interest of "ease," BASIC is a set of rote operations with little coherent logic. By comparison, Pascal and C are spare, lovely, logical forms that lend themselves far better to conceptualization. If you are just starting out in programming, this highly opinionated adviser would say skip BASIC — begin with C.

If you are limited to a computer that only speaks BASIC, though, it would make sense to give priority to investments in the best color graphics card and monitor you can afford, then program mostly still graphics and photograph them in sequence off the display with a 16-mm camera. This way you can take advantage of the highest-resolution images possible with your computer, even with a slow writing speed (that is, a refresh buffer that doesn't refresh the screen very quickly) that makes animation impossible to program. With a BASIC compiler that includes graphics statements and structured programming (such as Microsoft's), and with a hard disk, some completely in-computer animation (as opposed to that achieved by combining computer images with 16-mm film animation) is possible. This would most likely be mixed with the former sort of combined animation. The final product would thus be fully realized only on film, with some scenes animated in-camera from series of computer-produced frames and others filmed as live action of moving images on the computer screen. Owners of early generation IBM PCs and inexpensive compatibles most often will be using these techniques. The needs of such programmers will be addressed in the next chapter.

4.5 Beyond BASIC

Programmers and animators bring widely different experiences and preferred programming environments to the making of computer animation. Even though C seems the most efficient language for our purposes at the present time, it is far more important to understand the conceptual reasons behind an operation than merely to see it programmed out in C (or any other language). Since other languages continue to be used by some programmers of animation, it also makes sense to keep everybody talking to one another, by always beginning discussion on the conceptual level.

This is precisely the strategy taken by the developers of SIGGRAPH's core standards for graphics. The conceptual levels for graphics-making used here — (1) hardware, (2) application data base or data structure, (3) graphics system, (4) application program, (5) meta-program, user-made software — basically coincide with levels determined by SIGGRAPH for their programmer's model of interactive graphics (see Figure 4.1). Meta-program software does not enter in here, and "hardware" is broken up into input devices and display devices.

4.6 A Beginning Analysis of the Parts of a Graphics Program Package

The three levels of information along the vertical axis of Figure 4.1, though analogous to any sort of complex program's subroutine breakdown into frame buffer (graphics system), operating system (application program), and long-term-storage data base (application data structure), need explanation to both neophytes and experienced programmers. Here subroutine functions are rather different from batch and various sorts of micro applications programming. The application data structure, as a graphics data base, is very different from the usual batch data base. The data structure must store all the information for describing any objects to be depicted. The usual ways to do this, as pointed out in Chapter 1,

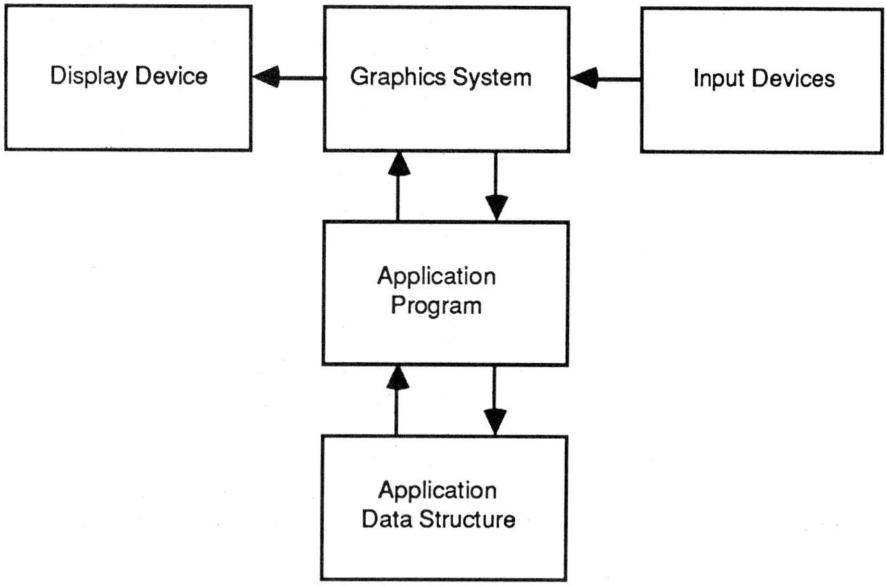

Figure **4.1** The SIGGRAPH programmer's model of interactive graphics

are either in terms of fractals or as geometrical primitives. In either case, the data structure contains

1. geometrical coordinates to define shapes
2. data for attributes of these shapes such as color and texture
3. data for how these shapes may be connected together.

In other graphics applications the data structure may also contain nongraphic information, such as the price or supply availability or stress characteristics of a depicted object in the data base. This type of extraneous information is not usually useful in animation, but as a creative programmer you may indeed think of some appropriate use for this capability.

In fact, because of the dominance of this nongraphical dimension in other sorts of graphics applications, off-the-shelf data base management systems (DBMSs) are often used (though often somewhat customized) to hold and access the data structure. Using a DBMS for animation has certain drawbacks, unfortunately: geometrical coordinates in a frame buffer involve more complex information that must be processed quickly than the average batch; the more lifelike the animation is to be, the less likely a commercial DBMS can handle it. As adaptations of DBMS programs for microcomputers become more common, however (and as micros increase in power), it seems increasingly tempting in turn to adapt a micro DBMS for graphics.

The application program is like a shuttle, a traffic cop for information, or, in the typical metaphorical comparison of computer to mind, the ego that decides where information ought to go — to or from the id (application data structure) and superego (graphics system). The application program is what a user identifies with as the "program." It uses the operating system to read and write to and from the data structure, allowing a user to specify images to be lifted and transferred to the graphics system, or vice versa. Indeed, the application program also can be thought of as a cushion above the operating system. As a plush cushion it is highly developed, so that unsophisticated users may interact in simple ways to create and manipulate images; as a hard cushion it allows a more programming-minded user to more quickly extract complex images from the system.

The graphics system, too, is a cushion. It shields the application programmer from having to know the specific architecture of the display system, as part of its frame buffering function, but its design need involve few tradeoffs between comfort and speed: in this case the two are fairly synonymous. The frame buffer(s) within the graphics system must be capable of being instructed by the applications program to accept input from devices such as keyboard or tablet and to store that input. Preferably it will be able to mix input with data already forming an image, without needing to send it down to the data structure first, but it should also be able to mix in material from the data structure.

As has been mentioned previously, the more frame buffers the better; the graphics system should be able to throw the contents of each onto the display screen as quickly as the user wants, while it continues to receive instructions from the applications program to perform other actions on images in other buffers.

Foley and Van Dam say, in *Fundamentals of Interactive Computer Graphics,* "Interactive graphics programs are different from batch programs in that they tend to be *event-driven;* that is, they wait for the user to do something, react appropriately, and wait again." In fact, the same could be said for any program meant to be used interactively by relatively unschooled users. An animation program (depending upon the hardware and memory resources on which it can draw) need not work so simply. Images should continue to move or replace each other on the screen, supplanted by ever-alternating and/or refreshing frame buffers, even as the user commands change in the graphics being presented. The bigger the "cushion" the application program provides, either the less quickly the system is able to respond to the interactive user, or the fewer choices it allows the user to make. Thus, the more interactive a graphics generator is, the less likely it is to be a true *animation* graphics generator. Given the tradeoffs involved in generating graphics at all with limited memory, in the case of a micro-based system, the more interactive, the less graphics.

For these reasons, programmers who would construct the finest possible animation with any given hardware had better plan on setting up a "hard-cushion" system with which they (as all-knowing creator) will be able to interact well, but which less sophisticated users may not be able to make much use of. On the bright side of user-friendliness, almost any conceivable animation problem can be solved by a highly interactive system, so long as that system makes use of sufficient memory. Turnkey devices such as the Bosch–Fernseh FGS-4000 and Lucasfilm Pixar imaging systems share the same basic model that has been described in this chapter. By building their "soft-cushion" application programs over a hardware bed with immense memory in temporary and long-term storage, high processing speed, and multiple frame buffers, they can maintain interactivity along with high animation speed, diversity of effects, and resolution quality. Not having such resources at their disposal, most programmers must sacrifice either interactivity, speed, diversity of effects, or resolution.

4.7 Logical Steps in the Graphics Creation Process

To create a picture of something with the sort of graphics package that has just been described, you must first know what it is you want to create a picture of. This may sound very simplistic, until you try to quantify and analyze what goes on when people draw pictures with simple tools like pencils or brushes. The artist may start with a complete idea of what to create, or only a vague idea, or no idea at all. This more or less vague idea grows and changes as images take shape. Using turnkey paint programs, it is possible to proceed this way via computer as well with a pencil. But with any sort of nongraphical, language input used to define images, the user must start out with concrete ideas of what the final product will look like.

It's just as well to get used to this, because the process of animating images demands an equal or even greater degree of precise planning from the start. In this game you've got to be methodical. If you think of yourself as intuitive, doodle out your intuitive images on paper or in a paint program until you come up with models for the final images you wish to generate by computer and animate. (Well then, if we can doodle in a paint program, why not set up a graphics package that allows that painted image to serve as the basis for animation? Soon, soon.)

A model of the image the graphics maker wishes to create is the first step in creating that image. The model may itself be a picture, or it may be a mathematical function that the programmer expects can be represented graphically, or it may be a list of physical parameters for an object (that may or may not actually exist). The first and second cases are easy to visualize. The third, it may surprise some readers to learn, has for a few years been exemplified each fall by automobile commercials that have been created with computer-generated images of the product before the product actually existed.

The model, once complete, must be described to the application data structure and to the graphics system. The most basic way to do so is to list physical parameters in a program that correlates those parameters to some sort of mapping system. Any object model may be described as a set of points and lines and/or planes, of various color and texture designations, or perhaps as a character string, occupying precise positions on a Cartesian grid of either two or three dimensions. To get a bit more complicated, the model may be described as *a set of any number of sets* of any sort of combination of points, lines, planes, etc. Each of these component sets is a *primitive,* which may be thought of as any sort of image building block. A primitive can be a simple point or line, or a mathematically describable polygon, or some odd, complex shape. Of course, mathematically describable points, lines, or polygons make very useful primitives, because their algebraic descriptions fit neatly into algorithmic solutions to the problems of representing any image model, after which they are easily converted into code.

It may be easy to understand how points and lines may be combined in an algorithm to solve the problem of any image to be represented, and at the same time to be dubious that polygons can be used as primitives to describe realistic objects. For example, say you wish to create a two-dimensional image of a human hand. Can one simple ellipse, such as that in Figure 4.2, be used to represent the hand? It doesn't seem very likely.

In these equations, A is the angle from horizontal (X axis) in a clockwise direction. If RY > RX, the ellipse is longer in the Y direction. (If RX > RY, the ellipse would be longer in the X direction and RX = RY would result in a circle.) If you don't understand how these equations define an ellipse, don't be too worried yet. Deriving shapes from equations will be covered anon.

Now, Figure 4.2 doesn't look very much like a hand. In Figure 4.3 the

Figure **4.2** An ellipse on a Cartesian grid

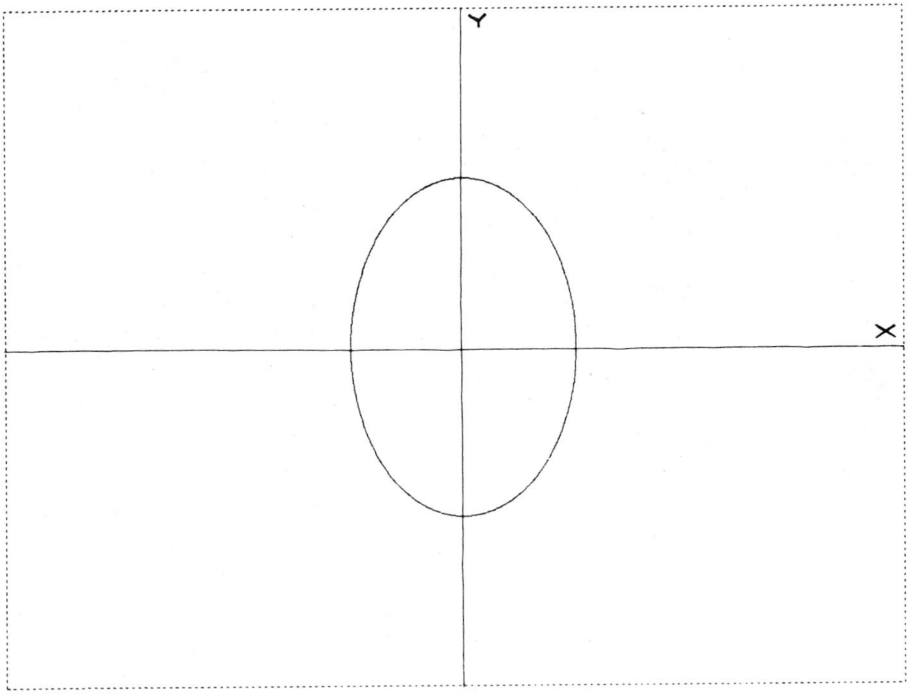

FIGURE 4.2

An ellipse on a cartesian grid represented by:

$$X = X_1 + RX * COS(A)$$
$$Y = Y_1 + RY * SIN(A)$$
$$RY = 3RX$$

same ellipse has been placed in a context that indeed allows us to identify it as a hand, even though you may well still maintain that it doesn't much look like a hand. To be generous, let's agree to call it a stylized hand. But to be honest, if such stylization is all our computer animation can achieve, what's it worth?

Put in a context changed only slightly again, the 2D mannequin in Figure 4.4 has quite acceptable hands. This is, obviously enough, the same stick man that we could only generously call "stylized" in Figure 4.3. After having seen him up close there, we may still notice that his hands are no more than simple ellipses. But if we were to first enounter him in Figure 4.4, or say the same size as in 4.4 but surrounded by other pictoral detail, as in Figure 4.5, we might just assume we're not seeing much detail because the fellow is quite far away.

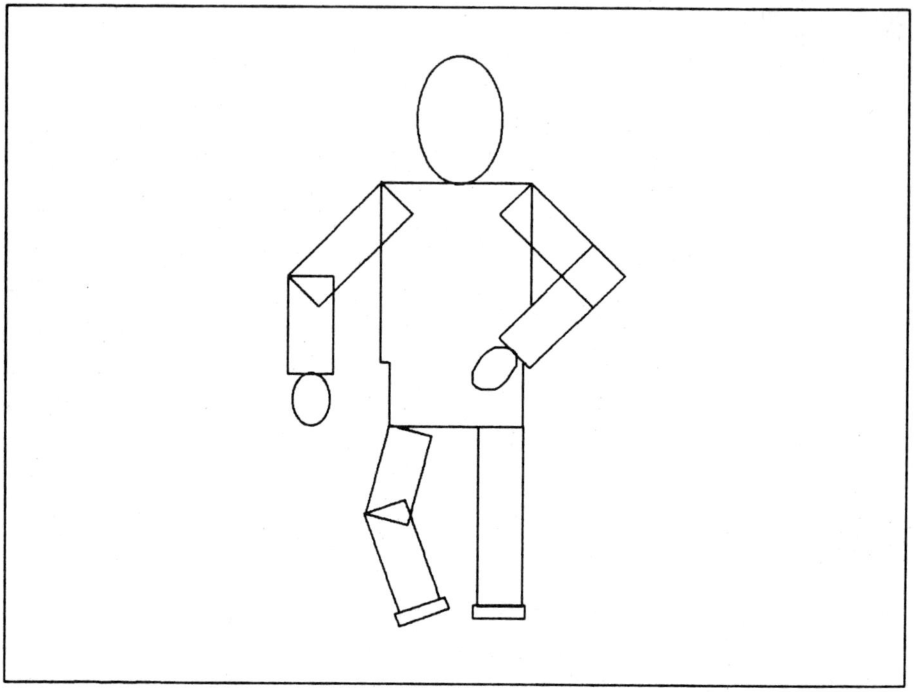
Figure **4.3** A low-resolution man

Figure **4.4** Same man, but less of him means higher resolution

Figure **4.5** Low-res man in a low-res world may just add up to a coherent and interesting style

This is all indicative of another side of the problem of measuring the coastline of Britain, described in Chapter 1. Detail increases in importance the closer you look at it. Distant objects don't need to be presented in nearly as much detail as closer objects. What *is* necessary, from the artist's standpoint as well as from the viewer's, is consistency of style. In psychovisual perceptions of reality, what seem like properly detailed hands from up close do not look like ellipses from far away — they look like small and out-of-focus, somewhat elliptical, flesh-colored lumps of what are probably hands. In an animated scene, viewers will accept any degree of stylization, but will not accept a properly detailed hand turning into a properly detailed ellipse at some distant point. Though the perception of this must remain subliminal to a viewer, it would be fatal for an animation designer not to understand what needs to be done.

It may be just as well that we find it hard to assemble a perfectly detailed hand by computer simulation. In fact, the missed approximation of reality that most computer animators routinely come up with has resulted in a typical computer-animation sort of stylization that audiences look forward to, and that probably evolved mostly unconsciously on designers' parts. But this style of somewhat-off-reality can grow tiresome, too. How much fresher a truly consistent and meaningful animation style made of boxes and ovals would be to the familiar cliches!

On the other hand, representing hands as ellipses all the time has limitations, too. And we can do better. We can, using very little more inventiveness, represent a hand as a combination of ellipses, as in Figure 4.6. Here the basic concept of using an ellipse to represent an entire hand has been slightly modified, to use somewhat changed ellipses to represent the stem and fingers of a hand. Notice how the algorithmic equations tie the fingers into their proper positions relative to the base and to each other, by localizing each ellipse's central point relative to the largest (central) ellipse's central point. We have not defined any points in this roughly simulated hand to specified coordinates on the grid, so that by first defining the coordinates occupied by the central ellipse, then changing those coordinates, the entire hand will move together. Yet by changing the definition of any of the central points of the ellipses that represent fingers, the fingers can be moved independently, too.

Figure 4.6 may be merely the hand of a stylized cartoon character, but it can be made either far more realistic or far more interestingly stylized without resorting to any basic forms other than ellipses. For example, it is surely easy to see how fingers may be made of three ellipses each, connected end to end. Fingernails and warts can be made of other el-

Figure **4.6**

Two-dimensional hand made of a combination of ellipses, defined by the following equations:

$$X = X_1 + RX * COS(A)$$
$$Y = Y_1 + RY * SIN(A)$$
$$RY = 1.5(RX)$$

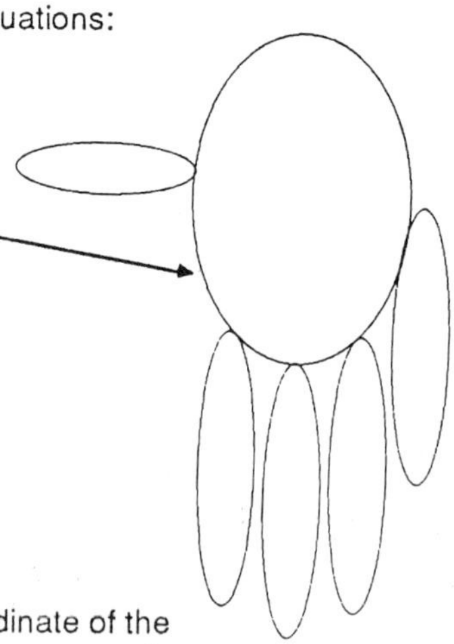

$$RB = 0.2 * RX$$
$$X_2 = X_1 - 4RB$$
$$B = X_2 + RB * COS(D)$$
$$C = Y_2 + RC * SIN(D)$$
$$RC = 5RB$$

Where *B* represents the *X*-axis coordinate of the determining point of the ellipse, *C* represents the *Y*-axis coordinate, and *D* represents the radius from (X_2, Y_2) to (B, C).

lipses, localized by central points defined in relation to the immediately larger ellipse on which they are fastened.

Moving in a different direction, instead of using more ellipses to make a more realistic hand, let's imagine some classical animation (see Appendix A) in which characters bounce and jiggle as they move. From frame to frame, we might redraw the hand in Figure 4.6 so that it expands and shrinks, perhaps as fingers walk across the screen. So much of the fun of animation lies in caricaturing physical movement like this; if you let your fingers walk across a table, you may notice that when a finger presses on the table it gets just a little bit rounder, and when you raise it, the finger (now under no pressure) looks slimmer. By counting out how many seconds such a movement ought to take, then dividing the result into frames (24 per second if you will animate by filming off the computer screen, 30 per second if you have enough memory available to animate the image in the computer and transfer directly to video), you can figure out how many changes to make in the ellipses to create the illusion of a balloon-like hand walking across the screen.

4.8 Design Goals

A simple set of equations defining one ellipse can extend into a fairly complex algorithm. There are several benefits to using similarly defined ellipses for building more complex objects and then animating those objects:

Programming ease. This is many-leveled. It is easier to write a bugless program (or to later debug a program) that contains many similar equations for similar shapes, rather than many very different sorts of equations mixed together. Calculations are not so confusing, and errors are easily recognizable. This sort of program also can be written quickly, considering the programmer need not look up and adapt many different sets of equations for many different shapes.

The program runs quickly. Simple shapes take less memory and thus less time to output to the screen. This is also somewhat intertwined with the third point, design elegance. To look forward to that a bit, a program that combines the same few equations over and over is one that allows the programmer room to find all possible shortcuts. Fast running speed (and its corollary of relatively low memory requirements) means it may be possible to achieve in-computer animation of a scene. Just how possible depends, of course, on many factors, but it never hurts to use shapes as simple as possible in any image.

Design elegance. ''Elegance'' is used here in the sense of something fully achieved with the smallest possible effort. That ''fully achieved'' is an important part of the definition. Making all the parts of an image out of similar primitives gives the whole a unity of form at the same time that it makes it easier to produce. The result may not be realism, but it is coherently true to its own style. This concept is particularly important for animator–programmers working with micros or other less-than-ultimate equipment, where compromise is always part of the game. Realism may be more than is attainable, but design elegance can be perfectly compatible with compromise solutions to programming problems. Design elegance is most often preferable to realism — not to call the two incompatible. They can operate together or apart, luckily for animators who find that equipment exigencies obviate all possibility of attaining realistic images.

These ideas do not pertain exclusively to the ellipses used to demonstrate them. Some other all-purpose shape would do just as well, generally speaking. Though roughly circular primitives (such as ellipses) feel roundly comfortable and approximate the curves of humans and other natural phenomena, various polygons have other advantages. Polygonal primitives have two major advantages over any continuously changing form such as an ellipse. For one, flat edges connect easily to each other. The least realistic thing about the ellipse model of a hand was that the fingers were never really joined to the palm. You could cut flat edges off the ellipses at points where they are to join, but this is a complex procedure (one that is worthwhile, surely enough, and will be explained later in this book) and uses substantially more code and memory. To connect one flat edge of a rectangle to another rectangle, it is only necessary to place them side by side. To keep them connected, it is only necessary to define the position of the second in relation to the first, as was done with the ellipses that were used to make a hand.

The other way in which *some* polygons have an advantage over rounded forms for use as primitives is how they match the needs of raster scanning and pixel mapping. Pixel maps are grids. They are especially conducive to the drawing of straight horizontal and vertical lines. In fact, if one has a picture made up entirely of horizontal and vertical lines, even a ''low-resolution'' raster scan system may easily reproduce that image with perfect resolution. An image of a square can be reproduced perfectly by any raster scan system. Rectangles therefore make perfect building blocks for other images — perfectly adaptable to the scan and memory system, that is. Circles built of many combined rectangular primitives look really circular only if the rectangles are so small that stair-stepping cannot be noticed.

Using polygons with more than four sides as primitives allows for some of the same benefits as using rectangles. Octagons, for example, can be plotted so that half of their perimeter is always made up of straight verticals and horizontals; furthermore, octagons connected to octagons on any side will appear to be solidly attached. Such polygons also offer certain of the benefits of rounded figures: for example, an octagon with two extended parallel sides resembles a finger about as much as an ellipse does. The right octagon can look much more like the palm of a hand than any ellipse, or than any rectangle, either.

In other words, for any imaging project, some particular sort of primitive shape(s) will be most nearly ideal. Setting your programming goals at the start of any project certainly involves determining what sort(s) of primitive(s) to use. Making that decision involves consideration of all the factors in the design and animation process: what sort of hardware is at your disposal, how much time you have to produce the image, how complex is must be, what the coherent "look" will be, whether it is to be more or less realistic, etc.

Another factor not yet mentioned is *view.* The display where an image is to be generated is more properly thought of as the *view surface.* The more realistic the picture, the more its resemblance to a photo may be generally understood; but the view surface is really more akin to the focal plane of a camera before a picture is taken. Like a camera, the CGI screen can be "aimed" at any angle and distance from the image to be simulated. Perhaps the most compelling reason to create images in three dimensions is that the view surface may act as a *synthetic camera,* switching to various different viewpoints of the scene. With two-dimensional pictures, too, you may well want to switch viewpoints; to a certain extent, a changing view on a 2D scene can remain realistic, and after some point the new view will look exactly like a certain type of turnkey video animation trick that has been overly popular in music videos: an image captured in an oblique window.

In fact, instead of thinking of the view surface as a synthetic camera, you might think of it as a magic window. Thinking of the synthetic camera's snapshots as *windows,* a concept familiar in all sorts of general applications programs that became popular in the early eighties, allows you to relate the images you make to the ways that windows are used in so much software. This is something new for animation, and will surely inspire new sorts of moving images.

Whether you can change views of an image (and to what extent that view can change) is a function of data base size within the graphics system, and also of having that capability built into the application program. Here is a major reason for having a "deeper" picture behind the view surface than ever may be shown on the actual screen. Of course, all is compromise in this business; a system operating on limited memory may have to slow down so much between two views of the same scene that animating those images becomes impossible within the computer and must be done externally, on film or video. How much you wish to change views must be balanced against the time image transformation takes, and on that time lag's effect on the animation process. How much you are able to change views depends on how much of an unshown picture there is to take a new view of, with similar compromises already mentioned elsewhere. Most often there are no easy decisions on all these compromises, and programmer–animators wind up muddling through with the highest possible investment and fewest possible plans. The more that can be planned out, based on the subject of the animation to be made, the better the finished project will look.

4.9 Production Planning

There are still more factors to take into account when planning a graphics project, but all would seem to be best introduced a bit later, after less complex topics sink in. The most important lesson that can be learned from facing all these daunting compromises is to establish a technique for conquering them at the beginning of your project. Otherwise, problems may become unmanageable later on.

It may seem paradoxical, given the great technological advance the computer is supposed to represent, but the best way to solve problems at the start is to make a *storyboard* (see Figure 23 in color insert). A storyboard looks like a comic strip, with each frame depicting an essentially new frame of the moving-picture-to-be. Written instructions next to each frame tell anyone who looks the storyboard over just what image changes happen when (animation storyboards are often timed to the frame, or at least to the second). By forcing yourself to write out just what you plan to do, right at the beginning you can solve the problems that would arise later; even if nobody but you ever sees the storyboard, it forces you to communicate better with yourself.

A storyboard allows you to take a second step in the production planning stage, a *production schedule.* This involves a close look at the storyboard, to relist each image or complex part of an image in an order that groups it with other, similar images or duplicate images. Animated films have often made use of the same segments over again in different spots; these are known as "cycles" (see Appendix A). Next to each group of like sequences, roughly describe the process that will be used to create them. With all of the above figured out, you will probably then want (or need) to assign a target date for completion of each stage of the project. Give yourself some leeway by building into the timetable what traditional animators call a "pencil test" stage (so called because in traditional animation incomplete pencil drawings are made and animated before the final, full images are created): that is, a dry run.

From the production schedule, you can proceed to algorithms. Isolate each group of like images and solve the problems that each suggests. Your description in words of the images to be created must be transformed to mathematical equations; then those equations can be changed to the next step, program code. (In many cases images will be made and manipulated that require little or no programming, if you have already programmed in the basics from past projects, or have programmed your system for turnkey-style, easy user interaction. In these instances, animators can move directly from production schedule to image production.) It all adds up to a four-step model for *pre-production:*

1. storyboard
2. production schedule
3. algorithms
4. programming.

Of course, you can't begin to make a storyboard until you have a sense of what is technically possible and desirable within a given system. Thus these four steps do not necessarily follow in chronological order, but sometimes exist side by side, changing each other as more research or imaginative ideas change them. After whatever changes have been wrought by innovation at a mathematical, programming, or other production stage, the best way to keep a handle on where the whole production is going is still to go back and reform the production schedule and storyboard.

4.10 Input Transformation

There are smaller steps, not really explained yet, that fall between pre-production steps. All of these are part of what the SIGGRAPH Core system calls *input transformation* — a phrase that begins to suggest what must be done with the information in the storyboard. Most CGI systems rely on a grid system of X and Y coordinates for 2D images and X, Y, and Z coordinates for 3D image plotting. A bare beginning has been made at explaining how to make a model of the image to be created, so that it can be understood by the computer. That model need not originate mathematically, but at some point it must become mathematical to be understood by the machine. For example, a storyboard hand drawing may serve as a basic model; to render it mathematically, an intermediate step might be to reproduce the drawing on graph paper, draw X and Y coordinates on the paper, and assign values to all points in the drawing. These points could then be entered directly into a graphics system that will plot them on a similar grid.

If this sounds like a lot of work, imagine a very similar input transformation that involves a digitizing tablet. A bit of code would instruct the graphics system to accept coordinate data from the tablet; then the storyboard image could be drawn directly on the tablet. In other words, with an adaptable input transformation stage, you can produce storyboards by CGI, too.

Whether the storyboard is on paper or already resident in computer memory, you may still wish to go through the stage of transforming ideas for images into equations for polygons or other programmable primitives. Why do this for an image that has already been painted on a view surface, with coordinates already entered in memory? There are several possible answers. As in the examples of Figures 4.3–4.5, using primitives can allow you to move a part of an object based on its relation to another part of the object. A painted image may be composed of many primitives, each of which may be one or a few pixels square in size. This complicated assemblage of pixels must be wholly or partially repainted to move part of it: in partial repainting, if a character is to move its arm from one frame to the next, the whole first frame can be duplicated (given a system with frame buffers that can hold both) and the second changed only by redrawing the arm. Moving a primitive in relation to another primitive within the frame is a whole different procedure for animation. Given 3D images, it is necessary for any kind of visualization; even in 2D, it yields a different look and often more efficient, elegant animation than redrawing each frame of painted image. Painting directly on a tablet can be combined with primitive modeling in various ways, by using the painting as a storyboard-like source of ideas about what primitives to use, or more complicatedly, by making applications programs that treat parts of the painted image (which is made of *very* primitive primitives) as second-order primitives to be remodeled.

In any event, any object must be described to the graphics system in a way consistent with its output from the graphics system. The input transformation must mirror the *output transformation* to come, so that a given primitive looks the same when it comes out of the system as it did in definition on the way in. As was described in Chapter 2, some distortions may enter in here, based on the peculiarities of differing pixel length or width, from the computer's interior view surfaces to the final display's view surface. Similarly, the display's 5:3 ratio curved screen can be easily distorted when filmed by a 16 mm animation camera; the optical solution for this latter problem is analogous to the in-program correctives that may be necessary for the former problem. Unfortunate examples are the many competitive (and otherwise perhaps high quality) graphics cards for the IBM PC family that create internal grid/view surfaces not precisely correlated with many other color display monitors' grid sizes. Pairing hardware that matches as closely as possible would be wise; if not, correctives must be built into programs.

4.11 Interactive Programming

Yet another goal in developing an efficient applications program is some way to see interim results of what you are programming. In non-graphics applications, this would have little relevance, but imagine drawing a picture without knowing precisely how it looks during the process, and you've begun to see some of the difficulty of programming CGI. Painting images on a digitizing pad, with fairly simple software enabling you to display what is being drawn as it is drawn, is one way of solving this analog interface problem. For directly programmed images, it is necessary while programming to keep in mind an ideal of interactive program structures. You should program images in relatively incomplete segments, to view the progress of your labors bit by bit, then combine portions of programs that have proven successful. A vast length of code that is meant to produce and animate a full screen image — and somehow doesn't — is far harder to debug than bits and pieces of the big picture, assembled along the way.

CHAPTER FIVE

BASIC Graphics on the IBM PC

There are many other books and magazines full of advice on animation in BASIC with microcomputers, and some of these have been included in the Bibliography. All, however, also seem to have as a firm goal that all images and animation must be totally a product of the single personal computer at hand. The goal throughout this volume is different: the best and most realistic animation possible, given each animator's budget limitations. Within this goal, large data bases offering different view surfaces might be programmed in BASIC, but would take a long time to realize; preferably, the computer would be assisted by a film or video camera or videodisk to make animation. I will assume this to be a likely case for perfection-oriented readers.

A more serious problem is pointed out by a quick look at existing micro animation texts. Display monitors and graphics cards for home computers tend to be none too good, so existing advice on making PC graphics in BASIC emphasizes the relatively low-level work that can be shown on the typical home micro display. But not only are displays and graphics cards improving of late, the IBM PC and cards available for it have some peculiarities that may be exploited for better images by the savvy user.

In other words, image-making owners of not very souped-up PCs can now graduate from kindergarten pictures to at least the first grade — with some new hardware, a full understanding of the old hardware, and good programming.

CGI makers who are working with souped-up PCs along with other equipment can still benefit greatly from a detailed awareness of the graphics-making characteristics peculiar to their PC, so the following should be of interest to all classes of laborers in these vineyards. Many concepts that will be elaborated in depth in later chapters will be introduced here, in a simpler way and as they relate to BASIC programming.

Even impatient and advanced readers would be advised to at least skim along here in proper chapter order.

BASIC is a much more supple language that many micro users suppose, and it is capable of being used to produce very good animation if only it is not coupled to a slow, memory-poor computer and low-resolution display, as is so often the case. The reader most interested in this chapter will be one who prefers to do most programming in BASIC and needs a background in that language's graphics vocabulary that can be applied to the more advanced chapters to come.

5.1 IBM BASIC Graphics Structure

The IBM PC can use PC BASIC to generate graphics in a few different ways. Using BASIC's SCREEN statement will bring up the choices: *mode, burst, apage,* and *vpage*. *Mode* chooses from text display or, with IBM's own color graphics card, either low-resolution/color or higher-resolution monochrome graphics. Other cards allow both graphics modes to display color, with more limited colors at high res and more choice at low res. *Burst* determines color or monochrome display. *Apage* and *vpage* identify the text screen that is in use; depending on how much data is assigned to each, the IBM text display mode can support as many as eight "pages" (in a very-low-resolution mode), which is another, text-oriented way to say eight frame buffers. Unfortunately, in the color graphics mode all memory must be allocated to just one frame at a time.

With IBM's own color graphics card, in the high-resolution mode each pixel on the screen is controlled by one bit of display (or buffer) memory, with 640 bits/pixels to a line and 200 lines. This means the full screen has much finer horizontal than vertical resolution, and also means that if you try to build a diagonal by stair-stepping one bit up and one to the side, the line will rise over three times higher (or faster) than it moves sideways. This slope factor (640/200, or 3.2) must be built into any planned images; a circle programmed for equal horizontal and vertical pixel size would come out looking like an ellipse that is 3.2 times higher than it is wide.

In the low-resolution/color mode, the IBM card assigns two bits per pixel horizontally, for 320 pixels per line, with the same 200 lines. Even though resolution is lower, the closer correspondence of 320/200 (or 8:5) to the 4:3 screen ratio of most CRTs and of NTSC television means that most of the time graphics can be planned without the bother of a slope correction factor. When absolutely proper scale is necessary, a short

BASIC program can correct for it (this will be presented later in this chapter). Of course, the two bits/pixel allow color — only four at a time, in IBM's case.

If you must choose between these two modes on this color graphics card, the choice would not always gravitate toward low-res/color, even when the goal is color graphics. If you are planning to animate film shot off the CRT screen and have a film camera with sufficient registration (see Chapter 12), it pays to shoot three "passes" through the film camera, one for each of three primary colors. Creating monochrome images that are shaded properly for filtering into each color will result in a full-color image with effective resolution significantly greater than that of the CRT, because of some overlapping of images for each pass. (Of course, images can be overlapped and superimposed in the same way for the low-res/color mode.)

It would be preferable, though, to begin with some other color graphics card. Several are available that offer significantly higher resolution and color capabilities than IBM's, and perhaps by the time this is being read IBM also will offer a more advanced graphics card. (See Appendix B and Chapter 2.) The AT&T VDA has been mentioned already; this exemplary board not only offers 256 by 256 pixels with 256 colors, but 8 bits per pixel, MS-DOS and C bindings, a library of primitives, and the rudiments of an applications program.

The documentation for any graphics card should specify memory locations for the screens it can create. For example, the IBM card allocates a graphics page with the locations of bytes of memory numbered from hexadecimal &HB8000 to &HBBFFF.

5.2 Hexadecimals

IBM BASIC uses the hexadecimal (base 16) way of referring to numbers, and IBM uses the "&H" prefix to let you know the number is a "hex." Other references may be used, too (and will be in later chapters), but for now we will follow IBM's notation. In a hexadecimal world, digits 0 through 9 serve their usual purpose, and the symbols A, B, C, D, E, and F represent the decimal numbers 10, 11, 12, 13, 14, and 15. Thus, &HB8000 is equivalent to 753664. The last byte the IBM card allocates to screen mapping, &HBBFFF, equals 770047. The total number of bytes IBM allocates to the graphics page is &H4000, or 16384. As you can see, multiples of binaries come out to easily remembered, short, even numbers when calculated in hexadecimals — which is precisely the reason they are used.

To convert a standard base-10 number to hexadecimal:

1. Find the largest power of 16 that may be subtracted from the base-10 number.
2. Find the largest multiple of that power that may still be subtracted from the base-10 number.
3. Subtract the result of Step 2 from the base-10 number, and repeat Steps 1 and 2 with the sum of this subtraction.
   Repeat this step until the subtraction yields less than 16, or until you have reached a sufficient decimal place.
4. Assemble the multiples of powers you have obtained into columns of diminishing magnitude, left to right.
5. Beginning on the right, convert each multiple of a power into a hexadecimal digit and bring all together into one number, preserving place settings with zeros if necessary so that the rightmost column represents the final sum in Step 3, the second column represents multiples of 16^1, the third column represents multiples of 16^2, etc.

For example, 770047 is larger than 16^4 — 65536 — but not 16^5— 1048576. That's Step 1.

Step 2: you can subtract 11 • 16^4 — 720896 — from 770047, leaving a remainder of 49151.

To continue (Step 1 repeated), the remainder, 49151, is larger than 16^3 — 4096 — and (Step 2 repeated) is also larger than 11 • 16^3 — 45058. Subtracting this leaves a remainder of 4095. You can continue calculating the next hexadecimal places; here is the whole thing in a more schematic form:

770047	=	$11(16^4)$ + 49151	=	&HB0000	+ 49151
49151	=	$11(16^3)$ + 4095	=	&HB000	+ 4095
4095	=	$15(16^2)$ + 255	=	&HF00	+ 255
255	=	$15(16^1)$ + 15	=	&HF0	+ 15
15	=	$15(16^0)$	=	&HF	
TOTAL =				&HBBFFF	

Converting from hexadecimal to decimal is a little easier. Just multiply each hexadecimal (people often simply say "hex") digit by the power of 16 represented by its place in the hex number. A hex number with three places to the left of the (hexa)decimal point has a 16^0 column, a 16^1 column, and a 16^2 column, analogous to a decimal number's 10^0, 10^1, and 10^2 columns.

For example:

$$\begin{aligned} \&HB8000 &= 11(16^4) + 8(16^3) + 0(16^2) + 0(16^1) + 0(16^0) \\ &= 11(65536) + 8(4096) + 0(256) + 0(16) + 0(1) \\ &= 720896 + 32768 + 0 + 0 + 0 \\ &= 753664 \end{aligned}$$

Each power of 16 corresponds to commonly attainable bit and byte multiples, and thus to screen and resolution measures. This is a coincidence of multiples of the basic binary building blocks dividing evenly into 16. Each of the decimal numbers 0 to 15 may be represented by a four-bit binary or by a one-digit hex. Hexadecimals are useful for any machine-language-level programming, but are usually not necessary to an understanding of programming in BASIC, C, or other high-level languages. Except in graphics, that is: being able to think in hexadecimals allows the graphics programmer to better visualize pixel arrangement on the screen and in the computer's memory. In the chapters on C ahead, you'll want to use hexadecimals or octals (base-8 numbers, which are just about as useful) for machine-level operations with C.

This need to visualize the pixel map is a good example of what was referred to in Chapter 1 as a structural difference between graphics programming and other programming. Graphics-making is not purely an exercise in logic, as is most other programming, though it certainly does involve a large element of this. Making pictures also involves that old intuitive sort of feel an artist has for materials. Even if these materials are arrangements of numbers, the artist will be better off understanding how they are mapped, rather than treating the screen as a frame with magical workings underneath.

5.3 Bit Mapping

The eight bits in every byte of IBM color card memory each control one pixel in SCREEN 1 (as it is designated in IBM BASIC), the high-res monochrome mode, and are allocated at two bits per pixel in SCREEN 2, the low-res color mode. The first memory location addresses the first eight pixels at the left of the first line at the top of the screen, 753665 (&H8001) addresses the next eight, and so on across the line, 80 bytes or 640 bits per line. At the end of the first line, the next location skips to the third line to string another 640 bits and pixels, starting with byte number 753746. After the third line comes the fifth, and so forth to the bottom odd line (the 199th). The even-numbered lines are only filled in, in series, after the odd. Given any memory location on an even-numbered line, the eight-pixel-wide location directly below it will be

B = A + 8192

where *A* is the original location and *B* is the desired address immediately below; 8192 is half the number of memory locations allotted. Given any memory location on an odd-numbered line, the eight-bit-wide location immediately below will be

B = A − 8112

because 8112 = 8192 − 80. Adding 8192 to a location on the bottom, 200th, line will reach a similar location on the top line.

The only difference between the high and low-resolution screens is that one uses one bit per pixel while the other uses two. With one bit per pixel, there are enough bits to make each line hold 640 pixels, but only enough information per pixel to code each 0 or 1 — which could, theoretically, symbolize any two colors. With two bits per pixel, there are only enough bits available to make each line hold 320 pixels, each twice as large. But there is enough information available per pixel to code each 00, 01, 10, or 11. These can be used to symbolize any four colors the computer will allow you to choose from. Those four colors can be referred to as a *palette,* meaning all the colors immediately accessible to a given pixel. The IBM card allows a choice of two palettes of three colors each, and in addition allows a designated background color (coded 0) from one of sixteen possible colors. Only one palette and one background, and thus at most four colors may be used per screen (see Figure 5.1).

Imagine using a color graphics card with sixteen bits per pixel. This might be allocated to provide a choice of *over 32,000* colors per pixel, since there are 32,768 (2^{16}) possible combinations of 16 bits. Or, eight bits might be allocated to represent any of 256 (2^8) colors, then other bits might be used to partition the screen in some way that allows a choice of different palettes for different pixels, or perhaps different luminance settings (see Chapters 1 and 8). No matter what other color possibilities were assigned to the other eight bits, any pixel could be colored any of 256 • 256 possible ways; that is, again 32,768. In the chapters that use C to

Figure **5.1** IBM PC graphics card colors and their codes

<table>
<tr><th colspan="2">Background Colors</th><th>Palette Colors</th></tr>
<tr><td>0 Black</td><td>8 Gray</td><td>Palette 0</td></tr>
<tr><td>1 Blue</td><td>9 Light Blue</td><td rowspan="3">0 Background
1 Green
2 Red
3 Brown</td></tr>
<tr><td>2 Green</td><td>10 Light Green</td></tr>
<tr><td>3 Cyan</td><td>11 Light Cyan</td></tr>
<tr><td>4 Red</td><td>12 Light Red</td><td>Palette 1</td></tr>
<tr><td>5 Magenta</td><td>13 Light Magenta</td><td rowspan="3">0 Background
1 Cyan
2 Magenta
3 White</td></tr>
<tr><td>6 Brown</td><td>14 Yellow</td></tr>
<tr><td>7 White</td><td>15 Bright White</td></tr>
</table>

demonstrate more advanced graphics possibilities, we'll construct frame buffers with just this many color possibilities. It can be done in BASIC, too, though it wouldn't be displayable on the standard IBM graphics system. But once you understand how this stuff works in further chapters, you'll be able to implement it in BASIC, assuming you have a graphics system running BASIC that also allocates enough memory for the job.

5.4 Coordinate Systems

Addressing pixels by allocated bytes of memory is one way to map pictures. A way more often used is a superimposed grid with vertical (y) and horizontal (x) axes and coordinates (and with z, or depth, coordinates when working with 3D). Such a grid is usually set up with the (0,0) point (the origin) at center, or at either the top left or bottom left corner. The IBM PC graphics card sets the origin at top left. As can be seen by comparing Figures 5.2 and 5.3, a point having the same relative position on screen has a different-sounding address in each manner of dividing the graph. The top-left orientation of the PC makes its entire graph correspond to the lower right quadrant of a Cartesian system with central origin. The PC's x and y-axis numbering systems run only positive integers, but in directions that would be negative in the Cartesian system. We'll use the PC's numbering system here, to avoid confusion.

Setting the origin at the top left, or any corner, is fine for depicting a world of limited size; but as we will see in further chapters, it is often more convenient to think of one's graph as a part of an unbounded co-

Figure **5.2** IBM PC coordinate system with (0, 0) at top left

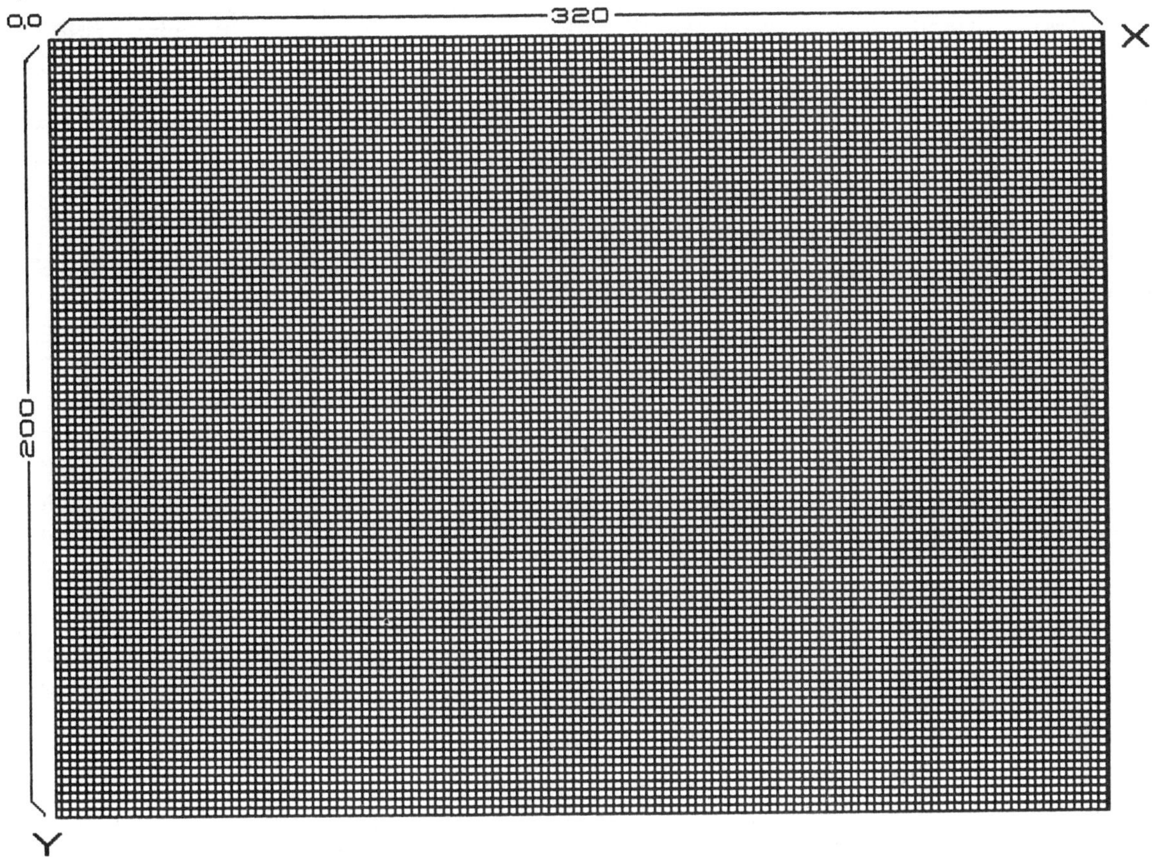

ordinate system — also known as a "floating point" system. A display of any given size can be thought of as a window on a portion of such a floating point system; so can the pixel map within the computer. A display window is more accurately thought of as a viewport, and might be equivalent to the full size of the screen, or to a smaller portion of it. Both viewports and windows can be used to close in on or withdraw from that floating-point "world coordinate system," showing more or less of its geography, as the "synthetic camera" creates images that look like a film camera's zooms, tracks, and pans. Windows, viewports, and their part in synthesizing all of this will be discussed in depth in Chapter 7.

A great deal of packaged software featuring "windows" is available

Figure 5.3 IBM PC coordinate system with (0, 0) at center

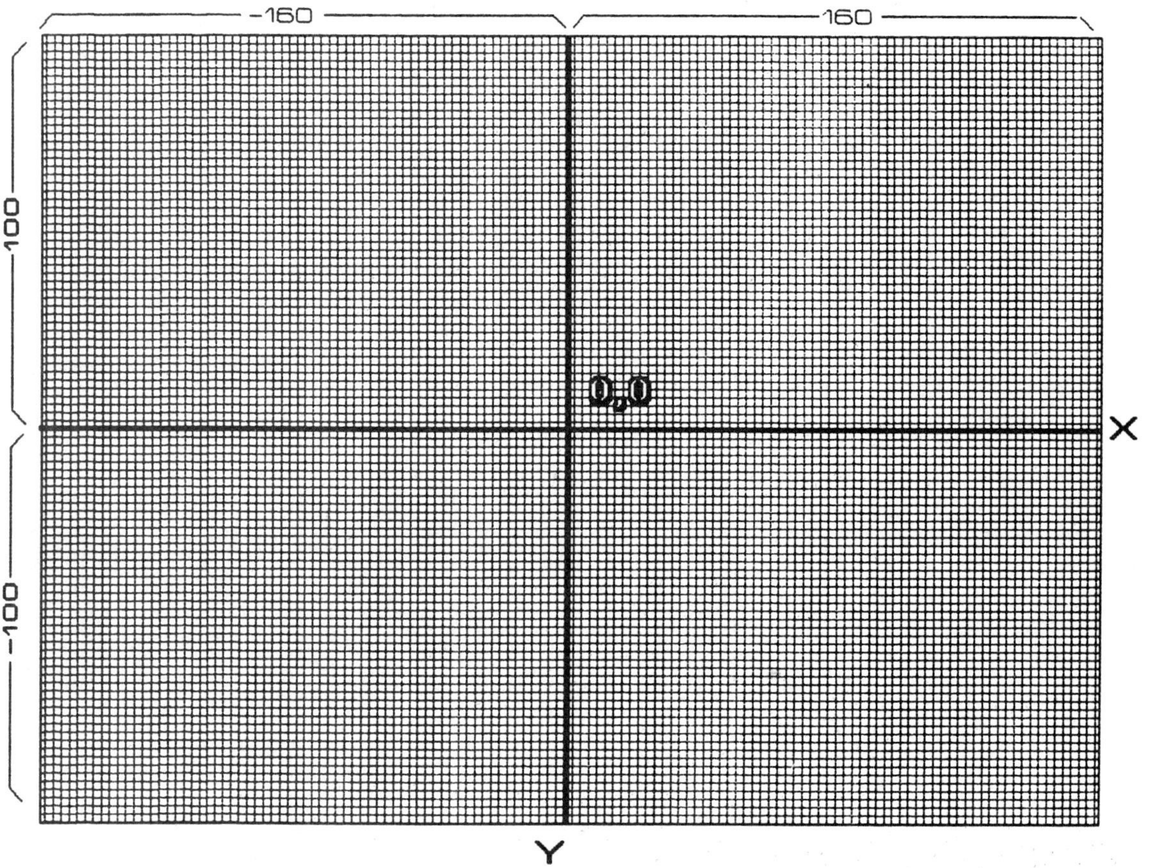

for the IBM PC. Most of this is of little use to us, as it is structured to use rather difficult-to-change viewports to show various simple graphs or text. You can make your own window software for the PC that is fairly supportive of animation, as is explained further on in this chapter.

5.5 Basic BASIC Animation Graphics Vocabulary

The basic method we can use to address bits is the same in the simple IBM color card and in a more complex card such as AT&T's, even if the better card uses a centrally oriented Cartesian grid, uses more bits to represent each pixel, or has other fundamental improvements. A BASIC program can easily be written to address each pixel in a screen and color each in any way made possible by the card you use. Several BASIC statements may be used in this process. DEF SEG defines the portion of memory to which your instructions will refer. To select background color and palette, IBM Basic's COLOR command is followed by a code number first for background color, then for palette. A setting might be

```
COLOR 1,1
```

(Other cards' COLOR statements select colors in slightly different ways.)

KEY and CLS are not exclusively graphics commands, but they affect graphics more than most operations. KEY shuts off the soft key display (that is, the on-screen prompt line), and so should be included early in any graphics program. CLS clears the screen — and should thus be used early in the program to start fresh, and also any other time when the whole image is to be rebuilt.

To those experienced only in film or video animation, this may be a difficult concept to understand. In these older methods of animation, it is taken for granted that an entirely new image supplants a previous one several times per second. Computer CRT displays are typically refreshed 30 times per second just as TV images are (see Chapter 1), so it may seem natural to make the same sort of wholly new images for single or double frames. Animating via computer, however, makes possible selective movements. If, say, only a character's arm position is to change, that change may be programmed alone, and the rest of any previous image will remain on screen. Indeed, a direct statement — CLS — is necessary to clear the screen. Clearing the screen and moving to another image is an intrinsic part of the film animation process; on film, it is easy to do for either mundane or dramatic reasons. Since every programming statement takes up some of a limited amount of memory and lengthens computer reaction time enough to possibly risk smooth, "real-time" animation, it may be noted that CLS, which produces something like a film "cut," is a far more costly achievement within its relative universe.

Now to the real building-block BASIC graphics statements: PSET and PRESET. Each turns on a pixel to the color indicated. Both are written in the same format:

```
PSET (x,y) [,color]

PRESET (x,y) [,color]
```

The (x,y) coordinates refer to the pixel being addressed. It can be addressed just in terms of such coordinates if a Cartesian grid has been programmed in, as will be explained further on in this chapter, or addressed by the hexadecimal location allotted in memory. The color can be identified by code number, as in Figure 5.1. The command format, again, is

```
COLOR [background], [palette]
```

In the high-res monochrome mode, PSET and PRESET select only from dark or light, with 0 or 2 (on any palette) standing for dark and 1 and 3 standing for light. Also, each command may be used with no color specified, in which case each has a default setting. The only difference between the two commands is that PSET's default color in any given palette is 1, and PRESET's is 0.

It may quickly become apparent that PSET and PRESET are the essential communications used by bitpads, or digitizing tablets. Being able to turn on each pixel independently, to any allowable color, allows you to draw the most complex pictures. Without a bitpad, the only way to know what you are drawing with these instructions is to draw an image first on graph paper, then program in the coordinates for the entire picture. A good tablet removes the intermediary step of programming each pixel command.

5.6 Point and Line to Plane

Creating pictures only by defining points certainly has its limitations. Programmers will be anxious to move on to defining lines and various planar shapes, and packaged paint and bitpad systems would seem to do all that can be done by programming with PSET, PRESET, and other point-oriented commands. Both paint-system makers and impatient programmers ought to give thought to what can be achieved by programming images point by point, as we discuss more complex operations involving lines and planar shapes. Many techniques to be discussed also will have application to programming one point at a time. Pictures thus created can be, hopefully, just the sort of new and innovative graphics never envisioned by makers of paint systems that slavishly imitate (while electrifying and memorizing) the possibilities of older media.

The task of explaining the increasingly complex representation of points, then lines, then planes, calls to mind the title of Wassily Kandinsky's 1926 book, *Point and Line To Plane,* in which the artist tried to lay a scientific foundation for painting. Kandinsky's "science" was more arbitrary mysticism and pseudoscience than the genuine article, but the work remains relevant despite its failures, chiefly because it helps explain the thinking behind Kandinsky's art. And Kandinsky achieved a tremendous expressiveness out of points, lines, and shapes that would be mostly very easy to program. With most computer animators and illustrators totally involved in a quest for photorealism, some of the old-fashioned spirit of Modernism would be an overdue breath of fresh design, too.

Images drawn by precisely identifying each pixel may be fine for still graphics, but the technique creates problems for animation. Moving any object so depicted would involve reidentifying each pixel of a changed object in a new location, and doing so many times for persistence of vision as the movement progressed. Film and video animators may be used to such redrawing, but some more advanced BASIC statements offer a better way. LINE, coded in the form

LINE (x_1,y_1) - (x_2,y_2)

draws a straight line between any two sets of coordinates. (A line made of one command obviously takes less memory and is easier to animate than a line made of individual pixel commands for each point along its way. A fairly simple interface program can thus allow tablets, too, to be used to draw lines.) In a slightly different form,

LINE - (x,y)

draws a line from the last point defined in the program line above to the new point defined in this command.

In other words, in the following program, line 20 puts you in the color graphics mode (assuming you are using an IBM color card), turns off the key line and clears the screen. Line 30 specifies a red background and palette number 0. Line 40 draws a line from the coordinate (20,20)— that is, 20 pixels to the right of the top left corner and 20 pixels down from the top left corner — to the coordinate (70,50). Line 50 draws a line from the last point mentioned, (70,50), to (70,80).

```
10 'line demonstration
20 SCREEN 1: KEY OFF: CLS
30 COLOR 13, 0
40 LINE (20,20) - (70, 50)
50 LINE - (70, 80)
```

When the program is run, the image will look like Figure 5.4.

The full format of the LINE statement also includes the ability to enumerate the line's color, a few selections for line style, and simple ways to build boxes. For example, we could change line 50 of the above program to

```
50 LINE - (70, 80)  ,0
```

to draw the line in the light magenta background color (see the chart in Figure 5.1). Why one might want to draw a line in the same color as the

Figure **5.4** Screen image of a short program (see text)

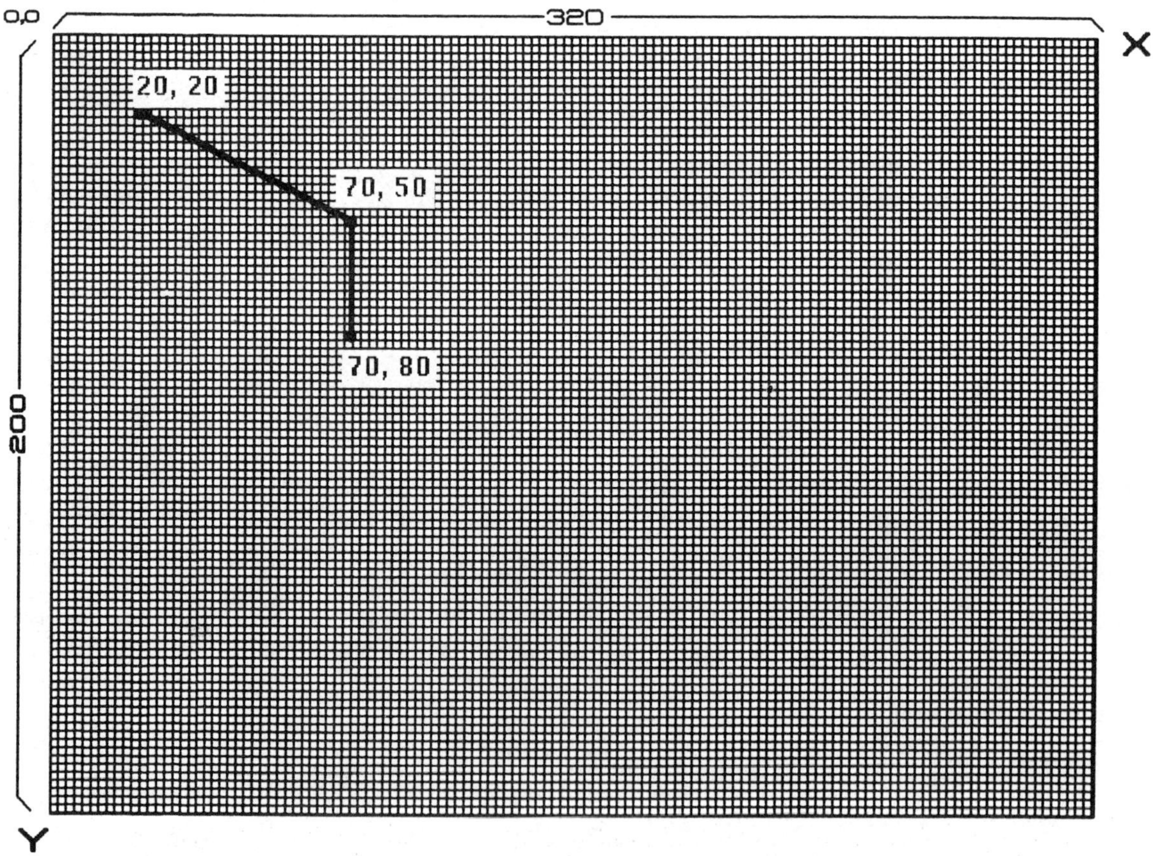

background is soon to be discussed. If we add a line to the program, such as

```
60 LINE - (65,50) - (250,180) , ,B
```

we are instructing the graphics system to draw a box that uses the specified coordinates as upper left and lower right diagonal corners. Only perpendicular boxes can be drawn with this command. The format for the command, you will notice, includes a spacing comma for the color position. We have not instructed the graphics system to draw this line in any particular color, but the format demands that color must be enumerated before *B*. (The system will choose the default color, as has been explained.) A somewhat different box can be drawn by changing the command slightly, to

```
60 LINE - (65,50) - (250,180) , ,BF
```

This creates a filled box — filled with whatever color the line was to be drawn in, that is. Style also may be enumerated for lines, but not for filled boxes. If you add the program line

```
70 LINE - (65,50) - (250,180) , , , [number]
```

you can choose a style for the diagonal line spanning the box made by line 60. Styles are simply dotted patterns, choosable from any 16-bit binary. To create a style, draw or think of a series of 16 consecutive pixels, as in Figure 5.5. Give each pixel either and "on" or "off" color, then count out the resulting pattern in binary numbers, then convert the binary to hexadecimal. Plug the hex number into program line 70 for a dashed line.

5.7 The Hidden-Line Problem

Lines may be drawn in any color, including the same color as the background. In animation, as objects move they hide parts of their defining lines, or parts of other objects' lines. The "hidden-line problem" con-

Figure **5.5** A 16-bit line style pattern resulting in 0001111010010000, or &H1E97

off	off	off	on	on	on	on	off	on	off	off	on	off	off	off	off

tinues to be addressed at length in computer graphics research, because real-time animation demands constant hiding and recovering of lines that define images. In BASIC, one of the few ways to address the hidden line problem is by drawing lines in the same color as the background. Such a line still exists, even if it can't be seen; at any point in space or time where it must reappear, it can be recolored with a simple line of code. The line defined in the example program's line 50, running from (70,50) to (70,80), is the same color as the background. It is also covered by the box defined by program line 60. If the box is to be animated so that (70,50) – (70,80) is exposed, the line can be recolored simply by repeating program line 50 with one of the palette colors specified, and all of this can be included within an IF, THEN statement.

5.8 Relative Coordinates

A much fancier, yet quite simple BASIC command really brings us within range of the ellipsoid hand algorithm begun in Chapter 4. STEP relates a line or point, or any other shape, to other coordinates that already have been programmed. Let's say we add a few lines to the earlier program:

```
10 'line demonstration
20 SCREEN 1: KEY OFF: CLS
30 COLOR 13, 0
40 LINE (20,20) - (70,50)
50 LINE - (70,80)  ,0
60 LINE - (65,50) - (250,180) , ,BF
70 LINE - (65,50) - (250,180) , , ,&H1E97
80 PSET (250,180)
90 LINE - STEP (30,10) ,2 ,B
100 LINE STEP (5,0) - STEP (5,10)
110 LINE STEP (0,8) - (30,0)
100 LINE STEP (5,0) - STEP (5,10)
110 LINE STEP (0,8) - (30,0)
```

Line 90 creates a red box (color 2 on palette 0) that extends thirty pixels to the right of the last point enumerated — (250,180), mentioned in line 80, — and ten pixels down. PSET must be used to set the point to serve as a reference for STEP. Line 100 illustrates another use of STEP, drawing a line that starts five pixels to the right of the reference point and moves to a point five pixels to the right and ten down. Line 110 draws another diagonal from eight down from the reference to thirty to the right from the reference. If the reference were changed, all these lines would move with it.

STEP can be used with LINE, PSET, PRESET, or CIRCLE.

5.9 Circles

The CIRCLE statement takes the format

CIRCLE (*x,y*) [*center point*] [,*radius length*] [,*color*[,*start,end* [,*aspect*]]]

The color definition here works the same as color definitions thus far presented. Starting and ending points for color allow pieces of the circle's arc to be colored separately. (IBM PC BASIC, and most computer languages, only understand arcs and angles as defined in radians, not degrees. One radian equals 57.2956°, since 2 pi radians = 360°.) If you wish to define starting and ending points for circles or their coloring in terms of pi, you will have to first enter a program line defining pi (3.1416 should do for any pictures one can draw on the PC). "Aspect" in the CIRCLE format refers to the screen aspect ratio, which has great bearing on whether a circle will end up looking like a circle or like an ellipse. Remember that in the IBM color mode the coordinate map's aspect ratio is 8:5, but the typical monitor screen has a ratio of 4:3; there is a 5/6 difference between these ratios. If you do not define the aspect for a CIRCLE statement, IBM BASIC will assume a default aspect of 5/6 to make the circle look like a circle. (In the high-res monochrome mode, IBM BASIC assumes a default aspect of 5/12.) You can always choose another aspect and draw an ellipse, though in an ellipse the radius measurement must constantly change, so it is necessary to go through some algebra to arrive at a formula that continuously relates the two variables. With very similar calculations it is possible to draw an ellipse in BASIC without the CIRCLE statement — and as you may have guessed, an ellipse drawn with CIRCLE must have its major and minor axes aligned perfectly horizontally and vertically ("aspect" is only meant to adjust the vertical-horizontal relationship). The math to be introduced in later chapters has equal relevance to calculating ellipses in BASIC, so read on, ellipse fans.

For now, to make this section's program turn out a somewhat Kandinsky-like end product, I'll add a brown circle, with the statement

```
120 CIRCLE (30,75),30,3
```

Run the program on your PC and , if you think "Program With Brown Circle" is not quite a masterpiece, customize it.

There's nothing like a window for animation graphics versatility . . . unless it is BASIC's DRAW statement, which is used for several types of "string" graphics operations. Stringing, windowing, painting, drawing, definitions of viewports, axes, pointing, rotation — all of these are the sorts of complex statements that are often hard to find definitions for even in BASIC instruction books, yet they are (along with the statements already defined in this chapter) what allows BASIC to remain interesting even to demanding graphics programmers.

We'll take the simplest terms first.

5.10 PAINT

The PAINT statement has the format

PAINT (*x,y*) [,*color*] [,*boundary*] [,*background*]

By specifying a set of coordinates, a whole area that has already been enclosed by lines can be filled in. If nothing has been enclosed enough for the graphics system to recognize a distinct area, the whole bit map will be painted the specified color.

The color can be specified from any available on the palette, or can be assembled by "tiling"; that is, assembling a pattern of variously colored pixels. Tiling can be a way for the memory-poor (such as anybody stuck with IBM's graphics card) to give the effect of more colors. If you are in Palette 0, for example, and have only green, red, and brown available, a background color of blue, judiciously tiled in various combinations with the palette colors, can create the pointilist effect of any hue in the rainbow.

To create a tiling pattern, you could either use a sheet of graph paper to doodle possible patterns, or write a fairly simple program that uses lines or boxes to make an enlarged grid, which can be experimentally painted with various colors. (You also could create a window for the same purpose, once you learn how to do so.) The basic tile pattern grid can extend to as many pixels horizontally and vertically as you wish, but each line of pixels must contain the same number of columns; the grid must be perfectly rectangular. Convert the colors into their palette number representations; convert the numbers (0,1,2, and/or 3) into binaries; then convert the binary numbers, read across the grid horizontally, into decimals (see Figure 5.6). You will need to use a program line to define the

Figure **5.6** Making a tiling pattern

tiling pattern (background 0, palette 1) = background/palette numbers =

red	blue	green	blue
brown	red	blue	brown
blue	brown	red	green

2	0	1	0
3	2	0	3
0	3	2	1

binary pattern = decimal (horizontal totals)

10	00	01	00
11	10	00	11
00	11	10	01

decimal	total
128 + 8	= 136
128 + 64 + 32 + 2 + 1	= 227
32 + 16 + 8 + 1	= 57

tile as one or more strings of characters. The format for this line (using the arbitrary numbers in Figure 5.6) is

```
TIL1 = CHRS$(136) + CHRS$(227) + CHRS$(57)
```

Then, in a PAINT statement, you can enter TIL1 in the [,color] position.

You'll recall that PAINT supposes that a bounded area exists around the specified coordinates to be painted. In the *boundary* position of the PAINT statement you can specify a color for the boundary itself, by choosing a number of any color from the palette. The final part of the statement, *background,* allows tile painting over an already painted area. The procedure for tiling here is the same as just described, but background tiling will automatically cease if two lines in a row repeat identical coloration that already exists.

5.11 WINDOW

IBM BASIC's WINDOW statement has the format

WINDOW [[SCREEN] (x_1,y_1) - (x_2,y_2)]

The first set of coordinates in this full statement refers to the upper left corner of the display screen; the second set to the lower right corner. Basically, the statement transforms the screen's coordinate system. If the first set of coordinates is set at (0,0) and the second set at (2,2), for example, the whole screen will be used to represent four pixels, and those pixels will be spread proportionally across the screen. WINDOW can be used to create an instant close-up on anything represented in the coordinate map, which can now be thought of as a universe with any selectable part viewable on-screen. Successively smaller or larger windows can also be used to simulate zooms.

Only when using the SCREEN option do the first set of coordinates specified by WINDOW refer to the upper left corner of the display screen and the second set to the lower right corner, with the positive direction of the vertical axis being downward, as is normal for the PC. The command

WINDOW (x_1,y_1) - (x_2,y_2)

changes the positive direction of the y axis to upward, uses the first set of coordinates to refer to the bottom left corner of the screen, and the second set to refer to the top right. The reason for this confusing change is that an infinite floating-point coordinate system must be thought of with (0,0) at center, and the very existence of a window immediately makes us think of the pixel map as only a piece of the whole world coordinate system. With (0,0) at center, the top right quadrant would correspond to the axis and coordinate direction set up by WINDOW. The question is, why did IBM choose to usually go with a coordinate system originating at top left? The reasons will become clear in the next two chapters.

For any number of more complex programming operations to come, you may wish to use the WINDOW statement just to change the coordinate system to the more standard form. The origin may also be set at the center of the screen — or anywhere else — by providing lines for the axes, then defining the center point:

```
100 LINE (0,100) - (319,100): LINE (160,0) - (160,199)

200 CX = 160: CY = 100
```

Obviously, the WINDOW statement may also be used to flip any image upside down. If specified window coordinates do not share the same aspect ratio as those to which the original image to be windowed has been mapped, the image can be flattened or stretched either vertically or horizontally. Successively graded aspect ratios for windows can make an object seem to change perspective; combining such grading with zoom can help give the impression of a track or dolly shot.

(Even some filmmakers confuse the looks of zooms and track or dolly shots. Each has its synthetic-camera equivalent, so it is important to differentiate them. A film camera's zoom is an adjustment of optics, with no movement by the camera, that appears to move the subject closer or farther by continuously shifting apparent focal length. Perspective never changes in this process, though depth of field flattens as the subject is brought closer. In a track or dolly shot, the camera physically moves closer or farther from the subject, actually moving through the scene and constantly changing perspective while focal length remains constant. Full 3D imaging is necessary to fully simulate a track, though tracking can be partly simulated by stretched perspective in windows — a type of simulation sometimes referred to as 2-1/2D. Zooming is a simple matter in 2D images.

(Pans and tilts are the subject of a more subtle confusion that also must be resolved by computer animators. Panning is generally thought of as sideways movement of the camera, parallel to the subject, with a tilt being the vertical equivalent. In fact, this would be a sideways — or in the case of a tilt, vertical — track, something not often done. Panning is a sideways, and tilting a vertical, *pivoting* of the camera. Sideways or vertical track shots are unusual in film, due to their relative difficulty and expense, but they are sometimes done to create an oddly attention-getting, yet subtle look. Several of Stanley Kubrick's films may be the best examples of extensive use of such shots; they allowed him to achieve a cold, hard-edged, techno look. Sideways or vertical movements parallel to the image plane are far easier to perform with a synthetic camera than true pivoting pans. This is one part of computer animation's cold, hard-edged techno look. Achieving the fluidity of an analog pan is difficult in computer animation, but not impossible. Perhaps a pseudo-analog pan could be used for an oddly attention-getting, subtly warm and natural look.)

Unfortunately, because of the limited bit: pixel ratio of the IBM PC graphics system, windows that enlarge images often develop strange and unwanted features in the process of expansion, and must be corrected. For like reasons, line styles and tiling effects cannot be made finer as images shrink.

5.12 Viewports

The IBM BASIC statement VIEW works with WINDOW to define a portion of the screen that is actively addressable. When VIEW is used, drawing can take place only within the viewport; the rest of the screen can continue to display images, but will not be addressable until the viewport is changed again to include some part of it. The complete format for VIEW is

VIEW [[SCREEN] [(x_1,y_1) - (x_2,y_2) [,*color*] [,*boundary*]]]

Simply stating VIEW, with no options, makes the whole screen the viewport. VIEW with coordinates specified identifies the area of the screen to be the viewport. VIEW SCREEN maps the image onto the entire screen, but only allows interaction in a viewport area defined by coordinates. The *color* option allows you to fill the whole viewport with one of the colors from the palette. *Boundary* allows a palette color to be used to draw a box around the viewport; without using it, no boundaries will separate the viewport from the rest of the screen area.

Whenever you use VIEW to map an image into a different section of the screen, you produce a dichotomy between the original coordinates with which the image was mapped and the new coordinates it will occupy. The viewport's coordinates are not quite a subset of the original image's, as in windowing, since they may be just plain different. A new term is necessary to take in the floating point universe concept and the original image map. Both can be called *world coordinates,* as opposed to the physical coordinates represented in any window, viewport, or screen display at all.

Because you may get confused as to where any image is located in each set of coordinates, IBM BASIC provides PMAP and POINT commands to tell you. If a given point has physical coordinates (PX,PY) and world coordinates (WX,WY), then

```
PX = PMAP(WX,0)
PY = PMAP(WY,1)
WX = PMAP(PX,2)
WY = PMAP(PY,3)
PX = POINT(0)
PY = POINT(1)
WX = POINT(2)
WY = POINT(3)
```

and POINT (*x,y*) gives the color of any pixel at the specified location. These statements can be used to label coordinate points as part of the image, or they can be used as ongoing information within a graphics system programmed for interactivity.

5.13 DRAW

DRAW allows you to string together a set of coded commands. There are so many different ways to do this that it would be difficult to enumerate them all here, so have a close look at your manual. Only the most useful formulations of DRAW for our purposes will be reviewed here.

In DRAW's coded vocabulary, U stands for up, D for down, L for left, R for right, E for an up-and-right diagonal, F for a down-and-left diagonal, and G and H for the remaining diagonals. All of these are moves from the last point specified. B signifies a move that is not drawn. All DRAW instructions must be included within quotation marks. If the last point specified in the last program line prior to using DRAW was (0,0), then, a program line such as

```
100 DRAW "BD100 U20 E10 H10 D20 F10 G10"
```

first moves 100 lines down where there is room to draw, then draws a hexagon.

All of the above are relative coordinates, continually strung on to the last instruction. DRAW also allows absolute coordinates, coded M.

```
DRAW "M 100,100"
```

draws a line from the last entered point to the coordinates (100,100).

DRAW strings can be defined and then called up by name, too. For instance,

```
100 STHEX$ = "U20 E10 H10 D20 F10 G10"
200 DRAW STHEX$
```

first defines STHEX$, then draws it. This is a very exciting possibility! It allows images to be drawn as primitives, then very simply plunked into a program, and an image, as often as necessary.

DRAW also allows us to rotate any drawn image. The code for this is TA, for turning angle, and is specified in degrees from −360 to 360, with the positive direction being clockwise and the negative counterclockwise. (Yes, here, suddenly, the PC understands degrees, not radians. Consistency is not the hobgoblin of small-computers.) The format for a DRAW rotation is

DRAW "TA [*degrees*]; [*string name*]"

So that

```
120 DRAW "TA 75;STHEX$"
```

would redraw the hexagon at a 75° angle. If this line is tacked onto the two lines of program shown above, this would be the second time STHEX$ has been drawn. With no instruction to clear the screen, both STHEX$ drawings would coexist.

DRAW statements deal only in physical coordinates. Once they are completed they may be included in a window. Though they may be drawn over the physical space a window occupies, however, they obey the physical coordinates of the screen and are not part of the window.

5.14 GET and PUT, BLOAD and BSAVE

GET and PUT are operations very similar to DRAWing a defined string. GET stores and PUT retrieves arrays of information. The format for GET is

GET (x_1,y_1) - (x_2,y_2) ,*array name*

The coordinates identify the top left and bottom right corners of a rectangle with sides parallel to those of the screen. PUT has the format

PUT (*x,y*) ,*array name* [*action*]

Its coordinates identify the top left corner of the area to receive the information in the array. There are several ways to perform this operation, and they are determined by *action*. The most interesting of these, for our purposes, are: PSET, which replaces whatever was on the screen with the stored array; AND, which presents the array image, along with whatever was already displayed; and XOR, which allows complementary display with two successive uses possible over the same space (after two, the original screen image reappears). In other words, the *action* possibilities of PUT allow rudimentary animation.

To save any graphic image on disk, first use DEF SEG to define the memory segment your new file is to occupy. Then the command format for BSAVE is

BSAVE *filespec, offset, length*

with *filespec* filled by any valid file name, *offset* representing the distance from the beginning of the memory segment to be used, and *length* indicating the number of bytes of memory to be saved.

The loading format is

```
BLOAD filespec [,offset]
```

To load a file, first define the memory segment (DEF SEG = &HB8000, most of the time). Use the *offset* option only if the file has been saved with an offset value.

5.15 Computer-Assisted Animation Via the PC

As was stated at the beginning of this chapter, we're not really very interested in the simple and rough-looking animation that is possible internally with the PC. All of this sort of animation is done with the terms already reviewed, plus some others — chiefly having to do with alphanumeric ANSII characters that have little to do with higher-level animation. Unless you want your animation to be on the level of a home video game, animation made totally within the PC is not so interesting. Any command that can make an image move to a precise display spot, repeatedly, is a boon to animation, but doing the whole job inside the computer — as anybody who has been programming along with this chapter's instructions knows — does not allow sufficient writing time for complex images. I said "we" are not quite interested in the very rough real-time work that can be done totally within the PC. If you are, see the Bibliography listings for a few PC graphics texts not aimed at professionals. This book may have delved into such instructions perhaps a bit more quickly than graphics-programming beginners and amateurs would prefer. The assumption here is that the average reader will be more interested in video output to a still-frame video recorder or videodisk for editing into animation, or a final product on film via output to a film recorder or filming off the CRT. If the last-named possibility is your method of choice, remember to compensate in programming for the aspect and color differences between film and the computer, and make an effort to find a movie camera with the best possible pin registration, as always with animation. (In 16 mm, an inexpensive old Arriflex is often the animation camera of choice; in 35 mm, Arris and Mitchells are most often used. Old Mitchell cameras are inexpensive enough and dependable enough even for student investments.) In any case, animation combined with some sort of live action is a constant goal of many animators, so it makes sense to set up a film or video system that can do this.

CHAPTER SIX

Programming Graphics and Animation in C, and Beginning the Palette Choice Program

6.1 Introduction to C

Every programming language has an environmental influence on the way that tasks are accomplished. One long-established direction of computer graphics design has been to explore graphically this influence: the relationships of math, machine, and language. Another, complementary direction has been to try to work beyond the peculiarities of hardware and software to create images with either photographic realism or some other style that seems totally independent of the computer system that produced it. C is a wonderfully supple language for all sorts of applications, including graphics. Not least of reasons why, moreso than perhaps any other language, C facilitates either of these reflexive or nonreflexive sorts of graphics styles.

A self-understanding style seems more interesting to this commentator. The grammatical and syntactic structure of C Language is so elegantly logical that animation written in C really ought to take advantage of the opportunity to allow the end product to demonstrate and explore some of its constituent logic. Interactive programs meant for end users (a lá videogames) would seem the best way to do this, and some attention will be given to this in Chapter 10. Meanwhile, this chapter will explore some of the characteristics of C that are most useful for animated graphics. Far moreso than in Chapter 5's similar discussion of BASIC, ideas for animation projects should spring naturally to mind as you become familiar with the language's possibilities.

Readers with an advanced understanding of C probably will be considering skipping to the next chapter, but the aim here is to introduce C with critical reference to graphic animation. There should be something even for experienced programmers to glean....

C has been called both a high-level and a low-level language. Its low-level, or machine-language-like aspects are direct operations on bits and memory addresses, with operators closely tied to the capabilities of hardware. These characteristics are all of great importance to graphics programmers. High-level languages typically operate on no smaller units than individual bytes; operating on bits may be possible, but in other languages, it is about as graceful as picking up dimes with your toes. Operations on bits, however, make greater use of scarce memory — thus, individual bits control pixel characteristics in most display systems. Being able to directly address a bit memory map increases processing speed and reduces the memory needed for running a program, useful for any graphics and especially useful for animation. And C's bit operations are relatively easy to learn and use.

C's high-level characteristics can be called very high level indeed, if high-level is thought of as equivalent to more portability. C does *not* include I/O (input/output) at all; the language leaves I/O peculiarities to its operating system. Because the shape of output is what graphics makers are particularly interested in, the degree to which we can utilize C's portability is limited. The operating system and library functions must be large parts of our work. The more you understand C, though, the less of a limit this will seem. And C often has been called one of the easiest programming languages to learn; it engages the logical mind and involves less rote than other languages.

What is a library function? How should you choose among operating systems? C was written for use with Unix, and this has certainly been the most common combination. But many versions of Unix are currently available, and they can be quite different from each other. There has also been something of a software boom going on for C, what with Xenix adapted from Unix, MS-DOS recently adapted for C (MS-DOS was adapted *down* from Unix in the first place), simplified versions of C becoming available, etc. C is a highly *un*standardized language (although an ANSI C standard promises to change that), and different versions of C get along best with different operating systems. Your choice of operating system may just be limited by what is supported by your hardware manufacturer.

With all of these complications, however, the basics of C are fairly constant. Most programs in this book were developed with Microsoft C, the Microsoft C compiler version 3.00, and MS-DOS version, 2.00 but they ought to be applicable to most C environments. Don't take the authorial system as an endorsement of these products; there are many fine C Language products.

Some advice: It doesn't seem to make too much sense to get involved with CBASIC or some other supposedly simplified or hybridized version of the language. Standard C is not all that hard to learn, so why bother with a "simplification" that must cut down on versatility? In the second case, hybridizing C's lovely form looks kludgy from here. Otherwise, it seems hard to go wrong with the various available Cs, compilers, and operating systems; just make sure they all match each other.

C is very structured, and allows an infinity of functions to be created within its structure. "Functions" in C are more often called "subroutines" in other languages. Programmers can create their own libraries of functions, or can purchase ready-made libraries. The choice depends on whether your required tasks are represented in a given function library, whether you can afford to buy it, and whether you'd rather go through the nuts and bolts of developing your own functions for tasks at hand. C is such a rich language that any number of different functions may be combined in programming to accomplish the same task, and some will inevitably be more efficient than others. A standard function library is typically supplied with your compiler, and libraries also are available for specific sorts of operations. A function library for C graphic animation for micros seems like a great idea; many graphics and screen-control libraries are commercially available, though I'm not aware of a really fine one for animator's purposes — which just may be a fine opportunity. Operating systems are nonspecific function libraries that include I/O, or even perhaps can be said to specialize in varied I/O instructions.

A language that allows libraries of functions to be kept on file also allows programs that call functions from different files. Graphics makers can set up parameters for all sorts of images or movements, then call these functions into one animation job or another as needed. C is made for such modular programming; it speeds program development, debugging, and adapting existing programs for other jobs. High-level functions order overall processing in a general way and call low-level functions to manipulate data details. In the very structural universe of a C program, each function has its place, and each doesn't care how other functions manage to get their jobs done, as long as the job is done when that function is called.

Such modularity is what allows for C's portability. A compiler that hooks Function A into a VAX, for example, runs entirely different code from the same operation detailed to an IBM PC. But, assuming each machine has enough processing power to perform what is asked of it, Function A can be shuttled unchanged from one compiler to another. Where particular instructions must be changed to adapt code from one computer to another, all those changes may be defined together as, say, a set of VAX 11/780 instructions, with an interactive user interface fitted in front of the program to turn on or off that set of instructions.

C programs may at first look very strange to anybody with experience in other programming languages. Lines aren't numbered, both upper and lower case letters are used, symbols are used extensively (though there aren't all that many of them), and, perhaps most confusing, numbered series or arrays always start with 0. Don't let all of this throw you. Good programming practice always includes extensive documentation, and it's easy to include extensive notes in any C program as you go along.

There isn't space in this book to go into a full explanation of C, but a few good texts are recommended in the Bibliography. These should have any interested reader writing fairly complex C programs inside of a week. What *is* necessary here is a critical examination of what in C is particularly relevant to an understanding of making graphics. This is easier said than done; those familiar with graphics making in C might well ask, "Where do you draw the line?" — the line, that is, between what in C is more relevant to graphics and what is not. So much of C's way of doing things can uniquely affect the end product. For some all-too-interesting aspects of C, the line has been drawn at the above conceptual discussion; below, some C statements worthy of deeper review with respect to graphics will be looked at. In the chapters ahead, other concepts in animation graphics will be illustrated with reference to C.

Perhaps this chapter and the next few should be brought together into a subbook called "Meditations On C For Graphics And Animation." These few chapters (6, 7, and 8) will enable you to put together a basic high-resolution graphics package in C, including programs for frame buffers, palettes, paint, texturing, and modeling.

These programming chapters are *not* meant, however, to be a text on C! They are meant to suffuse the graphics-making process with an esthetic built around knowledge of the tools used to do the job, and to introduce graphics makers to programming, programmers to graphics, and each to the other. A text on C is highly recommended for anybody who would make the most of this volume, and for anybody who would make computer graphics and has access to a machine that can run the language.

6.2 Fundamentals

First, some C fundamentals for those with no background in the language (readers who speak some C will want to skim toward Section 6.4 or 6.5): All C programs have a **main** function that may, in fact, be the entire program, but more often pulls together all subsidiary functions and presents the program to the compiler for action. A simple sort of C program looks like

```
main ()
  {
  printf ("C is a wonderful language for programming graphics.\n\n
     We'll advance from text to graphical output as\
soon as possible."\n);
  }
```

The output of this program is

```
C is a wonderful language for programming graphics.

We'll advance from text to graphical output as soon as possible.
```

The **main** statement tells the C compiler that this is where to begin to execute the program. Since **main** is the first statement to appear in the program, this is also the name of this particular program. The parentheses following **main** contain nothing, telling the compiler that the **main** function contains no *arguments,* or parameters. The curly braces contain all the action of the function; everything within them will be assumed to be part of **main.** The **printf** is the text print command, and like any other statement within a function, it acts upon everything within a following set of parentheses. Quotation marks set off what is to be printed, with the exception of certain special symbols, denoted by a backslash (\). One such symbol is the plain \, which allows a string constant (the quotation marks here hold a string of character constants) to extend to another line without affecting program output. Another is **\n,** which inserts a new line in the program output. Checking your C system documentation, you ought to find backslash characters to insert single or double quotation marks, form feed, vertical and horizontal tabs, etc., into your string constants.

A semicolon ends every C statement.

Spacing is almost entirely noncritical in C. The way this program has been indented is entirely to enhance readability, with one exception: after the \, if the next line were indented, those spaces would be part of the character string output, so the line beginning with ''soon'' must start at the left margin. The same program could be written

```
main(){printf("C is a wonderful language for programming graphics.\n\n
We'll advance from text to graphical output as\
soon as possible."\n);}
```

but this would be extremely bad form. Similarly, continuous documentation is only to be expected from any well-written program. The symbols * and *\ enclose any explanatory notes not to be run as program instructions, so you also could have written the above program this way

```
main ()   \*program to print my opinion of C, and also to*\
          \*forecast a future direction for the discussion  *\

   {
   printf ("C is a wonderful language for programming graphics.\n\n
       We'll advance from text to graphical output as\
soon as possible."\n);
   }
```

6.3 Constants and Variables

In C, any character, number, or character or numerical string can be either a constant or a variable, but variable names must begin with a character or an underline (_). A variable's *data type* must be declared before it is used. Usually, all variables are declared at the top of the program or function in which they occur. Different C systems allow somewhat different data types for variables, but some basic data types are **int**, **float**, **double**, and **char. Int** stands for integer and **char** for character. Type **float** can be used for storing floating-point numbers (those with decimal points), and **double** is for floating-point numbers between -1 and 1, to much greater accuracy than numbers stored in a float variable. Exactly how many decimal places can be stored in float or double variables will depend on the system hardware. Generally speaking, a 16-bit CPU will allow each expression half or less the number of decimal places than will a 32-bit CPU. This is definitely an instance of possible non-portability to watch out for in any program. Even more critical, using variables that take up more memory space than necessary is wasteful of an item in short supply. It may be handy to keep a range of values in mind for each data type. For 16-bit CPUs, Figure 6.1 lists byte requirements and value ranges for C's data types. Your particular C system may have other data types.

You may notice that character values are given numerically. This is because, in C, characters do have additive integer values: e.g., $a = 1$ and $A = 27$. These values are, of course, distinct from the ANSI memory-position value used to represent each character. In the next several examples, integer values will be used most often, because these simple programs won't need variables with all that much accuracy. Graphics

Figure **6.1** Data types, required memory, and ranges of possible values

Data Type	Bytes Required	Value Range
char	1	-128 to 127
unsigned char	1	0 to 255
int	2	-32,768 to 32,767
unsigned int	2	0 to 65,535
long int	4	-2,147,483,648 to 2,147,483,647
unsigned long	4	0 to 4,294,967,295
float	4	±1.7014111E38
double	8	±1.00E307

programmers must inevitably progress, however, to addressing memory positions or operating on bits and bit fields; then choosing the right sort of variable will be far more critical. Think of these variables as envelopes for numbers. Conserving memory demands that the smallest possible variable ought to be used every time, but it must be big enough to hold its package accurately.

It is important to understand the difference between constants and variables. The expression

$$32 + 82.5 = i$$

is a constant expression; *i* can only equal 114.5. If *i* has been declared an **int,** however, the expression is variable; *i* could equal any value that might be assigned to it by a function, as long as it is an integer value. The variable *i* is then said to *call* the function whose product equals *i*. If no value is assigned to *i* other than its value in the expression 32 + 82.5 = *i*, then *i* will equal the integer sum of 32 and 82.5, or 114. The decimal will be lopped off, since an integer may only be a whole number. The format for declaring the data type for a variable is

```
int    integer_variable
```

This would declare the variable called **integer_variable** to be of type **int.** The label **integer_variable** is a fully valid name for a variable, though on some systems only the first eight characters of a string count toward defining a variable name. In the interests of portability, it makes sense to limit names to eight characters. Other valid names are sum

I

guess_what_this_variable_is_called

_what?

The last may be confusing, because the subline in the first position takes other meanings to some compilers. Examples of invalid variable names are

all_my$

your name

2toomuch

float

Variables may not start with numbers (2toomuch), contain the dollar sign, or contain an empty space. They also may not use anything with a special meaning to the compiler, like "float."

Basic arithmetic expressions are the same in C as in most usage: −, +, *, /, and =. C also has a modulus operator (%), which gives the remainder of the first value divided by the second value. As you might expect, multiplication, division, and modulus take precedence over addition and subtraction, so that

$$2 + 3 \% 3 / 2 = 2 + \frac{(3 \% 3)}{2}$$

$$= 2 + \frac{0}{2}$$

$$= 0,$$

not 1 as would be the case if all operations had equal precedence and were simply calculated from left to right.

Other operators that are very commonly used in C are of the *relational* sort. These combine two common signs and imply a testing operation. For example, the operator == translates into English as "proves equal to." Combined with an **if** statement, you can say

```
if{

        x == y \*...(to be continued)*\
```

then go on and say what might happen if this is the case. This is very different from saying $x = y$ in C: $x = y$ assigns x the value of y. $x == y$ tests whether $x = y$. The relational operators are listed in Figure 6.2.

Relational operators are great for use with **for, while, do,** and other *looping* statements, and with **if, else, switch,** and other *decision* statements. In many ways these operators and statements are the guts of how to manipulate objects and characters in animation; it is easiest to introduce them by giving examples with simple numbers, then move on to their use with matrices that represent two or three-dimensional objects. Their relevance to animation will soon be apparent.

First, though, a little more rote learning. The symbol % is also used in C to symbolize a certain kind of calculated program output: %**d** tells the **printf** function to display the decimal integer value of the next argument presented to it. Other characters after % tell **printf** to return other sorts of calculation results: %**ld** displays a long decimal integer value; %**o** will display an integer value in octal notation; %**x** will display an integer value in hexadecimal notation; %**f** displays float and double variables; %**e** does so in scientific notation; %**c** displays float and double variables; %**e** does so in scientific notation; %**c** displays the value of a character variable. There are probably other possibilities for specifying output data types in your C system; check your documentation.

Okay, let's illustrate some of this by looking at a program on page 99 that does something pretty simple, like calculate a square.

This may seem like a lot to go through just to calculate a square. But once you understand this format, even at this basic stage a similar program can be built that might help out in animation. Other chapters have talked about how natural movement usually starts slowly, speeds up, then tends to end slowly. Logarithms are one of an infinite number of ways

Figure **6.2** C's relational operators

Operator	Meaning
==	proves equal to
!=	proves not equal to
<	proves less than
>	proves greater than
<=	proves less than or equal to
>=	proves greater than or equal to

```
\*Program to calculate the square of any integer*\

main ()
     {
     int      square, number;                    \* Here we declare two integer    *\
                                                 \* variables, called "square"     *\
                                                 \* and "number."                  *\

     printf ("Enter any integer.\n");            \* Aha! This is an inter-         *\
                                                 \* active program!                *\

     scanf ("%d", &number);                      \* "Scanf" instructs the system to*\
                                                 \* look for user input; the entire *\
                                                 \* desired input is to be an inte- *\
\* ger, so scanf's first argument," ", looks only for a % answer.                  *\
\* Scanf's second argument, &number, uses an operator not yet                      *\
\* introduced, &. & is a "pointer," used to assign the value of                    *\
\* % to "number. (Pointers will be very interesting to animators,                  *\
\* and will be discussed later.) Notice that a semicolon must                      *\
\* end every C statement.                                                          *\

     square = number * number;

     printf ("The square of %d is %d\n", number, square);

                                        \* Here printf takes three arguments, the     *\
                                        \* last two filling in %d positions in the    *\
                                        \* first. The first %d is filled by "number"  *\
                                        \* and the second by "square" because this    *\
                                        \* is the order in which arguments have       *\
                                        \* been stated.  *\

     }
```

to represent such movements mathematically. (In fact, the inventor of logarithms, a contemporary of Shakespeare named John Napier, meant the term to define the totality of these infinite ways of mathematically representing acceleration or deceleration. It was his friend Henry Briggs who limited the term to describing what we think of as a logarithm. Remember Napier to realize that as a computer animator you are part of a long tradition of emulating natural movements with numbers.) A program much like the one above can calculate a log. If you have access to a system running C, why not try your hand at writing one as an exercise?

All you will need is a formula for calculating logarithms, which, pardon a confusing bit of rhyme in this example, will serve as your algorithm. I prefer not to present the formula for a logarithm here, but to send any reader who doesn't know it back to an elementary algebra textbook to find it. Why so cruel? Because much of the process of creating computer images involves hunting through miscellaneous mathematics exercises to find algorithms which, when presented graphically, solve some pictoral problem. You may as well get used to it now.

Of course, just knowing the log of a number doesn't move a character along its course in logarithmic progression. But a looping statement can do this nicely.

6.4 Program Looping and Recursive Functions

The general format for a **for** statement in C is

```
for (initial_expression; loop_condition; loop_expression)
    program statement;
```

The three expressions in parentheses set up the loop environment; the "program statement" can be any C statement that will sensibly act upon the situation set up by the loop. For example,

```
\* Program to introduce the for statement, illustrate re- *\
\* lational operators, and incidentally generate a table  *\
\* of all powers of 2 up to 10 and their values*\

main ()
      {

      int  power,  two_to_this_power;

      printf ("Table of Powers of 2\n\n");
      printf ("power number   2 to this power equals\n")
      printf ("-----------   ---------------------\n")

      two_to_this_power = 1

      for (power = 1;  power <= 10; ++power)
           {
           two_to_this_power = two_to_this_power * 2;
           }

      printf ("  %d           %d\n",  power,  two_to_this_power);

      }
```

The program's output will be:

```
Table of Powers of 2

power number    2 to this power equals
------------    ----------------------
      1                   2
      2                   4
      3                   8
      4                  16
      5                  32
      6                  64
      7                 128
      8                 256
      9                 512
     10                1024
```

So much explanation may be in order here that commentary within the program would take up too much room, so let's talk about this program in standard text. First, with a few **printf** statements, a format was established for presenting results. The contents of those first three **printfs** easily could have been enclosed within one **printf**, just by using new-line characters, but since the program reads more easily with separate statements, and since memory compromises are not crucial in this program, three statements were used.

Next, one of the program's two declared integer variables, **two_to_this_power,** was set equal to 1. Then came the **for** statement, setting up a loop for various possible values of the integer variable **power.** The statement first sets the value of **power** to a minimum of 1, then also to anything less than or equal to 10. The third part of the loop, **++power,** is C's *increment* operator; it is equivalent to saying **power = power +** 1, which is to say it will continually increment **power** by 1. Since it is part of this **for** loop, it will only do so until the value of **power** reaches 10, as specified in the second argument of the loop.

The expression **++power,** or **power = power +** 1, is a *recursive* function. That is, the expression on the left of the equation is defined in relation to itself as changed by another operation. There is a feedback relationship between right and left sides of the equation that keeps the variable continually changing its value until, perhaps, some declared limit has been arrived at (as in this **for** statement). Recursive functions provide grist for philosophical thought, and they also make for a good way to animate an object.

Both results spring from the very human sort of action recursive functions describe — a variable defined by its change in relation to something else acting upon it. The idea defies the usual notions of an object as either a closed, inert system, or as solely a part of an exterior system that acts upon it. Recursion as a way to define anything is a philosophical ground exactly halfway between Descartes's wholly internal definition of existence ("I think, therefore I am" — and it would be a mistake to think this credo has nothing to do with Descartes's coordinate mapping system used for all computer imagery) and Alan Turing's definition of independent intelligence, which has led to so many advances in computing: "if it acts like it thinks, you can't prove it doesn't," might be a too-bastardized paraphrase.

What does all this have to do with animation? For example, let's say you have already gone through all the programming necessary to define the variable **Dancing_Bear** as something that looks uncannily like a still image of a dancing bear; also, assume you have defined the variable **cha_cha_step** as the full sequence of changes that overcomes **Dancing_Bear** in the course of one additive step of the Cha Cha. Then

```
Dancing_Bear = Dancing_Bear + cha_cha_step
```

would be all the code you'd need to keep moving **Dancing_Bear** through step after step of the Cha Cha. Does the Cha Cha have a few different steps? Well then, a few different variables, not in a loop but in a "nested" format,

```
cha_cha_step1,

cha_cha_step2,

...

cha_cha_stepn,

cha_cha_step_default
```

are what is necessary to lead **Dancing_Bear** through everything that affects its character in the course of a complete Cha Cha. Keep this in mind as you come to the section on nested statements, in a few pages.

Recursive functions will also loom large in your future associations with interactive programming in C. They allow a *data tree* or *list* to be very efficiently combed through, step by step. Just as a dancing bear can be animated one step after another, so a user of an interactive program can progress from one stage of an animated story to another as the user chooses action.

This discussion is dancing ahead a bit fast. Back to the program. You'll notice that the next part of the **for** loop is another recursive function, this one a multiple, not an additive incremental. Since my particular C system is not one of the versions of C that use a special symbol for the multiple recursive function, the statement is written out in the same form as the simple **Dancing_Bear** statement.

You may notice, too, that this last part of the **for** loop has been enclosed within its own set of curly braces. This is because, when you get down to it, the action of a **for** loop is a typical C function. In this case, it has been written as just part of the **main** function, but it could also stand as a separate function, one that took the results of other functions, like the definitions of **Dancing_Bear** and **cha_cha_step,** acted upon them, then passed them on to a **main** function for output to the compiler. More on functions is coming up later in this chapter.

If you bothered to put together a program to find a logarithm after reading the last section, you can add a logical **for** loop to that logarithm algorithm and quickly come up with a program that lists logs; that is, a program that can calculate each in-between position in any sort of natural movement that can be represented by a log. The next step after calculating each position would be to write a program that actually fills in each in-between position, which many computer animators refer to as "tweening." Now, while a Napier logarithm by definition takes in all natural movements, the log formula you are likely to have found in an algebra text would be for a Briggs logarithm, a special case of natural movement. One such natural movement you could represent with a standard modern (or Briggsian) log is the trajectory of anything shot out of a cannon. Napoleon has been quoted as calling Briggs' work on logarithms his favorite book; his adaptation of logs as algorithms for calculating trajectories was the basis of an empire. You, too, can conquer the world — of computer graphics — with inspired use of a few simple formulas to be found in old algebra books.

6.5 while, do, Image Flipping, and Color Cycling

Any **for** statement can be translated into a **while** statement that is an almost equivalent loop. The format of **while** is

```
initial_expression
while (loop_condition)
      {
      program statement;
      loop_expression;
      }
```

So when do you use a **while** and when do you use a **for**? With some degree of subjectivity, **for**s are usually better for loops scheduled to end after a predetermined number of feedbacks, and when the initial and looping expressions, and the looping condition, all involve the same variable. The **while** statement can handle complexity a little better. For example,

```
\* Program to demonstrate "while," and also to reverse any*\
\* integer's digits -- with significance for graphics ex-        *\
\* plained in notes.                                              *\

main ()
      {
      int  number, last_digit;

      printf ("Enter any integer, I'll twist it around. \n")
      scanf ("%d", &number);

      while (number != 0)
\* meaning: while "number" proves not equal to 0*\
            {
            last_digit = number   % 10;

                                    \* This operation, as you           *\
\* remember, gives the remainder of "number" divided by 10. The  *\
\* remainder of any integer divided by 10 is its last digit           *\

            printf ("%d",  last_digit);

                                    \* Here the last digit,              *\
\* derived by the last operation, is printed. This "printf"          *\
\* contains no new-line character (\n), so the next thing to be      *\
\* printed will follow on the same line.                              *\

            number = number / 10
            }

                                    \* Yet another recursive func-      *\
\* tion here; the effect of this is to shift to the next left-       *\
\* ward decimal place.  And since the while loop closes immediately*\
```

```
\* afterward, it loops back on itself continuously till "num-     *\
\* ber" != 0. Thus each successive remainder prints in the       *\
\* space on the same line till the number equals 0 within the*\
\* loop, and the digit-reversing operation is over.              *\

          printf ("\n")  \* This line is not strictly necessary,  *\
                         \* but please think about why it is bad  *\
                         \* programming practice to leave it out.*\
          }
```

This program's output is

```
Enter any integer, I'll twist it around.
```

If you then enter, say, 112055, the program would answer

```
550211
```

on the next line. With a particularly slow CPU, you'd be able to see each digit come on, one at a time, left to right. Transpose this operation from the one-dimensional world of integers to a two or three-dimensional plotted graphical universe, and it is certainly still valid. In fact it achieves a typical turnkey video graphics system trick: flipping an image. As soon as you learn how to construct a matrix in C, later on in this chapter, you'll be able to construct an image-flipping engine. And, if you remember previous chapters' discussions of pixel coloring by bit coding (Chapters 1 and 4), then as soon as you learn to use C for operations on bits, you can use a simple variation of the above program to cycle through a palette of colors. Color cycling is often used in animation to change a scene from winter to summer or from daylight through sunset to night, or in music videos to suggest druggy influences.

The **do** statement differs from **for** and **while** in that the conditional statement comes after the body of the statement, not before. In use, a **while** or **for** statement may just wind up doing nothing, if the original condition is not met. For example, in the last program, if a user entered 0, the program would completely bypass the rest of the **while** statement and return no result. Rephrasing this program as a **do** statement would allow it to go through the loop at least once, even if the user entered 0. The program would look like

```
\* Program to demonstrate the "do" statement and to reverse *\
\* the digits of an integer.   *\
```

```
main ()
     {
     int  number, last_digit;

     printf ("Enter any integer, I'll twist it around.\n")
     scanf ("%d", &number);

     do
         {
         last_digit = number % 10;
         printf ("%d", last_digit);
         number = number / 10
         }
     while (number != 0)

\* As you can see, a "do" statement must be followed by a  *\
\* "while" or "for" statement if conditions are to be set.      *\

     printf ("n");
     }
```

6.6 If, Else, Nested Statements . . . and a Color Palette Program Begins to Take Shape

```
if (you want to glean what you can about graphics)
  you will methodically devour these pages
```

This is a perfectly formatted **if** statement in C, except that its arguments are written in English. If a *specified condition,* as contained in the parentheses after the statement **if,** is met, then the *program statement* that follows will be executed.

But what happens if the condition is not met? Setting up an **else** condition allows a second program statement a chance of being fulfilled. For example:

```
if (you want to glean what you can about graphics)
   you will methodically devour these pages

else
   watch TV,and idly wish someone would discover you
```

Now, to get really precise, an **else if** construct can be used to compound this statement even more:

```
if  (you want to glean what you can about graphics)
    you will methodically devour these pages

else if (you don't care about computer graphics anymore)
    trade the book in for a glossy magazine

else
    watch TV,  and idly wish someone would discover you
```

Of course, this statement implies there must be a contradiction between the **if** and **else if** clauses. To make a complex **if** statement that does not necessarily imply a contradiction, you must use *nested* if statements. For example:

```
if  (you want to glean what you can about graphics)
    you will methodically devour these pages

if  (you then don't understand a concept presented)
    you will work hard to master it

else
    watch TV,and idly wish someone would discover you
```

As you might guess, it is possible, and often desirable, to nest other statements, too. In fact, in writing the algorithm above (for that is what it is), a **while** statement almost popped in. Here's how it would look:

```
if  (you want to glean what you can about graphics)
    you will methodically devour these pages

if
    while (reading)
    (you then don't understand a concept presented)
    you will work hard to master it

else
    watch TV,and idly wish someone would discover you
```

The interesting algorithm being developed here will provide more grist for discussion later. For now, to bring these statements up to C level, look at a different example of their use:

```
\* Program to illustrate "if," "else if," and "else," and also to  *\
\* randomly suggest matching colors from 2 restricted palettes.   *\
```

```
main ()
      {
      int     color_to_match;

      char  palette;

      long  *cobblue, *turquoise, *babyblue, *powderblue,
            *midniblue, *silvblue,

            *blu18pcgrey, *blu50pcgrey, *blu75pcgrey,

            *IBMblue,  *blrd19, *blrd28, *blrd37, *blrd46,
            *blrd55, *blrd64, *blrd73, *blrd82, *blrd91,
            *CocaColared;

\* The list of long variables that belongs in this program has been  *\
\* cut off in the interests of space. Since there's a lot to explain      *\
\* here, this won't be done in the program, either; see text below. *\

      printf ("The graphics system you are using can\n\
display any 16 colors at once out of a\n\
total of 256. This program exists to\n\
help you choose from two palettes of 15\n\
other chromatically close colors to\n\
match any one color that you choose. Be-\n\
low is a list of all 256 possible co-\n\
lors. Choose the basic color you wish to\n\
work with by typing in its number. Press\n\
the return key.\n\n\
\
Then EITHER choose a palette of the\n\
closest possible colors by typing\n\n\
\
C\n\n\
\
(be sure you have used only lower-case\n\
letters)\n\n\
\
OR choose a palette of colors with far-\n\
ther chromatic values by typing\n\n
\
F\n\n\
\
Be sure you have used only lower-case\n\
letters.\n\n");

\* This program should fit nicely on a prompt screen, or window,  *\
\* within a paint program. So the introductory statement above    *\
\* has been formatted with newline characters to be displayed in *\
```

```
\* 40 character lines. It could have been written within the pro-    *\
\* gram using many more characters per line, with the line sepa-    *\
\* ration character (\) not necessarily coinciding with the \n      *\
\* character governing OUTPUT line separation-- but this would     *\
\* be asking for confusion, and probably a bug. This way, the      *\
\* text you see in the program is what will be seen in program     *\
\* output.          *\
\* Except, very importantly, there is a bug here! Something very *\
\* logical is being left undone in this program. Can you guess     *\
\* what?          *\

   printf (" 1.CobaltBlue %x                2. Turquoise %x\n",
                                               &*cobblue, &*turquoise);
   printf (" 3. Baby Blue %x                4. Powder Blue %x\n",
                                               &*babyblue, &*powderblue);
   printf (" 5. Midnight Blue %x            6. Silver Blue %x\n",
                                               &*midniblue, &*silvblue,);
   printf (" 7. Blue/18% Grey %x            8. Blue/50% Grey %x\n",
                                               &*blu18pcgrey, &*blu50pcgrey);
   printf (" 9. Blue/75% Grey %x           10. IBM Blue %x\n",
                                               &*blu75pcgrey, &*IBMblue);
   printf ("11. 10% Blue/90% Red %x      12. 20% Blue/80% Red %x\n",
                                               &*blrd19, &*blrd28);
   printf ("13. 30% Blue/70% Red %x      14. 40% Blue/60% Red %x\n",
                                               &*blrd37, &*blrd46);
   printf ("15. 50% Blue/50% Red %x      16. 60% Blue/40% Red %x\n",
                                               &*blrd55, &*blrd64)
   printf ("17. 70% Blue/30% Red %x      18. 80% Blue/20% Red %x\n",
                                               &*blrd73, &*blrd82);
   printf ("19. 90% Blue/10% Red %x      20. Coca Cola Red %x\n",
                                               &*blrd91, &*CocaColared);

\* The program ought to continue on and list 256 colors, but this *\
\* will do for an example.  *\

   scanf ("%d", "%c", &color_to_match, &palette\n);

   if (color_to_match == 1 && palette == C)  \* Yes, && is being *\
                                              \* introduced here;    *\
\* see text for a full explanation, but read it now as "and."       *\

      printf  ("A palette of the closest 16 colors avail-\nable\
includes:\n\n Turquoise  %x\nBaby Blue  %x\nPowder Blue  %x\n",
                              &*turquoise, &*babyblue, &*powderblue);

\* Only three colors have been listed here, in the interests *\
\* of space. 16 should be listed, but you get the idea.      *\
```

```
    else if (color_to_match == 1 && palette == F)  \* You may have *\
                                                   \*      already real-*\
\* ized that there's a problem with asking for a close or far pa-       *\
\* lette to be chosen as C or F. See if you can figure out a solu-      *\
\* tion to this bug before one is explained in the text.                *\

        printf ("A more distanced, yet still chromatically\n\
close palette includes: \n\n30% Blue/70%Red %x\n20% Blue/80% Red %x\n",
                                     &*blrd37, &*blrd28);

\* This lying program is getting even lazier! Now there are only    *\
\* two choices given when 16 are promised! Oh well, you get the  *\
\* idea....     *\
    else if (color_to_match == 2 && palette == C)
          printf ("A palette of the closest 16 colors avail-\nable\
includes:\n\n Cobalt Blue %x\nBaby Blue %x\nPowder Blue %x\n",
                                     &*cobblue, &*babyblue, &*powderblue);

    else if (color_to_match == 2 && palette == F)
          printf ("A more distanced,  yet still chromatically\n\
close palette includes:\n\n30% Blue/70%Red %x\n20% Blue/80% Red %x\n",
                                     &*blrd37,  &*blrd28);

    else if (color_to_match == 3 && palette == C)
          printf ("A palette of the closest 16 colors avail-\nable\
includes:\n\n Cobalt Blue %x\nTurquoise %x\nPowder Blue %x\n",
                                     &*cobblue, &*turquoise, &*powderblue);

    else if (color_to_match == 3 && palette == F)
          printf ("A more distanced,  yet still chromatically\n\
close palette includes:\n\n30% Blue/70%Red %x\n20% Blue/80% Red %x\n",
                                     &*blrd37, &*blrd28);

\* The program should go on and on and detail all possible color *\
\* palette choices, but you've already got the idea. Of course,     *\
\* you may not understand some of the C jargon used in each         *\
\* choice, but the text below will explain all (hopefully....)      *\
\* Just remember that the last choice offered in a nest of "if,"    *\
\* "else if," and "else" statements must be an "else"-- so,         *\
\* skipping to the end...      *\

    else (color_to_match == 20 && palette == F)
          printf ("A more distanced, yet still chromatically\n\
close palette includes:\n\n Cobalt Blue %x\nTurquoise %x\n\
Powder Blue %x\n",
                                     &*cobblue, &*turquoise, &*powderblue);
  }
```

Though this program may seem long and complex, even in compressed form, it is actually not very complex — just long. Even in the form presented, this program would run perhaps twenty of this book's pages if each of the twenty color choices was presented with two possible sixteen-color palettes. With a full 256 colors listed and two palettes of sixteen choices presented for each, count on one hundred pages of code, and this program isn't even complete! First of all, there are two bugs in it, both mentioned in notes in the program. You were asked to guess, in each case, what the bug might be. The first would have been obvious if you were reading the program on a computer screen instead of a printed page: the user instructions are longer than one screen of an average twenty five text lines can display. There must be some way to "turn the page" on-screen, for which we'll have to develop a program. That program will do double duty for clearing the display and presenting a new frame of animation, too. The second bug had to do with user input. What if the user doesn't do what is asked?

And then you surely noticed the many long variables listed at the beginning of the program, all with asterisks in front of them. An asterisk (*) in front of the name of a variable implies that the variable is a **pointer.** When pointers are explained, a few paragraphs on down the line here, you will begin to understand just how much code this program really needs to succeed in its present form. For now, let's define a pointer as a variable that points to some other value, one that may be defined in another function or file. In the case of this program, the pointers are referring to some sort of definitions of colors that would allow the program to print out a sample of each color wherever the pointer for that color is to be printed.

This program ostensibly exists to present palette choices to a paint program user. Does such a program *really* have to be over one hundred pages long in C? No, but remember it was said that this is a very simply written program in present form. Let's first come to an understanding of its current form, then see what we can do about each of the many drawbacks of the program. To settle any lingering suspense, we should eventually be able to get the full program — all 256 colors and two palettes of sixteen choices — down to five or ten pages of code (depending on how copiously it is documented), much of which will be shared with other programs. I use "we" not royally, but because the whole thing won't be written out here. You'll have to help.

6.7 Compound Relational Operators

Let's not start at the top of the program this time, but examine some of its midsection first. Specifically, we were talking about **if, else if,** and **else** statements before being so rudely interrupted. Check out the way these things nest in this program, one after another to a total of 512 nested statements in a full 256-color program.

You will have noticed that each of these statements is a **compound relational** test, without necessarily knowing up till now that this is what the thing is called. The == business implies a relational test, as you'll remember, and now the relational test && has also been used in the body of the same statement. This test is known as the **logical and.** There is a complementary relational test, as you might already know or hope, known as the **logical or.** The symbol for a logical or is ||. Both of these operations have lower precedence than any arithmetic or relational operators, and && has higher precedence than ||. Whenever you encounter these expressions in C you can assume they mean "and" and "or," just like in English.

The precedence of && and || leads to some interesting possibilities. For one, any of the program lines could have been rephrased to say something like

```
else if (color_to_match == 3 &&palette ==F||
        color_to_match == 4 && palette == F)
    printf (\"...\");
```

This statement now says that if either Color 3 and Palette F are chosen or Color 4 and Palette F are chosen, **printf** will display the same palette (the example cuts off before listing the palette colors, but only to conserve space here). If Color 3 and Color 4 are indeed very close chromatically, there is every reason to save some program space and use the same far palette for each. Because of the relative levels of precedence of all the relational operators in this statement, there is no need to set any of its individual operations off in parentheses. Remember, however, that if you want to change the meaning so that

```
else if ((color_to_match  == 3 || palette ==F) &&
        (color_to_match == 4 || palette == F))
    printf (\"...\");
```

you could do so simply by adding parentheses. Excluding **else,** which makes for clumsy English, this statement now says: "**(else)** if the color chosen is 3 or the palette chosen is F, print the following list of colors, and, if the color chosen is 4 or the palette is F, print those same colors." This would be a valid C statement, but is has no place in the current program.

Go back to the former double compound statement. Assuming that the total of 256 colors were evenly spread around a realistic spectrum wheel, we could save exactly one quarter of the necessary nest of **if, else if,** and **else** statements by just doubling up on palette listings in the F, or farther palette case. In the closer, C palette case, if we doubled up we'd either wind up giving back the same color as one of the complementary choices, or would have to avoid giving the absolutely closest color as a choice. Neither is a good alternative (unless absolutely starved for memory space), so we can't save any program lines in the case of C palette choices.

6.8 switch

The **if–else if** chain is so commonly used in C that there is another, synonymous expression available to simplify matters. This is the **switch** statement. The format for **switch** is

```
switch (expression)
 {
 case value 1
    program statement;
    program statement;
   ...
   break;

 case value 2:
    program statement;
    program statement;
   ...
   break;

 case value n:
    program statement;
    program statement;
   ...
   break;

 default:
    program statement;
    program statement;
   ...
   break;

 ...
 }
```

In other words, one switch after another can turn on or off until all the **if** or **else if**-type possibilities are used up, upon which you come to the default possibility, which is equivalent to a final **else.** Putting the **if, else if,** and **else** statements from the program into this form would look like

```
switch (color_to_match)
  {
   case == 1:
      if (palette == C)
        printf ("A palette of the closest 16 colors avail-\n\
able includes:\n\n Turquoise %x\nBaby Blue %x\nPowder Blue %x\n",
              &*turquoise, &*babyblue, &*powderblue);
      else
      printf ("A more distanced, yet still chromatically\n\
close palette includes:\n\n30% Blue/70%Red %x\n20% Blue/80% Red %x\n",
             &*blrd37, &*blrd28);
      break;

   case == 2:
      if (palette == C)
      printf ("A palette of the closest 16 colors avail-\n\
able includes:\n\n Cobalt Blue %x\nBaby Blue %x\nPowder Blue %x\n",
              &*cobblue, &*babyblue, &*powderblue);
      else
      printf ("A more distanced, yet still chromatically\n\
close palette includes:\n\n30% Blue/70%Red %x\n20% Blue/80% Red %x\n",
             &*blrd37, &*blrd28);
      break;

   case == 3:
      if (palette == C)
      printf ("A palette of the closest 16 colors avail-\n\
able includes:\n\n Cobalt Blue %x\nTurquoise %x\nPowder Blue %x\n",
              &*cobblue, &*turquoise, &*powderblue);
      else
      printf ("A more distanced, yet still chromatically\n\
close palette includes:\n\n30% Blue/70%Red %x\n20% Blue/80% Red %x\n",
             &*blrd37, &*blrd28);
      break;

\* As before, we'll skip ahead to the last case.              *\

   default:
      if (palette == C)
      printf ("A palette of the closest 16 colors avail-\n\
able includes:\n\n 30% Blue/70%Red %x\n20% Blue/80% Red %x\n",
             &*blrd37, &*blrd28);
```

```
        else
        printf ("A more distanced, yet still chromatically\n\
close palette includes:\n\n Cobalt Blue %x\nTurquoise %x\n\
Powder Blue %x\n", &*cobblue, &*turquoise, &*powderblue);
    }
```

A few notes on this are in order. You'll have noticed that no argument follows the **else** situation nested within each case. In the original program, **else if** was used for all of these situations, and each situation had to be specified. However, for example, when case == 1 there are only two possibilities for action, either a C or F palette choice, and there is no need to use an **else if.** A default-style **else** will do. When we come to the last case in the program — Color 20 in the truncated version shown or Color 256 in a hypothetical full version — there is no need to specify that number, since all other possibilities would already be accounted for.

6.9 Flags

It has just been suggested that C and F constitute an either/or sort of choice in this program. Computers are great at either/or choices. C and F just happen to be an either/or because the conceptualizer of this program was too lazy to provide more than two palette choices. But if two palette choices were really all one ever wanted to provide, the program could be somewhat simplified again, by making the C or F choice into a **flag.**

You know, of course, that computers are the technological expression of binary logic. Everything a computer does is a complicated combination of either/ors, yesses or nos, and really, when you get down to it, pulses switched on or off. The basic language of the machine is a combination of ones and zeros, and the communications of any high-level language must be translated down to combinations of ones and zeros for the machine to act upon the instructions. One reason that C is such an efficient language is that it is able to reduce many sorts of expressions to an elemental on/off switch. Any expression that you can reduce to such a switch will run faster and save memory.

A flag is any simple declarative statement that C can evaluate in a true or false sense. C will read "true" as a one, and "false" as a zero. Some of the statements that have already been introduced can be evaluated by C in exactly this way. For instance,

```
variable == 0
```

can also represent a test of whether the variable is false. If it is equal to zero, it would be equivalent to saying it is false. If it is not equal to zero, it could equal anything else, of course, but in the binary mind of the C compiler (that's who you're conversing with whenever you program in C), "not equal to zero" essentially means "one," until it is necessary to think of the variable otherwise.

If you remember your relational operators,

```
variable == 0
```

can be expressed oppositely as

```
variable != 0
```

which could mean not only "does *variable* prove not equal to zero?" but also "is *variable* false?" If what you are interested in is whether a variable or a statement meets a certain condition, it is easy to set up a true-or-false situation. It equals either something (true) or zero (false). Assuming that the relational operator is positioned within an **if** statement,

```
if (variable != 0)
```

is equivalent to

```
if (variable)
```

This last is precisely the form a flag takes. This flag can be read in English as "if the variable is true."

The symbol ! can also be used as a *logical negation* operator with a flag. As may have been evident from its part in the **!=** relational expression, **!** used alone can be thought of as a binary flip operator.

```
!expression
```

negates the logical value of the expression, and is most definitely never to be confused with the unary negative operator, used for negative numbers. If you say

```
if (!variable)
```

it means, "if the variable is false."

In any situation where only two cases are possible, the situation can be represented with a true-or-false flag, which will communicate to the C compiler more quickly than other ways of stating the same thing.

In the palette program, the user was presented with a choice of palette C or palette F. Since this was an either/or choice, a flag can be used to simplify the statement

```
if (palette == C)
```

to just plain

```
if (palette)
```

as long as C has been set equal to one first. This is not a terrific help for the program at hand, but flags will be very helpful many times in the future, as on/off switches between any sorts of choices.

6.10 The Unexpected Input Bug

You may also remember that the definitions of C and F for the palette variable made for a bug in the program. What if, asked to choose C or F, a user answers with "c" or "f"? C and c represent quite different values in the C language, and the answer "c" would do absolutely nothing. What if the user answers with "C", including the quotation marks, or V or G or D because of clumsy fingers? Nothing at all would happen, as the program now stands.

So, we have a bug in the program that has to do with the C and F inputs as well as any improper input. What if, asked to key in a color number from 1 to 256, the user answers 257? What is needed is some sort of default statement, to tell the user something like, "Either you made a mistake or you are joking. Try again." A loop is needed, too, in this case, to go back to the beginning of the program. Let's go back and change the program again. We'll put the whole thing back together again, too, since we need to make changes both at the beginning and at the end of it.

Here's how the program would now look:

```
\* A recoding of the palette program, using flags and clearing *\
\* the unexpected input bug *\
```

```
main ()

   int      color_to_match, palette, close = 1, far = 0;

\* This is new. *\

    long     *cobblue, *turquoise, *babyblue, *powderblue,
             *midniblue, *silvblue,

             *blu18pcgrey, *blu50pcgrey, *blu75pcgrey,

             *IBMblue,  *blrd19, *blrd28, *blrd37, *blrd46,
             *blrd55, *blrd64, *blrd73, *blrd82, *blrd91,
             *CocaColared;

\* The list of long variables that belongs in this program has been *\
\* cut off in the interests of space.          *\

    printf ("The graphics system you are using can\n\
display any 16 colors at once out of a\n\
total of 256. This program exists to\n\
help you choose from two palettes of 15\n\
other chromatically close colors to\n\
match any one color that you choose. Be-\n\
low is a list of all 256 possible co-\n\
lors. Choose the basic color you wish to\n\
work with by typing in its number. Press\n\
the return key.\n\n\
\
Then EITHER choose a palette of the\n\
closest possible colors, by typing\n\n\
\
close\n\n\            \* This should make it harder   *\
\                     \* for any user to make an error. *\
(be sure you have used only lower-case\n\
letters)\n\n\
\
OR choose a palette of colors with far-\n\
ther chromatic values by typing\n\n
\
far\n\n\
\
Be sure you have used only lower-case\n\
letters.\n\n");

    printf (" 1.CobaltBlue %x                    2. Turquoise %x\n",
                                                 &*cobblue, &*turquoise);
    printf (" 3. Baby Blue %x                    4. Powder Blue %x\n",
                                                 &*babyblue, &*powderblue);
```

```
printf (" 5. Midnight Blue %x          6. Silver Blue %x\n",
                                          &*midniblue, &*silvblue );
printf (" 7. Blue/18% Grey %x           8. Blue/50% Grey %x\n",
                                          &*blu18pcgrey, &*blu50pcgrey);
printf (" 9. Blue/75% Grey %x          10. IBM Blue %x\n",
                                          &*blu75pcgrey, &*IBMblue);
printf ("11. 10% Blue/90% Red %x  12. 20% Blue/80% Red %x\n",
                                          &*blrd37, &*blrd28)
printf ("13. 30% Blue/70% Red %x  14. 40% Blue/60% Red %x\n",
                                          &*blrd37, &*blrd46);
printf ("15. 50% Blue/50% Red %x  16. 60% Blue/40% Red %x\n",
                                          &*blrd55, &*blrd64);
printf ("17. 70% Blue/30% Red %x  18. 80% Blue/20% Red %x\n",
                                          &*blrd73, &*blrd82);
printf ("19. 90% Blue/10% Red %x  20. Coca Cola Red %x\n",
                                          &*blrd91, &*CocaColared);

  scanf ("%d", "%d", &color_to_match, &palette\n);

int  color_to_match (x)
  int x;

\* Because it is a pointer, an operation finally to be explained  *\
\* below, "palette" contains either "close" or "far," as entered  *\
\* in  scanf. "close" now has been set equal to 1, "far" to 0,     *\
\* so "palette," when next called upon, will equal either 1 or 0.  *\

   switch (x)
     {
      case == 1:
          if (palette)  \* now "palette" is a flag *\
          printf ("A palette of the closest 16 colors avail-\n\
able includes:\n\n Turquoise %x\nBaby Blue %x\nPowder Blue %x\n",
                 &*turquoise, &*babyblue, &*powderblue);
          else
          printf ("A more distanced, yet still chromatically\n\
close palette includes:\n\n30% Blue/70%Red %x\n20% Blue/80% Red %x\n",
                &*blrd37, &*blrd28);
          break;
      case == 2:
          if (palette)
          printf ("A palette of the closest 16 colors avail-\n\
able includes:\n\n Cobalt Blue %x\nBaby Blue %x\nPowder Blue %x\n",
                 &*cobblue, &*babyblue, &*powderblue);
          else
          printf ("A more distanced, yet still chromatically\n\
close palette includes:\n\n30% Blue/70%Red %x\n20% Blue/80% Red %x\n",
                &*blrd37, &*blrd28);
          break;
```

```
        case == 3:
            if (palette)
            printf ("A palette of the closest 16 colors avail-\n\
able includes:\n\n Cobalt Blue %x\nTurquoise %x\nPowder Blue %x\n",
                    &*cobblue, &*turquoise, &*powderblue);
            else
            printf ("A more distanced, yet still chromatically\n\
close palette includes:\n\n30% Blue/70%Red %x\n20% Blue/80% Red %x\n",
                    &*blrd37, &*blrd28);
            break;

\* We'll skip ahead to the 20th case. This time, this last listed  *\
\* color will not be the final, default case of the switch state-  *\
\* ment.     *\

        case = 20:
            if (palette)
            printf ("A palette of the closest 16 colors avail-\n\
able includes:\n\n 30% Blue/70%Red %x\n20% Blue/80% Red %x\n",
                    &*blrd37, &*blrd28);
            else
            printf ("A more distanced, yet still chromatically\n\
close palette includes:\n\n Cobalt Blue %x\nTurquoise %x\n\
Powder Blue %x\n", &*cobblue, &*turquoise, &*powderblue);
            break;

        default:
            printf ("Either you made a mistake or are joking.\n\
Try again.\n");
            scanf ("%d", "%d", &color_to_match, &palette\n);
        }
    }
```

Only a few changes really have been made here. For one, **palette** has now been declared a type **int** at the beginning of the program. It could have been so all along, since type **char** is a subset of type **int** (characters are also integers in C, but not vice versa). It is good practice, however, to keep your characters declared type **char** so that in cases when a variable must be declared an **int** because it must change to an **int** value that **char** could not be used to represent, this will be obvious to any reader or debugger from the beginning.

While changes were being made to the user input, it made sense to make things a little more "user friendly." **Close** and **far** are variable names with even more meaning than C and F, and the instructions now offer less chance of confusion. Yes, it is quite okay to declare a variable's constant value right at the start, and here is a perfect case for why. At the bottom of the program, the default statement has been changed to take care of improper user input. Declared equal to 1 or 0, **palette** can now be a flag, because it contains the values **close** or **far.** Why? **palette** is a pointer. Pointers can help the program in other ways, too.

6.11 Pointers

Pointers constitute yet another possibility for pulling data together that makes C a most efficient language for graphics. A pointer may be used like any variable; it must be defined by data type before being used, and it may be assigned all sorts of changing values. But pointers also contain a direct reference to another value. If

```
*pointer = x
```

then wherever this pointer is used in the program, the compiler will read **x**.

One might well ask, why not just use **x** to mean **x?** For one, **palette** in the palette choice program is a pointer. It contains whatever meaning the user types in to view a close or far palette. We want **close** or **far** (1 or 0) to be contained in **palette** so the program can sensibly refer to the user entry data. A pointer such as **palette** can be made to contain any of many possible values, all of which are part of an expected set of possible values to be treated in a consistent way.

Many pointers were listed as type **long** at the beginning of the program (each had an asterisk prefix). These pointers were then referred to later on, but the pointers were never defined. This is evidence, to anybody who knows a pointer when they see one, that the program is incomplete. It has been built to have each of these pointers refer to data that does not exist in the program. Each of these points to a definition of a color. Those definitions may take up a few words of code or many lines of code but each can be accessed by a one-word pointer. (In a section of Chapter 7, ''Operations on Bits,'' some of these definitions will be built.)

Obviously, pointers are also a great part of the very versatile modularity of C. Build the definitions for many colors, or movements, or any applications at all, keep them in separate functions or files, then bring them into the program at hand, when and where necessary, with a pointer and a few other instructions. The basic parameters of a graphics system can thus be built and swapped around among various jobs with a minimum of effort to customize the system for each job.

To get down to detail about pointers,

```
data_type *pointer;
```

can define a pointer anywhere in a program before it is used, but good practice says to do it at the top of the program or function. This was the way all those **longs** were defined in the palette choice program. A pointer can also be defined

```
pointer = &x
```

as long as the variable **pointer** has already been defined as of the same data type as the variable **x.** This was how the **palette** pointer was defined, in the **scanf** statement. Pointers *cannot* be defined in both ways. To have defined **palette** at the top of our program as

```
int *palette
```

instead of

```
int palette
```

would have been confusing to the C compiler, because we'd have really meant **palette** to be defined as a pointer to the **scanf %d** input later on, but the compiler would assume the pointer **palette** to be already reserved for a different object. Pointers defined in either way can be used equivalently.

Finally, as we move on to more complex C data forms of multifunction programs, arrays, and structures, be aware that each can be filled with pointers to other complex constructions, filled again with pointers to others, and all may be pyramidically accessed by a pointer. If you remember the way an ellipsoid finger was defined in BASIC in relation to another ellipse forming a hand (in Chapter 4), you will know why it is indeed very useful to refer to one image in relation to another, and not directly. C allows this to be done with far more complex images than the commands available in BASIC.

6.12 Why Write This Program Providing Variable Palettes?

Before moving on in defining C constructs in relation to graphics, how about stepping back for a bit to consider this program from an algorithmic criterion?

Look at those two palette choices, first C and F, now **close** and **far,** and a flag. They just happen to be an either/or because the conceptualizer of this program was too lazy to provide more than two palette choices. A much more usable program would provide, say, sixteen variable palettes of sixteen colors each for any of the 256 color choices the program assumes can be made. Now that the program has been greatly simplified, using **switch** and **||**, you might be tempted to provide those extra choices. Before going any further, however, it seems reasonable to think out what our real needs are.

The first need that prompted dreaming up this program was for some sort of palette selection guide for a larger paint program. Other palette selection guides usually just present any number of colors at a time for the user to choose from. How do other programmers choose which colors to include in which palettes? Who knows? If system hardware is versatile enough to allow use of, say, any 256 colors at once out of a possible 32,000, programmers most often assume palettes should be organized according to nearest chromatic values. Otherwise, programmer and user alike would lose track of them all. If system hardware allows, say, use of any sixteen colors at once out of 256, programmers most often want to include a wide range of color values within the small sample available—so a palette for the latter, small system might simply include all of the primary and secondary colors (that is: red, yellow, blue, green, cyan, magenta), a few more complex colors, and white and black.

Now assume that, like me, you have access only to a small system allowing display of but a few colors at once. This program may be written for the parameters of sixteen possible colors out of 256, and you may be able to use four out of sixteen or sixty-four out of 1024, or 256 out of 256 — no matter. The important thing is you have fewer colors available at any one time than you'd rather use. Knowing only as much C as you may from this book alone, you can certainly customize the program to your system specifications. But the problem remains: if you only have a few colors to use, do you flaunt it and produce some garish picture with splashes of blue, red, green, and yellow? Or do you go in for a little subtlety? Sometimes you may wish to do one, sometimes the other . . . So you want a variable palette program.

So you may optimally want several variable palettes made available to any system user. On the other hand, you may feel that, as the chief user of your system, you are perfectly capable of choosing the precise colors you want to combine in a palette, merely by picking the perfect sixteen out of 256 available (or the perfect four out of sixteen, or whatever else your hardware makes possible). Then you would want to write a very different program, one that presents each of the color choices your hardware is capable of, and allows you to choose any number that system hardware will support. This alternative will be most interesting to artists who know their own minds, while the program we've been honing in the last few sections will be of most benefit to designers of interactive systems meant to cue possibly inexperienced artist/users to pleasing color choices.

In the light of the program's intended use, some details about it become clear. All those **long** pointers, for instance:

```
long    *cobblue, *turquoise, *babyblue, *powderblue,
        *midniblue, *silvblue,

        *blu18pcgrey, *blu50pcgrey, *blu75pcgrey,

        *IBMblue, *blrd19, *blrd28, *blrd37, *blrd46,
        *blrd55, *blrd64, *blrd73, *blrd82, *blrd91,
        *CocaColared;
```

These were grouped into three sections for an esthetic reason, not to meet any technical requirement of C. (Isn't it nice that C allows them to be grouped in this way without altering program execution in the slightest!) The first group of variable names were taken from paint chips supplied by a neighborhood home improvement shop. The second group is taken from the labels of a few handy photographer's grey cards last used for performing gamma tests as described in Chapter 2. The third group describes colors constructed along a continuum blending precise amounts of two constant, definable colors: IBM Blue with Coca Cola Red (these names are routinely coded, with "blrd19" meaning "10% blue, 90% red"). Exactly how each of these colors can be made in C will be detailed in the next chapter, under "Operations on Bits."

Which of these colors are most people capable of making, in any objective sense? When it comes to actually designing colors, some precision is necessary. Names like turquoise, baby blue, powder blue, midnight blue, and silver blue may be more evocative to many people than "10% blue, 90% red," but "10% blue, 90% red" is far more evocative to a C program. The latter is not nearly evocative enough to instruct a C compiler in how to order the bits of a particular pixel so that it does become a bluish red, but it is a step farther in the right algorithmic direction than calling the color, say, "purply brick."

When faced with the problem of how to name anything in C, some workable compromise between C and English will always be necessary. I tend to prefer names like blrd19. You might prefer something like silvblue. Each of us ought to be consistent, whatever we do, because the more names, the harder it will be to remember idiosyncratic language.

In all cases where a system user has to make color choices, it's most helpful to have the color actually represented onscreen. Words don't describe colors all that well, so in the palette program colors are to be shown next to their names in the printed list of choices presented to the user. This presentation is far from completely programmed. For one thing, the program as written assumes that the user's hardware includes a color graphics card and monitor that are capable of running ASCII characters and color graphics at the same time. It may work on a system that cannot normally display both, but that has a high-resolution color graphics display and card — assuming that the programmer can use C to twiddle with bits and pixels enough to form a full character set. As mentioned in Chapter 2, many quite well-designed graphics systems are built around two monitors and two output cards: a color system for the end-product graphics and a monochrome card and display used for all programming instructions. Such a system is quite easy to put together, and it also can solve a dilemma as to how to run the palette program, with slight modification. The program would send palette choices and other color information to the user in a window on the color screen, and if text is a complicated achievement on the color screen, output the color list and all other text only on the monochrome screen.

To understand some of the other complications in implementing the concept outlined (but not yet achieved) in the program, more linguistic explanation is in order. Each step of the way, we'll also be able to clean up the program more and more.

CHAPTER SEVEN

C Functions, Structures, and Arrays

7.1 Developing Algorithms: Top-Down or Bottom-Up

The **if else** construct was exemplified in Chapter 6 with

```
if  (you want to glean what you can about graphics)
     you will methodically devour these pages

if
    while (reading)
    (you then don't understand a concept presented)
    you will work hard to master it

else
    watch TV, and idly wish someone would discover you
```

This is the beginning of an algorithm.

Figuring out what sort of programming tools to use to accomplish any task usually is a process of constructing an outline for action, first in English or in algebra that imitates the logical processes possible in C, then in more and more refined algorithms. From the beginning you want to format your language as much like the eventual programming language as possible. So, to clean things up:

```
if  (want_to_learn == you)
    you = read * this_book

if
    while (read * this_book)
    (you != understand)
    you = work_harder
```

```
else
    you = watch_TV
```

Now, assuming all of these variables have been defined properly, this program would actually run in C. Of course, not yet enough C vocabulary has been presented here to enable you to define these variables properly, but after reading this book and a good text in C, it will be quite possible, and fun, to do so. Before giving more vocabulary, however, some observations about this example are in order.

First, this is a very *top-down* method of developing a program. While the general outlines of action are presented in a C-like manner, no details of images or action have been filled in at all. It is possible to begin an algorithm this way, then develop more and more detailed algorithms for each individual part of the whole. It is also possible to work the other way. Once you have developed your own image and action libraries, you will be able to think conceptually in a *bottom-up* manner, too. That is, playing around with various sets of program files or algorithms for object primitives (basic building-block shapes) or small movements, you will build larger, more complex objects and movements, and finally develop those into characters, stories, etc.

It is probably fair to say that most professional computer animators tend to work bottom up. They put in many hours and years of their lives developing polished small movements, because it is in the details that animation either looks compelling or ultimately appears to the average audience like an interesting technology for the future that still needs a lot of work. This tendency to work bottom up from areas of intense research results in the interestingly idiosyncratic way many computer animators have of showing some processes that are in development to clients. The clients say, "Oh, let's do something with that image," and image *X* winds up being a TV commercial for anything from hash to soap to cars, or could equally wind up the costar of a feature film. Traditional animators more often tend to work top down: a conception for a whole work leads to the detailed plans for each part. Planning a project top down may include a lack of attention to detail early enough in the project to really solve problems the right way. Some combination of both planning directions is necessary for any properly done project, so some top down examples are being thrown in throughout this discussion.

The basic logical statements of C already reviewed can be used equally well for top down or very detailed applications. Complex animation movement can be represented by nests of **switch**es, **if**s, **else**s, etc., and complex static images can be built this way, too. After coming to an understanding of what character animation is all about by reading this book's "Interviews With Animators" and "Looking Backward" chapters, and by perusing some books listed in the Bibliography, it ought to pay to look again at the above algorithm and others like it.

Algorithms can *represent character,* and must be made to do so if animated characters shaped by those algorithms are to really be characters. Many writers like to think of the characters they create as if they have minds of their own, and have grown to be what they are without the putative creator knowing or planning the final outcome. This may well happen, to a limited extent, to the animation scriptwriter, too, but animation must be far more carefully planned than other art-forms that depict character. Novelists can rip up pages, live-action movie directors can change dialogue on the spot, actors can ad lib as they feel organically part of their creation. Animators will find that one deviation from a plan often involves thousands of others. Thus animated characters are usually best realized when fully planned in advance.

Thinking top down in a structured, C-like way is also conducive to making the end product a reflexive examination of the animator's computer and language tools. This needn't always be the case, of course, no more than anything written in English need be a lesson in proper English. But good writing in English serves as an exemplary language lesson. A comparison to computer languages stretches a metaphor somewhat, because in English or any other traditional language a reader sees the very same "code" produced by the writer. In a computer language used to make graphics, animation, and many other sorts of end products, a viewer does not see the code, only its product. As traditional language writing is once removed from spoken language, computer language output is twice removed from the original plan for communication — the algorithm. Animation output may shed light on its method of construction in more or less subtle ways. Of course, the whole subject of a film or tape may be *How to Make Animation in C.* The computer animator's equivalent of *Singin' in the Rain,* a film about movie-making, may be a more entertaining and elegant way to include reflexive ruminations; though this certainly would not teach anybody how to make animation in C, it might just be an object lesson in elegant programming to others who already have some programming knowledge. I think of the Fleischers' *Out of the Inkwell* series, discussed in Appendix A, as a wonderful set of lessons in this vein from traditional animation. (See, too, Peter Wollen's *Signs and Meaning in the Cinema* for a discussion of reflexivity as related to live-action films.)

In the above algorithm, various possible characters were imputed to a variable called **you.** These nested character possibilities add up to a more complex — and realistic — sort of character. It is a character defined by its movements, which is what character animation is all about. If **you** moves to read, or to work harder, or to watch TV, in each case **you** becomes a different sort of character.

Of course, the characterization of **you** depends on how fully all of the variables in the algorithm are defined. Each of those variable names was chosen to mean something in a way that makes sense in English, though as yet, the names mean absolutely nothing to a being that cannot understand English, a being such as your C compiler. But "common-sense" variable names are an important part of good programming practice. They help get algorithms into shape so that writing the actual program comes easier, and they keep the program understandable for the writer, for anybody else who has cause to go into the code, and for debugging.

Defining a variable such as **you** is obviously a more complex undertaking than any of the variables defined so far. **You** would, unfortunately, need to be defined by many, many functions working in organic harmony — far more functions of far more complex data arrangements than any currently available computer memory can hold. Oh well, so much for cloning you in computer memory. On the other hand, a representation of some few sides of your personality is about all anybody could expect from an animated cartoon.

7.2 Functions

A function is an independent set of statements that, when executed, performs a single specific task. A clearly defined group of actions may be performed by a single function, but if a programmer has any doubt about that group's logical similarity, it may be best divided into more than one function.

As was explained in the last chapter, all C programs are built of functions. All of the programs shown so far in this book have been single-function programs, each ending in a printed-out result. Functions can also come to results that do not get printed out, but are passed to other functions to be used as parts of logical processes that may result in graphical output, or may result in yet other results passed to other functions. The whole philosophy of C is built upon the notion that it is far more useful to divide complete jobs into many functions — each called by another until, finally, all are joined together and outputted by the main function — than to contain all the details of program operations within one main function as has been done thus far.

The main function never nests other functions within it. The closing curly brace of the first function listed in a program must precede the opening curly brace of the next. It does not matter, though, in what order functions are listed. For instance, the following two-function program may be listed interchangeably either way:

```
\* first run-through *\

main ()
   {
   printf ("This is the first line of program output.\n");
   middle_func ();
   printf ("This is the last line of program output.\n");
   }

middle_func ()
   {
   printf ("This is the middle line of program output.\n");
   }


\* second run-though *\

middle_func ()
   {
   printf ("This is the middle line of program output.\n");
   }


main ()
   {
   printf ("This is the first line of program output.\n");
   middle_func ();
   printf ("This is the last line of program output.\n");
   }
```

The output of this program, either way, is

```
This is the first line of program output.
This is the middle line of program output.
This is the last line of program output.
```

Either way, when **middle_func**'s name is called within **main,** the output of **middle_func** is inserted in **main** at that point.

The format for writing **main** all along has been

```
main ( )
```

and any function name takes the same form. The parentheses are there to hold the arguments that the function takes. Since both of the functions in the program above have empty parentheses following the name, the compiler allows neither to take any arguments.

To arrive at some understanding of the role of the function, let's work first with variables and applications simpler than **you** and its action in that beginning of an algorithm above. Functions, like full programs, are begun by stating a problem algorithmically. For example, say you want to get the absolute value of any number. Absolute value may be one of those elemenatry algebraic concepts you remember as having almost no use in real-world problem-solving, but it will be quite useful in programming graphics. Just one example is the need to adjust data addresses from the negative side of a coordinate map to the positive side, or vice versa, as an object moves across the screen.

To always keep a variable's value absolute, you can say, "If *x* is less than zero, make *x* equal −x." That's your algorithm; the function that implements it is

```
int    absolute_value (x)
       int x;
       {
       if (x < 0)
            x = -x;

       return (x);
       }
```

The last line of the function, the **return** statement, is always an option for any function, and always takes this form. It returns the value of **x** to **absolute_value.** Any other function can then call up **absolute_value** at any point, and this function will perform its built-in operation just like any C library statement you have been memorizing. The variable **x** was declared as an **int** variable, by the way, so if anybody used this function on a **float** or **long** value, the number would be cut short.

The coordinate system for graphics will be of at least two dimensions, and here is where absolute value sometimes gets difficult: The dimension *y* can be positive while *x* is negative, and vice versa. The **absolute_value** function can be adapted to deal with this:

```
line_cross_inversion (x, y)
     int x, y;
     {
```

```
if (x < 0)
    x = -x;
if (y < 0);
    y = -y
return (x, y);
}
```

The argument **x,** and now the second argument, **y,** were still declared to be of type **int,** because you can expect to be able to treat individual pixels as nondivisible integer values (unless you are twiddling bits, but bits are never referred to directly as some fractional part of a pixel, like a single decimal value). Using **int** for any reference to pixels is the most economical data type possible.

Now any **(x,y)** coordinate may be operated on by **absolute_value** to become an absolute value. Remember, however, that **x** and **y** have been declared as variables only within this function; they are **local** variables, belonging to **absolute_value** only. If any **x** or **y** appears in any other function in the same program, it is a wholly different **x** or **y**. It is always good programming practice to use different local-variable names in functions to be used together, to keep them distinct in your (and any other reader's) mind; some overlap will be inevitable, however, when it comes to **x**s and **y**s.

This definition of a local variable applies entirely to **automatic** variables — variables that have no other characteristics in other settings, or *non-local* characteristics. Local variables also may be typed **static.** That is, they may be assigned initial values (or assume the unassigned default value of zero), but *each time a function is called, static variables retain the values they are given in that function.* The next time the static variable comes up, then, its new assigned value will be a product of the function's actions upon the last assigned value. A **global** or **external** variable, called an **extern** in some C systems, will retain its value throughout a program, even if it is defined within only one function.

7.3 Arrays

Arrays are sets of ordered data items. Placing values in an array allows you to access any or all of them. Many different types of sorted data lend themselves to easy listing and access in arrays. For example, all the colors listed in the last chapter's palette choice program could have been included in one or more arrays (see Figure 7.1), making the program far simpler.

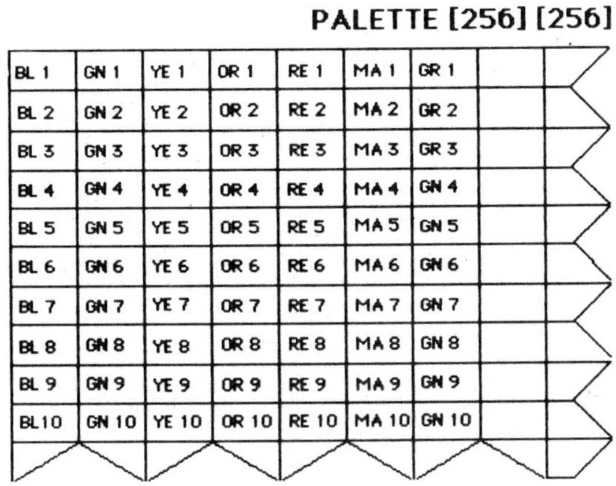

Figure **7.1** Numbered colors on a palette matrix of 256 by 256

The format for specifying an array is

```
data_type array [number of values]
```

The whole array can then be assigned to one variable, as in

```
x = array [100]
```

Or, by putting the array on the left side of the equal sign, just one of the positions in the array may be assigned to a variable or constant:

```
array [100] = x
```

In this case, only element **[100]** of **array[100]** is equal to **x.**

Looping statements can be used to sequentially address each member of the array, and any other function can refer to the whole array as a variable or to any of its elements alone. Arrays can be accessed by pointers, and even can be made up of pointers.

How about an example here:

```
long pal[256] =
    {*cobblue, *turquoise, *babyblue, *powderblue, *midniblue,
    *silvblue, *blu18pcgrey, *blu50pcgrey, *blu75pcgrey, *IBMblue,
    *blrd19, *blrd28, *blrd37, *blrd46, *blrd55, *blrd64, *blrd73,
    *blrd82, *blrd91, *CocaColared};
```

An array with 256 possible members has been defined, though only 20 members have been specified. The first array entry is numbered 0, not

1. This is perhaps the most confusing little idiosyncracy C has to offer. All arrays start with 0, and end with the number *before* the total one would assume the array had if its first entry were 1. In other words, the final position in this array is 255.

Now, just imagine rewriting that palette program and arranging all of the possible colors as members of an array of 256. The closest colors chromatically to any color **x** would be located in the 15 array positions immediately surrounding color **x**. That is, the close palette would always consist of

```
while (close != x);
for (close > x - 8; close < x + 8; ++close)
```

This would be able to present all the contents of the array of 256 colors that fit the close description of any of those 256 colors. The far palette would always consist of

```
for (close > x - 256; close < x - 241; ++close)
```

In fact, considering how much simpler the whole program now would be, it would make sense to offer a possibility of any of 16 possible palettes, running from

```
for (palette > x; palette < x + 16; ++palette)
```

to

```
for (palette > x + 240; palette < x + 256; ++palette)
```

But, when you get down to it, 16 different palettes is certainly enough for simplification into an array. An array of arrays? Why not? (As long as enough memory is available in each array listing to hold what will be stored there; there would be problems with high values in types **char** or **int**, but probably not in long for our purposes.) The choice, though, is whether to use two sets of arrays, or more simply to construct a two-dimensional array: a **matrix**. Matrices work just like arrays, but in at least two dimensions. Whatever you have learned of matrices in math, statistics, or philosophy, realize that in C they are arrays of more than one dimension. They must be declared of a certain data type, and then of a certain maximum size:

```
int matrix[200][320] = {
                        {a, b, c, d, e},
                        {f, g, h, i, j},
                        {k, l, m, n, o},
                       };
```

defines a matrix of integers measuring 320 columns and 200 rows. This happens to match the pixel distribution on the IBM PC's color screen, just to pique any flagging interests. Pay attention, though, to the order in which rows and columns must be specified after the matrix name: *rows first, columns second.* This is exactly opposite the normal order in which coordinates are listed in (*x,y*) axis forms. Matrices are the C programmer's chief way of referring to coordinate maps, and C prefers the *y* coordinate listed first, *x* second in any two-dimensional array. Oh, well, so they didn't build this language with graphics in mind from the start. This confusion can be responsible for many a stupid bug (it has for me!); just try to keep *x* and *y* — that is, *y* and *x* — coordinates straight.

Most of the space in the matrix above has been declared empty (while available for any input), with only the first three rows and four columns having any entries. Pay close attention, too, to the precise format of the entry listings; each is followed by a comma, except the last in each row, whose comma comes after the curly braces. This precise syntax actually makes the curly braces separating the rows unnecessary, if the matrix is initialized full. Since the matrix above was initialized with many empty positions, if it had been identified in an otherwise equivalent way,

```
int matrix [320] [200] = {a, b, c, d, e, f, g, h, i, j,
                          k, l, m, n, o};
```

then it would be defined so that only the first row had a few occupants.

A matrix measuring

```
long palettes [256] [16]
```

might just do very nicely at holding all of the palette program's possible palette choices. This matrix would include all colors, repeated sixteen times, just so that each column would be a discreet, easily addressable palette of sixteen colors. A matrix measuring 16 by 16 would hold every available color without wasting memory, but we would have to think of a more ingenious way of simply accessing each palette list to use it. How about

```
long pal_matrix [16] [16] = {\* let's not go overboard by
                                listing all 256 colors--
                                just pretend they're in here*\}
```

with the closest of sixteen palettes of sixteen accessed by

```
while (color_to_match = x)
for (pal1 = x;  pal1 < x + 16;  ++pal1)
```

and an equivalent loop for each of the fifteen other palettes. Each **for** loop would be placed in one of sixteen positions in the **switch** statement, all followed by one **printf** statement capable of handling whichever list of palettes were chosen. With all 256 colors listed (as pointer elements of a matrix) and choice of not two but sixteen palettes, the entire program would be shorter than Chapter 6's truncated program of twenty colors and two palettes.

The only problem with such a recoding of the palette program would come with any palettes chosen toward the end of the array. The counting mechanism (+ + ______) would need to somehow be able to double back to the array's beginning for consecutive colors in the spectrum. Sad to say, the increment operator doesn't work that way in an array in C. The simplest solution to this problem is to simply expand the array by fifteen colors and include the first fifteen again at the end.

Finally, it may already be apparent that there's no real need for a two-dimensional array here; a single dimension will do just fine, now that data handling has been simplified:

```
\* A recoding of the palette program, using an improved array *\


main ()

  int        color_to_match, palette;

  long    *pal_array[271] = {*c1, *c2, *c3, *c4, *c5, *c6,
                                   \*...*\ *c271}

\* We'll save space with shorter color names, and make the program *\
\* more portable, too. Also, to be sure you're reading these pro-  *\
\* grams carefully, something new is being introduced here. Notice *\
\* how the entire pal_array has now been called a pointer; that is, *\
\* it is an array of pointers. Now it is no longer necessary to as- *\
\* terisk each pointer in the array; all members have been declared *\
\* pointers.      *\
```

```
    printf ("The graphics system you are using can\n\
display any 16 colors at once out of a\n\
total of 256. This program exists to\n\
help you choose: either any palette of\n\
16 chromatically close colors, including\n\
any one color that you choose, or any\n\
of 15 other palettes of chromatically\n\
consecutive colors. The palettes are\n\
numbered 1 to 16, in order of distance\n\
from the color you choose. The screen\n\
(the graphics screen, in a two monitor\n\
system) will display all 256 colors.\n\
Choose the basic color you wish to work\n\
with by typing in its number. Press the\n\
return key.\n\n\
\
Then choose a palette by typing 1 for\n\
the closest possible palette, to 16 for\n\
the farthest.\n\

\*...............................................*\
```

7.4 A Parenthesis: Looking Forward to Addressing Memory Directly, and Knowing When to Do So

So far so good, but let's truncate the program here while rethinking the next step. Before, 20 colors were listed in a **printf** statement, with pointers used to fill in actual colors next to each name, as if this were always possible. In fact, combining alphanumeric characters with graphical output is usually only possible by working entirely within graphics mode, then reformatting characters to be used like any graphics primitive. Virtually all computers' text output modes involve screens formatted into lines and columns ready to receive standardized characters. The format is put together in the first place by exactly the same sort of process that will be necessary to program graphics. In other words, if you want to program text and graphics together, you've got to find or create a graphics system that will accept and display it all. But the system packaged into the IBM PC is typical: it has two modes, one for text, one for graphics, and the twain don't meet. There are not enough pixels, nor small-enough pixels, in the graphics mode to allow characters to be built out of pixels and still get a good number of lines and columns of text on the screen.

Creating a system of text displayed in the graphics mode involves directly addressing memory, then forming typography. Among the object primitives mapped to such a graphics system would be digits, letters, etc. For anybody with an interest in typography, this can be a most creative area of computer graphics. For someone who needs characters only as programming instructions or simple text output, it seems like a lot of effort.

Given a computer without a preformed graphics mode, ordering your own graphics system involves mapping out a frame buffer that is a certain number of pixels long, wide, and perhaps deep, perhaps deciding on the number of bits per pixel, and setting up a coded set of colors and shades. All of these are tasks that the typical color graphics card accomplishes, then presents to the user/programmer as an environment to twiddle with. The palette choice program as written will work with a color graphics card that allows standard text and mapped colored areas to be displayed together in the same frame. Among color graphics cards that do not allow this off the shelf, some can be programmed readily in C to do so, and others can't be adapted without great difficulty, or even adapted at all. In either case, you'll have the tools you need to accomplish the task later in the book, in combination with a C programming text and documentation about your system hardware.

How worthwhile is all this programming in order to fill the needs of the palette choice program example here, and perhaps for many other programs as well? Lack of portability is unfortunately an important consideration. Programming directly tied to memory addresses is programming tied to a particular machine. Even another machine from the same manufacturer is likely to be incompatible with the code. The benefits of such low-level programming are still often necessities for graphics applications: economy of memory often demands that graphics and animation be programmed this closely. But the price, in terms of compatibility, is high. Wherever possible, it ought not to be paid.

Maybe we can figure out a way to avoid that price in this program. Doing so involves really understanding the program's purpose and final output. The full program entails display of 256 colors, allowing a user to choose any of them on which to base a palette. Even without any color names or other text on the same screen, intelligible display of 256 colors cannot usually be done all at once; a few pages of information are necessary. This relates to one of those two bugs pointed out when the program was introduced in Chapter 6: more than a page of output is presented for the user's interaction, yet there is no mechanism in the program to change pages. Perhaps this bug can be solved at the same time as the program can be made more portable to differing color graphics presentation systems, and at the same time making it better reflect realities of use.

Taking the third point first: is it really necessary for colors to be named as well as shown? What user/artist would ever choose colors by name (especially since monitor variations would make the "same" color different from one hardware system to another, even using precisely the same software)? Yet there must be some labeling system for the colors, to give the user a way to key in a chosen color. Perhaps colors could be displayed in a few pages of information on the graphics screen and labeled there in numbers that would be simple enough forms to be displayed even on the lowest-resolution screen. The user could then choose colors by number, as before, but without reference to a name. Or, the text part of the program could list corresponding names, if you prefer, just the way it has.

7.5 Clearing the Screen, and a Quick Look at the Preprogrammer

Remember that at the beginning of Chapter 6 it was noted that most specific I/O tasks in C would be part of the operating system. Now that it can be taken for granted that all readers understand what a C function is (or at least are well on the road to understanding), the roles of the C operating system and of libraries in C will seem much clearer.

The example at hand is a "clear screen" or "begin screen" sort of command. Neither is part of the standard vocabulary of C, but both are commonly supported by C libraries, and by Unix and MS-DOS. All are really systematic sets of files of C functions, made to be called up into any program where they can be used.

The whole contents of another program file can be included in any C program, by a statement such as

```
#include <file_name>
```

The hash mark must precede the **include** statement, and the statement must be listed at the very top of the program. (In some C systems, the < > are not used.) This same "preprocessor" sort of command can serve to define any term, using the **#define** statement, and to build "conditional compilations" with statements such as **#ifdef, #else,** and **#endif.**

These statements take on similar meanings to standard C **if, elseif,** and **else** commands, but can be used to set definitions of terminology that relate to entire programs or files of programs. They can be used to enhance program portability, by defining exactly the changes that might need to be made to run a program on one computer or another, as in

```
#ifdef IBMPC
#include <PCclear_screen>
#ifdef VAX11780
#include <VAXclear_screen>
#endif
```

If you are flying with a self-made operating system and don't feel you can afford any of the available C function libraries, you may well develop your own **clear_screen** files for inclusion in your programs, but this is highly unlikely and recommended only for those whose purpose in computer graphics is to waste time. With any function library, you are most likely to have available a set of functions for combined inclusion in your programs, because so many of these functions will be necessary for routine tasks such as clearing the screen, setting cursor position (the **put** and **get** series of statements), and so forth. For example, Microsoft C's standard I/O ''header'' file (because the preprocessor listings are headers listed at the top of any program) is called **stdio.h.** It must be **#include**d for any program that would use a **get** command (such as **getchar,** which reads any character input), **put** (such as **putchar,** which puts a character in a given place), or any other file-oriented, constantly defined functions.

If you include a standard I/O file that includes in turn a **begin_new_screen** sort of command at the beginning of your palette choice program, then, you can call that function at the appropriate place in the program. You can also use header statements to preprocess the particular things that must be changed in the program if it is to be run on one type of system or another — or to **#include** the parameters of any particular graphics system you construct, for use with program after program.

Now, you can rewrite the palette program again, with these statements included, in a typical example of top-down programming. The actual details of the other files **#include**d into the program would not affect an understanding of the way the palette program worked, so long as these other, undetailed functions did what they were supposed to do in the program. You can do this; I won't tinker further with the palette program for a couple of chapters, until some other snazzy techniques can be brought to it.

7.6 More on I/O

A little bit of a bottom-up view, for a change.

Programming graphics can get quite system-specific. There is a limit to just how specific any general book on the subject can afford to get — or needs to get, given the existence of function libraries within C compilers built for various machines — yet some generalities tend to be applicable to many situations. The IBM PC and compatibles will be taken as exemplary, and as the case most likely to be meaningful to many readers.

Standard C-library I/O functions are of use, but unfortunately of only limited use for the PC; this situation, again unfortunately, can be generalized to many other small computers. In the example of the PC running C with MS-DOS, the C compiler sets up three files to handle interaction: a standard output file, **stdout,** a standard error file, **stderr** (for error messages), and a standard input file, **stdin,** which is normally directed for input from the keyboard. In stdout, the standard I/O function **printf ()** and the **put** commands may be used, as well as the analogous file-oriented functions **fprintf (), fpute (),** and **fputs ().** Both **puts ()** and **fputs ()** output a string of characters, the former to the display, the latter to the display and to a file. To speed up display, **stderr**'s purpose may be manipulated a bit; it exists to display error messages to a display or file separate from the standard output messages, on the assumption that you may not want all that error information saved in the same place with desired information. But since it uses another buffer file for output information, it may be used as an alternate buffer for *desired*, nonerror information, too. Files may be directed to **stderr** by using it as an argument of a **fprintf (), fputs (),** or **fputc ()** statement.

All of this applies basically to text output, an insurmountable limiting factor to using this method of output for graphics. (An understanding of this output method, however, can lead to development of your own analogous, but more complicated, output system for graphics, as will be seen.) The PC (and compatibles) also has a ROM chip that holds basic I/O services (known as ROM-BIOS) as firmware. The functions of this chip were responsible for the graphics capabilities of BASIC reviewed in Chapter 5. C can also be used to interface with ROM-BIOS routines; in fact, it does so for all standard output as described so far in this chapter and in Chapter 6. ROM-BIOS can also be called directly, using assembly language or one of your C library's DOS interface functions. (Microsoft's C library supplies three of these for use with MS-DOS, and other vendors supply analogous functions for this and other operating systems.) Directly addressing ROM-BIOS immediately reduces program portability to any computer using the same operating system, but this is still more portability than is achievable with the third, and more common graphics alternative.

As might have been apparent from Chapter 5 and BASIC, ROM-BIOS's graphics capabilities are rather limited. If what you need to do can be done with ROM-BIOS, great; it will program fast, run fast, and be portable to other machines that may be otherwise dissimilar but do run the same operating system. The IBM PC's ROM chip just doesn't hold all that much memory though; it makes a rather small frame buffer. Designers of the newer generation of microcomputers, like the Amiga, have picked up where IBM and compatibles left off, by building ROMs with a far larger set of BIOS routines (you could take off the "B" for basic, and call these ROM-IOS chips) that are capable of holding usable graphics frame buffers. Using the C library's DOS interface commands to call ROM-BIOS routines in the Amiga is a very attractive way to program graphics, for programming ease if not for portability (because you'd need not only another computer running the same operating system, but another Amiga with the same ROM chips).

Finally, the third way of putting program output onto the screen is what is usually most conducive to making animated graphics: memory mapping. Most computers, including all the micros this author is familiar with, have memory-mapped displays. This implies that a block of memory controls the screen as its slave. The particular block of memory that does so for the IBM PC was discussed in Chapter 5. In BASIC or C it is possible to change the specific bytes of display memory (but it's far easier in C), a technique sometimes also known as direct display, or video RAM access.

Even if you have a machine such as the Amiga, which allows an extensive set of operations with full pixel control under ROM-BIOS, most often it will make sense to use direct memory mapping. Directly addressing memory means the very most efficient use of memory, and the fastest possible running speed, both of which can be of paramount importance to animation or even still pictures. If there's one lesson this book may have already served to impart, however, it's that all uses of memory involve trade-offs. The price of direct memory mapping is a complete lack of portability to any other than an identical system; future upgrades in hardware for your own system may also necessitate some arduous recoding.

A combination of pointers, arrays, and some bit-level operations allow direct manipulation of memory, so back to arrays, but now in discussion related to the central problems of graphics making.

Figure 1 By Maija Beeton, Fantastic Animation Machine

Figure 2 By Maija Beeton, Fantastic Animation Machine

Figure **3** By Maija Beeton, Fantastic Animation Machine

4

6

5

7

Figures **4–7**
Madonna
By Maija Beeton,
Fantastic Animation
Machine

Figure **8** "Sexy Robot" by Robert Abel & Associates, for NFPA

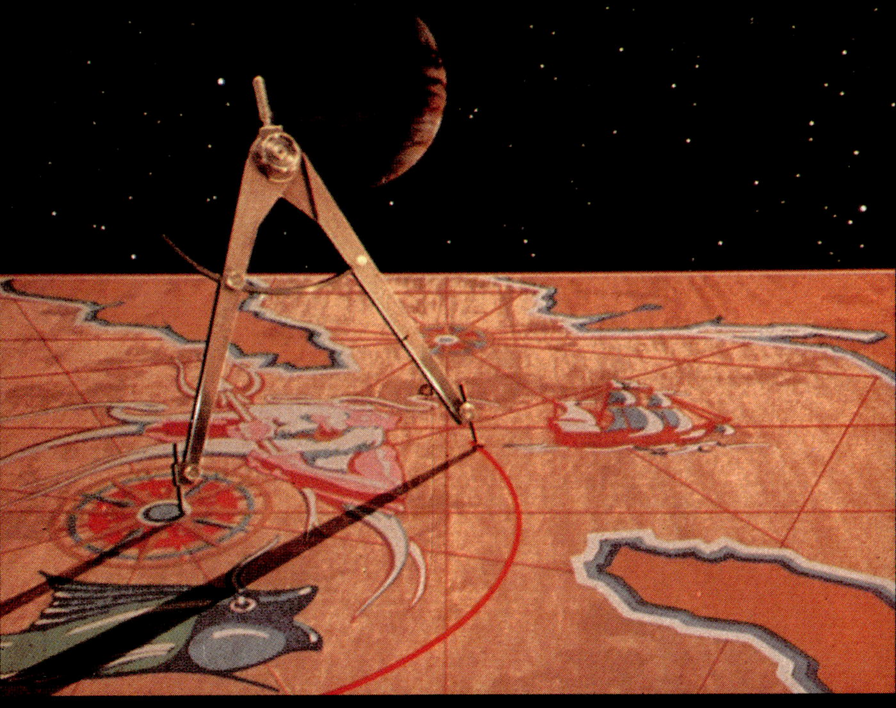

Figure **9** "Line" by Robert Abel & Associates, for TRW

Figure 10 by Robert Abel & Associates, for High Fidelity

Figure **11** "Hoover" by Robert Abel & Associates, for Hoover

Figure **12** "Glider" by Robert Abel & Associates, for Panasonic

Figure **13** Bo Gehring & Associates, for Apple

Figure **14** Bo Gehring & Associates, for KCOP

Figure **15** Bo Gehring & Associates, for ABC

Figure **16** Bo Gehring & Associates, for NTech

Figure **17** "Bottle Lift," produced by Charlex for Colorado Cooler Company

Figure **18** "Dinosaur," promo for Nickelodeon produced by Charlex for Fred/Alan Inc.

Figure **19** "Flappjazz," promo from Kids Club for USA Network, produced by Charlex

Figure **20** R/Greenberg Associates: "Streets of Fire" Effect for Universal Studio

Figure **21** R/Greenberg Associates: "Lifeforce," Trailer

Figure **22** R/Greenberg Associates: "Cinemax Special," Opening for Cinemax/HBO

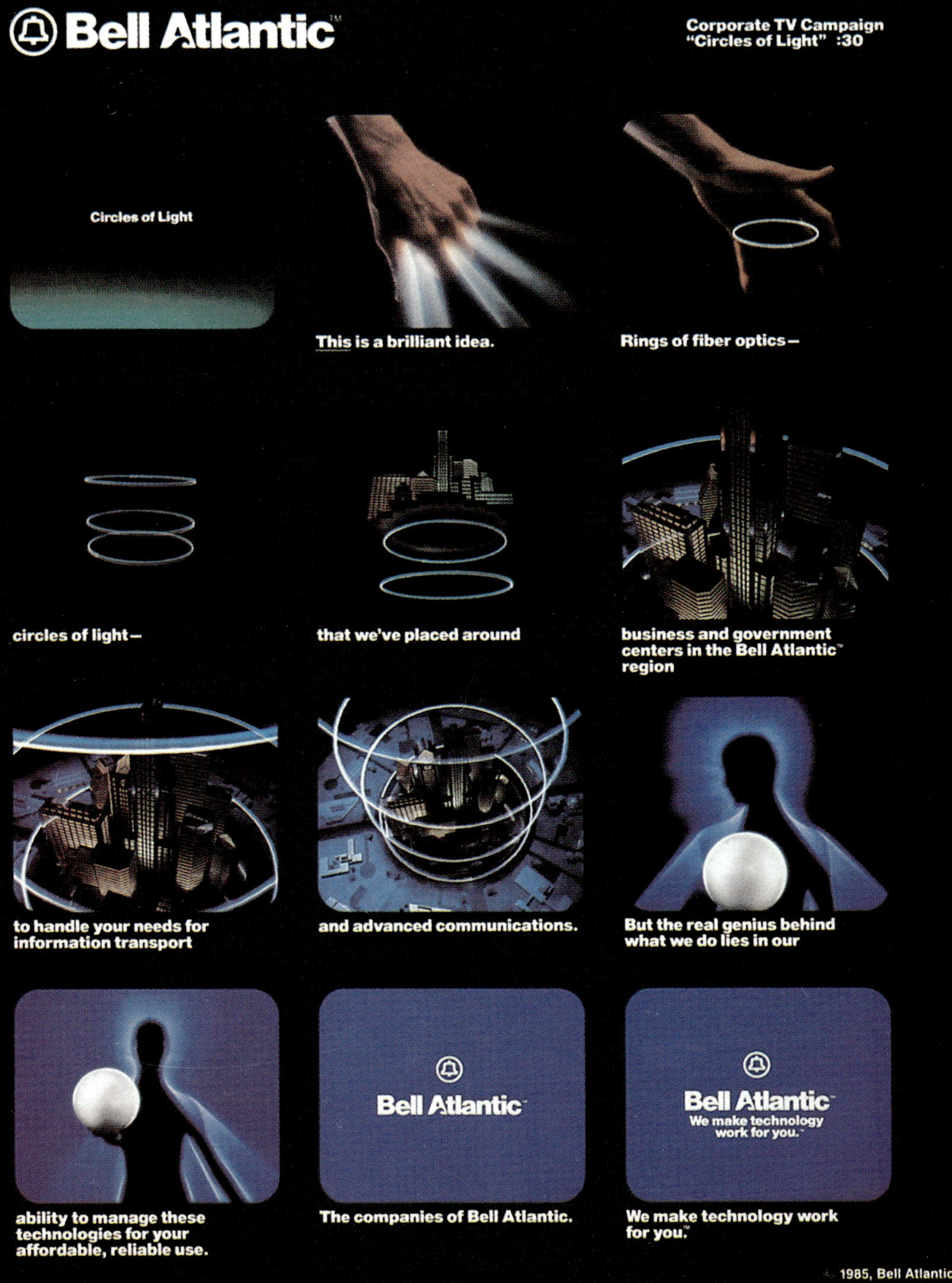

Figure 23 R/Greenberg Associates; "Circles of Light," Ketchum Advertising for Bell Atlantic.

7.7 Structures of Arrays of Arrays of Pointers to Memory Locations: The Basics of Commanding the Screen

A one-dimensional array is a simple list of items belonging to a set, as has been explained. As the palette program only begins to demonstrate, a lot can be done to allow a one-dimensional array to form a logical picture. Graphical pictures become possible in C through use of two-dimensional or three-dimensional arrays. Technically speaking, arrays can be made in more than three dimensions, too, and a thread of experimental work throughout the 35-year history of computer graphics has been to take advantage of this to depict two or three-dimensional images that include the reflections or influences of other, only suggested dimensions. Though this may seem to be a subject more fit for Chapter 9, "Topics in the State of the Art," many-dimensional arrays have had very practical uses in computer-aided design for several years; that fourth dimension may just be full of data on wind resistance, the fifth may be a pricing dimension, and so forth. For now, even three dimensions are more than are necessary to demonstrate the basics of graphics programming.

Say you're working with a hardware system that allows a display of 256 vertical by 256 horizontal pixels. An array

```
screen [256] [256]
```

can be used to represent that screen. It can be tied directly to the screen by using the screen-controlling memory locations in pointers at each element in the array. A pointer contains another value; each of these blocks of screen-controlling memory would then contain a pixel from the frame buffer, and would easily transfer it to the screen. In some other I/O program, in which the frame buffer array could be **#included**, these pointers would do their job. The I/O program code could include an array looking something like

```
*screen [256] [256]  = {
                        {pointer_to_buffer00, pointer_to_buffer01,
                        \*...*\}
                        }

\* Notice here that the entire array has been declared a  *\
\* pointer, which simply allows every element in it to be *\
\* a pointer.       *\
```

Something has been left out of the definition of **screen[256][256]**: the data type. There is also something very important about memory location

0,0 that has so far been left undiscussed: how big it is. These two forget-me-nots must have a good deal in common. Assuming that each memory location applied to a screen pixel is one byte, which is also the size of a variable type **int** or **char,** the entire array **screen[256][256]** can be declared either of these data types. Referring back to the last chapter's chart on data types on page 96, you can decide what type the array would be with two bytes assigned to each pixel, or more.

Referring back to Chapter 1's discussion of the optimum bits per pixel for defining color, intensity, and other parameters, it must be apparent that we're going to have to split some bytes here to release pictoral energy. First let's investigate how to contain a byte-sized value in a pointer variable, then move down to the subatomic world of bits.

Whenever a variable is defined in C, whether it is a simple data type, an array, or even more complex, the compiler reserves one or more locations in memory to hold the values contained by the variable. Defining a pointer variable is like making one of those anticlimactic box-inside-a-box presents: the memory location holds the address of another memory location. What is held inside the second memory location could, in fact, be a third memory location; pointers can point to pointers pointing to pointers, and on. Members of an array, whether they are pointers or not, have some complementary capabilities, especially for graphics purposes. They can be declared right at the start, as was ***pointer0** above, or they can be assigned individually to the array at a later time. Using a pointer allows you to access an individual (or any number of) element(s) from a larger array, and the entire array may be acted upon by any standard C operation. All together, stacked combinations of arrays and pointers allow a basic graphic map to be built and mapped images made of certain values on that grid to be treated as a separate array, or as part of the first.

One other major way that C can group elements is relevant here: the *structure*. Arrays are great for grouping constants or variables that have some semblance of order — that are meant to fit into certain positions in a list or a matrix, like pixels. Structures hold elements whose relationship can be much more tenuous. Take the concepts ''foot,'' ''arm,'' and ''head,'' for example. Each may be the name of a two or three-dimensional array of pointers to pixels, and they may logically go together in the creator's mind as parts of a character. Putting them all into a structure is what groups them for the compiler. A typical structure in C graphics might be

```
struct body
{
```

```
head [ ] [ ]
foot [ ] [ ]
arm [ ] [ ]
}
```

A structure is always announced by the term **struct,** followed by the structure's name, in this case **body.** The structure's data type also must be announced before the structure is used. The structure above should, logically, have a few more members, assuming that each member array corresponds to an image of what the cursory reader would assume it does. (This need not be the case, of course.) Structures behave, en masse, very much like individual variables. The structure above could be declared at the beginning of a program, outside any function, and could apply as a global variable to all functions in the program. It also could be local to a particular function, and if the arrays that are members of this structure were globally declared outside the function, they would be totally unconnected outside that function, and connected within the structure only within the function.

Thinking top-down again, the uses of this last procedure in graphic animation can be many and mind-boggling. Not so subtly, one character's arm in one function can be another character's arm in the next function. More subtly, structures can be members of other structures, or members of arrays, and can add up to a complex combination of structured attributes that change as a depicted object moves or is acted upon by other depicted object structures. Perhaps this is the kernel of what animation in C is all about.

But, to move back to bottom-up thinking, all of these wonderful creations have to be tied to pixel reality, don't they? Exactly how to address a byte of screen memory on a particular computer depends on the peculiarities of the computer's graphic address system and language, and on the compiler and operating system. As was seen in Chapter 5, IBM's own PC graphics card uses one byte to control eight pixels. In BASIC, a byte was addressed by a DEF SEG statement, then the bits tweaked with PEEK and POKE statements. The pointer is the C equivalent of a PEEK or a POKE in BASIC, but instead of just PEEKing or POKEing, it allows all the logical operations possible in C to be used on the value contained by the pointer. Unfortunately, in a situation where one byte controls eight pixels, C doesn't allow us to expand much in terms of coloration. (C does allow a vast increase in animation possibilities over BASIC, as will be seen soon.)

The limited parameters of the IBM PC graphics screen do not prevent us from using some other, larger block of the PC's memory to partition into an imaginary screen — a frame buffer whose parameters may be much more encompassing than the standard PC screen. This frame buffer may be built to correspond to the actual dimensions and bit-per-pixel parameters of some other computer system, and in this way graphics can be built in the IBM PC for eventual running in, say, a supercomputer. The frame buffer's purpose also could be used as a larger graphical universe, with the 320-by-200 graphics screen serving as a small viewport on a portion of it. Or a frame buffer may serve both purposes. Building it would involve an array of pointers to locations in a block of memory. A *macro,* or preprocessing definition, would set those pointers to a precise block for the IBM PC, and another macro would set them to a different block of memory on a different machine, depending on which were **#included**.

For precise details on how to address a given block of memory, you'll have to check the instructions accompanying your operating system and compiler, but the whole frame buffer can be built without knowing more than the generalities of the hardware to be involved, up to the stage where it is tied to a specific block of memory. You don't even have to be sure of how much memory many sorts of variables (which could be pixels or groups of pixels) may take up; memory can be allocated dynamically to variables, depending on how much memory the values that fill the variables need to take up.

7.8 Dynamic Memory Allocation

If a programmer using C wants to define an array that may contain as many elements as, say

```
buffer [400] [600]
```

this may be based on the reasonable assumption that the best possible display system available to the programmer will show 400 vertical pixels by 600 horizontal, and that screens with less resolution will also be usable by this array. That is, if only 320 of the 600 horizontal positions and 200 of the 400 available vertical positions are filled, the array can handle things just fine. What happens, though, when that Hollywood producer in the sky likes your stuff and makes a better-than-ever-imagined display system available to you, Childe Genius, and you now want to transpose the program to a buffer with resolution of 4000 by 6000?

In this case, you'd have to go back and change the value of **buffer,** then recompile it. Now, you may say this is a complication you're willing to deal with, given the circumstances, but as pessimists may have realized, the example given above was a mite simplistic. You are likely to need make many changes in the sizes of many arrays, because a final program is likely to contain all sorts of arrays that refer to other arrays. C supplies a tool which, at the same time, handles this inevitable need to expand arrays and other variables and also contracts them to the minimum possible size: programs run faster when the variables contain smaller values.

Dynamic memory allocation is the name of this game. The functions that allow it to happen are, most likely, part of your operating system (and less likely a part of standard C), but they are so commonly used that most C systems use them equivalently. These functions are **calloc, malloc,** and **free.** The **calloc** function takes two arguments, specifying the number of elements to be reserved and the size of each element, usually expressed in bytes. The **malloc** function takes only one argument, just a specification of the number of bytes to be allocated. The **free** function takes this same single argument, like **calloc** and **malloc,** and returns a pointer to the beginning of an allocated memory block. Both **calloc** and **malloc** thus allocate the block with a beginning, but an open end, and **free** gives the block back to the system.

The **sizeof** unary operator is very useful for these functions. In the form

```
sizeof (variable)
```

it will determine the amount of memory that any variable, including an array, or any data type (**int, long,** etc.) takes up. The **sizeof** operator creates an automatic numerical value that the C compiler can use as part of a **calloc** or **malloc** function, without the programmer ever really needing to know just what that value is.

The format for **calloc** usually is

```
calloc (number_of_elements, sizeof (array_name));
```

and for **malloc,**

```
malloc (sizeof (variable));
```

Both of these functions may be used for any application needing dynamic memory allocation, including arrays; if **calloc** is available, it's obviously the best suited for arrays with a number of elements to be reserved. Usually, **malloc**'s single argument must be of type **int,** signed or unsigned, and it returns a pointer of type **char,** which may be changed to any other data type being used, simply by declaring that other data type before calling the function. The details of **calloc** are usually a little looser, but details for both this and **malloc** will vary in different C systems. The main point is, either function should be built into any array whose size, or the size of whose elements, may need to vary.

The form for doing so would be

```
long array_name [y] [x];

array_name = (long *) calloc (x * y, sizeof (long));
```

Here the array has been specified to be of type **long,** so the **calloc** function must also be specified type **long.** This is done by a sort of pointer that is new to this discussion, a **cast operator:** (**long** *). This points a data type to a statement in the midst of an operation, so long as it is used before that statement comes to the C compiler's attention. The operation could equivalently read

```
long array_name [y] [x];

long calloc (x * y, sizeof (long));

array_name = calloc
```

but the cast operator makes things a bit neater. Either way, because array_name has been declared of type **long,** each of its elements may be of any size up to the maximum that a **long** will hold; in this case, that's good enough, and the **calloc** specifies

1. that the number of elements in the array is **x * y,**
2. that their maximum size is **sizeof (long).**

This may be considerably larger than you may ever envision any element being, but because memory will be dynamically allocated, there is very little difference in memory usage or running speed between this statement and specifying, say, **sizeof (1000),** assuming you are sure each element will never exceed the bytes needed for 1000. There may be more or less of this slight difference on different systems; try running a program each way to a stopwatch, if you are curious.

Such a test would be a simple **benchmark.** Running benchmarks is an important tool for developing any complex program. (Graphics and animation are almost always complex.) Once you have a program debugged and working, there's usually more than one way to tinker with it to get it working better — to get it to use less memory or take less time. Running benchmarks and retooling programs for ever better operation makes the difference between programs that merely do their job and great programs.

7.9 Operations on Bits

Most computer systems use the concept of a byte as a most convenient memory building block, composed of eight bits, or primary building blocks. Given that bits are binary, eight binaries in a string, ranging in value from 00000000 to 11111111, can represent 2^8 values, or from 0 to 255. Or, with the leftmost bit being a sign indicator, 127 positive and 128 negative values. This latter is the most commonly used **twos complement** notation, with a leftmost 1 meaning negative and 0 meaning positive. C assumes twos complement notation is in use, so that a variable of any type counts only positive values, or 2^7 values per byte — unless it is **unsigned,** as in a declared **unsigned int, unsigned long,** etc., in which case possible values are doubled to include negatives.

Significantly, it hardly matters whether half of the possible values of a byte are positive and half negative; different combinations of values, of any sign, may be assigned in C to stand for some sort of external meaning.

There are, then, all these many possible meanings in any byte, yet bytes usually remain undivided by programmers, and so much of the computer's power to hold information is ignored. Of course, a byte that holds less information can be processed faster than a byte holding a lot of information, but on the other hand, any quantum of information held in a few bits can be processed faster than the same information stored in byte-sized chunks (sorry). Computer programmers moved to the byte standard decades ago, as memory started to get cheap enough to make the move possible, because programming in bytes was to step away from machine language toward a higher, more portable level. But operations on individual bits have continued to be necessary in many applications where there is simply no choice but to pack information as tightly as possible. Graphics, especially on a micro, is exactly such an application. Part of what really allows C to shine in graphics is its capacity for performing low-level bit operations and integrating the results with high-level, fully portable programs.

Let's take a brief look at that frame buffer that's slowly being built in this chapter.

```
unsigned char buffer [256] [256]
```

would imply a grid with each pixel represented by an array element (remember "pixel" simply stands for "picture element") of type **unsigned char:** that is, one byte per pixel, or 256 possible values per pixel. With 256 possible values per pixel, the graphics system could allow 256 colors, any or all available on the screen at the same time. These are the basics, at this writing, of at least one commonly available PC color card (AT&T's). Of course, if the computer system being used somehow has enough memory to allow two bytes per pixel — declared by calling the buffer an **unsigned int** — this would allow not just 2×2^8 values per pixel, but 2^{16} or 65,536 values. The best raster graphics systems allow at least half this many color value possibilities. When talking C on the byte level, **char** and **int** were lumped together as the smallest data types, and used pretty much interchangeably. With packed information on the bit level, however, the difference from one to two bytes per pixel can be enormous.

In Chapter 1 it was suggested that 16 bits per pixel is really what we ought to have at our disposal for accurately determining coloration. Eight bits per pixel may just have to do for many micro users, but a fair amount is possible with 256 values for any pixel. The IBM PC color card provides two bits per pixel in low-res color and uses each possible value to represent one of a total of four colors. To put it bluntly, I hope you can afford more. But think positive: if you have the memory but not the graphics screen, you can create a frame buffer built for bigger display capacity, then lust for the day you will have the hardware to implement it.

C's bit operators are listed in Figure 7.2. The last on this list, ones complement, is a unary operator; all the rest are binary. All of these bit operations can be performed on any integer data type, whether **short, long,** or **unsigned,** but they cannot be used with types **double** or **float.** You can't break a bit, so there's no need for any but **int** types.

When any of these binary bit operations is performed on two values

Figure 7.2 C's bit operators

Symbol	Operation
&	bitwise AND
|	bitwise inclusive OR
^	bitwise exclusive OR
<<	left shift
>>	right shift
~	ones complement

of different sizes, they are aligned to the right and the smaller is extended leftward with zeros to match the number of bits in the larger value. If the shorter value is signed negative, so that the leftmost bit is a sign indicator, that bit is automatically shifted all the way to the left and the spaces between are filled with zeros.

AND

When two values in C are ANDed, their binary forms are compared bit by bit, by corresponding positions. If two corresponding positions in the two compared values are both one, AND returns a one in the result number. If either of the values or both have zero in the same place, that answer number place is a zero. So

```
111 & 000 = 000

101 & 100 = 100

0011 & 1001 = 0001
```

Make sure you don't get this bitwise AND confused with the predicative pointer sign & or with the logical and, &&.

Inclusive OR

The inclusive OR (|) is also a bit-by-bit comparison. Here each bit that is a one in the first compared value OR the second value produces a one in the result. So

```
0011 | 0101 = 0111

100 | 100 = 100
```

Exclusive OR

The exclusive OR (^) works the same way, except that it returns a one only if just one of the two compared bits equals one. If both do, then a zero is returned, So

```
0011 ^ 0101 = 0110

100 ^ 100 = 000
```

Left Shift, Right Shift

Left shift literally shifts all bit values in a number to the left, and right shift does so to the right. Each does so by a specified number of places. For example,

```
0011 << 1
```

shifts the value of 0011 one place to the left. A bit variable that contained the value 0011 would become 0110 after the operation.

```
b = b << 1
```

is a recursive way of stating this, and

```
b <<= 1
```

is another way of saying the same thing. If $b = 10101$ and it is unsigned, then

```
b >>= 2
```

will set b equal to 00101. Zeros are always shifted in, from either left or right as necessary, to fill out vacated places; these shift operators never bring bit values around from the other side of the number, as might be expected.

Shifting to the right or left by a number of places equal to or greater than the number of bits in the datum operated on does not produce a reliable result in most C systems; though such an operation may seem, sometimes, to be a convenient way to zero out a value, don't do it.

Ones Complement

This simply flips the bits of the number it operates on, so that if b = 1, ~b will be equal to zero. Although we often think of bit numbers with zeros in the most leftward place(s) just for spacing purposes, remember that if $b = 01$, $\sim b$ will still be zero. The ones complement flips the numeric value of the bit number. It is one of many flag-like statements in C; don't confuse it with ! or $-$.

7.10 A Parenthetical Note on Octals and Hexadecimals in C, and a Program for Converting Bases

It's about time to mention that the way octals and hexadecimals are recognized by C is different from the notation the IBM PC recognizes in BASIC, which was mentioned in Chapter 5. C recognizes any number that starts with 0, followed by digits 0 to 7, as an octal, and any number starting with 0x or 0X as a hex. Just like in BASIC, the extra digits needed by a hexadecimal number are supplied by A, B, C, D, E, and F; these may also be in lower case in C.

It ought to be pretty plain how confusing it would be if the C compiler had to read &H for a hex; it would think a pointer was being used. So, more rote here, unfortunately.

It also ought to be pretty plain how useful octals and hexadecimals are for dealing with bits; with eight to a byte it makes even more sense to refer to them in either of these bases than in binaries. But then, keeping track of which bit is where can get confusing, with so many different bases in use. Keeping track of which bit is where is, however, exactly what you have to do to build a color-coding system for pixels. Here's a program that can help all that back-and-forthing from one base to another. It will be helpful, too, to cure any lingering disabilities in making programs of more than one function, and to introduce a few new ways of doing things.

```
\* Program to convert any positive, base-10 integer to any *\
\* base from 2 to 16 *\

int new_number [64] = (int *) calloc(64, sizeof (int));
n = 0;

long  int old_number ( )
long  int temp
      {
      printf ("Enter the number to be converted.\n");
      scanf ("%ld, &temp);
      return (temp);
      }
```

```
int base ( )
int temp
        {
        printf ( "What base do you want it to be converted to?\n" );
        scanf (%d,   &temp);
        if (temp  <  2  ||  temp  >  16)
                {
                printf ("You must choose a base between 2 and 16.\
Choose again. \n");
                scanf (%d, &temp);
                }
        return (temp);
        }

convert  ( )
        {
        do
                {
                 new_number [n] = old_number % base;;
                ++n;
                 old_number  =  old_number  /  base;
                 }
        while (old_number  !=  0);
        }

show_new_number
        {
        static char digits [16 ] = {'0',  '1', '2',  '3',  '4',  '5',  '6',  '7',
                 '8',  '9',  'a',  'b',  'c',  'd',  'e',  'f' };
        int  next;

        printf  ("The converted number = ");
         for (--n;  n  >=  0;  --n)
                {
                next = new_number [n];
                printf ( "%c\n",  digits [next] );
                }
        }

main  ()
        {
        old_number  ( );
        base  ( );
        convert  ( );
        show_new_number  ( );
        }
```

Okay, what's this program about? Explanatory notes were left off in the interest of succinctness, so let's go through it line by line. At the start you know you're in for a multifunction program, because variables are defined globally, outside of any function. The **calloc** function is used right in the definition of the **new_number** array, to use minimum memory right from the start. (This program won't use very much memory in any case, but it's always good practice to dynamically allocate memory where it may be useful in the future. How about if this program were merged in with several larger ones and used on a wimpy machine?) Also at the top, **n** is set equal to zero. It may change later, but it will start at zero.

The first function is **old_number** and it simply accepts the user's input of a number to be converted, then stores it in itself with a return. A variable named **temp** is locally defined within the **old_number** function, because we need a place to store the value entered before it is returned to **old_number.**

The next function, **base,** is basically a replay of **old_number,** with a slight twist to allow for improper input. The possibility of improper input to **old_number** — an entry beyond the capacity of a **long int** — seems so remote it hasn't been provided for. Of course, this is probably exactly where the program will mess up, someday, somewhere!

Actually, **old_number** and **base** are intimately connected in a fine way to be represented by a structure. Both could be replaced by a structure and one function that looks like this:

```
struct  number_and_base
     {
     long int old_number;
     int     base;
     };

get_input  (x)
struct number_and_base  x;
     {
     printf  ("Enter the number to be converted.\n");
     scanf  ("%ld, &x.old_number);
     printf  ("What base do you want it to be converted to?\n");
     scanf (%d,  &x.base);
     if (x.base  <  2  ||  x.base  >  16)
               {
               printf  ("You must choose a base between 2 and 16. \
Choose again. \n");
               scanf  (%d,  &x.base);
     }
```

Unfortunately, because the structure has been used as an argument by the function, this is not perfectly portable code; some old versions of C won't run it. You could get around this by using a pointer to the structure, but I won't. The authorial system runs this as is (with the appropriate change in the main function at the bottom), so do it with a pointer as an exercise, if you like.

On the other hand, using a structure for this program complicates things a bit more than before. The situation is just so simple that a structure is hardly needed, even if logically the combination of **number** and **base** fit so neatly into a structure. Here is a valuable-enough programming lesson to make this whole digression worthwhile: It may be logically elegant, but if it takes longer and is harder, don't bother. Programming philosophers may cringe, but in animation in particular, this maxim will serve its users well.

Okay, now to the **convert** function. It always looks difficult if a program is presented before you have a chance to understand the algorithm behind it (so the next chapter will present its more complex topics as algorithms), but here the purpose is at least partly to impress you with that difficulty. Sooner or later, you will probably need to go into code and figure out what in the world it is trying to do. I hope you have figured this little function out already. Doing so is a process of

1. keeping in mind the purpose of the function,
2. calculating what each contained operation would do to a typical value contained by a variable acted upon.

Keep these in mind, keep a C textbook by your side, and eventually you'll be reading as if your parents sang to you in C in the crib.

Here the **do** statement refers to the variable member of the array. It is set equal to **old_number** % (*modulus*) **base**. The modulus is an operator that's so rarely used that its definition has been saved for this special occasion. Based on the calculations described in Chapter 5 for obtaining a hex number from a decimal, the hope here was that you'd take a fling and guess what the modulus must mean. Enough teasing; the modulus produces the remainder of a division operation. If **old_number** = 10 and **base** = 2, then, 10 % 2 = 0.

The calculation of a new base involves a progressive process of continually dividing a number by the base-to-be, then placing each remainder in successive right-to-left places representing $\textbf{new\_base}^1$, $\textbf{new\_base}^2$, $\textbf{new\_base}^3$, etc. The modulus comes in very handy for this, and so does an array, to successively hold each remainder in a string. This is a logical, nongraphical array, but an array nonetheless. The **++n** cycles to the next element in the array, and the next statement recursively resets **old_number** to **old_number/base,** as the formula for another base necessitates. The **while** statement ends this cycling once **old_number** is completely transferred and equals zero.

By the way,

```
old_number = old_number / base;
```

could have been stated equivalently as

```
old_number /= base;
```

This is a shorthand as common as **++n** for $n = n + 1$. Be warned.

The final function before **main** is **show_new_number**. This function starts out by defining a local variable array called **digits,** whose data type is **static char.** Being static, it is initialized to zero, yet will retain its value outside the function. The sixteen elements of the array (all type **char**) are named in single quotes ('). This means they will be printed as part of a character string with no spaces in-between. No, this has not been described before, and there are lots of other details about character strings this book cannot afford to introduce, since they are, for the most part, not very germaine to the graphical concepts presented here. If you really want to get into programming graphics or anything else in C, though, you'll want to study more about character strings in your C text.

Here a decrement operation is used within a **for** loop involving that same global variable **n** used in the last function. It must be decremented here because, if you remember the discussion in Chapter 5, the new number must be assembled left to right. The assembly is accomplished by

```
next = new_number [n];
```

then by using **next** as a variable member of the **digits** array in the **printf** statement that follows.

Actually, this program is pretty elegant, especially at the end of this function. It pulls values into a variable, then pulls the variable into an array, all in very economical form. Kudos are accepted, but not all that meaningfully; the code runs economically and reads elegantly partly because it implements a simple formula that's been around forever, and partly because the program's author has had the chance to learn from other, very similar programs in countless programming texts. This one improves on others wherever I was able to do so easily; it combines nice features of several. It is not nearly original. Much of your programming work will not be original, either. When there is a simple problem to solve that has been solved before, don't reinvent the solution — adapt others'. This approach applies, too, to how to find algorithms that can be used for graphical representations in all sorts of published places: borrow and adapt. In this program, credit is too diffuse to bother beyond making this point; otherwise, just give credit where it is due.

7.11 Accessing Bits Within Variables

Now that everyone's up to speed on dealing with the various bases involved, let's use some of Section 7.9's bit operations to fill a bit field of packed data.

Some background: Information can be packed into bits in two ways in C. One is to simply represent the data inside a normal type **int** or **char,** then access individual bits with the bit operators. The other is to define a structure called a *bit field.* Which you use may well depend on what your system hardware demands that you use. For example, a graphics card with 256 available colors per pixel may code each color as a successive value. Either method would do well here, so you may as well use the easier.

The first, simpler method will be discussed first. Assume an unsigned **char** or **short int** array element (one byte) represents a pixel, and you want to pack bit data to represent color choices. Assume the graphics firmware system described above. Accessing the pixel is as easy as naming the array element. Giving it a color involves

1. knowing the code number of the current pixel color
2. knowing the code number of the color you want the pixel to assume
3. changing bit values to the new code number.

For example, suppose the current code number is 0, which on this system is black. Suppose you want to access the code number of puce, which is 200. The pixel could simply be set equal to this, as in

```
pixel = 200;
```

Since **pixel** already would be defined as a one-byte entity with a certain location in a matrix, this numerical assignment can only refer to its bit value. Don't confuse this with a statement like **pixel = [200]**! The latter doesn't even need a two-sided equation, and one good reason not to use such a simplified form when defining an array member is to avoid the confusion.

When you want to change bit values of pixels, more complex methods may be necessary. The eight-bit binary for 0 is 00000000. The unsigned eight-bit binary for 200 is 11001000. There are any number of sequences of different bit operations that could be used to change the first binary into the latter, and which you choose would be very much dependent on what fits in with the rest of your program. For example, suppose something puce (bit value 200) collides with something golden oak (bit value 100) to produce some other color. Perhaps that other color ought to be mauve. Please don't assail this book if these colors don't join that way! The most accurate way to assign color names was mentioned in Chapter 6, but let's have a little fun. The bit value of 100 is 00100100. Mauve should be the product of some bit operation between puce (11001000) and golden oak (00100100). If the two values are inclusive-ORed, they produce 11101100, or decimal 238. If you can, you may want to assign 238 to mauve, so that when the time comes in the program, you can state

```
pixel = pixel | 100;
```

which can be stated equivalently as

```
pixel |= 100;
```

This is hardly a realistic situation for most users or programmers. For the most part, we're not in the business of assigning colors to bit values, but accepting the bit values that hardware manufacturers give us, and working with them. The hardware manufacturer has to set a certain combination of phosphors equal to Color *X*, then give *X* a code value. So if the manufacturer says puce is 83, golden oak is 210, and mauve is 3, and you still want the first two to collide and form the third (and you can't take the easy way and just say **pixel = 3**), then you must figure out some most efficient combination of operations to get from either 83 or 210 (the pixel had to be one or the other before the animated collision) to 3.

Take 83, for example. Its binary is 1010011. Decimal 3 is binary 11, or to fill out bit spaces, 0000011. Shifting right six places, then using the inclusive OR would change 1010011 to 0000011.

The statement

```
pixel = pixel >> 6 | 3;
```

Figure **7.3** Order of precedence for all C operators

<table>
<tr><th>Precedence</th><th>Type</th><th>Operator</th></tr>
<tr><td>15</td><td>primary</td><td>() [] -> .</td></tr>
<tr><td>14</td><td>unary</td><td>! ~ ++ -- - (type) * & sizeof</td></tr>
<tr><td>13</td><td>arithmetic</td><td>* / %</td></tr>
<tr><td>12</td><td>arithmetic</td><td>+ -</td></tr>
<tr><td>11</td><td>bitwise</td><td><< >></td></tr>
<tr><td>10</td><td>relational</td><td>> >= < <=</td></tr>
<tr><td>9</td><td>relational</td><td>== !=</td></tr>
<tr><td>8</td><td>bitwise</td><td>&</td></tr>
<tr><td>7</td><td>bitwise</td><td>^</td></tr>
<tr><td>6</td><td>bitwise</td><td>|</td></tr>
<tr><td>5</td><td>logical</td><td>&&</td></tr>
<tr><td>4</td><td>logical</td><td>||</td></tr>
<tr><td>3</td><td>conditional</td><td>?:</td></tr>
<tr><td>2</td><td>assignment</td><td>+= /= -= *= %= <<= >>= &= ^= |=</td></tr>
<tr><td>1</td><td>sequence</td><td>,</td></tr>
</table>

works because > > has greater precedence than |. It would also work if > > and | were of equal precedence. Can you figure out what the result would be if the precedence of | were greater than > >, and the statement were made without parentheses?

Many operations have been described already in this book; there are a few in C that haven't been explained here and are not listed in figure 7.3. The bitwise operators **&**, | and ∧ are lower in precedence than any arithmetic or relational (<, >, < =, and > =) operators, but of higher precedence than **&&** or ||. The operator **&** is higher than | and ∧. The operator ~, like a unary −, has higher precedence than any binary operation. The two shifts, < < and > >, are lower in precedence than arithmetic operators, but higher than relationals.

If you haven't guessed already, you can't use arithmetic operators for bit operations. That's because, for example,

```
pixel + 1
```

would increment array elements.

7.12 Bit Fields

Now to the more complex way of accessing bits. Chapter 1 presented many variables involved in color besides a simply named color value. Any color system must deal with red, green, and blue basic components, and with hue, saturation, and brightness. Excepting the metacolor influence of texture, every natural color represents a combination of a different intensity rating of each of these basics. For realistic color depiction, we might divide the bits used to define each pixel into six subgroups, with each "bit field" standing in for either red, green, blue, hue, saturation, or brightness.

With only decimal 256 to play with in each element of a type **char** array, there wouldn't be too much subtlety in each of the six rating categories. With a type **int** array, however, each pixel could contain sixteen bits, which would be sufficient for such realistic depiction.

Remember from Chapter 1 that there is more than one way to skin this cat. Standard "composite" television systems use "luminance," or *Y*, and two "chrominance" ratings, *U* and *V*, to represent a composite of all six color variables. This was a choice made in deference to concurrent luminance-based monochrome broadcasting of the 1950s, rather than to conserve on encoded information, but it has this effect for us now. Graphics programmers should be aware that, in designing the standard composite TV system, the engineers of the fifties realized that human perception of color resolution is much lower than our perception of luminance resolution. Luminance needs to carry far greater detail, and chrominance can be skimped on with still "acceptable" results. At least, this has been the case in television for decades, and the average viewer doesn't much mind. Film gives roughly equal chrominance and luminance resolution (both being much higher than video's); in previous discussions of resolution in this book, this fine point has been avoided. Besides the total numerical pixel difference between the two media, the far higher color resolution of film has some objective effect on perceived resolution. How much? Relatively minimal, but since we're splitting bits here, and in a limited-memory system every bit counts, be aware that while a compromise similar to television's will be beneficial (that is, create a much larger bit field for luminance and smaller fields for *U* and *V* chrominance), like any compromise it has a downside.

How much larger should the luminance bit field be than the others? Various psychovisual experiments have come up with various combinations, certain of which are more complicated formulas, based on the human eye being more sensitive to changes in hue than changes in saturation.[1] In constructing a frame buffer, all of this ought to be taken into

---

[1]For more information on composite TV, see relevant SMPTE Recommended Practice numbers, Society of Motion Picture and Television Engineers, Scarsdale, NY. Also see various papers on psychovisual work by the New York Institute of Technology Computer Graphics Lab and Chapter 1, *Computers for Image-Making,* by David Clark.

account. In the end, a sixteen-bit type **int** might be broken up into something like eight bits for luminance and four each for U and V, or eight each for Y and U in one pixel, and $[Y \times 2^8, V \times 2^8]$ in the next; the possible combinations are many. The point is, somehow bit fields must be determined.

Let's assume we want a bit field of $Y = 8$ bits, $U = 4$ bits, $V = 4$ bits. In memory, the full sixteen-bit pixel would look something like Figure 7.4. This would be achieved by defining an unsigned **int** array which has at most, arbitrarily, 256 elements in each of two directions and has a top left element called **packed_pixel:**

```
unsigned int   screen [256] [256]
                                    {packed_ pixel,};
```

Now we can arbitrarily assign fields of bits inside **packed_pixel.** Whose memory does Figure 7.4 refer to? Our own human memory! All the computer knows at this point is that it has sixteen available bits in **packed_pixel.** They may or may not all presently equal zero, as in the top line of the diagram. To set them equal to zero, you can apply a **mask,** a set of beginning bit values. The simplest such mask would set

```
packed_ pixel &= 0
```

A more complex mask might set all U values to 0 and all other values to 1. Since U has the four leftward bits, such a binary number would be 0000111111111111. That is, decimal 4095, or perhaps more conveniently, 0xee0. To make this mask, just say

```
packed_ pixel &= 0xee0;
```

or

```
packed_ pixel &= 4095;
```

Figure **7.4** Bit field assignments in **packed pixel**

0	0	0	0	0	0	0	0	0	0	0	0	0	0	0	0
Four Bits Assigned to U				Four Bits Assigned to V				Eight Bits Assigned to Y							

This involved at least one of us having to calculate the rather more complex hex or decimal for 0000111111111111, instead of that for 0001000000000000. The latter equals decimal 4096 (hardly simpler), or hex 0xf000 — much simpler! So we could set the mask this way:

```
packed_pixel &= ~0xf000;
```

Even simpler, we could say

```
packed_pixel &= ~(0xf << 12);
```

Aha! Suddenly the beauty of hexadecimal numbers for this business comes out! So does the simplicity of using the << operator, instead of having to do much base-conversion calculating at all. You don't have to remember decimal places for bit operations, just bit field locations. (As you well know, the parentheses in the statement above are necessary to counter the higher precedence of ~ over <<. You don't have to go overboard with using hex numbers; if you think of 12 places as decimal 12, use it.)

Now you may see that it is an easy matter to set the computer's memory to correspond to your own idea of what the *U*, *V*, and *Y* bit fields ought to look like. First set the *Y* field (it doesn't really matter which you set first, but since Figure 7.4 arbitrarily uses the eight rightmost bits for *Y*, let's take *Y* first), then *V*, then *U* to whatever value it ought to have. Say we want the very brightest luminance level available. With eight bits assigned to *Y*, there are 256 available levels.

```
packed_pixel &= ~0xf0;
```

does it. Now we have sixteen possible levels of *U* and sixteen possible levels of *V*. Say the two combined chrominance levels that add up to the color we want are **U = 0xe** and **V = 0x4.** We could left-shift each value, as was done with the mask for *U*, or to put the whole set of fields together, all the values for *U*, *V*, and *Y* could be added together and assigned as one large value to **packed_pixel.** Since **0xe** = binary 1111, **0x4** = binary 0100, and **~0xf0** = **0xee** = binary 11111111, the whole **packed_pixel** might be defined as equaling binary 1111010011111111, or either a hex or decimal equivalent. Wait a moment, you say, this is just as difficult as not using the idea of the bit field at all!

Instead of that complex mess, this is a perfect situation for a structure. Remember, the section on structures, in this chapter, said that arrays of arrays of structures are perfectly valid in C. Using a structure to represent a bit field of a pixel (which is created by an array of an array) is what allows the C compiler to see the bit field just the way you did in Figure 7.4. So, to define the bit field assignments for *U, V,* and *Y* as arbitrarily decided above, create a structure

```
struct  packed_ pix_struct
     {
     unsigned int  Y:8;
     unsigned int  V:4;
     unsigned int  U:4;
     };
```

The numbers after *Y, V,* and *U* specify the number of bits in each. This structure is now the perfect copy of Figure 7.4, without values set yet for the fields. Setting values is now a simple matter of saying

```
packed_ pix_struct.Y = 0xee;
packed_ pix_struct.V = 0xe;
packed_ pix_struct.U = 0x4;
```

The order in which bit fields are listed hardly matters now, as long as system portability is not a problem. Some C compiler systems will assign bits from right to left, others from left to right. Before running code that concerns bit fields on differing systems, check this.

Bit fields have an additional, and very large benefit over accessing bits without field assignments. Bit fields, as standard structure elements, can be used in normal C expressions. Arithmetic will work with them, and so will all C statements such as **if, switch, for,** etc. Because, as mentioned above, you never know exactly where the bit field is within its "word" (our sixteen-bit example is part of a two-byte **int** word) or data type, you can't use a pointer to a bit field. Neither can you partition bit fields into arrays, but for graphics you don't need to do so. Bit fields can extend beyond one word, so that if **packed_pixel** is an unsigned **int,** but you assign more than sixteen bits worth of bit fields, the C compiler will use the next element in **screen[][]** for the extra bits. This may be useful for some esoteric graphics applications, but is more likely to cause program bugs. Most important is the ability to use bit fields within most C statements. Bit fields thus can be altered in a systematic way, to vary colors and brightness according to the necessities of animation.

Now that the forces of the array, bit field, and logical C statements and functions are with you, conceptualizing graphics and animation systems should be a snap. Shall we?

CHAPTER EIGHT

Implementing More Complex Algorithms

8.1 Finishing the Palette Program and Building a Paint Program

About all that's left unfinished about the palette program that was begun in Chapter 6 are things that you now can do quite easily for yourself: more easily than this book can do the tasks for you, anyway. Whatever C system you use (if you are indeed using C), this book can't tell you precisely how to change screens for user instructions, or whether you can present colored patches and text together on one screen, or how to use two monitors. The subtext of Chapters 1, 2, and 3 was that learning the real guts of the matter *can* point you in the right direction as to what hardware to buy; consider yourself pointed. If you've already made the hardware plunge, this book should point to where to look in your system documentation for further instructions. On a more serious level, advice on how to construct each color depends again on your system hardware, on what colors you have available, and on how the system expects these colors to be addressed in C.

You should be able to use *U, V,* and *Y* composites to represent colors if your graphics card is built to work with a composite monitor. In this case, coding bit fields for colors will be easy to do. If your (probably RGB) graphics card wants an unfielded, simple additive bit code for any number of colors (perhaps 256, as in the palette program and the bit-accessing example in Chapter 7), this is just as easy, though less versatile.

All those pointers in the palette program were aimed not directly at colors, if you think about what's really necessary to the program, but at *patches* of color. One pixel of a color wouldn't accomplish very much, and even one pixel is really a patch of a specific size on a graphics screen. How big a patch on how big a screen depends again on your hardware, but the generalities of the situation are reasonably equivalent. You need a way to paint the screen to enable the palette program to do its stuff. Turning this observation around puts the horse before the cart; the palette program is really meant to be a subprogram within a paint program.

Here reference to a hypothetical system is again necessary. With differences in number of lines and pixels per line, and in bits per pixel available for color, almost any other raster paint system will be roughly similar. Assume a basic system, such as

```
unsigned int  *screen [400] [600];

struct  shade
        {
        unsigned int  Y:8;
        unsigned int  V:4;
        unsigned int  U:4;
        };
```

A quite serviceable system, this has somewhat better resolution than television and should allow pretty realistic color. There are more nearly optimal ways to organize bits for color, but their complications make them worthy of more advanced graphics makers. To define a color in this system, let's assume that

```
shade.Y = 0xb9;
shade.V = 0xa;
shade.U = 0xf;
```

will give precisely the shade you want. (Again, the only way to know this is through the workings of your own specific system — not only the graphics card, as has been noted, but, of course, also the colors the monitor is able to produce).

To make any pixel take the color **shade,** all that's necessary is to make that pixel a pointer to **shade:**

```
screen [y] [x]  =  &shade;
```

which implies that the whole matrix should be a matrix of pointers, and this is why it has been so defined above, in the form

```
*screen [400] [600]
```

(It hasn't been yet mentioned that pointers and arrays get along very well in C; they are almost the same thing, when it comes to memory usage. An array contains the addresses of other blocks of memory, and a pointer contains the address of one other block of memory; arrays are not much other than multiple pointers. An array of pointers is like a pointer to pointers.)

Of course, you want many colors; 256 ought to do just fine. Each of these colors will have to be defined as a particular structure combination of *Y*, *V*, and *U* values. This list of 256 structures can and should be itself contained within either a structure or an array. This new structure of structures or array of structures would then be linked to the first screen — that is, the screen on which a picture gets painted — any time a pixel points to one of the values in its list (see Figure 8.1). Essentially, an entirely new screen is called for, a palette screen which would contain colors to which individual pixels of the "real" screen could point. This would truly be a palette in an old fashioned, painterly way.

Figure **8.1** Linked arrays

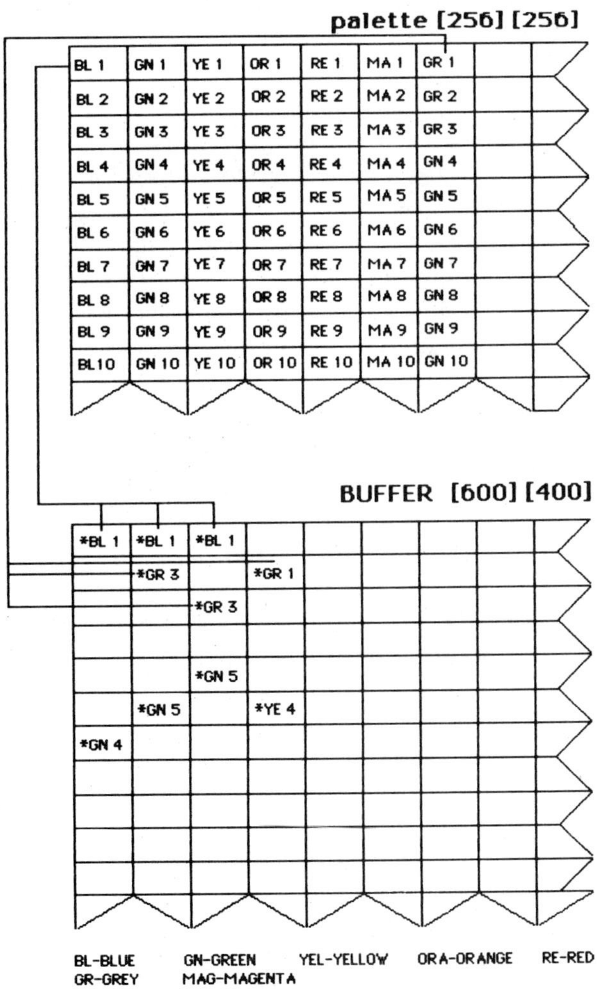

Either a structure or an array could be used to hold this palette. An array already has been used, in the later incarnations of the palette program, because it is more efficient for this purpose than a structure. The difference is appreciable when contemplating the original purpose of the palette program: to present a well-chosen selection of colors from the full palette of possible colors. Whether the smaller palette is an array within the array or, more simply, several consecutive elements within a one-dimensional array, you can cycle through the elements of an array with a good deal simpler code than needed to cycle through a structure.

The palette program honed over the last couple of chapters could therefore more accurately be renamed the "small palette program." It would **#include** as a macro a "large palette program," which would be, essentially, an array of structures of bit fields representing every possible color combination. If system hardware permits, the large palette program might contain, say 65,536 (2^{16}, or 0xf000) colors, with only 256 available for use at any one time. This is a very reasonable and common use of palette memory. It would involve a structure containing 256 different palette arrays, each of which contains 256 colors. Only slightly improved system hardware is necessary to support such a system of palettes, since the 16 bits used for each color are actually capable of 65,536 different combinations. Here it makes particular sense to use two-dimensional arrays to represent each of the 256 palettes, since you'd want to be able to view the array as a screen to make your choice. Such a "small" palette of 256 colors could quite reasonably be presented with just one or a few pixels representing each color, and a user could choose colors by pointing a pen at the screen or at a data tablet. This would save you the problem of providing a matched list of names. If you don't like pen and tablet input, a program much like the old palette program could cycle through "very small palettes" of sixteen colors, each color assigned to a large box on the screen with the color name indicated beside it.

The possibilities for elaboration are huge. You can surely figure out many other lovely features to add to this set of very realistic demands from a program that should be entirely within the reach of anybody who managed to slog through the last few chapters.

8.2 Structuring a Graphics Library

Any C program can be tacked onto the beginning of any other C program; each program you write is a modular resource for making other programs, like building blocks. There is no need to reinvent data structures for every program. The **#include** statement, which brings source programs into the one in use, already has been mentioned. If you have a C system to work on and have been programming along with this book, you already know the particulars of filing and of accessing program files. If you have not been reading in front of a keyboard, a few moments with a C system's documentation will acquaint you with file operations.

If you want to build a paint program, by extension you know you will need

- a large palette program, for inclusion in this and other programs that will also use the paint program
- a small palette program, for choosing colors from the large palette
- a frame buffer, defined in RAM, to assemble the chosen colors into a picture
- a program that handles output from this RAM buffer to the refresh buffer built into your hardware graphics system, which must scan the RAM buffer for presentation to the monitor screen.

The paint program itself merely controls how you access colors from the small palette and put them where you want them in the frame buffer's image. All of these other programs would need to be **#include**d in the paint program for it to work its magic. Figure 8.2 is a flow-chart sort of representation of the way each program draws on the others to support the paint program application. There ought to be a strong resemblance between this figure and the flow-chart-like illustration, in Chapter 1, of the user's model for interactive graphics: not an exact parallel, but close. Here the model is specifically geared to a *non*interactive, programmer's paint application in C, and it is in fact the beginning of a master algorithm for all the programs involved. The modular programs in the diagram may never assume anything like this relationship to each other for other applications, for which reason they are indeed separate modules. The next task is to set up the programs, one after another. They will be the first few programs in an image-programming library.

Creating the frame buffer is a simple matter of a large piece of code. Each of the elements in a large array must be named, but the whole process will be familiar to you from the discussion of arrays in Chapter 7. The frame buffer array is a passive block of memory (though it should also be dynamic in the sense that it expands and contracts to use only as much memory as it needs at any moment); it contains information fed into it by programmed functions, until other operations take the information out. Since it is a construct that doesn't act upon anything, a single

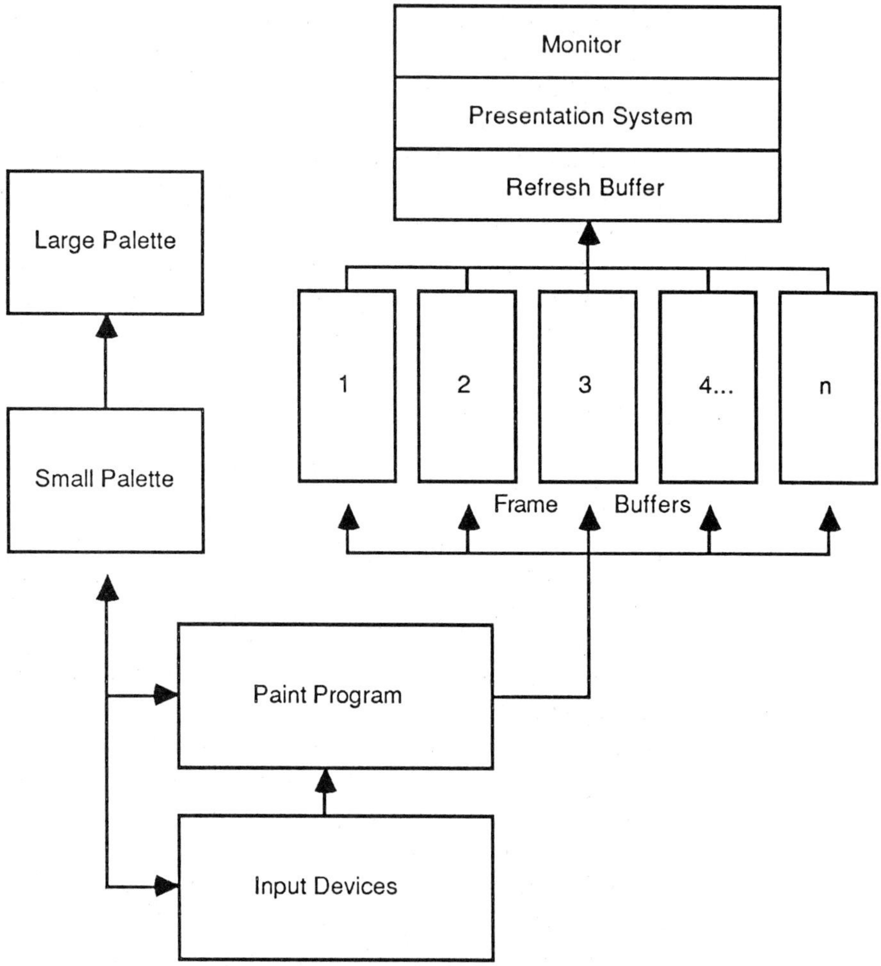

Figure 8.2
Modular programs joined for painting

frame buffer contains no functions. It could be entirely contained within one **main** function, then used as a macro wherever needed. As has been alluded to in past chapters, however, it's going to be very handy to have more than one frame buffer. With two, for example, a picture can be copied from the first to the second, then slightly changed in the second and animated by quickly showing succeeding frames. The RAM your hardware has available to use for frame buffering will determine just how many buffers you can construct and use at the same time. Each exemplary buffer to be constructed in this chapter would consume 960 Kbytes of RAM. With a couple of megabytes of RAM you could store any two of them there and alternate with others stored in long-term memory. Figure 8.2 shows five, for example. In the interest of conciseness, just enough code to give you the general idea for one buffer will be presented here.

One more, most important bit of advice on buffer building: If compromising between the number of buffers and the size of each, never compromise too much on resolution and available colors. If you *can* use sixteen bits per pixel and at least broadcast-TV resolution, and somehow choose not to, your reasons for doing so ought to be peculiarly, unimaginably good. Furthermore, just because your system may display a limited number of pixels on screen, you needn't limit all buffers to that screen resolution. A buffer can be built just as easily with precisely twice or four times or many more times the resolution of the eventual display screen and then scaled down to size by a simple macro command (described below) for output. The benefits of this are not merely the oft-mentioned one of portability to your future super system, but — perhaps much more significantly — it would allow you easily to zoom in on a picture with no reduction in resolution. Just change the scalar by which the image is multiplied to match screen size, and then transfer only a part of the buffer's frame to the screen's frame. Pans can be made this way, too, and limited animation. To do so, just incrementally change the portion of the frame buffer that is output to the screen.

The "presentation system" box in the figure would be partially occupied by your C I/O system, as a connection to graphics card and monitor. What you've got in a **stdio.h**-type file, or perhaps a special graphics I/O file should do the trick when combined with a means to access each pixel from the frame buffer. The "means" implied is actually another buffer array of pointers, or of some machine-level equivalent of pointers: beyond frame buffers and palettes, a third-level screen array! This is the refresh buffer, whose responsibility is to scan your RAM buffer's lines and throw their information to the monitor screen in a sixtieth of a second, and to do this thirty times per second.

Toward the middle of the last chapter, it was mentioned that an array of pointers *to pixel addresses, from the graphics-controlling-card firmware* was a reasonable way to arrange system output. This was a little bit disingenuous, for the purpose of a simple explanation of arrays and program output at the same time. An output program most likely would not be able to order memory locations in firmware into an array. Probably it would have to more laboriously code each memory location individually as some machine-language equivalent of a C pointer. Hopefully, you'll never have to write such complex code! You *probably* won't, since this is the business of companies that make graphic memory control cards. If you buy one that promises compatibility with your operating system's graphics I/O functions — and especially if your operating system is a popular and recent variant of UNIX — you'll be in great shape to run I/O out of the box with no custom coding. That's one module down, five to go.

The bottom box, labelled "input devices," needs no further introduction at this point. Either you wish to make your paint and palette programs respond to keyboard alone, or also to the more ergonomic devices like joy sticks, digitizing tablets, digitized video input, etc. If you go for the fancier inputs, you will have to modify standard system I/O (as in **stdio.h** or a separate graphics I/O header file) somewhat. Given the hundreds of companies making these things, precise advice on the subject is difficult; you'll have to rely on your hardware documentation. Adapting your operating system's I/O to the task should not be difficult, since late-version C operating systems already have macros geared to graphical input. Much the same advice applies if you elect to go with keyboard input only, with much less possible need for customization. As with the output module discussed above, if you run a common version of UNIX or MS-DOS and your tablet (or whatever) has been built for compatibility, you should have clear sailing.

That's two modules down. The others are more complex; let's put them together.

8.3 Building a Frame Buffer in RAM

Most of the details of the screen or buffer array examples presented thus far can be directly utilized in a frame buffer. The purpose of the buffer is to

- hold the graphical input,
- which is placed there by the paint program (and taken from the small palette program)
- and upon direction, to dump what is stored in this buffer into the presentation system.

To answer these needs, the code can be very simple indeed. It could look like this:

```
#define    BUFFER [x] [y]    buffer [y] [x]
#define    MAXX              600
#define    MAXY              400
```

```
main ()
     {
     static int    *BUFFER [MAXX] [MAXY] =
                   {
                   { (-300x) (200y),  (-299x) (200y),  (-298x) (200y), \*...*\},
                   { (-300x) (199y),  (-299x) (199y),  (-298x) (199y), \*...*\},
                   { (-300x) (198y),  (-299x) (198y),  (-298x) (199y), \*...*\},
                   { \* and so forth to MAXX, MAXY *\ }
                   }

     BUFFER [MAXX] [MAXY]  =  (int *)   calloc (2400, sizeof (int ));
     }
```

A few notes about this are in order. For one, the maximum number of elements specified in **calloc** is dependent, of course, on the number of elements listed in **BUFFER.** This number is arbitrary, yet convenient for many hardware systems. If your hardware system can support a maximum of fewer pixels, and if you have no opportunity to use a better system for output, you may or may not want to use less. If your system supports greater resolution, use what you can. The principle will be the same, whatever the array size.

A second comment concerning the **calloc** function: It is being used to conserve machine memory devoted to the buffer. On many systems, its effect is to say that a possible, but unused member of the buffer array is allotted no memory space. But you do probably want an unused pixel — on the final monitor screen — to do something or other, probably it should appear black. The definition of this frame buffer could have been written with

1. a statement setting all pixel pointers to zero (each would later be redirected to colors within the paint program), then
2. a structure statement setting zero equal to black in terms of color-coded bit fields.

That would have used a little extra memory; it is always preferable to conserve memory where possible, so what is called for is code in the presentation system (output) module saying that any pixel not defined by the buffer array is to be shown black. This usually is the default condition anyway, or else is easy to establish with most, if not all, graphics cards and operating systems.

Finally, **buffer** is defined as a **static int** — **static** so it will hold and increment assigned values when this may be necessary in future programs, and **int** to make use of sixteen bits per pixel. It is not an **unsigned int,** since negative values are being assigned to many array elements.

8.4 Macros to Redefine the Buffer Array

On the top, or header line of the program is a preprocessor statement that hasn't been used before. Its form ought to seem similar to **#include,** which has been used; **#include** is an oft-needed preprocessor statement for any serious programming, and the only one used so far in this book. Another tremendously useful statement is **#define.** Among other things, a **#define** "macro" — **#define**d terms are usually referred to as macros — can be used to reset C's standard **[y][x]** array form to the usual order of **[x][y]** and avoid untold confusion.

You'll also recall, from Chapter 7's introduction of the **calloc** function, the goals of system portability and conserving memory. A macro can be used to set the maximum number of elements in an array — to **[400][600],** for instance. Throughout the rest of the program, the array size can be referred to by the **#define**d maximum, and not by specific number. Then, if you want to run the program on a larger array, just change the **#define**d maximum once, in the preprocessor; it saves you the problem of searching through all program references to whatever is **#define**d, and avoids bugs that would creep in during that process. (If you run the average paint program on a larger array than it has been written for, it might occupy only a part of the array, or might run in an unpredictable way, or not run at all.)

To **#define** anything as a macro (and you *can* define anything to equal anything else as a macro, including writing full functions as macros), use the very top program lines, and anything to the right of the first unbroken term to the right of the **#define** statement becomes part of what is **#define**d. Don't use a semicolon (;) after macro statements, unless you want the semicolon to be part of the definition. If your definition must go more than one line, use a backslash (\ ) at the end of each line. Also, it is not necessary, but it is conventional among C programmers, to write all macros in upper-case letters.

Macros will make for a big change in programs yet to come in this book. From now on, assume they include the macros listed in the buffer program.

Macros do use up some scarce memory, so if you're really short of this precious commodity you'll sometimes want to work without them. Finally, the terms "header file," "library file," and "macros" have been thrown around here a little too loosely for any C purist; they are approximately the same, but not quite. If you delve deeply into C, the differences will assume greater importance. (Steve Schustack, in *Variations In C,* makes the differences clear; see Bibliography.)

8.5 Initializing the Buffer Array

The buffer's elements all have been set to standard Cartesian coordinate labels. Although it's something of an effort to program in all of this the first time, there are many benefits to doing so and very few drawbacks. (By the way, it need only be done once; your operating system should supply a function such as **strcpy ()** or **strncpy ()** for copying an array, and you can use this to build all buffers after the first.) For one, it makes all standard algebraic calculations and representations easier if you use standard coordinates. You'll recall that much the same change had to be made in BASIC for the PC screen, in Chapter 5. Now you surely understand the underlying reason for a screen with numbering systems starting at the upper left corner; it fits naturally with the numbering system of an array.

A simpler programming method could have been used to set all array elements to standard coordinates. The code would involve **if, elseif,** and **else** statements and would follow the same transformation method as that used in Chapter 5 for the IBM screen. An algorithm for it would be

1. Any x value < **MAXX** / 2 = $-x$.
2. Any x value > **MAXX** / 2 = x.
3. If x = **MAXX** / 2, $x = 0$.
4. Repeat the same steps for y.
5. Each x and y value should retain a variable, to appear in the form (__x) (__y)

You can do it. Or else you will just have to program out each pixel individually.

So far, the buffer array has been used with none of its elements named. They've all been pointers, since the array has been declared an array of pointers. As you'll recall from the opening discussion about arrays, in Chapter 7, the array elements can certainly be named, too — given values outside of what they point to — and the names certainly can be positions in an (x,y) coordinate system. Another benefit of coordinates with values is that, instead of the paint program needing to specify

```
BUFFER [y] [x] = &color;
```

to set a pixel to a color, now all that's necessary is

```
(x) (y) = &color;
```

Element *positions* in an array cannot be renamed, so the **[0][0]** position of the **BUFFER** array is still in the top left corner. What has been done to this array is not nearly the equivalent of what was done to move the (0,0) point to the center of the PC screen in Chapter 5. Here we have *both* numbering systems coexisting, *one inside the other.* And because both are linear, they will result in equivalent computations, as long as systems are not mixed up and each is treated coherently. For example, each of these statements does something similar, but gets a different result:

```
(200x) (-100y) - (100x) (50y) = (100x) (-50y);

BUFFER [500] [300] - BUFFER [400] [150] = BUFFER [100] [150];
```

In the statements, the values being added are analogous —**BUFFER [500][300]** is **(200x)(−100y),** and so forth — but the answers do not agree. **BUFFER[100][150]** stores **(−200x)(50y).** Be sure you understand never to mix computational systems. Sometimes it will be necessary to use the array-element positions for operations, as has been done, but whenever possible it will be easier to stick to computations on the values contained.

8.6 Beyond the Frame Buffer to the Paint

The paint program must

1. by whatever input method is preferred, let a user assign a color from the small palette to an individual pixel in buffer;
2. allow a user to choose a color, then draw a line with it, coloring each pixel along a path of the user's choice.

It might also provide other tricks designed to mimic real-world drawing and painting possibilities. For one, a choice of "brushes" would be nice, so that users could draw, say, a one-pixel-wide line, with one brush, or a 30-pixel-wide line, with another. A choice of textures within a specified color would be great to have; even better would be the ability to create and store a user's own choice of textures, or tiling. The ability to fill in a circumscribed area with a specified color or texture would also be very helpful. You'll recall from Chapter 5 that IBM BASIC has a few of these capabilities, and if you are familiar with any commercially available paint programs, you'll know that all of the above are standard on many programs.

C doesn't provide these capabilities with direct commands, but it does allow you to build them to a much finer degree of resolution, control, and beauty than does IBM BASIC. You can, with just about equal ease (or difficulty, to pessimists), develop more capabilities on a wish list of painting tricks, such as

- image flipping
- zooming in or zooming out
- warping or flattening the image
- inserting another image, from another buffer, into a portion of the screen
- animating painted images.

The ideal paint program would have facilities for all of these, and perhaps some others, too. Let's look more closely at each wish, and see what it will take to make it happen.

8.7 Assigning Color to Pixels

Certainly it is easy to continually program pixels for color, as opposed to writing interactive user code and using a data tablet, pen, etc. The benefits are

1. You never have to bother writing more complex code for system access by unsophisticated users.
2. You save on scarce memory — extra code takes up space.

The disadvantages are predictable: Nobody but a programmer can use the system, and perhaps far more important, you may feel you can accomplish more graphically with tools like brushes, preprogrammed textures, and other tricks. If you are working on a memory-starved system — like most micros — the only way to optimize graphic quality is to program all picture details fresh each time, with no easy user interfaces. Thus, getting the optimum picture would involve directly programming colors into a buffer. Any image changes, as in animation, zooms, pans, etc. could be done in the following way:

Use the buffer code example to make more than one: ***BUF1[MAXX][MAXY]**, ***BUF2[MAXX][MAXY]**, ***BUF3[MAXX][MAXY]**, etc. With more than one buffer, you'll probably want each in a fully separate program module to be **#include**d in the paint program. Each could also be a part of one whole **several_buffers** program, then you could fill the first with images assembled from your palette array.

Copy the first onto the second with one simple pointer statement, then make changes in the second that would imply whatever movement should take place between frames. Continue with this procedure through successive buffers till you've used all the buffers memory can afford. Output one buffer after another to the monitor screen; with enough buffers, and if your output is fast enough, you can animate a few seconds or more on the monitor screen, and film or videotape it. More likely, if your output is slower or your buffers fewer, save the output of each completed frame on disk, then bring each frame up to record single or double frames on film or video.

If your output system has the rudimentary versatility to allow you to see what you're doing to the frame buffer while you're doing it, this low-rent way of making pictures is not so hard to deal with, and can produce fully professional results, given acceptable resolution.

With just a little bigger cash investment, you can add a digitizing tablet or some other ergonomic drawing device, but this ups the memory ante significantly. Now we're talking nonprogramming user interface: an interactive system. This is the proper subject of Chapter 10.

For each trick that you may have seen commercially-available paint or animation systems offer, there is a programmer/artist's sort of solution, and a user/nonprogrammer/artist's interactive sort of solution. If you can program, a programmer's solutions are simpler. Let's make some lines, for instance. To paint one pixel at a time, you'd use something like

```
(69x) (-87y)  =  &blue;
```

Assuming that **blue** was defined properly by your palette program in terms of bit fields, and your palette program was **#include**d in the paint program, this would set the pixel at $x = 69$, $y = -87$ (that is: **BUFFER[369][287]**, or what would have been **buffer[287][369]**) to blue.

To make a line, you might first define a variable

```
int  *line [ ]  =  { ... }
```

This new pointer array called **line** could be laboriously set to contain one pixel after another in the buffer array:

```
{ (69x) (-87y),  (70x) (-86y),  (71x) (-85y) };
```

would define a short diagonal, and then ***line[]** would be set to point to a color from the palette program, just the way an individual pixel was in the buffer array. For any general cases or longer lines, though, it would make less sense to define a line this way than to build a line function, one that would define

```
line ((x1) (y1), (x2) (y2), *color)
```

as a straight line from the first argument's coordinates to the next, drawn in the specified color. Once you figure out how to make such a function, it should not be much more difficult to make other functions that utilize various algebraic forms known to have graphic representations that fit other sorts of lines.

Creating a straight-line function is straightforward enough. In the two-dimensional buffer array, **(y2)** will be a certain integer number of elements more or less than **(y1)**, and **(x2)** will be a certain integer number of elements more or less than **(x1)**. The line must extend **(y2) − (y1)** elements vertically and **(x2) − (x1)** elements horizontally. If **(y2)** or **(x2)** is smaller than **(y1)** or **(x1)**, respectively, the line would extend in a bottom-up or right-left direction. The increment and decrement operations described in Chapter 6 could easily give perfectly horizontal and vertical lines; used in combination, they can fill in a diagonal. Along the way of programming out this application, you will surely discover that with even less work, but most of the same basic ingredients, you can make a box function defined by the same two coordinates at diagonal corners, a function for two perpendicular lines connecting the two coordinates named in the arguments, a filled-box function, and a function for a box to be filled with any tiling pattern (with another argument added to the function, for pattern). In other words, almost all of BASIC's graphics routines are variances of the same few simple operations.

It would spoil the fun, and increase this volume's length unconscionably, to spell out each function envisioned here. If I can program any one, at this point you can figure out the rest.

```
line [ ][ ] ((ax) (ay), (bx) (by), *color)
     unsigned int  *color;
     {
     int x, y, temp [ ] [ ];

     if  ((bx) > (ax))
     for (x = (ax);  x ≤ (bx);  ++x);
     else
     for (x ≤ (ax);  x = (bx);  --x);

     if  ((by) > (ay))
     for (y = (ay);  y ≤ (by);  ++y);
```

```
else
for (y ≤ (ay); y = (by); --y);

temp [ ] [ ] = temp [x] [y];
return (temp [ ] [ ]);
}
```

To use this function, you would define the two coordinate positions as the first two arguments and fill in the color argument just as you would point to any color from the palette for an individual pixel. The local variables **(ax), (ay),** etc. have been substituted for $x1$ and $x2$, and so forth, because C doesn't know from subscripts: any value for x in "$x1$" or "$x2$" would be multiplied by 1 or 2.

Because all integers are involved here, the line that results may indeed be aliased. A very basic anti-aliasing system would be to plot two other lines immediately to either side of this first one, each of a color halfway between that used for the original line and the background color.

Of course, you wouldn't want to rewrite this function every time you wanted to draw a line. Rewrite it slightly into a full program, file it away under the name "line," and **#include** it at the beginning of your paint program. It will then act as much like a standard statement as **calloc ()**, a function from the operating-system library. A paint system library is begun! Boxes, filled boxes, setting all pixel colors within a circumscribed area equal to one pixel's color, constructing tiling patterns and filling boxes with them, etc., are now child's play for anybody who has made it this far; go to work!

8.8 The Large Palette

Compromises, ever more compromises. Here we've been contemplating the palette program, in one form or another, for three chapters already, and now its final form depends entirely on some tough decisions you have to make. A fairly ideal palette for a micro-based system would be a full sixteen bits per color, for 65,535 possible combinations of colors and shades. If your hardware supports this, great. The full palette can be stored in long-term memory, where it will take up less than 300 kilobytes. It would consist of 256 palettes of 256 colors each, just one of which would be held in RAM at a time as a "small palette," out of which your images would be made. Already there's compromise here: it is assumed that you would only rarely want more colors than this for a picture, and would rather save on available RAM. If this is not the case, it will be easy to customize code more to your no-holds-barred tastes.

If you must make do with less, oh so many more compromises lurk. It may help to write out an algorithm for the decisions you face, to be sure you give up only what is least excruciating. Remember that you may have to juggle the number of colors in the small palette against considerations of frame-buffer resolution, interactivity, etc. In any case, it will be just as easy to customize on this book's coding recommendations in a down-sizing way as to get swankier.

Two incidentals on the idea of swanky palettes:

(1) Computers are getting cheaper all the time. Write code for a better display system, and in a year or two you may be able to afford it. (Over the year-long course of producing this book, hard-disk memories have dropped ten-fold in price.)

(2) The palette system here will stick to a U = 4 bits, V = 4 bits, Y = 8 bits way of organizing bit fields. This is a compromise, too, of programming ease against slightly and esoterically better color resolution. You may wish to arrange things more complexly, based on psychovisual research. The amazingly subtle colors you come up with are avidly looked forward to in these parts.

The large palette program can perhaps best be organized by setting each of 256 columns to a specified brightness level (Y = 8 bits would yield 256 possible settings), with each of the 256 rows filling in all possible combinations of U and V (again 256). One peculiarity about arrays in C that has not thus far been noted here is that two-dimensional arrays are stored in memory according to rows — first all members of Row 1, then all members of Row 2, etc. This allows you to access any row within a two-dimensional array as an array of one dimension. The same is *not* possible for columns. For the palette you want to present 256 small palettes of 256 colors each. It would not make sense to have each of the small palettes supply only one, or even a limited number of brightness levels, since brightness seems to be subjectively viewed as more important to resolution than color. Instead, with each row presenting a broad brightness range and a limited chromatic range, it easily could serve as just the sort of "close" palette that was used in the original palette program. A "far" palette could be simply a different row, again supplying great potential brightness resolution.

Would these colors need to be named, as in the original palette program? This has been already discussed at length. If you've decided to do so, you may want to suggestively name each member of the **large_pal** array defined below (this is 65,535 names!). More likely, you'll probably go for the easier programming task represented here.

```
\* The basics of the large palette program *\

unsigned int  large_ pal [ ] [256]
unsigned int  small_ pal0,  small_ pal1,  small_ pal2,  small_ pal3,  \*...*\
                                                          \* to small_ pal255 *\
struct  color
      {
      unsigned int  V:4;
      unsigned int  U:4;
      unsigned int  Y:8;
      };

small_ pal0 ( )

      unsigned int small_ pal [256];
      struct  color;

      {
      while (color.V = 0  &&  color.U = 0)
            for (small_ pal = 0;  small_ pal < 256 &&\
large_ pal [small_ pal0] [0];  ++small_ pal0)
                  for (color.Y = 0;  color.Y < 256; ++color.Y)
                     return (small_ pal0);
      }

small_ pal1  ( )

      unsigned int small_ pal1[256];
      struct color;

      {
      while (color.V = 0  &&  color.U = 1)
            for (small_ pal = 0;  small_ pal < 256 &&\
large_ pal [small_ pal1] [1];  ++small_ pal1)
                  for (color.Y = 0; color.Y < 256; ++color.Y)
                     return (small_ pal1);
      }

\* Continue process for 256 functions, each for all values of Y and *\
\* with all successive possible combinations of U and V.              *\
```

The arbitrary nature of these palette choices will be emphasized just one last time. The *U* and *V* combinations depend on what your hardware expects to work with. Also remember that you can come up with other color combinations by arranging the basic function form only slightly differently. What you need now is a display function that will determine the form all palettes will take for preview. First you'd need to go back to the start of the program and make sure it **#include**s the buffer program —

```
#include <buffer>
```

— so that you have something to work with. Then a display function should specify that each patch of color depicting each different structure making up **small_pal0, small_pal1,** etc., should be shown on a grid of pixels. With 2400 pixels available and 256 colors to show, each can occupy nine pixels, with some room left over.

If the program is being made for a system with a pen and data tablet, it seems acceptable to group these nine pixels in a box for each color structure and to present the whole as a contiguous screen. The user would then be able to choose by pointing to a spot within a displayed smear of continuously changing color. If the program is being built for keyboard input only, larger patches of color may be needed, to allow room for a cursor to pick out the color. In this case, a command line also could be used to announce a name for the palette (a number would do just fine), allowing the user to choose the palette by keyboard input. Down the road, whether the user is expected to be a programmer (yourself, say) or not, there must be some way to allow for accurate choice of individual colors from the small palette.

Keyboard input is well standardized to an ASCII code for virtually all micros made. The code for each key should be listed in your hardware documentation (if not, it is listed somewhere in each of the C and BASIC texts listed in the Bibliography). Since you are thoroughly familiar with C's **scanf** statement, it will be easy to include any sort of expected keyboard input in your palette program. (It may appear easier to do this by making use of one of the operating-system or standard library functions for defining and moving a cursor. You will want to be sure, however, that you are not using a function that implies the screen is formatted into lines and columns of characters, and most such standard cursor functions work on this assumption.) You'll have to refer to the ASCII codes to make standard character input from the keyboard equal characters within the graphics-mode output, precisely because you're not working within that standard-format character screen. Instead you'll need to define each character in terms of pixels, which is a powerful incentive to hold down the number of characters you'll need (except for designers with particular interest in typography). To produce a pixel-grid character, it may help to study the way a dot matrix printer produces characters. Some pretty classy-looking letters and numerals can be made with a matrix of 24 by 18, and a legible character system can be made with as few as 4 by 10 pixels.

Designing characters, then, becomes a process that is exactly equivalent to designing any other static composition, including the patches that will designate palette colors for a user's choosing. Each small palette must be an array (a one-dimensional array will serve the purpose here) of designated several-pixel-square patches of 256 colors, which may also include characters (designed in pixels) naming those colors or the palette. Except in these details that you must choose to optimize your own hardware, it needn't differ very greatly from the last version of the small palette program, presented in Chapter 7. If close and far palettes are desired, as in that program, remember to access only half of each of two of the 256-row arrays in the large palette program.

8.9 Color Cycling

Color cycling is a pseudoanimation technique that can be accomplished in real time even on sixteen-bit CPUs. It involves cycling all the colors of a palette within a designated area of a picture, or over the whole picture, without changing line contours that define basic images. You also will want to use some form of color cycling just to view one small palette after another, to choose which to use. The same basic technique makes both possible.

One other major change that will be needed in the small palette program, from the way it was presented last, is just this need for color cycling. Before, the entire large palette was envisioned as 256 colors. We've grown more ambitious since then (or at least one of us has). Some mechanism is needed to cycle among all 256 small palettes and allow a user to choose among them. This process is really quite simple. The program must include a function, which might be called **cycle,** that would basically consist of a looping statement, incrementally presenting each small palette within the large-palette array, until a user input stops the cycle.

```
for (large_pal [ ] = small_pal0; large_pal < small_pal256; ++large_pal)
        display (large_pal [ ])
           while (!pal_choice);
```

This little bit of code implies that a "display" function has been already introduced, and also that a **pal_choice** variable has been initialized to certain conditions. The second matter will be explained first. In the small-palette program an input of some palette number was requested. In the examples given in Chapters 6 and 7, some number from one to sixteen was expected as an input to a **scanf** statement to designate one of sixteen palettes. Now, of course, you have 256 palettes to choose from, so the program ought to be modified to expect one of 256 numbered answers. These may as well be numbered from 1 to 256. This would allow **pal_choice** to be initialized to 0, then used as a flag here, and also previously, as the object pointer used by a **scanf** statement to read the user's choice of palettes. If no user input has yet been read, **pal_choice** will continue to equal zero, which the **while** statement implies. As soon as **pal_choice** has any value at all,

```
!pal_choice
```

will no longer be true, and the loop will end. Until the loop ends, palettes will cycle on screen (assuming **BUFFER**'s contents are being outputted to the screen). To contain the flag (initial value of zero) as well as 256 palette-choice elements, obviously **small_pal** must contain 257 elements. Exactly the same sort of code can be used within the paint program you'll be building to cycle colors within a palette within a specified area.

The specified area would be designated in a way analogous to the ''display'' function hinted at above, or to any output formatted to specific pixels in **BUFFER.** Here a display function must take an argument, to stand for whichever small palette is chosen, and map each color member of this array to a certain set of pixels, with any descriptive characters also mapped to pixels, and so forth.

Within a paint program, it is quite common to see colors cycled within a particularly bounded area of the picture, say the sky of a landscape. This is no easier or harder than any individual color or pattern used to fill in an outline. The process is described below. The colors used in the cycle can be customized easily — to sunset colors, for instance. It is just as easy to cycle among a portion of the colors within an array as the whole array; just set the loop to reach only from, say, element 0 to element 100.

8.10 Filling in Outlines and Defining Images for Animation

Several pages back a program was presented for line drawing, and it was suggested that a very similar program could be adapted to drawing boxes, then to filling in boxes with colors or patterns. Any outline specified with a **while** or **for** statement can be equivalently filled in by a coloring or patterning operation as the second half of the statement. A more complex outline, involving jagged and irregular lines, might involve a very complex statement with several **&&**s, but describing the outline would remain an easy, if tedious, task. If you need to describe the outline more than once, it would certainly be far less tedious to first set a variable — an array of lines, most likely — equal to the whole outline, then simply use the variable wherever needed in the future. Using an array of lines to represent an outline also allows the array to be incremented, decremented, or multiplied by a scalar; in other words, it allows any image to be animated.

To take an example used some time ago, suppose you have a character called **dancing_bear.** If **dancing_bear** were an array of several lines with a few other included elements being instructions to fill in colors or patterns, then **dancing_bear** could be copied into another buffer, certain elements or all elements could be changed systematically then copied into another buffer, elements could be changed again, etc. The original **dancing_bear** was conceived as a structure, and this has certain benefits over a simple array. It allows greater latitude in the changes made to various members of the structure at the same time. The ideal, certainly, would be for **dancing_bear** to be a structure of arrays, of lines, of color and pattern assignments (which are, as you know, arrays of structures), and so forth. When **dancing_bear** was introduced, readers without knowledge of C could only visualize the character in a top-down way; now you can build **dancing_bear** either top-down or bottom-up.

8.11 Analytic Geometry, Vector-style Graphics, and 3D

Curving lines or polygons defined by algebraic equations are a little more difficult to begin to understand than straight lines, boxes, and tiling patterns, but once you know what you're doing with the more complex equations used to define these constructs, they become every bit as easy to deploy in pictures as a straight line.

It cannot be the purpose of this book to give a course in analytic geometry, but an understanding of the subject is as much a key to designing complex creations as is an understanding of programming. A high-school text is recommended reading for anybody who is unfamiliar with the subject. Speaking as a relatively indifferent student back then, who forgot most everything in a period of a few short years, it is easy to get interested again and relearn and conquer the stuff when you have a purpose. What's the point of learning to plot parabolas in high school? Well, there's a little more point to the matter when you can use a series of parabolas to represent a mountain ridge in your animated masterpiece.

Analytic geometry for the purposes of computer graphics is like a tool kit. Look again at the ellipses used to form a rough drawing of a hand in Chapter 4; you will recognize that the equations are easily translatable into C programming instructions, and that all the ellipses used to create the hand can easily be grouped into either an array of ellipses or a structure of ellipses. Instead of rather simple ellipses, each part of the hand can be represented by more complex forms, if only you know the formulas. A library of formulas for geometric shapes is a library of algorithms for object primitives.

Using such constructs moves you beyond the realm of a paint program, too. Vector graphics were devised to draw shapes derived from equations without wasting memory on colors. Since most micro users have the capacity for raster graphics whether they like it or not, this book has concentrated first on building palette and paint programs. The buffer used to assemble your painted graphics can be equally well used to assemble vector-type images (these would not actually be vector images, because they would be built pixel by pixel; the difference has been explained in past chapters), which can then be filled in with colors or patterns.

Only through such vector-like graphics can a convincing illusion of 3D be made. Making 3D graphics starts out only incrementally more complicated than 2D graphics: build your frame buffers to three dimensions by adding a third array dimension of *z* coordinates. The third array need not be translated to the 2D presentation system — its evidence in terms of the shapes of images in the other two dimensions is precisely what we are after in so-called 3D images, no more. You may want to build a system that is capable of viewing *any* two of the three dimensions at once, however, and to therefore be able to change "camera" viewpoints on the scene. Doing so is as easy as changing the order in which the array is defined, from

```
BUFFER [x] [y] [z]
```

to

```
BUFFER [z] [y] [x]
```

which can be accomplished via a macro. You might want to look at a 3D image from a camera position beneath or above, or to one side or another; setting one or another of the dimensional arrays, **[x]**, **[y]**, or **[z]**, negative will do the trick. If you use the notation **(__x) (__y) (__z)** to represent 3D array positions, then to view a typically drawn image of a standing person from a point beneath the floor,

```
#define BUFFER [x] [y] [z]    BUFFER [z] [x] [y]
#define y                 -y
```

will do the trick with macros. The trick can also be done using far less memory, and on a temporary basis, by using the equivalent statements within a program. Redefining $x = -x$ will turn the person's back to the camera (assuming they faced front originally).

Realistic 3D images are much more complex, unfortunately, than what you'll get by simply adding on a [z] array. Objects represented in 3D coordinates must be scaled so that they recede realistically in space. Animated characters that move through space necessitate camera angles that don't merely flip to a negative image, but gradually rotate to that new point of view. Yes, you can recreate the image subjectively, using the Renaissance laws of perspective in painting, and give just as perfect a 3D image without more mathematical calculations. By the same token, you can do this using only two axes and a paint program, but some understanding of image-transform formulas in three dimensions will allow you to program all this stuff for quick execution.

8.12 Image Transforms

The simplest sort of image transform is a flip, or mirror image. As was mentioned way back in Chapter 6, any row or column of the 2D (or now 3D) array can be defined as a line that, when crossed by an image, flips the image in one or more dimensions. Even if the object flips in two or more dimensions when crossing any such line, this is a one-dimensional transform because the line crossed is one dimensional. Two-dimensional transforms require a *translation matrix*. Again, this is fairly standard analytic geometry turned to the tool-kit purpose of graphics.

For example, suppose you need to multiply an object in incrementally larger scalars, to simulate its coming closer. The simplest way to do so is to multiply all array elements by an equal amount, continually incremented. Next most simple would be to multiply x coordinates by one value and y coordinates by another, again continually incremented. An object thus scaled might get wider as it comes closer. Even more control over the transformation is achieved by multiplying the object by a matrix. To demonstrate, take a very simply drawn character, as in Figure 8.3. The x's in the diagram mark the pixels used; empty boxes are unused pixels; assume all are drawn the same color, to simplify the concept here. Of course, this also could be represented by the C matrix

```
array [][] = {
             {0, 0, x, 0, 0},
             {0, x, 0, x, 0},
             {x, 0, x, 0, x},
             {0, x, 0, x, 0},
             {0, 0, x, 0, 0}
             }
```

Now imagine multiplying this matrix by another matrix,

```
array [][] = {
             {0, 0, 2, 0, 0},
             {0, 2, 0, 2, 0},
             {2, 0, 2, 0, 2},
             {0, 2, 0, 2, 0},
             {0, 0, 2, 0, 0}
             }
```

or by this matrix:

```
array [][] = {
             {0, 0, 3, 0, 0},
             {0, 4, 0, 2, 0},
             {5, 0, 3, 0, 1},
             {0, 4, 0, 2, 0},
             {0, 0, 3, 0, 0}
             }
```

Figure **8.3** A simple character

		x		
	x		x	
x				x
	x		x	
		x		

In the first case the object depicted would seem to come uniformly closer by a power of x; in the second case, by a power of 2. In the third, the object would come proportionally closer (larger) on the left, and stay of more equal size toward the right. Presto! A canned digital video effect worthy of a music video or station ID. Used more subtly, the third matrix provides the basics of a change in point of view. Think what you can do with much more careful use of larger scalar matrices. Objects can be rotated through an angle θ (theta) from the point of origin by being multiplied by a matrix

```
array [][]= {
            {cosθ, sinθ}
            {-sinθ, cosθ}
            }
```

In algebraic form the transformation would be expressed as

$$x_2 = x_1 \times \cos - y \times \sin\theta$$
$$y_2 = x_1 \times \sin - y \times \cos\theta.$$

Positive angles are measured counterclockwise from x toward y; negatives can be used to move things the other way around. In 3D transformations, the right-hand axis of rotation in a positive direction for x would be y to z; for y it would be in the direction of z to x; and for z it would be in the direction of x to y. Left-hand rotation would be the inverse of these. Rotation and scaling in 3D are simple extensions from the same calculations in 2D.

Since every book on computer graphics listed in the Bibliography goes over all of these details — as do all analytic geometry texts this author has ever seen — a long discussion of the subject seems redundant, except in context with other, more advanced 3D algorithms. Next chapter is the place for that.

8.13 Windows and Viewports, Again

A viewport is a view on a clipped portion of the graphical universe. A window is a framed look into the contents of another buffer. The subject of viewports will come up over and over, in ever subtler ways, as you get involved with geometrical algorithms for 3D modeling. Every time a view of the whole buffer screen is clipped in a different way — to suggest movement, to establish a different camera angle, or as a dramatic method of revealing just part of a scene — you'll be finding new ways of using viewports.

Windows are less protean, but they do have uses in animation or still graphics. For example, say you construct an image of a room that's supposed to have a window (the "real" sort, with glass in it); a graphical window could be defined by the sash of the in-picture window, and the contents of some other graphical creation, perhaps a landscape or a monster movie you made and stored on disk eons before, could be the view through that window. This is not to imply that a window must be rectangular, or even of polygonal shape, or even of some regular shape. Say you have a closeup image of an eye, and want to show a reflection in it of what the eye may be looking at. A window used for the task would need to be very irregularly shaped to suggest the color and texture of the eye that holds the reflection. In fact, the scene in the window should be tinted, too, to the general color of the eye. All of this is not easy, but it is possible to do with windows.

Defining a nonmoving window is as easy as using the beginning of a conditional statement to set the window's boundaries; an **#include**d image in another buffer would be either clipped to fit the window or scaled to fit, or both. Changing the color of the enclosed image to match that of the eye or the room is just another clause of the statement.

A simpler problem needs a solution, too. Consider all the varied programs that must come together into a graphics system — large and small palettes, paint, each brush function, line, box, and texture functions, and geometrical line-drawing programs to be built out of the algorithms you find in math texts — each must be somehow accessible while using another. In a system built strictly for use by the programmer, all this involves is an **#include** statement and the code to call up a function or program. In a system built for interactivity, you'd want to provide some kind of menu within a window, which would open up to other windows with instructions for each operation. The approach is probably familiar from most recent software in almost any application. Indeed, much of the market value of graphics programming skills is to build programs for all applications with these lovely graphic touches. This sort of window usage is properly within the realm of Chapter 10, "Interactivity."

8.14 In-Betweening, and Calculating How Many Buffers You Can Afford

The tedium of animation is the making of all those in-between pictures — images involving no originality, but filling in frames of movement from one basic character position to another. Just being able to copy a whole image from one block of memory to another, then make small changes, then do it over again, certainly reduces the tedium factor dramatically. With at least eight frames per second necessary for animation, however, and twelve frames per second needed for smooth animation, a good bit of tedious work remains. A way to reduce the rote work even more is computerized in-betweening. That is, getting the machine to draw those in-between frames.

Lots of people have some sort of in-betweening program, but nobody has a perfect in-betweening program. The more complicated a movement is, and the longer its duration, the more difficult it is to program in enough variables for the computer to know how to fill in frames. Extraneous detail like color and picture information not associated with the moving parts also add tremendously to the difficulties of in-betweening — or "'tweening," as it is often called. In-betweening programs work best when they are simplest — when they are meant to deal only with vector-type line drawings on a black background. In any case, given the memory requirements, it will be a long time before more complex in-betweening programs are in the province of micros.

Thus, a trade-off is going to be involved in any decision to devise an in-betweening program. Getting those in-between frames with the method already described — copying the whole picture, changing details, copying again — cuts the need to recolor succeeding frames, add background, etc. Using a simple in-betweening program cuts the need to redraw the parts that move, but necessitates redrawing everything else. Some compromise is possible, certainly: you could use an in-betweening program to copy the movement, use the earlier method to copy the whole original frame, then devise a program to superimpose one picture over the other. Even then details would need to be touched up. If a character's arm moved against a landscape background, the coloring of the arm would have to be moved to the new arm position, and the landscape's detail would need to be extended to fill in the position vacated by the arm. What if these paint details were defined as existing within an outline, an outline that has now changed? Indeed, an in-betweening program could allow the color defined by the arm outline to change boundaries along with the outline. The trade-off is that such a program would probably not be workable in anything close to real time, but it would be much closer to real time than the compromise method to which it is here being compared.

As you might guess, in-betweening is possible only with at least three frame memory stores (not counting the one or two that are used for screen refresh, as part of the presentation system), and preferably several more; the buffers must be used

1. for the original frame,
2. for the end-of-movement position,
3. for as many in-betweens as possible, one buffer per in-between.

Here is where memory needs get particularly intense — all of these buffers must be resident in RAM. This, again, is good reason to limit the detail in each buffer, so that as many as possible can be squeezed in. In-betweening remains a natural for vector graphics; even though memory costs have dropped so drastically in recent years, the vast memory needed for raster in-betweening makes vector display devices (which are several times more expensive than raster monitors) begin to look cheap.

In-betweening *is* possible, and helpful, with raster graphics, and the large number of buffers needed to accomplish it is equally to be desired for ease of animation, even without in-betweening. A buffer with 600 by 400 unsigned integer pixels will use 960 Kbytes of RAM. Limit your in-betweening to two-color line drawings, and you can do without most of the palette and paint programs, temporarily, and their 100 Kb or so of RAM usage. Two megabytes of RAM is a pretty common fat RAM pack for a micro, as this is being written, which means the average micro user with this sort of investment could get away with two buffers with those other programs in RAM. In-betweening is not for Mr. Average Micro.

If, on another hand, you have more than the average micro to work with, and can put together, say, eight to twelve in-between buffers, then in-betweening is for you. An algorithm for going about the process is:

1. Compare each pixel of the original buffer to each pixel of the end-of-position buffer. For this purpose, comparing arrays is as easy as subtracting one from the other; where element values are equal, the result is zero.
2. Wherever there is a difference, average the difference and display the result in a third buffer. When subtracting to compare buffers, the subtraction result divided by two, plus the number subtracted, equals the average.
3. Repeat Steps 1 and 2 between Buffer 3 (the averaged buffer derived in Step 2) and Buffer 1.
4. Repeat again, between Buffer 3 and Buffer 2 (the end-of-position buffer).
5, etc. Continue to average and display results in other buffers, to the limit of buffers available.

8.15 Run-Length Encoding

If you remember back as far as Chapter 1, run-length encoding was mentioned as a possible way to save memory through dynamic pixel usage. For images with a great deal of detail, however, run-length encoding can use up to twice the memory of the simpler pixel coding method already detailed. Run-length encoding can be particularly useful, though, in the special case of in-betweening.

Actually, the fine details of run-length encoding will be somewhat different in different programming languages. It is possible to do in most languages, if not all, but not all have features that allow it to save memory. You might save more memory with run-length encoding in FORTRAN, vis-a-vis the sort of direct pixel addressing already described, than you will using C. Run-length encoding might be nothing but a headache to you in BASIC. Okay, enough mystification.

Even when drawing lines, this book has instructed you thus far only in a way to address pixels one-to-one. Even when the very next pixel in a line is to get precisely the same treatment as the one before it, it gets that full treatment. Instead, imagine taking advantage of the fact that two or three-dimensional arrays in C are stored in order of the row array — that is, all the elements of the first row across the array are stored in series, then all the elements of the next row across, and so on down to the last row of the array. If the array is three-dimensional, then the first row of the second *z* level is consecutively stored, and so on through all array elements. In an unsigned integer array measuring **[400][600]**, getting from **array[2][3]** to **array[3][3]** is a journey of two bytes, the length of the element. Getting from **array[2][3]** to **array[2][4]** is a journey of 400 elements, or 800 bytes. Run-length encoding can work efficiently along rows in C, and not efficiently at all from column to column. (To complicate things slightly, remember that a macro has been used to turn **buffer[y][x]** into **BUFFER[x][y]**; it is *still* rows that are encoded sequentially, but in **BUFFER,** rows are the second array listed.)

The information to be encoded in **array[2][1]** will be either the same as in **array[1][1]** or different. In other words, a flag can be used to test whether **array[2][1]** is different or not. If **array[2][1]** is not different, it must be painted the same as **array[1][1];** if it is different, it must be painted its different color. "Run-length" encoding implies that an entire run length of similarly encoded pixels along a line are encoded together. The flag feels out just how long the run length will be, and then the entire run is encoded.

Now, for a paint program with many colors and many color changes probably occurring between individual pixels, this sounds like a lot of rigamarole to go through, using extra time and memory. But imagine using a two-color drawing palette. Two colors, bit coded 0 and 1, are very compatible with the flag used to determine if a pixel is the same as the one before or different. Even so, if a pixel pattern of on-off-on-off were continued for some time, the extra step involved in the process would take precisely twice as much time and memory as one-to-one encoding. If only two colors are to be used, though, odds are that far more pixels will be one of them than the other.

Run-length encoding also may speed refresh buffer action and can be used there (where it will have been programmed by the manufacturer, not you) without being used in your own RAM or permanent buffer files. The refresh buffer is the buffer in firmware that serves as the transition between your buffers in RAM and the screen display; it can be coded to take all necessary information about an image in terms of run lengths of similar colors. The same caveat about detailed images applies, however, to run-length encoding in a refresh buffer; it would not make sense to make many-colored, complex images that must be read by such a presentation system. This is why, quite reasonably, run-length encoding is typically not used by manufacturers of graphics cards meant for raster systems (most micros included). On the other hand, run-length encoded presentation systems are quite compatible with vector images.

8.16 Vector Images Revisited

Vector images have been mostly ignored by this book, since it is presumed most readers are working with raster displays and are interested in full-color images. The vogue for vector images in animation was coincident with the relatively quicker mastery computer animators attained with them in the late seventies and early eighties, but their high-tech look (actually lower-tech than 3D raster images) went out of style quickly. The vector look may just coincide with some project goal of yours, however; what is and is not in style should not be taken all that seriously by those who would be style-makers.

Of more negative import to your prospects for working with vector images is the likelihood that you are working with a raster system. Using vectors will not save you a great deal of presentation time and memory if your presentation system does not use run-length encoding and you use a raster monitor, not a vectorscope. Displayed on a raster monitor, your vector images would have aliasing problems: they'd look pretty tacky.

Still, some introduction to the subject is in order. Constructing a vector-imaging system is so unlike a raster system that much of the buffer and palette array architecture designed over these last few chapters is irrelevant. You *do* need arrays of arrays to plot vector images, but don't need the elaborate bit structures to determine colors. Since vector images are defined by relatively few points along each line, not by all points as has so far been the case, the buffer array can be defined to hold a much larger number of *maximum* elements, for greater accuracy and images that are never aliased. The **calloc** or **malloc** function can be used to dynamically allocate array memory usage that can be very small indeed — any elements not needed to define lines would equal zero, which would imply black on the display. Even elements used to define lines would be simply white. Only one bit need be encoded per pixel to tell the difference. This means one byte of memory can control eight pixels, and a 960 Kbyte RAM buffer could conceivably hold an array measuring 2400 by 3200, as opposed to the 400 by 600 array it might hold in a raster system. If you have a vector monitor available, it would make sense to try some of the 3D modeling equations presented in the next chapter with such a vector system.

It *is* possible to get solid, full-color images from a vector system. Though this would defeat somc of its RAM-saving purpose, it would not defeat all of the RAM savings. Even with monochrome output, you can still use two bytes per pixel for coding colors. These could be interpreted by the presentation system as shades of grey, and a series of filters could be placed over the vector output for photographing in several passes on color film. If the picture were broken into RGB components, for example (easier than YUV for purposes of filtering), with each component filter coloring the shades customized for it, a combined image would thus be made of all the colors encoded. Just as much subtlety, and as many bits per pixel, are needed for this approach to color as the raster approach, so the vector grid must play the size versus memory-usage game in a tighter arena. The fact that vector images are defined by fewer points still reduces memory usage substantially, compared to raster systems.

The only problem with the above approach is that you've still only made a colored *line* image. To fill in the lines, you'd need to write a complicated program that must provide proper shading over full surfaces, which ought to be quite different from the shading of boundary lines. In fact, such programs, and systems such as this, have been in use for years at graphics production houses that invested in vector graphics early on and have continued to adapt their systems for increased versatility as much as they can. From this viewer's viewpoint, proper shading remains a problem in many products of these systems, and exhausted tales of hours of touch-up are common. It would seem to make more sense to start with a raster system, if you are starting in now. Proper shading over planar surfaces is a subject fit for, and well beyond, the next chapter.

CHAPTER NINE

Topics in the State of the Art

Maybe this is a misnamed chapter. What is state-of-the-art? How could we possibly get around to discussing it here without having to go through many ideas the s-o-t-a stands on the shoulders of? By the time we get there, the s-o-t-a will be someplace else, a couple of years ahead. A confession: the problem does not lie merely with any *reader's* base state of ineducation; this book is not being written by a guy spending his life pushing forward the frontiers. But then, frontier folk on the front line often can see nothing but their own individual targets.

So: Comments on what seems to be the state of the art to somebody standing just enough behind the lines to appreciate (he hopes) the full view.

9.1 Catching up with the Seventies

For anybody starting out in computer graphics now, there's a lot of catching up to do. Geometric 3D modeling with different types of primitives has provided fronts for exploration; algorithms for hidden surfaces, reflective surfaces, and textured surfaces of 3D models might be considered another related set of front-line experimentation; incorporating unaliased or anti-aliased lines and edges into all of the above (as part of the original model, not as a touch-up after execution) is a constant theme, with some sort of more efficient buffering being the likely solution; finally, there is the constant of making ever more use of ever more available memory and ever better display devices, to produce all of the above in full-color raster images.

A beginner's run through each of these topics is in order. So is more advanced research in all of it, but this is beyond the possibilities of a few pages. By all means, if you want to get and stay current with the cutting edge in computer graphics, pick up the various publications of SIGGRAPH cited in the Bibliography; there you will share the ideas of the top thinkers in the field. This chapter's goal is to get you to the point where you can make sense of these recommended readings.

The most common sorts of shapes to be used as object primitives for 3D modeling are polygons, patches, quadrics, and fractals. All of these already have been described to varying degrees of not very much detail; herewith more detail, adhering to as nonmathematical an approach as possible. Be warned, however, that to really be able to roll up your sleeves and work with these things, you'll need a rounded knowledge of algebra, calculus, and analytic geometry.

9.2 Polygon Meshes

Polygons can be used to describe any physical, natural phenomenon, but almost never can do so perfectly. Most things are curved, usually in unpredictable ways. Polygons are neither, but their regularity is what makes for their computational usefulness. They fill spaces — not perfectly, but if used carefully, close enough to pass. Close enough to pass is no small accomplishment; that's as good as computer graphics ever get.

A polygon mesh is a collection of polygons tied together at edges and vertices. Many different sorts of collections of polygons can be used to do the same job. For instance, unequally sized polygons might be cobbled together to fill a space as in Figure 9.1, or as in 9.2; or equal-sized polygons might be joined together as in 9.3. The possibilities are, certainly, endless. What is best is what works in a given circumstance.

Polygons may be represented in a program by the coordinates of their vertices, or by defining edge lines. Whatever method of definition is selected, it should lend itself to the simplest possible construction of forms for the job at hand, and also to easy debugging. When polygons are joined into a three-dimensional polyhedron, each polygon rests in a different plane; a polygon may implicitly define the plane it is on, or be partially defined by a plane that has been defined already. Defining differences between polygons and other planes, defining changes in polygons as they intersect planes: all of this is pretty elementary stuff for geometry, but it is the essence of defining 3D images to computers.

Figure **9.1**
Unequal polygons filling a curved space

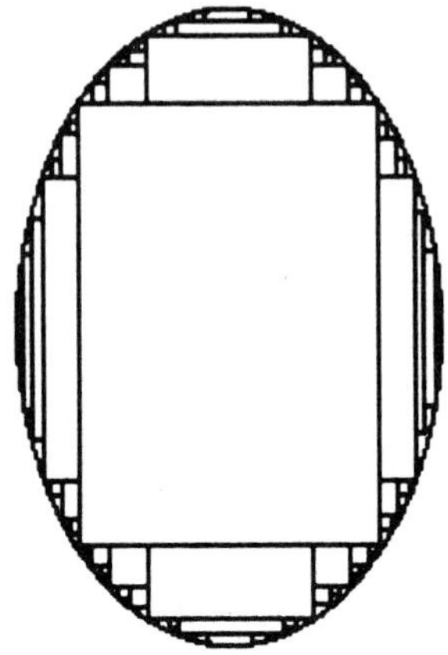

Figure **9.2**
Gridded Hermite patch

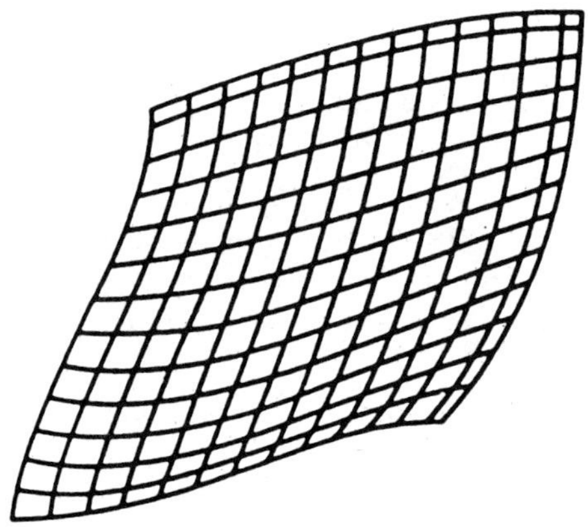

Figure **9.3** Bezier patch with sixteen control points plotted

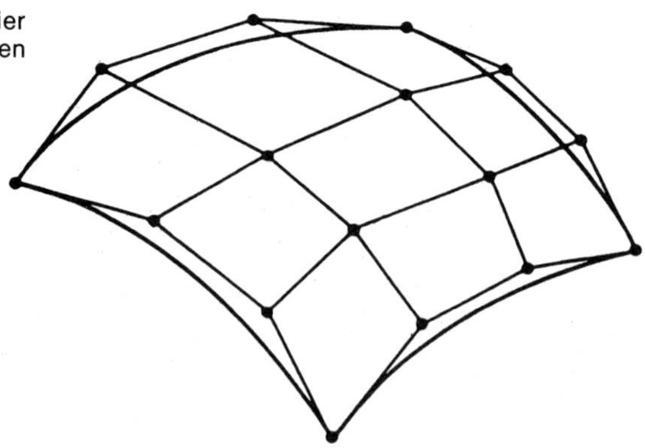

9.3 Curved Surfaces

Curved surfaces can be defined by many sorts of mathematical expressions, generally of a more complex order than those used to define polygons; they look more like reality than polygons tend to, although they are even more likely than polygons to be misrepresented through aliasing problems. Using curved surfaces to build 3D objects generally results in a more sinuous object than an equivalent polygonal rendering. Because it looks less machinelike, more natural, and yet in small unconquerable details still unreal, an object made of curved surfaces makes the most of the general ability of computer graphics to rivet our attention to the not quite real.

A few curves (among the possible infinity of forms) have found particular favor among graphics-systems designers. Among them are *Hermite* and *Bezier patches,* and several types of *splines.* Splines take their name from the metal strips stretched around aircraft hulls; they define space by stretching, usually in parallel, across a given curved surface. Figures 9.2 and 9.3 show Hermite and Bezier patches, respectively. These have been used since the sixties' pioneering computer graphics work of Steven Coons, John Whitney, Sr., and others to produce representations of matrices of differential and quadratic (thus ''quadric'' surfaces) equations. Now they are more often used, just as are polygons, as building blocks to represent natural shapes they circumstantially resemble.

9.4 Fractals

Fractals have been explained already in somewhat greater depth than these other techniques. They are at once a simpler and more subtle technique for rendering solids: simpler because they are not curved and exist in only one plane; more complex because a mass of recursive subdivisions of a simple shape, recombined in various ways, come closer to representing many natural objects than any other mathematical technique. Rocks, clouds, plants, natural heat-crack patterns, etc., can be made to seem very natural with fractals that individually have flat surfaces, yet collectively have a very complex texture. Curved-surface fractals (though memory-guzzling and time-consuming to compute) hold promise of eventually rendering even human or animal-like characters as convincingly as a photograph. The simplicity of working with fractals is a not-incidental part of their attraction: they can be made with less complex code than can curved surfaces.

Perhaps of even more interest, fractals can live more comfortably with lower-resolution, unaliased images than can curves. Curved surfaces veritably demand buffers and monitors with thousands of pixels in each direction. Fractals look better on better systems, too, but instead of betraying aliased lines and lack of detail when zooming in on an image of limited resolution, since fractals are infinitely divisible the fractal image can be easily subdivided again to provide more detail. This subdivision can be programmed to operate automatically for any window expanded to fill the screen, where other methods of modeling would need manual touch-up. On systems with resolution equivalent to a television screen, fractal modeling is the ideal 3D system. It may just be the ideal system for high-resolution, high-speed systems, too.

With a look back to the discussion of fractals at the beginning of this book, you may now be able to develop some fractal programs of your own, and you should be able to make good use of any fractal algorithms or programs presented in various SIGGRAPH journals.

9.5 Depth Cueing

Sometimes a 3D image rendered with perfect perspective still, somehow, does not look like it has real depth. After all, the final product is being viewed in only two dimensions. Proper shading and gradual loss of detail are cues that humans use to understand depth, and these must be provided too, to decode a 3D picture. Indeed, using these other means of depth cueing can obviate the need for the more complex and costly computations associated with the techniques for rendering 3D models described above.

Some very simple algorithms for depth clipping have been used to happy effect for years. Simply cutting off what is meant to be the rear of an object is cheap in terms of memory, and does provide the illusion that it is so far away it can't be seen. More effective is a gradual shading to signify the same thing; this may not be a real-world phenomenon, because shading has little to do with distance, but such shading mimics the fading-out-of-focus that we do experience with distance. Psychovisually, we tend to associate gradually darker shading with gradually less focus. This is fortunate for computer graphics makers, because providing gradually less focus is a far more difficult task and very expensive in terms of memory and time. Depth shading or clipping particularly help give a sensation of movement to animated objects.

9.6 Hidden Surfaces

The "hidden surface problem" continues to generate more and more state-of-the-art solutions, each flawed and each successful in its own way. Hidden edges and surfaces must be removed when 3D objects are filled in. To remove them "by hand," that is, by touching up with a paint program after models are mathematically derived, is always a possible solution, but rarely a best solution. What happens when you want to animate that object, turn it around, and show the surfaces you have removed?

In many ways, it's unfortunate that "wire-frame" vector images have not continued to grow from their popularity at the beginning of the eighties. With no need to hide edges or surfaces, a comprehensive aesthetic comes along with low cost. Now wire-frame images are so out of style that even architectural and industrial-design imaging systems compete for the best hidden-surface-removal algorithms and implementations, even though much of the time CAD users need to see those hidden (or hideable) surfaces!

To develop a hidden-surface algorithm, the basic question that needs to be asked of any two points defined in three dimensions is whether either obscures the other. This is akin to asking of two points, (x_1) (y_1) (z_1) and $(x_2)(y_2)(z_2)$,

1. Are (x_1) and (x_2) the same, and are (y_1) and (y_2) the same? If no to either question, there is no hidden surface. If both are yeses,
2. Which is greater, (z_1) or (z_2)?

Whichever is greater, that pixel, either (x_1) (y_1) (z_1) or (x_2) (y_2) (z_2), must be temporarily erased from view while still existing as part of the definition of the object being depicted and available for reappearance whenever it is no longer obscured.

If this is such a full statement of the problem (and surely you can think of a solution to the problem in a few lines of code as you read this), why have there been so many solutions to the hidden-surface problem? Testing for all the conditions described in the above preliminary algorithm can take a long time, and the best hidden-surface solution is one that is incorporated into the code for every rendering of a 3D solid object, hiding surfaces that ought to be hidden as they are created, hiding new surfaces as an object is viewed from a different perspective. Also, only a part of a larger image in the buffer is often viewed on screen. Hidden-surface removal can, of course, be accomplished only in the 3D environment of the buffer, but you don't want to have to go through the trouble of the procedure for an image that will be clipped by the viewport edge, anyway. Even more damning for simple algorithms, images may be hidden by more than one other image. Suppose one object obscures another; there is an obscured surface to Object 1, a front surface of Object 2 that is presently obscured but would not be if Object 1 were not there, and a surface of Object 2 that would be obscured by its front surface even if it were not obscured by Object 1. If you can help it, you don't want to have to test every array element of every surface of every object against every other in a complex picture. How much easier — more likely feasible, that is, for systems with smaller memories — it would be to compare all objects at once to those with the lowest *z*-axis values.

With curved surfaces, even finding out whether an object exists on a certain plane can be very difficult. The defining edges and quadratics need not affect all the pixels through which the image they contain passes — an image that exists unpredictably on many planes at once.

Here's more grist for hidden-surface problems: In the process of moving 3D objects around in a buffer, it is easy to make them take up certain of the same space. This may or may not be desirable. Think of the overlap necessary between arms and legs to make realistic elbows and knees, but then think of the realistic sense of collision and weight you want to create with a foot standing on a floor. Some surfaces ought to look and feel inviolable; others must be permeable. Permeable or translucent or transparent surfaces can allow dimmed, reflected, or refracted views of what they obscure, and not simply, totally hide it.

One straightforward, memory-saving approach to nonpermeable, nontransparent, nontranslucent surfaces involves directing the refresh buffer to scan the RAM buffer image in order of largest *z*-axis coordinates first. This makes the closest elements naturally obscure those farthest away, wherever occlusions occur. The procedure will not be possible with many graphics cards available for micros, but it is becoming more available all the time. Many packaged CAD systems are beginning to use this approach, and these systems are a driving force for new off-the-shelf equipment availabilities.

Using the refresh scan to do all the depth sorting required of complex images takes time, which slows down refresh to unacceptable levels. Other depth-sorting algorithms must be implemented alongside sorting in scan conversion to make the most of all levels of memory and keep images flowing quickly to the screen.

Here is what Loren Carpenter of Lucasfilm said in a recent SIG-

GRAPH *Computer Graphics* when introducing a new hidden-surface technique called the "A-buffer," for "anti-aliased, area-averaged, accumulation buffer":

> The first scanline algorithms did perspective, clipping, sorting, visibility determination, and "filtering" all at the same time. They resolved visibility at one point per pixel, and aliased terribly, although our standards were different then. In 1974, [Edwin] Catmull [then at the University of Utah, now director of the Computer Graphics Project at Lucasfilm] described the *Z*-buffer method. A *Z*-buffer is a screen-sized array of pixels and *Z*s. Objects, in no particular order, are examined to determine which pixels they cover. At each covered pixel, the perspective *Z* depth of the object is determined and compared with the *Z* in the array. If the new *Z* is closer, then the new *Z*, and the object's shade at this point, replaces the array's *Z* and pixel. This development started the trend toward modularizing the rendering process, as a *Z*-buffer could comprise the visibility section of almost any kind of renderer. Although extremely fast and simple, the *Z*-buffer aliases too much and cannot render transparent objects correctly.

To elaborate, scan-line algorithms, first developed in the late sixties, use the *scan-line coherence* and *edge coherence* characteristics of all the shapes in the frame-buffer image to create a final image in proper depth only on screen (not in the frame buffer), one scan line at a time. Scan-line algorithms only work well with shapes that exist along one plane, though that plane may be skewed in relation to any other planar shapes in the image. They calculate the position of the plane for any z coordinate based on the (x, y, z) positions of the edges of the planar object, so curved surfaces would fool the system.

The first task in any scan-line algorithm is the creation of an *edge table,* to sort the beginning and ending edges that any object shape occupies, for each horizontal line scanned by the refresh buffer. Entries in the edge table would be sorted according to

1. the x coordinate of the edge with the smaller y coordinate;
2. the incremental change in x when stepping from that scanline to the next;
3. the y coordinate of the deepest (highest z coordinate) vertex of a triangle, the two deepest vertices of a rectangle, the three deepest vertices of a five-sided figure, etc.;
4. an identification code number for the shape to which the line belongs.

A *shape table* would then list the following:

1. the coefficients that determine the shape;
2. color, shading, and texture information for the shape;
3. several other possible levels of information, to completely describe the shape.

The contents of both of these tables could be contained within a structure in C; they add up to a definition of an x coordinate edge for each z and y value of each object shape. Structures for each scan-line/shape would be compared to all other structures, to sort all edges (1) into an order of greatest to least y values, and (2) into order of least to greatest x values. The output system would then scan the buffer image in this double order of greatest y while least x.

Speed problems here must be readily apparent. The Z-buffer algorithm works faster, easier, and works with curved surfaces. It involves the use of yet another buffer, besides the frame buffer(s) used to devise the image and the refresh buffer used to scan-convert the image to the screen. This Z-buffer would have all z coordinate values initialized (as a **static** in C) to the largest possible z value. Here's the algorithm in pseudocode:

```
    For (each modeled object entered into the Z-buffer
(during scan-conversion))
    the output system calculates the z value for every
(x,y) coordinate;

    If (the z value of the shape is less than the initialized
 Z-buffer value.)1
    put  (z(x,y) into Z-buffer at (x,y))  and
    put (pixel value of shape at z(x,y) into refresh bufferr
at (x,y) );
```

Because the initialized z values are static, each new z value assigned by the program to any pixel will continually be compared to the next value looked at, and the program will continually sort pixels by the greater z value. The smaller the z value, the later that pixel is put into the refresh buffer. The very smallest go in last, in front of all other z values.

The primary disadvantage of this method is that it uses a full extra buffer to do its job. Secondarily, even in systems with memory to burn, it can't work with transparent objects. Also, since it makes an effective

---

[1]A MAXZ sort of macro would do fine for initializing the static int BUFFER[] [] [z] in the system devised in past chapters.

edge at every depth of a planar object, it will alias a diagonally skewed plane from all angles of view.

To solve problems left unsolved by the *Z*-buffer approach, Carpenter and his associates at Lucasfilm introduced the A-buffer as part of their REYES ("Renders Everything You Ever Saw") imaging system. (The A-buffer's first end-product demonstration to a wide audience was the "Genesis Demo" sequence in *Star Trek II.*) Instead of the frame buffer's pixels, the A-buffer uses fragments of polygons described by **pixel_structs**, each composed of two 32-bit words, one containing a *z* depth and the other either a color or a pointer that contains a list of fragments of shapes by which the fragment at hand is obscured. Carpenter's paper on the subject, thoroughly understandable to anyone with as much C as discussed in this book and just a bit of high school algebra, appeared in SIGGRAPH *Computer Graphics,* Vol. 18, No. 3, July, 1984. Since 32-bit words are probably beyond the reach of micro users, it would be less useful to have the process described second-hand here than to get used to going to the source.

9.7 Shaded, Reflected, and Textured Surfaces; Ray Tracing

After hidden surfaces have been removed, you'll probably want to shade, add reflections to, or texture the surfaces of the objects being depicted. Reflections can be painted on pixel by pixel, but this is a slow way to work. How much simpler and more accurate it would be, in the long run, to derive a formula that realistically describes the reflectance of the particular material your model should resemble, under the particular lighting by which you want it seen.

The first part of the task, in either case, is to get a feel for the way light, reflections, and shadows work. The *American Cinematographer's Manual,* the journal of the ASC, and conversations with cinematographers will be invaluable to any animator who wants to understand lighting enough to be able to simulate it. For that matter, serious study of optics and of Western figurative painting are so much cornerstones for the best work with lighting on film, and for all animation, that the importance of each cannot be overemphasized. (Using knowledge of mathematics, linguistics, and art — and gaining all too much knowledge of the art of war in the commercial marketplace — computer animators, male or female, are the ultimate Renaissance Men!) An understanding of the varied unscientific but psychologically effective ways lighting can be used can then allow best use to be made of mathematical formulas for simulated lighting.

Objects with a perfectly matte surface reflect predictable degrees of light in all directions in a diffuse pattern, to the extent of their "color temperature." (All colors can be rated in terms of the heat they would reflect from a standard lighting source, usually in degrees Kelvin; see the *Cinematographer's Manual* for the formulas and spectrum ratings.) The eighteenth-century Alsatian philosopher J. H. Lambert calculated that the amount of light reflected by a matte surface (I_d) is equal to the cosine of the angle θ between the vector direction (L) to the point source of light of intensity I_p, and a perpendicular, or normal vector from the matte surface (N):

$$I_d = I_p k_d \cos\theta,$$

where k_d is a diffuse reflection coefficient between zero and one, representing the variance of reflectivity of different materials. In other words, the reflectance of a perfectly matte surface is the same from any angle of view.

At the other extreme of reflectivity, a perfectly mirror finish will reflect all of the light from a point source, and thus all of its color (not the reflective surface's own color, which would presumably be nonexistent, independent of what it reflects), to an angle that is the inverse of that between the light source vector L and the perpendicular normal N. The angle of incidence always equals the angle of reflectance, but the visible light reflectance of a mirror is not the same from any viewpoint. If you view from the angle of incidence, you see the light in perfect reflection; as the point of view moves away from the angle of incidence, visible light decreases very rapidly.

Each of these situations results in a formula that is easy to turn into algorithms and incorporate into a modeling program. The point source of light must be specified, and its rays traced (thus "ray tracing") to the object model. For any pixel P, its full ray-traced color would equal its base color P_b times either appropriate formula. This method can reflect P_b-colored light from a mirrored surface and can be adapted for more than one light source, with any relative intensities. (Even with both types of reflectance at once from the same object. Though this would not be possible in the real world, this is not the real world.) No larger number of bits per pixel would be needed to do this; the formulas would be incorporated into a function to be used after modeling is completed, which would assign colors.

So far, these methods will work only for perfectly flat objects that are either perfectly mirrored or perfectly matte, each reflective of light that is perfectly white. What's needed are more complex algorithms to take into account surfaces that are

1. flat but "specular" to equal measure over the surface, that is, part-way between perfectly mirrored and perfectly matte;
2. some shape other than flat, with several more or less reflective surfaces;
3. multiplanar and specular, exhibiting reflectance that is in some places more mirrored and elsewhere more matte, some places lighter, some darker;
4. curved, exhibiting reflectance that is continuously brighter or darker and/or more or less specular;
5. meant to imitate some natural object with its typical reflective pattern, but whose method of modeling would tend to make it exhibit a different reflective pattern (e.g., a curved surface approximated by polygonal modeling).

These five points have been listed in order of the difficulty of reaching a formulaic solution. (Point 5 is, in fact, most often solved by painted touch-up.) Realistic lighting of three-dimensional scenes also must take into account differences in light. Rated in order of the difficulty of solving these problems in computer graphics, these are

1. differences in light intensity based on distance from the light source(s);
2. colored light, as original from the light source(s) or as reflected or transmitted from other objects in the scene;
3. partial shadowing, by either umbra or penumbra (total shadowing is a hidden-surface problem);
4. light that is itself specular, perhaps from a simple refracted source, such as glass, or from a source that is a complex of many different refractions or reflections, like water or bad or dirty glass;
5. diffuse light, perhaps from a source with a textured surface, like frosted glass.

All of the formulas, programs, and computing difficulties necessary to accomplish all of these combined tasks either realistically or somehow impressively are what add up to the business of ray tracing and other shading techniques. There is space available here only to go over the problems briefly, and there are not yet permanent solutions to most of them. New, better solutions keep coming along, and you will probably devise some, too.

Ray tracing has come to mean the tracing of light rays from an end viewpoint, as they bounce off objects in the scene, back to their points of origin. Doing so involves having solved all of the problems listed above, then breaking down the continuum of light viewed into a sufficient sample of individually traceable rays. Optimally, the breadth of one light ray ought to be the size of a pixel, assuming you've got a system with an optimal number of pixels (which would be an infinity of pixels, but we must compromise somewhere just to get started). Tracing rays from their end viewpoint, rather than from their origin(s), is necessary because of the infinity problem again. Light sources give off an infinity of rays in an infinity of directions; working backward limits the job to just what is necessary for a particular view on a particular scene. Tracing one ray at a time (and then each of the many possible simultaneous reflections of that ray one at a time) is a slow process, even on the fastest available computers. Parallel processing speeds things up, since more than one ray can be traced at once.

Reflections also may be mapped to surfaces, and so may textures. Subdividing a surface into fractals is one way to build texture. This, of course, makes tracing rays from each fractal much more complex than from the simpler original surface; if fractals are to be used for texture in noncritical lighting situations, the surface should be divided into fractals *after* the rays from the original whole have been traced. (Cheating is always allowed in this business, as long as it looks all right in the final product.) Mapping a premade, 2D tiling pattern, 2D painted image, or digitized photograph onto a 3D surface is another way to build texture. Mapping 2D images or patterns onto a 3D surface can be a much cheaper way of achieving a realistic lighting or texture effect than going to all the fine detail of modeling a perfect imitation of a natural surface or tracing all the light reflections that would bounce off a complex surface. It can also be a cheap way to get an unrealistic effect; stretched images made by turnkey video graphics systems have been overused in many a music video.

Mapping images or textures onto a 3D surface is a matrix multiplication operation analogous to enlarging or shrinking an image or mapping an image to a larger or smaller 2D surface, as described in past chapters. Mapping a 2D image to one flat surface of a polyhedron is precisely the same thing as fully 2D matrix multiplication (and this is the most common usage of the technique in 3D). Mapping the 2D image to a curved surface involves a matrix multiplier weighted to the defining formula of the curved surface. Mapping a single 2D image to a surface made of many fractals would involve mapping an equivalently sized, different piece of the picture to each fractal and is probably more trouble than it would be worth in terms of comparison to some other method of producing a somewhat similar textured image. On the other hand, mapping the image to the surface first, then dividing it into fractals, is an easy two-step for producing a very complex-looking, possibly dazzling surface.

Finally, it should be apparent from the discussions of both hidden surfaces and lighting that many different sets of problems combine to form *the* hidden-surface problem, and different solutions to many individual lighting problems must be combined into efficient and realistic-seeming lighting solutions. Efficient sorting of the multiple problem at hand into its components, in the proper order to reach the simplest possible solution, is an ever-important front in the state of the computer imaging art. Sorting information batches has been a traditional concern of computer science applied to all types of problems, certainly not limited to graphics applications. People coming into image processing from a background in solving information-sorting problems will find ample opportunity to make their own contributions to the state of the art here. Is knowledge of batch sorting as important to realizing good computer pictures as knowing the Old Masters of painting? Perhaps. Anyway, probably probability theory, surely artificial intelligence, and certainly many varieties of theoretical mathematics will continue to influence computer graphics and animation ever more strongly.

CHAPTER TEN

Interactivity

10.1 Where Is Real Time Now?

Somehow, a chapter called "Topics in the State of the Art" managed to avoid discussion of the s-o-t-a for animation, as opposed to that for nonmoving images to be animated later. Absolutely real-time movement in extremely high-resolution, 3D, nonaliased images may never be the s-o-t-a in computer animation, but we move closer to it all the time. Even now, real-time 2D animation in many-colored (if not full-color) medium resolution (that is, not quite TV) is being commonly achieved under limited circumstances.

"State-of-the-art" in animation implies all the goals and processes discussed in the last chapter, and it also implies constantly coming closer to real-time production. This last implication does tend to involve a divergent development. Real-time production implies interactivity. Many other s-o-t-a developments preclude either real-time production or interactiveness or both. Interactive systems that have sacrificed some real-time interaction for better resolution have been unsuccessful (think of the videodisk-based arcade games that briefly boomed and busted; more on this later), which leads one to conclude that interactive systems comprise a subclass of animation that involves goals, such as operating procedure and presentation, that are very different from the goals of other animation. Coming to understand the s-o-t-a in animation, however, implies an understanding of interactive systems, too.

There are three broad categories of interactive graphics animation applications:

1. graphics-making systems for nonprogrammers;
2. all sorts of general applications programs made more attractive to users through graphics and animation techniques, including

two subcategories: (a) programs meant for sophisticated users who take a good deal of effort to learn to interact with the program (such as spreadsheet and word-processing programs that incorporate graphics); (b) information systems requiring little or no training to use;

3. video games, which would tend to fit under (2b) if they didn't exist in different hardware and cultural environments.

10.2 Graphics-Making for Nonprogrammers

Let no vendor of turnkey graphics systems convince you that the first of these categories is not the easiest to program for. Indeed, with some solid top-down algorithmic thinking and a mastery of any given hardware and C system's I/O interfacing, readers who have made their way through each chapter to this point will be ready to build their own interactive graphics-creation systems. (There is space here only to outline the basics of planning interactive systems; interested readers would be advised to look into Foley and Van Dam's *Fundamentals of Interactive Computer Graphics,* listed in the Bibliography, for a deeper discussion of systems design.) To construct such a system:

1. Decide on all the capabilities you want it to have. Make a list of all the major programs needed, such as paint, palette, number of frame buffers, 3D modeling, etc., then of the smaller programs that fit within these, such as brushes, tiling, area fill, line styles, fonts (all of which would be programs callable from a paint program), etc. Decide on the resolution you will want each frame buffer to have, the bits per pixel and number of colors, the resolution of the display monitor, how many and which input devices, and the necessary I/O system to support all of this.

2. Settle on the appropriate hardware for the interactive system itself, and for designing software.

3. Draw up a top-down flow chart for the full program, as in Figure 10.1, then draw up flow charts for each subprogram, in data-tree form. Plan out interaction sequences carefully, so that they are as simple for users as possible. Certainly there is a trade-off here between ease of use and the memory available for more complex images and/or animation. It is a trade-off most efficiently resolved in this planning stage, before investing effort in program development. Pare down program options to the minimum necessary to fulfill the goals in Item 1; which also will result in greater ease of use. Here's a chance to review and reduce the list of goals in Item 1 and to think about how much you really want each option.

Figure 10.1 An interactive paint program

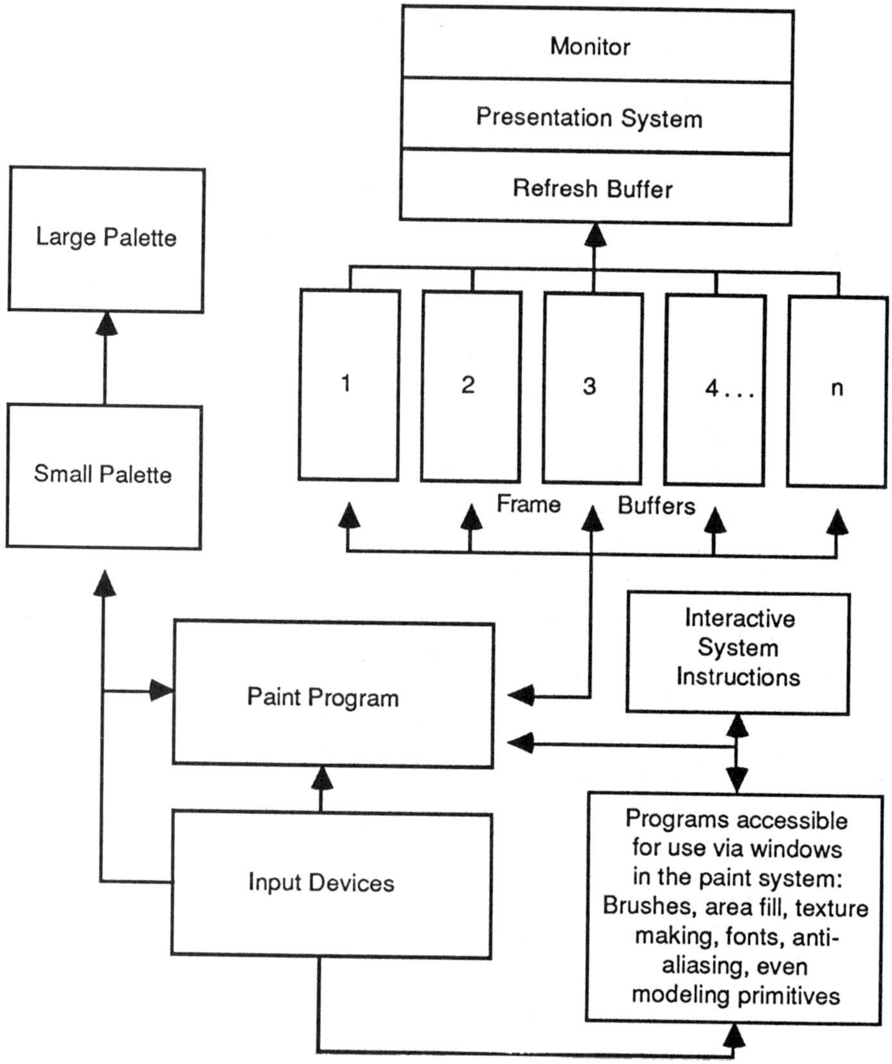

4. Build in a comprehensive system of prompts and help messages for the novice, but make it possible for experienced users to bypass them.

5. Foresee all possible user mistakes, even mistakes so completely wrong you'd think no one could ever make them. Build in error messages that tell the user what has been done wrong and error defaults that automatically move the user to the proper point to continue in the data structure. No mistake should necessitate restarting the program or backing up through a long series of menus.

6. Make it easy to learn. If there's no particular reason to do something differently from many other commercially available programs of all sorts, don't do it differently. For example, many programs for PCs use Function Key 1 for Help; it is reasonable to do the same, so the program will be that much easier.

In Chapter 8 two possible programming attitudes were alluded to: programmer's solutions to graphics creation or solutions for interactive applications. Only the programmer's solutions for a noninteractive system were presented then. Now it is time to look into doing things the interactive way. For example, just on the subject of input devices, you can't expect the average graphics designer to want to make pictures with a keyboard — not with the designer's livelihood or aesthetic principles at stake. Figure 10.1 shows how to modify the paint program presented in Chapter 8, and turn it into an interactive user's system. Input devices here should include a digitizing tablet with magnetic stylus, and digitized video input, alongside the keyboard. A joy stick or analog-style dial can be handy for such tasks as color cycling or cursor control; I have never had much use for mice or other such input devices, but this is highly subjective stuff.

Each of the modules of the paint and palette programs must be set up for simple input. Menus ought to present clear program choices, then scan for appropriate input. The programmer–user knows a brush program is **#include**d, for example, because the programmer put it there. Other users need to be told, and to be told in a simple way, to access the brush program, then how to access the right brush, then how to use it, how to stop using it, and how to move on to the next program choice. If the program as a whole is to run on one color monitor, the handiest way to present menus is within windows that can be looked into or closed at will. This is hardly a novel idea to anybody who's been observing the software scene lately — windows are everywhere since Xerox's Star and Apple's Lisa pulled down the first menus of icons a few years ago.

Now that you've come this far, you may want to begin putting together your own interactive paint program by writing out a comprehensive outline for its user interaction flow. For example:

1. Present a log-in screen with statement of copyright. Scan for appropriate log-in. Upon appropriate log-in, clear screen.
2. Present main help menu. It should state, " . . . "

and so forth. Build a plan for the program's flow the way you as a user would like to see it run, then build a program in pseudocode that provides this structure. Finally, convert the pseudocode to the real thing. Along each stage of the development process, even (perhaps especially) if you are not developing the program as part of a team, it makes sense to bring other people's advice into the project. They needn't be experts (though these are nice to have around); just plain sample users can help you find better ways of doing things, and also find those simple errors that creep into late nights at the terminal and can otherwise lead to eons of debugging.

Much of this advice goes for developing graphics for other applications programs, too. Graphics usually seem to be the sugar coating for general business applications; the task of making images integral to more efficient use of such programs can be a tremendous challenge, not least because it takes a lot of imagination to figure out how to do anything at all that's really useful. Bringing in insights learned in unlikely places — from video arcades, game theory, or favorite animated films — can be of help. More natural candidates for graphics use, such as CAD systems, are also more up-front in their challenges to efficient interactive design. Chapter 13 provides more information about possibilities here.

10.3 ROM, More ROM, and Real Time

Memory gets cheaper all the time. If you visit video arcades infrequently, each new visit is a futuristic shock of amazingly more-lifelike animations, all made possible by expanding ROM. Not every sort of ROM is relevant, though: games stored on videodisk had a brief flurry of experimental use and quickly sank to wherever unsuccessful products go. The videodisk allowed fully animated characters with better than TV resolution — far better than images stored on VLSICs — but did not allow nearly as quick interaction. In the split-second-reflex culture of the arcades, they were too slow. Only a year or so after the videodisk-based games disappeared, IC-ROM-based games were showing resolution that may have been clearly lower than TV or videodisk, but far more lifelike than ever. The state of the art for on-screen resolution in arcade graphics, as this is written, is about 256 by 256, highly aliased. This will surely continue to improve quickly, but even more of the continually-more-available-ROM will be designed into other sorts of resolution than nominal on-screen pixel count, and into higher levels of interactiveness.

To explain: The most common basic architecture for arcade video games involves

1. a much larger frame buffer in ROM (probably EPROMs, one-time programmable ROM chips) than the on-screen image. This frame buffer is completely filled with a background image and

predetermined but movable (within limits) window(s) for

2. one or a few smaller buffers stored in EPROMs and filled with already programmed images of characters. This window to a small frame buffer that contains a painted character is also known as a sprite.

The user's input devices control, within limits,

3. the screen as a viewport on the larger buffer and
4. again within limits, where the window(s) for the sprites will be located.

When sprites and/or the viewport are moved so as to come into contact with chosen positions in the large buffer array, predetermined pixel color changes may be activated, as well as extragraphical data changes, such as stored sound effects and point-scoring incrementation.

The organization of the larger buffer, of the windows and their contents as smaller buffers, and of the viewport will be mostly old hat to veterans of the last several chapters. For real-time image changes, input interfacing is really quite similar to what is necessary for an interactive graphics design system. The system must be programmed to scan for the coded input of a joy stick pushed in one direction or another. If the joy stick moves to the right, for example, the viewport moves a certain number of pixels to the right in relation to the larger buffer; holding the joy stick to the right would continue the viewport's movement at some easily determined rate, either constant or accelerating. Another type of input, be it a firing button on the joy stick or a foot pedal or something else, could be used to move the sprite(s), just as any window is moved within a scene. As the sprite's window comes into contact with a predetermined position in the large buffer, it can be made to change shape at the same time that the image in the smaller buffer occupying the window changes; thus the sprite seems to move.

None of this is difficult to accomplish, though all these sorted if/thens and loops add up to a complex, memory-intensive program. Planning each step in a pseudocode algorithm doesn't use any memory and may help you visualize the production process.

10.4 Pseudocode for a Video Game

#include <large_bufferful: a program for a 4000-by-4000 buffer that pictures a raceway>

#include <sprite_buf_1: a program for a small buffer picturing a race car>

#include <**sprite_buf_2:** same as **sprite_buf_1**>
#include <**sprite_window_1:** a program that inserts a window in **large_bufferful** that is tapered to the precise shape of **sprite_buf_1** and fills the window with **sprite_buf_1**>
#include <**sprite_window_2:** as above, for **sprite_buf_2**>
#include <**sprite_change_1:** a program that changes the shape of **sprite_window_1** and **sprite_buf_1** from full front to 3/4 face, upon reaching a certain coordinate point in **large_bufferful**>
#include <**sprite_change_2**>
#include <**second_sprite_change_1:** a program that changes the two programs for Sprite 1 at another point to be reached in **large_bufferful**>
#include <etc.>
define a **static int buffer [256][256]** as a viewport on **large_bufferful,** beginning at these coordinates: _____;
scanned input (joystick_move) = viewport move by ____ coordinates;
scanned input (button_press) = . . .

You get the idea. The question most often asked of me, and probably of anybody at all involved in computer graphics is, "When (or how) will video games advance enough that they get sophisticated, intelligent, movie-like action?" Let's face it, arcade games may never offer sophisticated characters to identify with and intellectually challenge, because that's not what the users of these games seem to want. If I were asked, though, when advances in memory and resolution will allow some of the same interactive techniques to be used for serious new stories and characters by serious new artists, I'd say it's probably already happening — it's too popular a dream not to be in the process of realization somewhere — but whoever's making the dream reality isn't telling the world yet. Maybe some readers of this book are making it happen.

10.5 Videodisk

Videodisk systems also are making possible wonderful interactive programs, without quite the hair-trigger level of interactivity of arcade games chock-full of EPROMs. It may take a second or two for an optical disk to access desired information, but this is fast enough for most nongame uses, and even for many sorts of games. Videodisks may contain animated subject matter as easily as live action, so in one sense they are not any more germain to this book than videotape. They make a good storage medium, and some can be set up to record single frames with ease, so they should see a great deal of use as recording devices for individual graphic frames, as detailed in other chapters. More and more videodisk players are able to randomly access individual frames within a close area of the disk, to assemble an animated sequence from separate still frames. There is real promise in programming players to do this (Sony's SM-70-series computer is configured to control Sony's videodisk players for just such use). While I have seen a great deal of corporate and educational interactive videodisk programming, nothing yet seems to have made good use of this wondrous capability for ad hoc animation of separate frames. It may still be too new and dazzling for anybody to have figured out a realistic use; surely it will be put to very good use in the near future.

CHAPTER ELEVEN

Home-Made Motion Control

11.1 Why Motion Control, Not CGI?

Perhaps most animators who work with motion control get involved as traditional animators looking for greater control over their medium. As such they tend to need computer and robot equipment that is compatible with their animation systems, and not the other way around. If you are just starting out, with no particular experience in motion control or CGI, why use motion control?

If your available CGI system is micro-based, it probably has very limited resolution. Maybe its resolution is adequate for TV, but what if you get a theatrical film job? Or what if perfect object models for stop-motion animation (that is, model photography with or without computer control) already exist? You might spend days creating pictures in a computer instead of shooting the models you have.

Even where models must be created, and even where a given production company has experience with both model photography and CGI, stop-motion is quite often used instead of CGI. Lucasfilm, for example, is an undisputed groundbreaker in both motion-control model photography and CGI. To this writing, most of the effects produced by Lucasfilm have been made with computer updates of traditional techniques: that is, motion-control model photography, computer-controlled traditional animation, and computer-controlled optical printing. The company's pioneering CGI work has been labor and time-intensive and has never accounted for a large portion of the firm's output. With hundreds of special-effects scenes to produce for a full-length feature, only traditional animation techniques provide sufficient resolution and are proven enough; only with computer control can the job be done quickly enough.

CGI promises to produce wholly animated feature films, but in the mid-eighties, motion control gets them done. In 1985, a silent 35 mm camera (such as the Mitchell or Arriflex mentioned below) hooked up to an animation stand and a $5,000 to $10,000 computer control system can produce feature-quality work. Doing the same with CGI necessitates a $100,000 investment or an acceptance of lower resolution than 35 mm film is capable of. That CGI price is shrinking drastically, while motion control costs will shrink only slightly at best, due to all the complex mechanical equipment involved. The fact remains that to make animation with very high resolution now, you need traditional equipment. To speed up production — which is to make some effects possible at all within budgetary constraints — a computer controls traditional motion.

11.2 Getting Started

Whether you call it motion control, computer control, robot control, or numerical control, it's the same thing: a computer used to precisely control mechanical instruments used in film or video production.

Some of the fanciest optical printers in the world are controlled by microcomputers running BASIC. Other languages, including C, will do the job too, but BASIC will work just fine. Have a look at Appendix A, "Looking Backward," for an understanding of optical printing, and you'll see how the programming task involved is simply a set of incremental moves of various camera controls. Other motion control applications in animation are horizontal and vertical animation camera systems. The vertical systems, as explained in "Looking Backward," are thought of as computerized animation tables; the horizontal as motion control tracks. For animation tables, motion control tracks, or optical printers, the need for computer control is basically the same: to allow for infinitely repeatable incremental movements.

Robot arms that will plug into a personal computer's parallel interface are available from a few vendors. Typically, these have from one to several gripping or prong-like moveable projections at the "hand" end. Making your own motion control system involves plugging these controllable moving parts of the robot arm into the manual camera or camera-mount controls of a film or still-frame video camera, and also using another robot arm, if necessary, to control the object being filmed.

The fanciest available motion control systems allow users to program moves by manually moving the camera or object — in other words, by using the robot arm(s) as input device(s). Programming for this sort of input is not at all difficult, but you will probably not be able to afford such luxury. Robotic input, however, is more a convenience than an additional creative tool for anybody who really understands what to animate before beginning work on a shot.

Now, there is little that motion control makes possible that is not theoretically possible with a well-planned and executed, manually controlled, traditional animation system. That's theory. In fact, being able to control animation by computer allows far more complex scenes to be built. Some stylistic innovations of the late seventies to mid-eighties are entirely due to the availability of motion control; "slit scan" is a case in point. The term refers to photographing light glowing through a slit in a matte. Slightly overexposing the shot (which often cannot even be helped, given bright lighting and film's tendency to fuzz a little in capturing bright lights) lets a halo form around the edges of the slit. This shot could be put to several uses. A scene might then be photographed through a reverse matte, covering only the area of the slit; these two shots would be superimposed in an optical printer, and the final image would show a glowing, haloed line at an appropriate place in the frame. Complex slit-scanned images can be made too; instead of a simple line, a several-line cutout may be used; or simpler slit scans could be superimposed over only each other, to make for a complex slit-scan pattern. In either case, the result is glowing lines or other shapes against a black background. Surely you've seen this sort of stuff in network and other corporate logos, in feature-film credits, and in spacey sequences. (Most are relatively simple sorts of slit scan; there are many more complex, and less visually hackneyed uses, limited only by the imagination of the animator.) Though the entire process is certainly possible without a computer-controlled camera, it's a lot easier with one, and wasn't thought of until the computer became available to help and to suggest the look as an "improved" sort of vector graphic.

Much of the best animation with models would be far too difficult without motion control. Think of a complex shot with several miniature models of giant things like airplanes, tanks, otherworldly creatures, etc., all colliding, blowing each other up, and so forth. To make the shot (assuming for some reason you can't use CGI to build it), you'd have to carefully map out the movements of each object in the choreographed whole. After tiny incremental moves, a frame of film is snapped, more incremental moves, another frame. All of the really creative work is in planning the shot, but without motion control, you could easily forget to move one of the many models just once or twice, in one or two of the thousands of tiny incremental changes needed. Just those tiny errors would mean months of work redone, whereas *with* motion control you'd program the whole shot, set the machine running, go to sleep, and wake up in a few hours with a complete shot! If there's a bug in your program, you may need another day to finish, but it's no great loss.

Obviously, this stuff doesn't come cheaply. At this writing, a robot arm with a joint and two controllable "fingers" that will plug into a parallel port and listen to BASIC costs $2,000. A complex shot like that described above may use several such arms, necessitating more than one PC for control, but on the bright side, industrial motion control systems sell for $100,000 and up. Cutting that price to a tenth just by doing your own BASIC programming is no mean matter.

The programming is the easiest part, though, and robots and computers may even be the cheapest part. Connecting robot devices to the camera and photography stand can be more difficult operations, and you may find yourself rummaging through every hardware store and junk shop in town to find idiosyncratically perfect fittings, or cultivating friends with machine shops that do precision metal lathing. The right camera for the job will be one that best fits the robot arm you use to hold it; many makers of customized computer-controlled animation cameras prefer using ancient, silent Mitchell cameras from the twenties (!). Not only are their controls fairly simple and easily reached, no camera ever made has had better registration. (That is, the system for holding each frame of film in the same steady position behind the shutter.) Old silent Arriflexes are also commonly used for like reasons. Though somewhat less adaptable, they are cheaper and easier to find than the old Mitchells.

CHAPTER TWELVE

Interviews with Leading Animation and Effects Designers

12.1 Clear Vision

A few interviews have been selected here for the light they might collectively cast on several areas of the computer animation and effects industry. Also, probably more significantly, those profiled here all have distinct, strong, and personal views on design for graphics and animation.

A clear vision of what graphics ought to look like is a prerequisite for making graphics that communicate clearly. This seems self-evident when put into a simple declarative statement, and of the very many designers in this field whom the author has interviewed, there is a direct correlation between the few with the sharpest design sense and their successful images. This correlation might seem most common-sense to traditional, noncomputerized animators and graphic designers; somehow, in a high-tech medium, people get to start believing it's the machines that are responsible for quality work.

It's reasonable for an artist of any sort to be scared by that constant confrontation with blank paper. When it's only you, a pencil, and the paper, there's no place to look for comfort. Many investments in computers have been propelled by a need for a bigger crutch than a pencil — something to help design the work. Turnkey systems seem to promise this — to work magic and to design creative work. Instead they most often are the crutches that make one designer's work look just like that of every other purchaser of that turnkey system. People who work on those machines are now more often referred to as "operators," rather than designers, and for many of them, rightly so.

It doesn't have to be that way; even animating exclusively with turnkey systems in a hackneyed medium, Charles Levi and Alex Weil manage to turn out original, lively, beautiful work.

What computer you work with is the least of it: Richard Greenberg has taken this to the extreme of preferring to make images so subtle that no one would know they were computer animated, except those who realize they'd be impossible any other way.

Robert Abel is a self-made pillar of the computer graphics world, yet says he's never liked space movies very much. He prefers using computers to make current the fantasies, like *The Wizard of Oz,* that inspired him as a child.

On the other hand, you don't have to spurn the high-tech look to produce good high-tech imagery: Bo Gehring originated much of the sort of imagery that soon became hackneyed in the hands of hordes of imitators, but somehow his work still looks fresh, so that anyone who has seen it can spot a new commercial on TV and say with certainty, "That must be a Gehring job."

Finally, computer imagery is as much part of computer graphics as it is part of the animation business; budding animators would be wise to take Jim Lindner's advice on hedging bets, because animation has historically been a hard way to earn a living, and there's no reason to believe modernized tools will change that.

12.2 Alex Weil's and Charles Levi's Charlex

"We went into doing video because there are 500 people doing good film effects," says Charlex's Charles Levi, "We can't do it better than all of them. Anyway, all I know is video. That's what I do." Charlex may be doing more than most to change the world's view of video animation. After their award-winning music video for The Cars ("You Might Say") the firm was deluged with work. "We're hot," admits Levi. "That sometimes means getting storyboards that parody The Cars video without an original idea, but on the other hand it lets us work with people who are really wonderful to work with. And we may be in this business quite successfully for 20 years, but I guess you're only hot once. . . . It's kind of fun."

Levi says he and partner Alex Weil first got into video by making animatics to support their rock and roll ambitions. Animatics is the largely unrecognized business of making pseudoanimation or very roughly animated drawings to bring storyboards to a state of life halfway between their paper form and full realization. Animatics are used extensively by advertising agencies, often for the additional measure of control they allow the agencies over the independent producers hired to transfer their storyboards to film, and sometimes to test audience reactions to commercial and product concepts. They are also sometimes used by animators or effects makers to more perfectly plan an intricate sequence. Animatics were a rarity before inexpensive (relative to film) three-quarter-inch, then half-inch video postproduction came along; with the coming of the first video effects devices, a sometime practice became standard business. Animatics are now commonly made of most storyboards for live-action or animated TV commercials. Levi and Weil were in the right place at the right time to get their share of this steady, profitable, but also usually unimaginative business, and to eventually use it as a springboard to animating finished commercials.

"There were two big stepping stones for us," says Levi. "We did the National Enquirer ads every week for two years — sometimes two spots a week. It was an ongoing way to express ourselves visually. It was an outgrowth of the animatics work — very inexpensive, very fast, we were able to churn it out using the same video equipment that we'd become familiar with. But it wasn't tightly scripted, and we were able to express ourselves. After a while, people got the point; they worked very well for the National Enquirer and that led to millions of things for us.

"The next big thing that happened was very much an offshoot of the National Enquirer: the Cars video. It's the only video we've ever done [at the time of this interview], and we lucked out. We had a good song . . . ."

The "You Might Say" video used 2D turnkey video effects to attach Cars star Ric Ocasek's face to the animated body of a fly, to stretch the face or the entire fly for appearances in mirrors, medicine cabinets, etc. from different perspectives, constantly pursuing a live-action image of the woman being sung about on the sound track. The animation and effects look as trashy as turnkey video effects can look, yet use their garish coloring and low resolution integrally: lyrics and music, visual action, and graphic look all have the same mood. The video was tremendously popular.

"We got boards from everybody based on the Cars video," says Levi, meaning that many an ad agency wanted to use the look Charlex had created to sell their products. "Well, let's just say that not everybody's was an aesthetic breakthrough. . . .

"You know, in a nonspecific way, one of the things that video represents to many people is a cheaper way of doing things. But with intelligent use of video — video as what it is, not a cheap brother to film — you can make some fresh images. . . . I'm not after trying to pretend that my tools are different from what they are. All I know is video; that's what I do. In many ways video is inferior to film, and in many ways the effects machines we have here — Quantel and so forth — are inferior to the machines other people have. On the other hand, many things are superior about video and video effects. For example, the effects come in much closer to 'real time' than with those ultimate-ultimate machines people are outputting to film for the higher resolution, so maybe you can capture a momentary inspiration with these machines that you can't with the others. If you explore these things, not only will you have something different, you may realize something new, something never done before."

Fresh inspiration and humorously tacky — but very highly designed — graphics were the combination that worked so well for Charlex's Cars and National Enquirer spots. Can this combination work for every situation? Of course not, but then, since their first booming success, Charlex has been muscling up in terms of staff and equipment to match their inspiration to the possibilities that come with higher resolution.

A different sort of possibility that arises with success is the opportunity to work with top people, perhaps even people whose work you've long looked up to and learned from. As a reporter waited to talk with Levi and Weil, other waiters decorated nearby sofas, all squeezed near two elevators at the gates of Charlex's overcrowded office. One was a distinguished-looking gentleman wearing shoulder-length white hair, sweatshirt, and sneakers. With constant nervous energy, he led his younger grey-suited companions in a waste-paper basketball tournament, as we all waited an hour and a half for Levi and Weil. They came in periodically to apologize for the delay — suddenly having more work than they'd ever dreamed of made scheduling appointments difficult. In fact, they'd inadvertently scheduled this interview for the same time as a conference on a logo for the soon-to-start music video channel, VH1.

"We're meeting with George Lois," said Weil. "He's been in the waiting room with you. One of the pillars. . . . Would you mind sitting in on our meeting and then doing your interview later?"

George Lois has devised much of the most entertaining advertising ever done, from the still-memorable Alka-Seltzer spots of the sixties on through this spot-to-be for VH1. Sitting around a conference table, Lois and crew brought out storyboards for the spot and traded ideas about it with Weil and Levi. A lot of hand gesturing and necessarily imprecise words went into trying to describe the feelings the animation should carry, the energy of the movement it ought to show. In an hour of discussing the ten-second logo, never was any particular technology for carrying out the project mentioned. "The tools are not what's important; it's the feeling," says Weil.

When a client comes in with a fully developed storyboard (most often the case in commercial making), what part of the end product is agency (Lois, Pitts, Gershon in this case) and what part is Charlex? The production company's share of the creativity may generally vary from near zero to more than half. In this case, it may well have been about half; in conference, Levi and Weil suggested some timing changes and a somewhat different explosion than shown in the storyboard. In a music video, "You Might Say," for instance, the production company can (and did, in this case) bear total responsibility for the visuals. "But, in a way, it doesn't really matter who thinks of what in a good collaboration," says Weil. "Lois's ideas here really fit what we might have liked to do anyway. Hey, it's always a cooperative medium."

"We didn't come into this from a technical background," says Levi. "When Alex and I were doing animatics, we were ignorant and abusive of all kinds of things; we just did what we wanted to do. If someone said, 'But that's off the 'scope [a video signal too high to be read on the oscilloscope, indicating overexposure that can quickly grow so great as to be unbroadcastable], but it looked good, we did it. I'm not really interested in equipment except for what to do with it. Most of what we do is special effects, video oriented. We hope we're helping to create a new form. It's actually some sort of sandbox here. Our stuff is more childish — human, really — than something 'high technology.' This is really a fussy place infested with a lot of creative people who are easily disgusted and bored, so you can't kid yourself about what's good."

12.3 The Brothers Greenberg

"R/Greenberg stands for Richard Greenberg," announced trade magazine ads taken out by R/Greenberg Associates. The new design firm had done so many amazingly different, technically difficult, and subtly designed projects in such a brief period in the early eighties that it may have seemed to many in the film and video industries like something controlled by a computer. Was their design approach the essence of subtlety, or was it personality-less? In fact, there are two R. Greenbergs at R/Greenberg Associates: brothers Richard and Robert. Robert has masterminded the company's quick growth as a financial and corporate manager; Richard is the chief designer and creative guts of the firm. Robert's abilities are such that the company recently moved into a 50,000-square-foot facility and grossed eight million dollars in 1984, only its seventh year in existence. Richard's abilities are such that the typical R/Greenberg graphic is so unnoticeably powerful that it hardly seems like a special effect, yet burns its way into viewers' brains almost subliminally.

"Nobody should know the work that goes into it," says Richard G.

Examples: the credits for the feature *Alien,* the bouncing, flying baby at the beginning of *The World According to Garp,* the fitting of the title character in *Zelig* into historical footage from other films, commercials with 747s cruising down Wall Street, or a Park Avenue populated only by thousands of Renaults, *Ghostbusters, Body Double, Purple Rose of Cairo.* With effects work for so many major features, often enough Richard Greenberg's sense of design seems quite like Leonard Zelig's personality: his goal is usually to blend perfectly, and as subtly as possible, into the necessities of the subject at hand.

After college, Robert Greenberg got a job with Royal Crown Cola. Seven years later, he was general manager of Royal Crown Cola of Canada and quickly getting less and less satisfaction on the job. He'd built the Canadian operation up from nothing, enjoying huge autonomy from the American bottle tops. "I wasn't as interested in the salary as the educational aspect, particularly in manufacturing," says Robert, who began to dream the entrepreneurial dream. His brother Richard was freelancing and teaching design at the Illinois Institute of Technology, but "the glory days of Mies van der Rohe and Moholy-Nagy were long gone at IIT," says Richard. "Even the echo was gone." He decided to open his own design studio in New York. It wasn't all that hard for him to persuade Bob to be his business manager.

Joining forces in 1978 was an ideal combination of financial and managerial acumen with design talent. "The same person can never do both," says Richard. "We were real lucky." They began with very little capital, struggled through a few early jobs, then landed the titles for *Superman.* "It was a real rush job, yet things took a lot longer than they should have because I couldn't afford experimentation," says Richard. "The premiere was a charity event at the Ziegfeld, with every luminary in New York there." Greenberg watched it with the audience and saw every imperfection, but no one else did. "Those technical things didn't matter at all, ultimately. By the end of the sequence they were ready to go with the film."

R/Greenberg Associates went with the film, too, and then flew on past it. Bob now finds himself running a sizeable company again and has just moved into New York's largest single-company production facility, a sleek, Bauhaus-style thing near Times Square. The growth has been a progression from design boutique with no in-house production capacity to design shop with its own optical capability, to a complete effects-design and "manufacturing" (as Bob often thinks of it) operation, and now to an emphasis on the combination of live action and all sorts of effects to meet the design idea.

The growth has involved an uncommon amount of career planning, for the film business. R/Greenberg wanted to make its own opticals, so as not to be at the mercy of others carrying out Richard's designs, but before doing so managed to negotiate a union contract (all major optical houses are unionized) that allows job flexibility, which the Greenbergs expected would come in handy as the firm expanded into all the new areas of special effects made possible by computers. The contract gave them the jump on competitors, and Greenberg would be, for a few crucial years, the most efficient design house for combined optical and other effects. The choice of New York as a place to start was a conscious and judicious decision by these two Chicagoans; R/Greenberg began just at the beginning of a boom in production there. The planning continues through integration of all types of filmmaking (live action, motion control, CGI) to what the Greenbergs see as their next move: the studio has gone online with a Cray-2 and is in the process of integrating all its equipment with the supercomputer. "We're at a kind of pre-Bach stage now in the movies," says Richard, "just approaching the point where images can be created synthetically and played the way we play music. It's happening faster than anybody anticipated, so fast that some of the vocabulary we've generated is beginning to wear itself out. I think Lucas has recognized that in the Star Wars trilogy — certainly he's gotten tired of spaceships zooming around. I think it's time for somebody to create a new vocabulary."

R/Greenberg's big break may have been *Superman,* but those titles are the least typical of Greenberg images. "If I have to see another thing pop and sizzle I'll throw up," says Richard. "In this symbol menagery, simple things stand out. Everything we do I don't love, but you can't hope to educate some 40-year-old art director. We hope to choose our projects where we can work well. . . . If our work is going to be criticized, I'd rather it were for being too simple, rather than overembellished. The work where we haven't made concessions holds up pretty well. It doesn't date."

That work now aims for a seamless congruity of living reality with special effects, but it's not just a matter of perfect matte lines. The combination has to say something in design terms, and say it quietly.

"We're seeing a basic change in the way people view narrative film. How much actual story does something have; how much is motivated by feeling?" Richard asks.

Yes, the brothers Greenberg are contemplating a feature, "but it's got to be the right one for our first," says Robert. "We've gotten several offers, but if we don't get one that takes advantage of what we do best, we won't do a feature."

What kind of feature would it be? The Greenbergs both choose their words slowly, carefully as projects, and never seem satisfied they've hit the right ones. To listen is to hear a self-torture for elusive truth. Robert, the business wizard, knows they can make a 10-million-dollar feature that looks like it cost many times more, seamlessly combining reality and fantasy. Richard wants to design a higher reality — to create a fantasy that is not just another pop "movie fairy tale." Yet that, as always, works simply and precisely.

12.4 Robert Abel & Associates

The new R/Greenberg studio is certainly an amazing technological toyland, but its stock of technological wonders pales beside the headquarters of Robert Abel & Associates. Not one motion-control track, but *nine* horizontal tracks, several computer-controlled animation stands, 360-degree motion-controlled boom arms, optical printers, front and rear projection systems, vector and raster graphics systems, all come in multiples at this hotbed of advanced imaging. All this and traditional cel animation, too.

The Abel business is a gun for hire that works on features, commercials, anything that comes along and a great deal at the same time. Thus it may be very hard to establish common threads running through all projects coming out of the firm: many bear much more resemblance to other work from the agencies and producers that commission them. But Abel's personal work, and his firm's major projects, almost always eschew the high-tech cliches of computer graphics. Not to say it isn't flashy, but Abel's is a whimsical flash.

"I was never interested in space," he says. "I was into *The Wizard of Oz, Gone With The Wind,* and the great fantasy movies of the thirties and forties. Man needs fantasy, from the cave paintings to space movies, but there must have been cave paintings that didn't strike people then as having much fantasy, just as there are space movies that don't have much fantasy. By nature, these genres, or any idea you want to communicate — they could be television commercials, which are no less valid than features or cave paintings — are abstract. How to describe and illustrate these ideas in a way that lets audiences get involved in the fantasy, that's always going to be the challenge.''

Abel is more bullish than even most animators in believing that the animation business will continue to grow strongly in the foreseeable future, and his is also a point of view that's probably more informed than most observers in and out of the industry. ''For one thing,'' he says, ''advertising is changing in ways that will help us tremendously. The change to shorter spots is beneficial because you need a more impressive image in only ten or fifteen seconds of air time. Also, people are going to want their product uniquely displayed; that's a constant concern of advertisers, but the trend is for products to grow less differentiated by anything other than image. I worried in the mid-seventies that our [animators'] share of the advertising dollar would decrease; instead it rose by eighty percent, to some twenty-five percent of the medium. [The rest being live-action commercials.] Our own business has grown by forty or fifty times. An example is that we had forty percent of the AT&T divestiture business. They need to constantly communicate to people, and to themselves, what is the nature of AT&T. The image of a company that does what they do *must* involve highly technological images, and this is also the way of so many other products and services.''

Some of Abel's most memorable images, however, have been very whimsical concepts for, in particular, Levi-Strauss and Seven-Up — seemingly low-tech products. The Levi spots were perhaps the height of psychedelia — a height only reachable with a few years of distance. This first Able image that the world at large sat up and noticed set the pattern for many of his impressive designs to come. It was a retrospective on a past style, using the latest in technology to accomplish what people working in the style years before may have only wished to be able to do. In the process, with rainbow-hued jeans floating like butterflies in extremely smooth animation, Robert Abel almost single-handedly showed the world that beautiful animation was still possible. In the seventies audiences, and animators too, had got used to ever-cheaper animation; it seemed no one would pay the price of quality work anymore (see Appendix A).

Even if Levi was a rare, deep-pocketed patron, Able managed to pull off Seven-Up spots that were if anything even more attention getting. Bicyclists rode through a stagey setting of bright, flourescent pastels, designed with a sense that would define a new California ''look.'' Both Levi and Seven-Up set seminal styles that continue to be mimicked so far through the eighties, set records for high production costs (long since topped), and served to break new ground in computerized animation. Though complex and new (for the time) technology went into these spots, the final product was a typical Abel combination of updated retrospection: Seven-Up's mood was old-time music hall, just like Levi's, realized in a more vivid way than ever. Similarly, Abel's more recent "Sexy Robot" spot is probably the full realization of the robot in the 1926 feature *Metropolis,* director Fritz Lang's vision of the lure of technology finally, perfectly, embodied. Comparing all these images, one might ask whether Abel might be treading conceptual water, continually updating old ideas with ever-higher animation technology. But with wonderfully realized images like these, why complain?

"'The creation of nonverbal symbolic images' can, I think, be the most important part of a definition of 'graphics,'" says Abel. "Working with powerful images, images that can carry a lot of meaning, that's very key to what any graphics designer should be doing. . . . The older ideas and styles can gain a new level of meaning, too, along with the old, realizing them in a new medium. Nothing is new; to communicate with anybody about anything, you have to refer to an image that can be recognized because it has been seen before, at least in part — mixing together something they've seen before with a fantasy they haven't. . . ."

This also would seem to apply to the value-added process of a commercial designer bringing life (fantastic or otherwise) to a product — such as a TV-commercial or feature-film storyboard. Abel believes "a designer is a person who tries to synthesize the essence of form, shape, or a series of images to create mood, an idea, etc., in order to sell a product, service, or object. That's as separated from an artist, who is into creating mood, feeling, what have you, not necessarily to sell something. The term 'artist' should apply to those designers who redefine their work, take it to the consummate level and open up communication to a wide audience. . . .

"Half the time our jobs begin with a call from our rep, who says such-and-such agency has an idea for a spot they want us to do — or else the agency calls directly. Either way we sit down with the agency producer, and quite often with the art director, in his office, and sometimes with the writer of the spot, too. If it's not a producer, it's an agency's creative director. If there's no [story]board, we'll talk it over and then come back with boards. If there is a board, we redraw it, make it what we think it can be."

In advertising, the client has to be kept informed every step of the way.

Describing an as-yet-unrealized animated fantasy to clients who may know very little about animation is a tough process, but one that technology has recently either made more difficult or improved tremendously, depending on who you talk to. Many computerized animators seem to be high priests of their mystical technology, masters of processes which are certainly difficult for the average guy to understand. Abel — and probably any really good animator — would prefer that everyone know what his technical solutions are; animation that is more understandable is less risky for clients. If all animators followed Abel's formula for computer-aided client communications, this would be another spur to animation-industry growth.

"On the phone or in meetings we describe how we see it, then soon after we draw up boards and discuss those. That's soon followed by a 720-frame [for a thirty-second commercial] animatic on the Evans & Sutherland MPS or the IRIS. Within one week they have a complete idea of what we're doing with their original concept. It used to be like the blind man and the elephant, but when we developed the capability to do animatics on the E & S flight simulator and both sides were suddenly looking at the same blueprint, misconceptions and problems disappeared. This system also lets us spec out a job pretty quickly, and we can all have a clear idea of what something will cost from early on.

"Related to this is the importance of keeping dialog as open as possible, not only with clients but within our operation. Everyone should understand the tools we're all using, and the people developing technology understand the needs of the artists on staff who can draw and render concepts. All of our work is done under our roof — there's no subcontracting, so we can control our own product. It's the old Hollywood studio system of Louis B. Mayer; you get the best movies that way."

Abel's company has designed many of its own computer imaging devices for several years. Most have represented far greater investments in development than equivalent technology that has been commercially available to other animators just a few months down the road, but inhouse hardware and software development has paid off for Abel in many ways, some less tangible than others. Certainly there is that few-month edge when nobody else can do what Robert Abel & Associates can; perhaps more important is the pervasive understanding of technological possibilities that informs this studio's work. If some of Abel's expensive early experimental devices sit unused while later, "store-bought" gadgets are in demand, the home-brewing process still pays its way, and commercial applications beckon.

Recently, Abel's company has brought to market its own imaging system, and a new in-house device is probably destined for the wider market too. In the words of Allen Debevoise, general manager, it is a new sort of digital film scanner that operates as a digital optical printer. "It will allow us to digitize live action and manipulate it. This kind of tool becomes a combination of, and replaces, all video and optical tools."

Heady innovations, out of the same tradition as the continuing research into film technology that the old studios used to subsidize. Robert Abel's artistic and technological ambitions form a consistent image.

12.5 Bo Gehring and Associates

In 1961, Bo Gehring quit Cornell University's electrical engineering program to weld metal sculptures. He had a couple of successful shows, but says, "I found I really didn't like working with my hands. But I liked design." Modern furniture and other consumer products with "high-tech" looks emerged from his drafting table through the sixties, in between Grand Prix motorcycle races. He eventually came to run a machine shop that built hydraulic disc brakes for motorcycles, and also laser holography cameras. Then came a contract to design and manufacture high-speed, computer-controlled drilling machines for printed circuit boards. "IBM was our first client," he says. "After that, I designed everything from camper tents to bowling-ball balancing machines."

In 1972 a headhunter brought Gehring together with Dr. Phillip Mittelman at MAGI. The company had developed programs for applications in nuclear physics, but also thought some of the software had applications in animation. The result was MAGI–SynthaVision, which Gehring helmed. First vector graphics, and then the very first high-resolution raster graphics ever made, and Gehring's MAGI–SynthaVision made history. Perhaps his most memorable design from this period was the "mothership" in *Close Encounters of the Third Kind.*

But Gehring was restless. Motion control enticed him, and so did the idea of having a company all his own again. He formed a new company, Gehring Aviation, exclusively to do motion-control animation of 3D models, then found that too restrictive. Now Bo Gehring & Associates uses whatever design technique is right for the job.

Bo Gehring was described as the "oracle of vector graphics" in an all-too-recent trade publication. The man who set up the animation production arm of MAGI, thus helping to set off the boom in computer animation a few years ago, has for the last several years involved his own company in "composite projects in many different disciplines. We're known for computer animation of all sorts, motion control, and we've now diversified into live-action and even cel animation."

If Gehring is, or was the "oracle of vector graphics," it was because his graphics set styles that others followed. He clearly does not seem to believe that vector images are always preferable to other sorts of images, and he continues, through changing technology and production genres, to create images that are uniquely dramatic. "The whole thrust of the industry is toward composite projects," he says. "You can do composite projects that are just as cliched as vector came to be, and we're seeing lots of those. That's already helped to give wire-frames a good name again."

Gehring sees clearly and admits to having suffered from industry problems of the mid-eighties. "When a Sacramento station wants an ID, I can't afford to do that anymore. It'll go to a guy working in his closet. . . . It's a buyer's market now; agencies can bid out projects to three or four places that are good, and they can jam a low budget down the production company's throat that precludes very-high-resolution work — and makes it more difficult to do highly imaginative work.

"I don't think the problem is too many animators, and I certainly welcome new talent into the business. There have always been too many animators, and there always will be. It's been a cost squeeze on the part of advertisers, reacting to other changes in the television industry, like the higher rates they pay the networks for lower viewing shares.

"Mostly, the situation doesn't hurt us, personally. Most of our bids are against just the other top companies — Abel, Greenberg, etc. But we're seeing fewer of the really creative *and* very expensive spots that do the most to advance the state of the art — like Abel's Levi's Brand spots of a few years ago. If you can't do it cheaply, it doesn't get done."

Also, he says, "when you talk about composite imaging jobs, and you're talking about raster graphics, the job gets so complex that no one makes any money. It's *very* expensive: you may be talking about a half hour per frame on the largest mainframe in the world. . . . If you go cheap on a complex composite image, it shows, and shows badly. Now there are some people who can do nice funky things with a low investment, but I think even they would rather be working at the top of the medium, technologically. It's a little hard to do this in an environment that's spawning so many uninspired graphics."

Gehring says, "The TV industry just cranks out more and more crap. When the average guy watching TV sees the average, very derivative and dull bit of computer animation, he may get to be preconditioned against all of what we do. The agencies get spooked very easily; they're very used to dealing with quickly changing trends. If somebody does a good Coke commercial with a football player, that's all you get for two years. We could feel a chill.''

Bo Gehring's company does very-high-resolution work, usually at the top end of the animation price range. He says somewhat over half is for TV commercials, and the rest is feature work. (But he expects that the demand for his sort of work will be more in the feature area in the near future; features' better resolution requires better graphics quality.) Whether a feature or commercial is in question, ''everyone wants something that hasn't been done before. But when you're in a situation, such as many agencies expect, where they have to tell you exactly what ought to go in the image, well, they'll put it in terms of something they've already seen. . . . You have to come up with your own interpretation of what they want — work within those limits — and still try to come up with something that's never been done.

''We've been luckier than other shops. By and large people trust us to get what they want. There's no single solution to attaining that trust, and sometimes jobs aren't very fun because of antsy relations with the client, but the ones that are fun more than make up for it. . . . Don't get me wrong: The market is overserviced right now, but in the long run it has to grow tremendously. Every network is complaining about difficulties getting programming, and this is a global broadcasting trend. Hardware is so far ahead of software. . . . ''

Bo Gehring & Associates occupies a relatively small studio in Venice, California. It's a boutique concentrating on design of very-high-end images; though several self-designed motion control tracks and computer systems devoted to high-resolution vector and raster graphics are on the premises, Gehring also does a fair amount of work in cooperation with other companies with bigger, faster computers. He frequently uses his minicomputers to ''front'' or program for images to be built at III (Information International, Inc.) in Hollywood or Cranston–Csuri in Columbus, Ohio. He says it makes the most sense, with technology changing so constantly and the movie business always being what it is, to avoid the path of taking on the heavy capital costs of a giant plant. Robert Abel, the Greenbergs, and most notably Digital Productions in Los Angeles (which uses a Cray X-MP supercomputer for animation) have taken this road and seem to be doing well; but Gehring knows the road from his days at MAGI. ''MAGI was getting killed on commercials. Money was made elsewhere, but animation just doesn't pay the way for very expensive installations, or not for many of them. The hardware is too expensive and yet too available. Software is a different sort of investment, and that's what people come to us for.''

12.6 Jim Lindner and his Fantastic Animation Machine

You wouldn't be able to classify most animators as businesspeople, but Jim Lindner and Suzanne Gavril, former marketing executives at Xerox — he an MBA, she a former advertising-agency producer, partners in Fantastic Animation Machine — certainly mean business. FAM makes animation chiefly with a 32-bit Ridge minicomputer running their own proprietary software in C and Unix, output to videotape. FAM also makes a device that digitally stores and manipulates live-action footage with, and as if it were, CGI. FAM makes and markets other software having little or nothing to do with animation, and has a computer typography division. A busy little business, of which animation is the small but cutting edge, and all wrapped up in one crowded midtown-Manhattan office.

''We're looking at this business as a business,'' says Lindner. ''Business graphics is a four-billion-dollar-a-year industry. Animation is *maybe, best case* — from all I've read and seen, if it's more than $200 million gross, total in this country, I'd be shocked. . . . If people in this industry ignore the Genigraphics and Dicomeds of the world, they'll be very disappointed.''

As a computer animation house, says Lindner, ''You're in a segment of a segment of a segment of the film marketplace,'' and that's not a very large business, either. His own strategy for FAM seems to be to use his firm's newly established beachhead in computer animation as a driving creative force into those related industries.

That's not to say FAM is not fully committed, in a similarly iconoclastic way, to animation. They have produced over one hundred spots since breaking with Computer Creations — a South Bend, Indiana, animator they began to represent in New York five years ago — all made on proprietary equipment.

Says Lindner: ''If you really think the solution to graphic communication is buying a piece of equipment, you're very naive. Software development is something that goes on here around the clock, all the time. And it takes a particular breed of person — somebody who understands what graphic design is all about and also understands programming and the technology. That sort of person is very much in demand, anywhere.

They *should* be even more in demand than they are, but some people do, somehow, have this idea that the equipment is the solution. I think they lose that idea pretty quickly.''

Lindner loved classical animation for years before ever going into the business; though he does not expect animation to be his major profit center as much as his drawing card, his love for it and his dedication to old-fashioned high-quality work is no less. He maintains contact with many traditional animators who may never want to touch a computer. ''Good design is dependent on its materials, but there are many constants between what was good about the old animation and what can be good about computer animation. There has to be a continuity here. Really fine animators have been, not starving, but let's say underemployed for years, ever since the big animation studios disbanded. Guys like John Canemaker — who does wonderful work, and who comes in here quite often to do some work — they seem to be members of a dying breed. There's a whimsical elegance to John's work — to so much of the best of animation. I hope that doesn't get lost among the machines.''

Clearly, there are different paths to the right design, as well as to successful animation careers. Would each of the companies run by the people profiled here take anywhere near the same approach to the same design problem? Probably not. Would each be an equivalently good response? Also probably not; all creators have affinities with certain types of projects and not others. There is room, in animation, for all distinctive design. Though a computer may seem like a good crutch that makes the design process easier, if anything ought to be plain from these interviews, imagination and sweat continue to be animation's constants.

CHAPTER THIRTEEN

The Market for PC-Generated Graphics

Why make either static or animated graphics on your personal computer, besides the fun of it? (As you are surely aware by now, it can often bring more agony than fun!) Television broadcasting often has been referred to in this volume as the standard by which much computer animation can be judged, and productions for television are indeed a major market for even micro graphics, providing they are either of sufficient resolution or have the right bold simplicity. Nonbroadcast television is a far wider market, as are many other business uses. To list a few:

- corporate video and nonmoving graphics for corporate communications
- advertising design
- publishing applications such as layout, typography, and illustration
- industrial design
- architectural design
- simulated learning situations such as flight simulation (the very first commercial application for computer animation)
- cartography, including mapping for various scientific applications like archaeology, geology (which implies such very commercial science as mineral exploration), and medical diagrams
- teletext and videotex-type data bank operations in many corporate, government, and educational networks
- as part of many other computer applications, making software "friendlier"
- finally, not least, in computer games

and there are probably one or two broad categories I've missed.

In all of these uses, the relatively low-resolution images of micro graphics are often quite high enough. Of course, people in the field will have seen quite poor-quality graphics from micros and may not believe that a micro is capable of the quality they need. Seeing is believing.

The only graphic industry where a maker of micro graphics often need feel not up to snuff is the movies and, to a lesser extent, broadcast television, but the animation and graphics opportunities and profits involved in the various industries named above *dwarf* those in the movies. The total movie and TV animation industry in the U.S. probably amounted to a maximum of $400 million in revenues in 1985, for example, and perhaps as little as $300 million. In 1985 the total revenues for U.S. computer-aided industrial design firms alone was on the order of *ten times greater.* The total revenue-producing activities of computer graphics in all of the industries listed are obviously far greater than what is normally thought of as the animation industry. They are growing fast and show all signs of continuing to spiral in growth far faster than movie and TV animation.

What sort of graphics are each of these industries looking for? Some details are called for. Read on.

13.1 Corporate Video

Many producers of corporate video expect that industry to grow a hundred-fold between this writing and the start of the twenty-first century. What is normally meant by ''corporate video'' includes any sort of sales support, training and service instructions, executive conferences and teleconferences, some subsidized programming on television, videotaped messages to stockholders, and any communications a corporation can convince itself are better put on video (except standard television commercials; these are another industry).

An industry is defined primarily by who does the work and where it is done. Corporate video producers are most often full-time employees of the company involved. They often hire outside expertise on a free-lance basis for individual projects, and this is the way most computer graphics designers get involved. There are many free-lance producers plying the waters of corporate video, too. For up-to-date lists of producers and information on the field, the industry organization to contact is the Internal Television Association (ITVA), headquartered in Irving, Texas.

Corporate video producers drool over computer graphics; they want these things very much to liven up dull productions, but rental time and free-lance work on one of the $50,000 to $100,000-class video effects devices have strained or been beyond many budgets. Micros will take over animation for this type of production, because the price is right. Demand for computer graphics in the business world guarantees that this market should continue to be by far the largest for micro graphics and animation.

Among the major growth areas within corporate video are interactive videodisk, teleconferencing, and, most important, something not quite video but quite meaningful to computer animators: custom-programmed instructional graphic software. To understand the importance of the latter, it is necessary to explain the demand for videodisk.

Interactive training, sales aids, and resource reference are what videodisks promise to do better than ever for corporations. Just in the auto industry, microfilm records of parts and service instructions at factories and car dealerships are being replaced by interactive videodisk; at the same time, these devices provide "point-of-purchase" interactive advertising on the sales floor. They are being incorporated into cars, too, and programmed with maps, service manuals, etc. The auto industry has so many uses for videodisk that it is likely to be hooked on the technology for a long time to come.

Producing interactive videodisks calls for a large investment. Businesses with smaller user networks that already have an installed base of microcomputers or terminals connected to a mainframe are logical customers for similarly interactive graphics that involve no full video and can run on their computer systems. In a word, this implies either videotex or interactive graphics, stored on floppy disk.

Videoconferencing is less obviously connected to computer graphics, but wherever there is a need to present graphic information in any video production, microcomputer graphics will be there.

13.2 Nonmoving Graphics for Corporate Communications

Slide shows and graphics shown directly from computer to video projector are presentation technologies very much allied to corporate video, but are most often thought of as a low-budget alternative. So much the better for micro graphics makers! All of the above comments on the corporate video market hold true here, too, right down to dealing with the same personnel.

13.3 Advertising Design

In advertising, many mock-ups and test layouts of print ads and comparable storyboards for commercials must be drawn and redrawn. In New York, Los Angeles, and Chicago, several commercial production houses have made their specialties in taking storyboards and using Chyron or Quantel-style effects to make "animatics," or roughly animated test commercials. All of these processes can be made more efficient and cheaper, with no quality loss, by switching to an appropriate micro animation system.

As of this writing, there has not yet been much of a move in this direction, which certainly convinces me that there is tremendous opportunity here. Making animatics is also a traditional way to break into the business of doing animation for television commercials.

13.4 Publishing: Layout, Typography, and Illustration

High resolution is required for any graphics work to be printed — far higher resolution than is available on any micro-based graphics system. Character generation of fairly high resolution can be done on a micro, however, because characters can be defined in a program not as collections of pixels but as individual, indissoluble 2D objects. This is a long way from the sort of graphics work covered in this volume, but its relevance is that the same micro system used for such typography may also be set up for use for mock-up layouts.

In the next few years, micros will be used for camera-ready layout of art, too. With a plotter that's capable of printing the product of the frame buffers created in Chapters 6, 7, and 8, magazine and book layout will never be the same. Laser printers that do the job are already in prototype as this goes to press. Already, micros have been used extensively for illustrations that are meant to have a low-res, micro "look," and also for relatively low-resolution news photos. People will keep trying to find graphical uses for micros in publishing, if only because they are so helpful on the "word" side of the business. When every editorial desk at a publishing company comes to have a micro on it, the graphic people next door start to get jealous. Who knows what manner of art will result? It won't be animation, but it'll be close.

13.5 Industrial Design

We move from the speculative to the most real of all micro graphics and animation uses. For many animation programmers, in fact, making cartoons is just fluff, and industrial design is where the serious action is. Three-dimensional design of any product, with coordinates automatically correlated into a list of specifications and the running of various sorts of simulated product tests in the design stage are now required elements of industrial design.

Military contractors and aerospace companies have been using large computer systems for design since the sixties, and the vast amounts of data that now can be commanded by large CAD (computer-aided design) systems certainly make using one preferable to designing on a micro. But now that small shops, making everything from machine tools to desktop staplers to precision medical equipment, also need to design by computer, micros are the tools of either choice or necessity.

Besides great similarity in hardware and somewhat less similarity in software, how much interchange is there between ''solids modeling'' and animation graphics? Software designers are in constant communication, trading algorithms, ideas, and job prospects at SIGGRAPH (the Association for Computing Machinery's Special Interest Group for Graphics) and National Computer Graphics Association (NCGA) conferences every year. Users are very different groups; one would no more expect to see animators (who are not programmers) involved in designing cars than automobile designers going to work for Disney. Fluid contact is definitely on the level of systems design.

13.6 Architectural Design

It might seem that much of what goes for industrial design ought to go for architectural design, too, but the situation here is quite different. Architects are more analogous to animators, in many ways, than to industrial designers. Architects tend to work in small firms that cannot afford large computer systems. Their educational training is often more artistic than technical, so architects have been as afraid of the computer as have practitioners of any art form.

All of this began to change at the beginning of the eighties, with micro design systems amassing enough power to be of interest, at prices that were affordable to the vast majority of architects.

Architects tend to be interested in the very same sort of modeling and data programs as industrial designers, so the animation graphics programmer will tend to have the same sort of interface with programmers of architectural graphics systems as with industrial design systems, with one major exception. Since there has been far more money invested for many years in industrial design systems, often enough software in that field is on a real cutting edge. Architectural systems designers, like micro animation systems designers, are followers of that edge. Thus, while animation and graphics programmers have less to learn from architectural programmers, there is more possibility of switching fields and contributing equally viable software.

Even moreso than in the industrial design field, architects are used to making demonstration models or pictures of their projects, allowing the lay public to visualize future buildings. At this writing, no micro graphics program exists to allow them to easily transform their computerized designs to such images, or to hire an artist to easily do so. Opportunity knocks.

13.7 Simulated Learning Situations, Such as Flight Simulation

The very first commercial application for computer animation was flight simulation. Whether funded by government, industry, or educational institutions, computerized learning situations have been all the rage for years. Does computerized learning show only signs of growth? Not quite. Many efforts amount to no more than books built into computer terminals and are thus far less efficient or transportable than books, unless they contain great chunks of interaction and animation.

The opportunity for animators here is vast, and challenging, too. If animators are not able to respond quickly to the challenge of making stimulating educational software, classroom computerization will continue to move about as slowly as it has. As of this writing, many educators outside the field of computer science talk about their small computers the way they have long spoken of other once-coveted gadgetry that now decorates closets in semiworkable condition. In corporations, too, training specialists are, if anything, even more anxious to employ computers, but complain of a dearth of engaging software. The solution is clear, and enough large institutions see opportunity here for the solution to be quite profitable, too. The quickest growth and greatest opportunities in the later 1980s are definitely in the corporate training and seminar businesses, which are fast growing to be value-added resellers (VARs) of hardware/software training systems, in partnership with the likes of IBM, AT&T, and their would-be ilk. Through the nineties, the business should enlarge and spread out, eventually becoming a major staple of off-the-shelf micro software sales.

13.8 Cartography

Maps are made by computer now. The frontiers of cartographic technique have moved in two directions. One is to include more and more information in data bases related to the map, so that as much data can be accessed as directly as possible from the map, allowing maps to be easily redrawn, based on altered or reordered data. This has been going on where large computer systems are available: chiefly in military-related industries and in exploration for natural resources such as oil.

The second frontier is occupied mostly by academics who try to achieve as much as possible of the gee-whiz stuff on their small computers. By definition, no one could want as much data built into their maps as anthropologists, who would like to assimilate geological, botanical, zoological, meteorological, and other data with their own "human relations area files"; all is pertinent. There isn't much monetary profit in anthropology, however, or in archaeology, botany, or zoology. Scientists must make do with micros.

In turn, it seems reasonable to surmise that ever-more-useful maps and other graphical data on ever-more-powerful micros will eventually lead to money-making industries in related fields. This has happened to geology, astronomy, mathematics, medicine, genetics, and other "hard" sciences, all of which have their highly commercial (if less theoretical) sides. Without the data that computers have yet to assemble, perhaps we can't imagine what such commercial applications for "softer" sciences might be, yet it seems safe to assume that graphical output will have a lot to do with them.

Finally, these disciplines are putting so many hopes into mapping and compiling data by computer that, as has happened in many other similarly competitive fields, those who get ahead (for better or worse) are likely to be the programming whizzes.

13.9 Teletext and Videotex

Neither of these technologies has set the world on fire, as both were supposed to along about the end of the seventies. With the hype and hoopla past us, however, it is easier to see the meaningful kernel of these systems for what it is and for what it is becoming in business, government, and education: a data bank of information that allows interaction and can interest relatively unsophisticated computer users with limited motion graphics. Such a system need not be as universal as television and the telephone to find many profitable uses.

Videotex systems are currently being used as bulletin boards at many universities and large corporations. They differ from the average data bank only in that they offer graphics. As the average company's computer system increases in graphical presentation capabilities, that average company's data bank is likely to start employing more and more graphic information and to become de facto videotex. It is already happening quickly; there is an accelerating need for artistically oriented programmers, as well as for graphic designers without programming knowledge, to keep these systems supplied with lively images.

13.10 Making Software "Friendlier"

Generally speaking, this is the promise of computer graphics in many fields. Pictures — especially moving pictures — can be the sugar coating that makes information enjoyable, interesting, and better retained. Business and home-computer programs for all applications are making more and more use of animation, in order to attract and keep users. With memory prices falling through the floor, general applications programs have increasing latitude to include graphics. The challenge is to design graphics that advance the program — that do more than just coat it with sugar. For designers who can meet that challenge, opportunities are vast.

13.11 Computer Games

Combining moving images with game theories — something else that computers are very proficient at — has already yielded a great deal of work. And it has had a fad that came and went. In a commercial sense, computer games may never again seem so big a deal as they did at the beginning of the eighties, but my inclination is to believe this book is written at a temporary low point between fad and an eventually strong and growing industry. The movies were once a fad visited in arcades, with limited — one might say brain-damaged — stories of limited length and of limited interest to anybody of a certain maturity. As image and sound rendering capabilities increased, the curiosity became both a huge business and a high art.

What computers bring to moving pictures are the animation and effects with which this book is concerned, as well as interactivity: real-time game playing. Computer games may presently be at a nadir of faddishness, because their capabilities in both graphics and game-playing began to seem naive and boring. As both improve, who will be able to resist the powerful lure of an entertainment form that allows us so much power to play out fantasies?

The presentation form that evolves for computer games is an important problem for designers to solve. A great deal of the popularity of motion pictures, even when shown on television, is the ability of many people to be involved together. Computer games, in an arcade or at home, can be as exclusive and exclusionary as a book; we're often told that many people don't like to read because you do it alone. Whether a computerized society will evolve toward lonelier art forms, or whether entertainment entrepreneurs will come up with mass computer games (probably something of both) will have as much to do with what sort of people we are in years to come as movies and TV have had to do with what sort of people we are now.

13.12 What Television and the Movies are Looking For

Now that we've looked at all the other, higher growth areas for graphics and animation, we come back to the greatest opportunity area now for finely crafted animation: television and film. Even as other areas surpass these in terms of total opportunities, now and in the near future these will remain the big leagues. The most noticed work of the highest quality, performed at the highest profit, will continue to be shown on these screens in the foreseeable future.

How do you break in? Makers of micro graphics are in a good position to break down the doors and demonstrate their talents. Even though hardware may not be capable of producing high enough resolution for theater or broadcast, most PCs can be configured at small expense to at least be able to show what one's talents would be with the right hardware. A special-effects craze is now moving into its tenth year since the first *Star Wars* arguably started things off, and shows no signs of decelerating. On the contrary, special-effects madness has spread to most commercial and music video makers and to every local TV station, video production center, and industrial filmmaker. If you can show you know how to make this stuff — and more important, know how to make it both cheaper and better than before (half of which micros are great at and half of which is up to you) — opportunity will beat a path to you.

Even one of the classic ways of failing to make it in a popular medium, by producing work that is too rarified and highbrow for the market, seems to have lost its relevance to computer animation. Of course, corporate logos don't tend to look like the animation in *Yellow Submarine* just now — images must match what they would represent — but television uses up any sort of image you can throw at it, to sell something or other. There's always somebody seeking to tie your fresh new image to their tired old product.

How you break in will have a lot to do with where you are, geographically. If you don't mind living in Los Angeles, opportunities are diverse. New York offers similar opportunities, with more emphasis on television commercials and corporate video and less on TV series. Both offer equal exposure to theatrical features (give it a few years of effort to make it all the way there), local TV, industrials, music video, etc. In both cities, talented programmer–animators will probably find work with an animation house already geared up to use their talents.

TV commercials are also a large market in Chicago, less so in such places as Toronto, San Francisco (which of course has Lucasfilm nearby, often thought of by animators as Mecca), Boston, Houston, Miami, and occasionally other active cities in North America. Television stations form the largest job market for animators, perhaps even in Chicago, and certainly in other major cities. Washington, Atlanta, Dallas, Denver, Salt Lake City, Montreal, Vancouver, and Columbus, Ohio, all have sizeable computer animation companies or several TV stations that are interested in producing a good amount themselves. In medium-to-small cities, the TV station is the best place to job hunt.

If at this point you think you need to go to Hollywood to make it in computer animation, you must have just started reading. On the other hand, if you want to make feature films, they don't generally come out and recruit.

CHAPTER FOURTEEN

Where's the Future?

In the last chapter some mention was made of future business probabilities in various markets for computer animation. A new generation of minds weaned on micros will make that future happen in ways not totally foreseeable, but we already have a great deal of evidence as to what forms future computer animation will take, if only we examine the present.

Ideas are a result of people interacting with environment. Animators working with machines produce work that reflects those machines. Those whose concepts of animation are mostly informed by past, noncomputerized practice may tend at first to use computers to more easily realize ideas engendered by the traditional animation media, or they may take inspiration from societal ideas of what computers represent. Eventually they will come to have new ideas based on exploiting newly discovered capabilities of their tools.

Animators coming basically from a computer background have tended to produce work that often seems unsophisticated, judged from the standpoint of general art culture, but that solves interesting problems and achieves beauty in the eyes of fellow hacking animators. They also take inspiration from societal ideas of what computers represent, though the society of people raised on computers is somewhat different from that of animators raised on Bugs Bunny and Mickey Mouse —, and quite pertinently, yet more different from those raised on high-art or on any other art traditions.

14.1 Beyond Realism

For a pertinent example, "realistic" challenges of representation in perspective often seem naive from a high-art tradition. All of this was done in the Renaissance; now for a free and intelligent painter to use perspective, the Renaissance solutions and aesthetics can be called up only as a self-conscious statement about that technique. This has long been an important issue for many artists. In socialist countries "realism" is dogma, with other forms of art sometimes proscribed. In the West the tyranny of the mass marketplace has usually made it far easier to sell crude attempts at pictoral realism than any other sort of art.

Computer animators are still in the stage of being happy to be able to represent three-dimensional objects with realism. What is sophisticated technologically seems crude artistically. It is comforting to think that a new era of art is dawning with the computer, and that its art ought to be judged in new ways. This is no excuse, however, for computer artists to fall into old traps.

The measure of computer animation against high Western art was brought up not to weigh aesthetics but to begin to understand comparative aesthetics. Setting aesthetic parameters is an arbitrary, faddish game. Its very arbitrariness, however, is predicated on whatever environments the conscious aesthetician or the un-self-conscious artist responds to. The game is played within rules. Discovering the rules allows a full picture of the game and likely pictures of what it will be in the future.

14.2 Interactivity

Speaking of games, the importance of interactivity to developing forms in computer animation is easy to see. Animation in the past and most of the present involves only passive interaction on the part of the audience. If audiences are going to be able to choose story lines in branching structures, this is an obviously new art form. Animation has already been changed as a result; one example is the sprite, which evolved in video games to make the most of motion possibilities with low resolution against a static high-res background. Whether or not sprites would have evolved as part of computer animation's repertory without video games (and in fact, it seems logical that they would have) is less relevant than that

1. they have evolved as they have
2. computer animators think of sprites in the context of what they have been used for in many video games.

The branching structure of interactive programs, the influence of game theory on animation, influences of the technologies of videodisk and other storage media, arcades and other trappings of the general game culture all are changing animation in important ways.

But how? An attempt to understand should begin with an examination of the forces affecting all computer animation, including the (as yet) small subset that is interactive animation.

For example: Even with numerous instances to the contrary, computer animation is most often used to make cool, hard, futuristic images. Advertising agencies and movie producers call traditional animators when they want something warm and fuzzy. When they want something cold and hard they call on the known computer people. Many, if not most traditional animators now produce their warm and fuzzy images with paint programs on computer terminals, but their work is no more thought of as computer animation than poetry written with a word processor would be thought of as computer poetry. "Real" computer-generated imagery is identifiable by its style. To computer poetry afficionados, as to those who like to play chess with computers, it would be an easy task to construct a parody of a typical computer poem or chess game without recourse to a computer, but it would be much harder to do so than to have the computer grind out its own self-parody. So, too, for us it is easy to envision drawing by hand typical sorts of computer animation images. It would be a senseless exercise, considering that a computer would make the task so much easier. But why is there such a cliched computer animation look for computer animators to constantly, unconsciously parody?

A lack of inventiveness is the simple answer, which leads, properly, to an exhortation to all new computer animators: do not be caught in the same traps. A more complex answer is needed, though, to be able to see the traps.

14.3 What are the Cliches?

1. smooth metallic surfaces
2. "mechanical," machinelike movement
3. bright colors
4. technology as hero at the center of attention
5. futuristic, science-fictiony subject matter

The first two or three are directly related to technological limitations — not that these are hard and fast limits, but it is easier to make images that function within them. In the early years of computer graphics it was difficult even to perfect smooth metallic surfaces and machinelike movement, so computer animators are to be sympathized with for still finding these to be desirable goals. For animators working on micros, these are goals just as difficult as they were on larger computers a few years ago.

It is for animators working with large systems to worry about going beyond these cliches, and for micro animators to just try to live up to them!

All of which makes "cliche" something of a misnomer. It may be no more cliched to make CGI with machinelike movement than to write a sentence with a subject and a predicate. The first two items on our list are part cliche, part structural imperative.

The third, bright colors, is a different sort of phenomenon. Micro users may indeed have to contend with color limitations, but much of the most familiar computer animation has involved film recording off a monochrome vector image. The animator then may filter the film with as much color variety as film allows. Animation made on large raster graphics systems can take advantage of, typically, 32,000 colors, yet basic, bright colors predominate. Why? An answer is as close as a look at most traditional animation; here, too, bright, basic colors predominate. Why?

The early Technicolor process, dominant until the middle 1950s, was partial to bright, basic colors. Since then, the animation palette seems to have muted somewhat, but also has remained very influenced by all the great classic animation of the Technicolor years. Long-time animators explain that bright, basic colors communicate clearly and simply. Simplicity is an artistic virtue enforced by the difficulties of the traditional animation process, but a real virtue nonetheless in communicating with a mass audience.

The last two cliches listed are not so much caused by technological limitations, but by the necessary interests of most people who would devote themselves to working so closely with machines. The machine must be the center of its user's attention after all that labor, so the animator makes it the star of the product. The result, though, often seems to be feature films, TV commercials, music videos, etc. that are chiefly interested in high technology. Why should TV station-identification logos commonly show robots and synthesized cities on channel after channel from one side of America to the other? No technology previous to computer animation has so given visible identity to our society's worship of technology.

Now this may be a fad, due to be replaced soon by the sort of warm, back-to-nature images that were popular in the late sixties and early seventies. During that last back-to-nature cycle, the country was also bombarded by images of technology gone astray: war, environmental damage, cities self-destructing. Warm, natural imagery was certainly a reaction to the other sorts of images people had to face all the time. All of the ugly images of the horrors of technology certainly still exist, but they don't make the evening news all that often. Americans have come to accept that technology exists without being news anymore, so we entertain ourselves with the notion of technology as hero. Considering the investment (fiscally and emotionally) in technology being the hero that can lift us above our problems, we are likely to keep looking for images that glorify it. Computer animators, with lives invested in their own technology, are not likely to be as interested in any other sorts of images, anyway.

This is not to imply that styles are not likely to change. They are, and will, within a high-tech framework. Probably the most interesting stylist to be working for years at the forefront of computer animation is Robert Abel. His work has been strongly influenced by the Art Deco and Art Moderne revivals, but his images are not at all interchangeable with his models from the 1920s to the forties; instead, they are obviously high-tech images that make bows to earlier styles with some graceful nuances. Abel's work has been slavishly imitated and rarely duplicated, as it has defined styles in television commercials. The imitators typically miss the main point Abel's work makes: it comments on a source, often one expressing naive technological optimism, from a contemporary high-tech vantage.

Abel's TV commercials thus mirror many concerns (in a much more commercial way) of independent video animators whose after-hours experiments with the video effects machines they typically have had day jobs operating have mostly been shown only at nonprofit cooperatives in major cities. The relative quality of often amateurish videos is not at issue; their very common attitude of cynical fun with technology is, like Abel's more visible work, an underside to the high-tech heaven of most computer animation.

As computer animation styles may change, this attitude is a next likely alternative. There won't be anything pastoral about it, and it's not likely to be antitechnology, either. Rather, it will represent attempts at a deeper understanding of the human–machine interface. Animators won't cover over their tracks, they will expose a bit of the workings of the way they produced an image. Micros will fit in well with this aesthetic; they will even help to mandate it, because it is easier to make wittily imperfect images with a micro than to go for feature-film or station-logo style perfection. Micros are spreading to a wide and widely talented new group of animators, and this is where seminal new styles will come from.

On the other hand, CGI and motion control capabilities have lately evolved to the point where photorealist effects are possible, if very expensive. Mostly, photorealism has been confined to images of cars and other machines in television commercials. No process as expensive and difficult, and as highly organized as CGI has been, readily lends itself to irony or self-deprecation. Even as CGI attains the realistic capabilities of live action and optical work, the sense of fun in the work is often likely to remain unsophisticated.

Animators working with large computers cannot resist the urge to put together the programming power to realistically represent what seems like live action, even of fully animated people. It may be surprising today to realize that, in the first flush of the computer animation boom of the late seventies, animators and the press wondered how soon it might be before actors were obsolete. Live action certainly will never be obsolete, but it is being augmented by unobtrusive, very-high-resolution animated images. Richard Greenberg's work on the Woody Allen movies *Zelig* and *Purple Rose of Cairo* stands out as prototypical here. Of course, these films are very sophisticated comedies, which would seem to prove false the contention that an investor in expensive technology is not interested in laughing at that investment. Unfortunately, or perhaps fortunately, Woody Allen's films seem idiosyncratically unconnected to the dominant trend.

André Bazin long ago pointed out that photography commands attention because of the presumed reality of whatever is depicted. Seamlessly realistic special effects also can exploit that power, but more often now operate on a different sort of audience expectation. Audiences know the images of a *Star Wars,* for instance, are nowhere to be found in the real world; special effects have become the show. It is no coincidence that special effects are most at center stage in futuristic and militaristic concoctions; that movie magic can depict all of this convinces even sophisticated audiences that eventually techno-magic will make it happen. The American popular aesthetic has always involved flashy hyper-reality, from wax museums to Disneyland. Computer animation lends itself to this aesthetic, and turns Bazin's reflections on realism in motion pictures inside out: because it can be faked, it will someday exist. Computer-animated epics frequently function as boosterism for a remarkably consistent vision of a future parochial technocracy. Such images are obviously inconsistent with irony or self-deprecating humor, and such an attitude does tend to turn its bearers into pious frauds. Define "pious" as "dutiful" and "fraud" as "simulation" and suddenly you've got a bland description of the job of computer animation.

How is a dutiful computer-simulator to avoid becoming a pious fraud? Care about the meaning of your images as much as the making of them.

A micro investment is easier to laugh at than a hulking, multimillion-dollar animation engine. The long-range trend favors less awe in animators', their patrons', and the public's contemplation of Big Tech.

14.4 The Future Audience

Changes in allied technologies will affect computer animation, too. High-definition television and ever-better TV monitors are raising the resolution ante for players entering the game. More complex entertainment distribution means quicker opportunities for newcomers to break in. These changes make it all the more important to try to understand the reasons people want to see animation. Who is watching, and why? Without understanding the answers, it will not be possible to take advantage of the changing entertainment industry structure. Markets for animation outside of entertainment were adequately considered in Chapter 13. Some of these also will impact on entertainment, though, and must be considered in that context here.

Saturday morning has always been a prime time for animation on television. Now that Saturday morning has spread to home video, to satellite networks that show children's programming every day, and to other places in and out of the TV schedules, "Saturday morning" is no longer the appropriate name for the animated children's programming industry it is still often used to describe, but it is the easiest to use. The Saturday-morning industry, the mainstay of many (if not most) professional animators for many years, only recently has been changed a great deal by the computer, as well as by the above-described fragmentation.

Home video companies have discovered that children's programming is very lucrative for the same (often overlooked) reason it had so long been an unchanging backwater of television: Children are happy to watch the same program over and over again. What allowed TV programmers to send out an unvarying diet allows home video retailers to *sell* their product to consumers, instead of renting it, in the pattern typical for most tapes. Thus the wholesalers sell more tapes to retailers.

Children like to memorize television shows, and for some reason, perhaps because the colors are bright and the animals talk, they often prefer animation, too. It is not certain that children have swallowed the high-tech look of CGI, since there is so little shown on Saturday morning TV. Perhaps its paucity in the schedules of programming aimed at children is related more to traditional animation companies' dominance of the market. More important, it is more expensive to make CGI than computer-assisted traditional animation, and Saturday morning has always been a ruthless domain of lowest-cost production. It is possible, however, that while slightly older children flock to movies that feature large doses of CGI, young children do not respond to the hard-edged high-tech look. As that look becomes cheaper to achieve, the Saturday-morning results will be interesting to see.

The computer-assisted, turnkey paint and animation package is the real revolution in Saturday morning — or perhaps "counterrevolution" is more accurate. This technology is allowing animation to be made in the U.S. at the same low prices foreign producers were able to charge when the industry was labor-intensive, and the general quality level has improved, too. This compounds opportunities for animators, since all those low-quality series of recent years now have short rerun lives against the tougher competition.

It has never been difficult for thinking people to be disgusted by commercialism on Saturday morning, but the eighties have seen the rise of the toy that stars in its own program, produced and sponsored by its manufacturer. (*He-Man and the Masters of the Universe* comes to mind as a horrendous example.) Children are at least as aware of the trend to technology as hero as are older people. For animators, this points toward (perhaps all too disgustingly) commercial opportunities for those who would design toy and programming in a combined strategy.

14.5 Selling Our Children

Why be squeamish about exposing children to what adults revel in? Combined marketing of program image and advertised product is only a slightly more crass reworking of the marketing wisdom that goes into advertising cars within programs that feature car chases and soap in soap operas. Animators should be aware that their services will be better rewarded, by and large, in television commercials than in any other entertainment genre, and commercials require a look in tune with the programming they are meant to fit in with. Hard, cool CGI will thus continue to be used to sell cars, while music videos (commercials for record albums) will be more open to micro animation (and will not be able to pay as much for it) and softer, 2D paint program work will continue to sell soap. If animators would use an incongruous style, or even a fresh, new style in a commercial, they'd better be able to convince an advertising agency there's a solid, money-making reason to do so. To use a fresh, new style in programming, the program's producer must also convince advertisers of the same thing. In a more positive light, often a fine money-making reason is just to wake audiences up with something different.

14.6 CGI as News, and as Part of the Game

Commercials pay all bills on television, and inclusively have paid a large portion of the bills for technological advances in computer animation in recent years, because marketers have realized that the feeling computer animation can give of the machine as hero is perfect for selling machines. Just as commercials must try to blend with the programming they must fit into, programming must try to blend with the commercials it would attract. We therefore have CGI taking large part in sports and news programming, even if it might, on reflection, seem wholly beside the main point of the program. In fact, the more CGI established symbiosis between program and commercial, the more it is the subject of the program. Football programs, for example, lend themselves particularly well to computer-generated illustrations of strategies and statistics. This will not hurt football when it comes to carrying more and more advertising for machinery, and also advertising for nonmachine products (beer, for instance) to be sold to people who like watching machines. Baseball, by comparison, does not lend itself so well to explication by animated graphics; it is losing the ad dollar race to football, even though statistics do not indicate fewer viewers. Statistics do indicate baseball has fewer viewers who might buy cars and other machines.

14.7 Imagining Animation

Looking for a way to use computer animation somewhat less crassly, but still commercially? Music videos have allowed more artistic freedom in exchange for less payment because, though essentially commercials, they have a more marginal payback than standard commercials. Feature films allow more artistic freedom with budgets just as high, if not higher than TV commercials. The high stakes involved in feature films act as exactly the opposite sort of spur to the low stakes in a music video: novel talent is needed, at almost any price. That far more talented animators find opportunity in the low budgets of music video, instead of in the high budgets of movies, is attributable to the thousands of music videos now being made per year, compared to some two-hundred feature films. While there are comparatively few opportunities in features, when a few come along together that employ a great deal of computer animation, almost everyone in the animation industry seems to take part. This was the case with the Disney production *Tron,* for example.

But features and music videos are only slightly more free forms than TV. In the long run, producers in all forms look to animators for novelty and talented work to attract viewers. An awareness of which viewers programmers are trying to attract doesn't hurt an animator.

One definition of animation is the attribution of animate characteristics to inanimate objects. Traditional animators consider this breathing of life into a character to be the essence of their art. Many of them find they can easily transfer their art to 2D turnkey packages, but claim never to see any real character animation come out of advanced 3D systems. Imagine a car in an old-fashioned cartoon. Its grille is a mouth, it has eyes behind its windshield. Getting started in the morning, it coughs, does a few calisthenics, bounces around on silly-putty tires, then roars off. Now imagine a typical 3D CGI car. It looks just like a real car, except it drives off into the clouds, or builds itself out of a vector grid. This is a whole different sort of animation. Does the 3D car have character? Only in a limited sense. But it does seem more real than the first car, and so its ride into the clouds is far more breathtaking than would be a similar ride by Car A. As computing power for animation systems increases, the challenge to animators will be to combine the sense of reality possible with CGI with the sense of imaginative whimsy possible with traditional animation. When this starts to happen, so will a new golden age for animation.

APPENDIX A

Looking Backward

Some experience in making animation with computers gives rise to new ideas of what animation can be; the interaction between a technology and any art produced by it is always such an interchange. It has been no less so with traditional animation techniques. Although some of the technology that helped spawn the art of traditional animation may have little relevance to computerized animators today, a great deal of it is relevant. Far more relevant are many of the ideas and images of nearly a century of animation history before the computer was added into the animator's toolbox. Computers have wrought a revolution in the way animation is made, but computer animation is still animation, and its best works draw from that long tradition. (Unconsciously, its worst sometimes do, too.)

A.1 Before the Beginning

The very earliest predecessors of motion pictures were, strictly speaking, animation. Magic lantern shows utilized drawings and painted art even before photography was invented, as early as the eighteenth century; several pictures would be fitted into panes of a lampshade and illuminated one after another. After Peter Mark Roget (also author of the *Thesaurus*) came up with the theory of persistence of vision, in 1824, devices such as the Zoëtrope added a slotted viewfinder to the magic lantern, creating the same flickering illusion as the flipped edges of a book. With the addition of a set of flipping mirrors, the Praxinoscope created an even better illusion. By 1870, Henry R. Heyl had mounted a large number of glass-plate positive photos of drawings, with flipping mirrors to act as a shutter, and projected (with gaslight, the electric light being nine years away) the first animated motion pictures before an audience of 1,600 at the Philadelphia Academy of Music. He called his device the Phantasmatrope. Mostly, though, magic lanterns were to be found either in the parlors of wealthy gadget freaks or in penny arcades. They were thought of as small entertainments to be peered at by a limited number of people at a time.

Sound and movies were always meant to go together, at least by their American inventors. In 1888 Thomas Edison had finally come out with a commercial version of the phonograph he'd been working on since even before perfecting the carbon-filament electric light. He and assistant William K. L. Dickson had heard of Eadweard Muybridge's 1872 photographic studies of animals in motion, as well as the continuous projection, by the equestrian painter Meissonier in Paris in 1882, of the series of photographs of a horse race Muybridge had made in San Francisco in 1877. Edison wanted to attach a spiral strip of photographs to his sound cylinders, to project sound-synchronized motion. It didn't work, Edison tired of the project and turned it over to Dickson. Dickson worked with George Eastman (who had recently come out with the first Kodak camera) to provide strips of 35-millimeter celluloid film and perfected a camera and projector. His first Kinetoscope film was a talkie, with Dickson himself speaking. Soon Edison took most of the credit for the invention.

The movies were not solely an American creation, though animation seems to have been. William Friese-Greene may have invented movies in England in 1852, and Louis Leprince did so in France at about the same time as Dickson, but he and his designs disappeared mysteriously from a Paris-bound express train. Edison patented the Kinetoscope only in the United States, but within five years Kinetoscope peep shows were established all over the world. In many other countries people copied and improved on the Edison design; the most important of the improvements was the Lumiere brothers' Cinematographe. Through a loophole in patent law that Edison did not foresee, it was legal to show films made with these foreign cameras in America; through a lapse of his usually clear business sense, Edison viewed the Kinetoscope as proper only for peep shows, even while audiences flocked to projected programs in Europe. The Lumieres' films were shown at the very first permanent movie theater in 1896, in a wax museum at 55 West 23rd Street, New York City (an unmarked monument).

Edison's commercial oversight was lucky for animators, because his technical oversights made animation impossible with his Kinetoscope. The Lumieres' was a hand-cranked camera that easily converted to projecting the same film it had shot. Edison had a heavy investment in electricity and insisted that Dickson's invention be powered by electric motors. Since

Edison owned all patents for motion-picture manufacturing in the United States, no films could be made here legally without using an Edison-manufactured or licensed, electrically powered camera, and no motion pictures could be shown without using an electrically powered projector. This may seem like a good idea, considering the present reliability and ubiquity of electric motors, but early electrical motion-picture cameras were giant, immobile, balky devices. Single-framing was impossible with them, and single-framing was just what was needed to animate pictures. The Lumieres' camera was not only portable, it was far more reliable than Edison's. Though it took a practiced and talented arm to smoothly crank it at constant speed (Edison's electric cameras didn't move at nearly constant speed, either), it was not necessary to crank it for animation. The Lumieres' camera could be easily customized to single frame.

A.2 The Comics

Animation's beginnings may have been more closely related to the mass-circulation daily newspaper, an equally new entity in late-nineteenth-century America, than to live-action movies. In a time of many technological advances in printing, and also of the first tremendous growth spurt of the great northeastern cities, suddenly it became profitably possible for newspapers to distribute hundreds of thousands of copies. New York City, for example, had more than twenty dailies throughout the 1890s; the largest in circulation were flagships for the chains of Joseph Pulitzer and William Randolph Hearst. Between 1870 and 1900, total American newspaper circulation rose from 2.6 million to 15 million. It was a time of tremendous social unrest, too, and almost all papers of the day were as sensationalist as the worst of today's tabloids. Political cartooning had been a vitriolic feature of most American newspapers throughout the century; with unprecedented scandals to lampoon, unprecedentedly large readership that could barely read anything but cartoons, and publishers anxious to win circulation wars, the space given to political cartoons expanded, some became less political, and soon the first comic strips were born. Technology allowed the first strip to be printed in two colors. Appropriately, it was named "The Yellow Kid" (thus, "yellow journalism").

That the idea of motion pictures inspired the successive frames of the comic strip seems probable, but the only proof is the fascination movies held for many of the second generation of newspaper cartoonists, who came to the already established form in the mid-1890s. In 1895 J. Stuart

Blackton sold his first cartoon to the *New York World;* he would later found Vitagraph Pictures. In the 1890s Blackton gave "chalk talks," lectures during which he would quickly draw and partially redraw characters on a blackboard, making almost-animated stories. In 1906, *Humorous Phases of Funny Faces,* the filmed record of a Blackton chalk talk, became the closest thing yet to an animated film.

In 1897 Winsor McCay began working for the *Cincinnati Commercial Tribune,* and soon also began giving chalk talks on the vaudeville circuit. In 1911 he would make the first high-quality animated film, *Little Nemo.*

A.3 Special Effects

Things moved a little quicker in France, the movies' other birthplace. The different technology employed by the Lumieres was one reason why. The Lumieres' choice of subject matter — similar to that of many European live-action filmmakers — was another. In America, the movies began as a theatrical medium, because Edison's electrical camera was so big it could not be moved. Subject matter therefore had to come to the camera, and the first studio was built — a small, black-draped room nicknamed "Black Maria." With portable cameras, Europeans filmed the first documentaries. Audiences delighted to watch the most commonplace natural scenes projected in theaters (just as American audiences delighted in the most commonplace dramas). But the adaptable Lumiere camera also could be well used for what soon became known as "trick photography," and the emphasis on naturalism also brought about its own opposite when the magician Georges Méliès began to take an interest in the movies.

A.4 The Optical Printer

Most of the "Amazing New Technical Achievements" ever to be blazoned across a theater lobby had already been achieved by Méliès in a 1902 serial, *A Trip To The Moon.* Special effects thus began with science fiction in space. The subject matter, as well as the effects, have been improved in execution, but the repertory was not added to for a very long time. Méliès's chief invention was probably optical printing, and he also made some true animation, along with many old-fashioned sleight-of-hand-type effects. The first full animation was in the jerky movements of the outlined figures of Emile Cohl's 1909 film *Fantasmagorie.* Unfortunately, little information about this film survives.

More information survives about Méliès — chiefly, most of his films. Though he was as secretive about his processes as many magicians (including Cohl), the films betray most of their techniques of manufacture. But not all: it is not certain that Méliès ever actually *did* invent the optical printer; he may have done all of his effects in camera, on the original unexposed film. But whether or not he did invent the optical printer, his effects served the equal purpose of inspiring others to reinvent it.

Optical printing had been accomplished by the Lumieres almost as soon as they had made two cameras, but they did not realize its possibilities for effects. Basically, there are two ways to make a copy, or print of a film: contact printing and optical printing. To make a contact print, each frame of the original film is brought into physical contact with a frame of unexposed filmstock. A light shines through the original onto the new footage while it is in this brief contact; then the new footage is developed. To make an optical print, the process is essentially similar, with the all-important difference that the image on the original film is projected through a lens and the duplicate footage records a picture of the projected image through another lens. In other words, optical printing employs a camera aimed directly into a projector. The image thus filmed does not appear on any screen between the two, but only at a certain focal plane of air space: it is a so-called ''aerial image'' (another concept that would soon be important to animators).

Optical printing does not produce as clear a copy as contact printing can at its best, but it does allow various sorts of manipulations of the film image. For example, single frames may be shot of the original, the original may be played in reverse direction while copied, or multiple exposures may be made in the camera, all with precise knowledge of registration and exposure settings. Slightly out-of-focus shots can be brought back into focus, too, by focusing the camera at a different depth of the original. The common cinematic vocabulary of fades, dissolves, and superimpositions and the quaint, mostly obsolete vocabulary of wipes and irises are all made in the optical printer, and all were pioneered by Méliès. Most of these techniques he first performed totally in camera, by winding back film and superimposing another shot. By the later part of the *Moon* series, though, the complicated matting he used seems to imply an optical printer.

As perhaps the most interesting capability of optical printing, there is room for masks (known more commonly in the trade as ''mattes''), filters, and other images between the projector and camera sides of an optical printer. A stationary matte, in the form of a disk, would leave a completely unexposed circle in the middle of a duplicate film. In another pass through the printer, the circular matte could be replaced with its opposite, an iris covering the edges of the film, but leaving a circle open at the center. A different image could be used as the original, resulting in a final picture of two combined images. In Méliès' films, trains thus managed to charge through holes in tablecloths, along with other similar effects.

Méliès was an imaginative technician, but not much of an engineer or artist. It was for others to perfect his effects, both technically and aesthetically. Eastman Kodak's engineers came up with superior high-contrast monochromatic film that made possible the "traveling," or moving matte. Any normally filmed image of a moving object could be contact printed onto "high-con" stock. This copy could then be "bipacked," or sandwiched together with the original in the projector half of the optical printer. In a second camera pass the negative of the high-con image would be bipacked again with a totally different original, resulting in a composite image of the original moving object in a strange environment.

Spectacular trick images were made by Méliès and many followers in this way, but it wasn't until the Fleischer brothers' *Out of the Inkwell* series of animated films, in the late twenties, that anything with real aesthetic power was made of the technique. In these films the animator and his real world often appeared in the same screen space with Koko the Clown and Betty Boop, via optically printed mattes and an invention of the Fleischers' own, the Rotoscope.

Soon after Méliès invented it, the stationary iris matte was widely used by D. W. Griffith, who believed that the full scope of the screen should be used only for vast panoramas, and that intimate action should occupy smaller, matted portions of the screen. This is an aesthetic never much used by anyone since Griffith's day, but one that still might yield interesting further experimentation. Griffith's other habit of using irises, at beginnings and ends of scenes, was copied universally as part of film grammar, as a sort of sentimental cameo. But few filmmakers were able to invest it with nearly the image power Griffith could achieve, for instance, in a tight iris of a couple of frightened women that opens up to a wide battle scene. As the iris came to be a kitschy device, only Buster Keaton could think of a way to use it powerfully, by burning a hole in a tablecloth and letting the audience see the object of his love in a cameo iris made of the hole. This was in the 1926 *The General,* two decades after Méliès not only invented but technically perfected the process; it took almost as long for a few artists to figure out how to really use the technology as it did for most to forget about its once-shocking, now cliched, more vulgar appearances.

A.5 The Divergence of Shorts and Features

The film vocabulary that Griffith invented in live-action films in a few years, from his first one and two-reelers in 1909 through the first real feature film, the 1915 *Birth of a Nation,* would be as applicable to animation as to live action. In two key respects, however, Griffith's inventions affected animation very differently.

One involved the way Griffith was able to invest an inanimate object with what he called "character." In the 1911 *The Lonedale Operator,* Blanche Sweet holds two crooks captive with what they and the audience think is a gun. At the right dramatic moment, a close-up tells the audience that Blanche only holds a monkey wrench. Arthur Knight says, in his very popular *The Liveliest Art* (Mentor, 1959), "Griffith discovered [how] . . . to make *things* a dynamic part of the world through which actors move." Very soon, animators would come to make far more use of this discovery than live-action filmmakers ever have.

The commercial success of Griffith's megalomania would have an indirect effect on animation. The length of a motion picture reel had been fixed by the Edison patent-licensees' trust at ten to twelve minutes, because they assumed nobody would ever be interested in films longer than this. The first two-reeler, Griffith's 1911 *Enoch Arden,* was released as two separate films. Audiences demanded that projectionists show the two together, and in a year two reels became the standard length for "serious" films. Light comedy remained standardized at one reel. Griffith went to California and to other companies to be able to make longer and longer films, each very successful with audiences. Feature-length films were fully established by the three-hour *Birth of a Nation* and four-hour *Intolerance.* Approximately ninety-minute versions of each were most popularly seen, and this very quickly became a standard feature-film length. Comedies continued to be made as short subjects. For a long time, no animator would be able to amass the resources for a feature film; its laborious manufacture always has made animation something taken in small doses. The movie industry's quick split, right at the time of animation's birth, between long serious features and comedy shorts made a readily acceptable spot for distributing animation. This paired animated films with the live-action shorts of the great silent comedians, whose pratfalls were much like those of animated characters.

Both Griffith and Méliès were bypassed by the subsequent histories of their own creations. Though the creations of each were essential to subsequent filmmakers, the ways they thought to use their own inventions were stuck in the very nineteenth-century theatrical forms they had made outmoded. Each's decline was pitiable, but Méliès's was worse, a first major demonstration that animators lead more dangerous lives than live-action filmmakers. He had sold the rights to his films the only way he could, for a small fee per foot. Whoever bought them could make as many copies as they liked; by the end of his life Méliès was a pauper running a Paris newsstand.

A.6 Winsor McCay's Achievement

Back to chronology: At the same time that Griffith and William S. Porter were inventing the modern feature film out of the Biograph Studios in New York's Union Square, Winsor McCay had become very successful drawing the *Little Nemo In Slumberland* comic strip for the *New York Herald.* John R. Bray and Max Fleischer were both working in the art department of the *Brooklyn Eagle.* Other soon-to-be-famous animators were drawing comic strips across America. With McCay's *Little Nemo,* the 1912 *How a Mosquito Operates,* and in 1914 *Gertie the Dinosaur,* the animated film became a sensation. Gertie and Charlie Chaplin were the major new stars of 1914, and they had a fair amount in common.

Nemo, the eponymous Mosquito, and Gertie all were made in basically the same way. McCay knew that registration — locking each image into the same position to reduce jitter — was the most important problem to be solved. Each picture was drawn on translucent rice paper, so that crosses drawn in the corners of each could be matched against crosses printed on identical nine-inch-square mounting boards. The left and bottom sides of each board were cut to a precise ninety-degree angle and fitted into a wooden frame in front of a horizontal camera. Before being photographed, drawings were checked again and again for smooth movement.

Little Nemo included the first use of what animators call a "cycle," which might be more commonly thought of as a recycling of a series of drawings. In a series depicting the motion of a character chomping on a cigar to flip it from horizontal to near-vertical position, the same seven drawings are repeated six times, in both forward and reverse motion, to create three complete up-and-down movements of the cigar. The next films made extensive use of this technique, which not only made the greatest possible use of the drawings, but was also entertaining in its very repetitiveness. Gertie's way of rearing up on her hind legs while wiggling her brontosaurus body was the forerunner of many wiggles to come, from Betty Boop to Mickey Mouse to Bugs Bunny and every other loved cartoon character on up to Fritz the Cat.

McCay's work established many of the standard elements to blend into most future animation: sight gags and satire (McCay's was very gentle), silly-putty bodies and, perhaps most significant, animal anthropomorphism. (Rough-house comedy, very much a standard of most animation concurrent with and after McCay, is conspicuous by its absence in his work.) Popular conceptions of the characters of animals have been formed, ever since Gertie (who, being technically extinct, *only* could be visualized through animation), more by animation than from any other source. Is it because "animation" and "animal" are words with so much in common that one should so often have become the subject of the other? Perhaps it is more that the process of giving character to motionless images is an analog for anthropomorphism, or maybe animation's principal audience of children is also the principal audience for animal stories. Gertie's audience, however, was no more made of children than the cartoonish exploits of the contemporary Keystone Kops and Chaplin shorts. That this was the dominant sort of film when animation emerged, and that live-action movies mostly moved on to other subjects while animation grew to be more and more for children, is surely also significant.

Little Nemo was also the first color animated film; McCay hand-colored at least one print, by painting on each frame of the film surface itself as was common in the silent movie era. His color palette was not typical of hand-painted live-action movies; it was the same as the colors McCay used in his comic strips.

Smooth, very small and natural changes from one frame to the next were perhaps McCay's greatest technical accomplishment. He shot single frames of each drawing and made some attempt at making movements naturalistic —movements would begin slowly, accelerate, then slow down. From a computerized culture's point of view, McCay's accomplishment is indeed very large: his animation represents the first time any natural movements of any kind that take place over time were consciously re-created from a digital sample. Muybridge's studies of the movements of horses, preceding the invention of motion pictures, did the opposite of this, in his concept of breaking living movement into component static images. It was for McCay, far more than previous animators, not merely to imitate projection of captured live images with drawings, but to begin (an intuitive, subjective, artistic, but nonetheless beginning) analysis of how characters move. Among animators he was first to notice that when one part of a body moves one way, another part moves a different way, and each movement accelerates and decelerates.

A few other animators made these discoveries soon after, and probably did so independently (lending some backing to the "it's in the air" theory of the history of discovery). Wallace Carlson's animation, beginning in

1915, made the first full use of dramatically changing pseudocamera angles; Paul Terry's work, beginning in 1916, was even more advanced in some ways than McCay's; the work of the Fleischer brothers will be described in more depth below. All of these animators began, as McCay did, with newsprint cartoons.

A.7 The Factory System Comes to Animation

Registration — locking those drawings to be filmed rock steady — was essential for movements as fine as McCay imagined could be made. McCay's own registration system was good, but it was slow and involved some imprecision. Another essential for character animation as fine as McCay desired was a factory system; if many similar drawings could be held in precise register, then many animators and illustrators could share the tedious work of making repetitive images. The goal of quantity, however, was a more important spur than quality toward standardized drawings by platoons of illustrators. The first fortunes were being made in live-action movies by producers who had moved to Hollywood to be far from the enforcement of the Edison patent licensees. It was the moment when Henry Ford was conceiving the assembly line for making automobiles, and if only animation's parts could be standardized — if its pictures could be registered precisely — then it, too, could be made on an assembly line.

Raoul Barrè had been publishing comics about rural Quebec since 1901, and in 1913 he both invented the method of registration that would dominate animation until the computer and established the first large studio to make animation in quantity. Holes were punched in all paper to be used for drawing, and the paper was mounted on pegs; as long as the holes were the right size and distance apart, the image would be perfectly registered.

Soon John R. Bray also established an animation studio, making a comparatively crude product. But Bray was very sophisticated in ways other animators weren't; he was the first to patent many animation techniques, even though he had invented practically none of them. One important Bray concept (and a patented one, of course), was to print many copies of drawings to be used as backgrounds. Another was to attach solid cut-outs to the backs of drawings, which developed into yet another (this time original) patent, for cut-out animation: shooting a frame of a cut-out figure, moving it, shooting another frame, moving it again, single framing again. "Single frame" is a misnomer in Bray's case: his company's animation was characterized by many, many duplicate frames, long pauses in action, and jerky movements. At least ten images per second are necessary for persistence of vision; Bray's films often did not provide that.

The heart of Bray's process was to have artists draw foreground characters directly on prebackgrounded forms. From here it was only a slight leap of the imagination (assuming he knew about Bray's process from the patents, which is probable, but unknown) for Earl Hurd, a cartoonist in Kansas City, to come up with the basics of the cel animation process, which he promptly patented. Hurd soon went to work as an animator for Bray Studios.

A.8 Cel Animation

''Cel'' stands for celluloid. In the cel process, parts of complete images are drawn on transparent sheets. Each is registered by holes onto the pegs of the animation stand. Thus characters may move without disturbing backgrounds, or backgrounds may vary by scrolling to one side as characters move. Only what moves in each frame must be drawn anew.

By 1916 both Bray's studio and Barrè's were making a cartoon a week. In 1917, Bray and Hurd combined their patents into the Bray Hurd Company and promptly filed suit for patent infringement against Winsor McCay and others from whom Bray may or may not have stolen ideas. Subsequently, every animator had to pay licensing fees to Bray Hurd, a profit source that would eventually make that company far wealthier than Bray Studios' uninspired animation ever could.

Bray brought two other trends to animation. One, soon to extend not only to Walt Disney but to many a live-action film producer, too, was shameless self-promotion. His signature appeared on films in very large-face type:

An Animated Film by
J.R. BRAY,
THE FAMOUS CARTOONIST

Bray Studios' most popular cartoon series was built around the character Colonel Heeza Liar. As the beginning of an alliance between animation and military training that would eventually blossom with computer flight simulators, Colonel Heeza Liar starred in several World War I training films. This sort of product became the staple of the Bray Studios as it continued in operation into the 1970s.

Winsor McCay, disheartened by being sued for infringing on processes he'd invented, and perhaps by the concentration of business interests in what was to him an art, made only a few more, progressively half-hearted films. He then concentrated on his comic strip work from the twenties onward. After he died in 1934, most of his films were thought lost, until they were discovered in an advanced state of decay in a friend's garage in 1947. It took twenty years to restore them, upon which they became the highlight of the Animation Symposium at Montreal's Expo '67.

A.9 Rotoscope

The next great invention in animation's progress was in 1915, almost simultaneous with Bray's and Hurd's advances, but technically much more complicated. In fact, many animators have always insisted that "rotoscoping" is not animation at all. Named and patented by Max and Dave Fleischer, rotoscoping is the process of projecting live-action film frame by frame to trace drawings from it. The drawings can then be reworked in various ways and rephotographed, and even combined with live action, which became a Fleischer specialty.

The invention of rotoscope would prefigure the beginnings of many personal-computer companies sixty years later. Max Fleischer was art editor at *Popular Science* and loved gadgets. In an unpublished autobiography on record at the Film Study Center of the Museum of Modern Art he wrote, "I used up every cent I had on the machine—about $100. . . . We built the machine, but we had nowhere to work it, so our missus said we could use the living room, if we didn't upset it too much. . . . We did make the room look very bad, I guess. We had electric wires from the chandeliers, motors, etc."[1]

A.10 The Fleischers and Walt Disney

From the Fleischers' first films, *Tantalizing Fly* and *Clown's Little Brother,* the quality and cleverness were evident that would lead, in a decade, to

---

[1]I am indebted for this to Conrad Smith's *The Early History of Animation,* New York, 1975, where it appears on page 6. For complete references to this and other works on the early era of animation, see the Bibliography.

the greatest of black-and-white cartoons and at least one of the movies' greatest animated or live characters: Betty Boop. First Max Fleischer would learn every aspect of the animation business by going to work for John Bray.

The Fleischers' *Out of the Inkwell* series became the most popular animation of the twenties, and Betty Boop captured the spirit of the age as few animated characters ever have. The series' wit and artistry seem today to be the essence of the legendary spirit of their time — as few other parts of that legend could probably match on closer scrutiny. The spirit of the next age would also be embodied in one major character who led an orchestra of effects fully competitive with the Fleischers', even in 1928, when the Fleischers' sound effects, far and away the best of the early sound era, were raising Betty to new heights of stardom. The star of *Steamboat Willie* would soon surpass every other animated character in public affection; his name was Mickey Mouse.

When Mickey first appeared, he was an anarchic character like Koko the Clown and Betty Boop. Though nowhere near as sexy as Betty, he was not yet the virgin he later became. Mickey got involved in off-color gags worthy of contemporaries like the Marx Brothers, Chaplin, and Betty, but Mickey began to grow more wholesome even before the increased censorship of the 1930s enforced the moral fiber of Hollywood.

The Hays Office (a voluntary association of film producers that, like the Motion Picture Association of America ratings system in force since the sixties, self-censored to avoid a threat of external censorship) has gotten most of the credit for the movies' change in morality. The Hays Office was established in response to scandals of the early twenties, but its code only got tough in the thirties. Actually, it was only a part of Hollywood's self-censoring reaction to the country's increasing conservatism in matters nonpolitical, caused by hard economic times. Walt Disney sensed this public change more quickly than most filmmakers, partly due to his own innate conservatism, and partly due to his business conviction that cartoons ought to be aimed toward family audiences, as opposed to the Fleischers' more cosmopolitan directions. When Mickey Mouse cartoons started to grow more prudish and also more oriented toward children, it served to accentuate Betty Boop's sinfulness as it increased Disney's coffers. Betty became the subject of censorship campaigns, and the Fleischers modulated her morals a bit as she continued through the thirties, but the damage was done — her moment was over. High-living cartoon flappers could not be so easily identified with anymore, though in live action they continued (under a new label, "golddigger," purged of its pejorative), while tending to get married more often.

In more ways than the above, the Fleischer–Disney competition was an archetype for animation's and the movies' mass–class dichotomy. "Class" in cartoons takes some defining, since the animation medium was long reviled as even lower brow than the movies as a whole. Disney's inflated attempts at high-brow culture were one of the very inspirations of Dwight MacDonald's definition of the term "middle-brow." To use Susan Sontag's terminology, Betty Boop could be camp, but Mickey Mouse was only kitsch. In more common terms, the Fleischers assumed their audience to be capable of understanding irony, satire, and double meanings. While the early films show Disney quite capable of appreciating all of the above, he quickly decided that these were not for the masses. By the proof of his commercial success, he was right.

Disney's commercial success allowed him to build the largest pool of animators and illustrators yet — and eventually, ever — assembled; to make the first color animation, in the early thirties; to pay for the technical experimentation that went into highly improved animation devices; and to make the first — and for decades the only — feature-length animation. Not only the subject matter of his films, but the way he used profits to build an unrivaled arts–technology studio axis, set the precedent for the Lucasfilm animation–effects juggernaut of our time.

A.11 Disney's Competitors

Disney's competition was significant, even as the Fleischers' competitiveness waned. Warner Brothers, Columbia, and Metro–Goldwyn–Mayer recognized the value of producing their own animated short subjects, especially as expanding feature production and radio (and later television) soaked up live-action two-reel comedy talent into more lucrative genres. (By the middle thirties, only the lowest of comedy acts, such as the Three Stooges, continued to make short subjects.) The majors also had their own distribution systems, which Disney never achieved. They could count on profitably releasing and shipping shorts along with features, while animation became the surest way to supply the shorts.

In the beginning of the thirties, Warner was the major studio most likely to take chances (they had gone from near bankruptcy to vast success with *The Jazz Singer,* and would produce most of the films that realistically dealt with the Great Depression), and they took a chance on a couple of disgruntled Disney employees: Hugh Harman and Rudolf Ising. Together their names spelled "Harman–Ising," and they created the *Looney Tunes* and *Merrie Melodies* series for Warner before leaving to start similar traditions at M–G–M in 1934. Director Tex Avery came to Warner Brothers two years later; he trained Chuck Jones and Bob Clampett to be his animators, and together with Isidore ''Friz'' Freleng and others, they created Bugs Bunny and friends as the chief alternative to Mickey, Donald, and the Disney ensemble.

The styles of these competitors were more rough-house than Disney's, more hard-boiled and less sentimental. In a comparison far too simple by way of gross unfairness to Chaplin, it is often considered that Disney mined the Chaplin tradition of comedy, while the competition derived more from Buster Keaton. The Warner cartoons in particular, but also often M–G–M's, tended to be wittier, more often adult-oriented than Disney's, and were often imbued with a sense of satirical social consciousness that was entirely lacking in the Disney product. Stylistically and in content the opposite pole to Disney was at Warner, and others were located on a continuum somewhere in between. Despite this opposition, neither Warner's nor anybody else's animation was in any sense a continuation of the Fleischers' style or content; if anything, for several years Disney's style remained close to the Fleischers', until his characters fattened up and got ever cuter. *Out of the Inkwell* was sophisticated froth that no one would ever match, but *Looney Tunes* and *Merrie Melodies,* particularly after Avery and Jones came aboard, defined an angular, hard but surreal style which, along with their content, seemed very much of a piece with Warner's gangster and detective live-action genres. (Proving the lie of that common Chaplin/Keaton comparison, one might imagine Bugs Bunny or Road Runner with the subject matter of *Modern Times* or *The Great Dictator* much more easily than Mickey, Donald, Bambi, or Dumbo, but given the character of Hollywood in the forties and fifties, the Warner characters were never allowed quite this close to relevance, either.)

A.12 Technical Innovations

Despite Disney's increasingly syrupy content, the technical contributions of all the great animation studios of the thirties through the fifties headed in the same directions, with Disney indisputably in the lead.

The use of color was an area in which Disney led the way for animation as well as live action. Not only did Disney make use of color in quantity sooner than other filmmakers, the way he used it was special. Disney's artists (just who came up with various Disney innovations is often unclear, or at least unknown to this writer; new evidence would be welcome) quickly realized that there must be some unifying order to color in a scene. Good guys would have their dominant color themes, which would extend to their belongings and natural surroundings. Bad guys would have theirs, too. Tonal ranges would complement and clash just as did the themes they depicted. Obvious though this may seem, it is still usually not the case with most live-action films and is only slightly more often the case with animation.

Unity of picture and sound became a hallmark of a Disney film. By all accounts Walt Disney conceived of music and other sound scoring first in his earliest sound films, then matched action to the soundtrack. This extended soon to completely scripting all sound, including dialog, before any drawings were made. Disney characters often were shown in close-up, with lip movements perfectly matched to dialog; this is the one technical area where competitors rarely even tried to match Disney's quality. In the use of color and general inventiveness with sound, though, Warner, Columbia, and M-G-M took no back seats, and all of the major animation makers of those golden days shot at most single or double frames of every position, utilizing three cel layers on the animation table.

A.13 The Animation Stand

The three (and sometimes more) cel system was and is the standard for traditional animation. The animation stand would be arranged around a vertical axis, with the camera mounted on a tall column, facing down. The camera would use as highly accurate registration as possible, usually a 35 mm Mitchell. Even today some of these 50-year-old cameras are in daily use. The traditional animation stand is certainly still in use. To go on describing it: A leveling system makes sure the film plane of the camera is perfectly parallel to the tabletop. A precisely calibrated, sprocketed wheel moves the camera up and down. The top-level cel fits on a set of registration pins over a removable (either transparent or frosted) glass portion of the tabletop; with many holes and many or movable pins, it is possible to simulate live-action pans by precisely shifting the cel slightly for a series of still frames. The second cel rests on an exactly similar level below the tabletop. The third level holds a pan or scroll cel — a horizontally longer cel meant to hold the often-panned backgrounds of a scene. Frosted glass is usually used beneath the pan cel.

The table can be either bottom lit or top lit, for very different looks. In bottom-lit animation lights shine up from below the pan cel, shining through the drawings to give filmed images a bright luminous glow. A more natural look may be achieved with top-lit work, with lights situated to either side of and above each level. But top lighting is more difficult to control, so most cel animation is bottom lit.

More complex animation stands allow for aerial imaging, in which a projected motion picture or still frame is focused, from below, directly into the focal plane of the camera. That image may be combined with drawings on cels.

The three levels of cels in the animation stand, when exploited best, can give a complete illusion of three-dimensionality. Foreground objects can not only pass in front of background objects, but parts of foreground objects can, with proper planning and execution, be made to disappear behind occluding parts of the same object, as that object is split between cels. These are achievements that are difficult in computer animation, too.

A.14 Aesthetics of Hollywood Animation

The great Disney features — *Snow White and the Seven Dwarfs* (1937), *Fantasia* (1940), *Pinocchio* (1940) *Dumbo* (1941) etc. — did more than anything else to cumulatively reverse animation's low-brow image in the popular mind. Individual characters in those and other films may have been even more important in this change; the pathos and personability of a Jiminy Cricket could not be denied. Disney Studios sponsored art classes in Hollywood, beginning in 1932, that came to be seen as more prestigious and seminal as time went on. Theorists of animation, inside and outside Disney's organization, learned to think of animation not as a process of making drawings move, but of drawing movements.

''Character animation'' is the most important term to come into use at this time. Animators and theorists used it to mean a visualization of the character as a symbol of its style of movement, and the style of movement as symbolic of the interior forces of character conceptualized by the artist for that character. Dumbo or Pinocchio could be characters, and so could a tree. These were extensions of Griffith's ideas for all characters in motion pictures, but the sort of extensions that could be realized only with the art of animation.

This way of looking at character and movement was as much responsible for animation's golden age in Hollywood as technology or the army of animators that could be employed for a few dollars a week. Technology would advance, the army of workers would occasionally be reunited, but no comparable animation would or can ever be made without similar ideas.

A.15 Special Effects in Live-Action Feature Films

The tradition of optical effects that began with Méliès continued for a few years in France, notably in a few films by Abel Gance and René Clair. Gance used the optical printer to superimpose up to a hundred images and pioneered split screens (made with stationary mattes), painted stationary mattes, and various odd ways to move the camera. Clair's films broke no new technical ground, but, like Keaton's use of the iris, used effects with artistic vision. Painted stationary mattes, positioned directly in front of the camera while it filmed a live-action scene, accounted for most French special-optical-effect work in the next few decades, and they were a mainstay of effects in other countries as well.

Through the twenties and early thirties, effects work in the major filmmaking centers of the U.S., Britain, Germany, France, and the U.S.S.R was known more for different national (and certainly, individual) styles than for different technical achievements. Stationary matte work in Hollywood, England, and France tended toward lush, romantic scenes, and after a period of strong expressionism, so did the design work in Germany. Filmmakers in Hollywood and Moscow had some attitudes in common (surprising as that may seem, given antipathetic subject matter), in particular a desire to go out of doors and make movies that moved. The next major technical advance, rear projection, while invented in Hollywood, was put to use very quickly in the Soviet Union. Rear projection is a way to place actors in a scene that might be difficult or too expensive to film — in a traveling car, for one very common example. Actors would do their scene in a stationary, slightly rocking car in a studio, with a screen behind them. A film of the open road would be projected onto this screen from behind and filmed again as part of the whole scene. Rear-projected material looks much worse than the rest of the composite picture and is always readily apparent to the knowing viewer. These days it looks cheap; in those days it was the best that could be done, and was basically used for backgrounds, anyway.

From 1927 through the thirties, most of the film industry's investments in technical improvements went into advancing sound quality, and into color film. The erstwhile documentarian Dziga Vertov achieved visionary images with the optical effects in *The Man With The Movie Camera* (1929), but like Keaton's aforementioned artistic perfection of already invented devices, no really new technology was put to use. In the thirties the British film labs solidified their reputation for the world's highest black-and-white quality, helped along by the inability of British producers to afford color. The war cut back even on advances in color, while Eastman Kodak provided the compensatory advances of the smoothest black and white stocks ever produced, with fine grain that would be put to very good use in better traveling mattes.

Before the war, Hollywood optical effects experimenters had discovered that more effective traveling mattes could be made by shooting the original matte-positive subject against a blue screen. Because all film tends to be more sensitive to blue, the fine-grain panchromatic negative resulting from shooting the subject against a blue screen would achieve the highest possible outline detailing of the subject. When high-contrast negatives and positives are printed from the original, detail is preserved as much as possible. Even so, no matte is perfect, and with aerial-imaging animation stands becoming available, special effects makers were able to adjust mattes by hand, frame by frame. The matte quality thus attained in 1938's *Bringing Up Baby* (whenever ''Baby'' appeared with the stars, it was a matte) was a real advance, and technique improved even more with better filmstocks.

The next major spur to film special effects was the commercial advent of television. To keep audiences coming into the theaters, moviemakers expanded the difference between their product and that available on little blue-and-white screens at home. Color began its real takeover of most feature production in the fifties, and the various wide-screen, stereo-image 3D (with those absurd cardboard sunglasses), and stereo sound processes came in then, too. As part of this wave of technical improvements came the first films to emphasize special effects as a major part of their subject matter since the time of the First World War.

The films of George Pal in particular stand out in this era, in which filmmakers worked equivalent special-effects magic with Greek, Roman, and biblical myth, as well as classic science fiction. Big myths and big effects have been associated in the minds of audiences and filmmakers ever since. Pal wasn't alone or even particularly original: Cecil B. DeMille's remake of his own silent, *The Ten Commandments,* and William Wyler's remake of the silent *Ben Hur* were also part of this trend. DeMille's career was the exemplary Hollywood one of always hopping onto a trend and making pedestrian but ''spectacular'' creations a la mode. The big effects in the originals of these biblical remakes had most of what Pal put into his films, and those originals were copies of other effects films before! But Pal's movies were lively, unabashedly low-brow, and made for children, where his far-more-distinguished competitors aimed their deadwood efforts so much higher. Perhaps more significant, Pal's main subject matter was glorification of fancy machinery; this preoccupation of special effects movies has come back in force.

In *The Time Machine,* probably Pal's most memorable, the machine is the central idea of the movie. The evolutionary consequences of a rigid class system was H. G. Wells's chief concern in the novel, and this almost disappears in the film; to my knowledge there has been no room for any such concern in any big studio special-effects movies since Pal's, either.

A few makers of low-budget black and white science-fiction films shared Pal's lively way of matching myth with gadgetry and were just as formative for the generation of filmmakers that would rise in the mid-seventies to unite computer effects with mythic subject matter. But the strings and rubber bands tend to show in most of the "B" movie effects; their subject was influential, even as their technology was so laughably low as to be inspirational, too, on other levels. (Fond parodies of these films have been a rich comedic genre for the eighties.)

It was in the fifties that animation and optical effects were first united on a regular basis to attain special-effects objectives in feature films. While no new technical ground was broken in Pal's movies, for example, a goodly amount of animation was mixed in with optical effects to achieve his visual goals. Animation also made an appearance in a dream sequence in one of the greatest feature films of the era: Alfred Hitchcock's *Vertigo.* Opticals were common in the big-budget art films of George Stevens (*Shane, Duel in the Sun, Giant*), and were made so superbly that even practiced eyes have a hard time finding any tell-tale matte lines.

If movies were to be a spectacle that could lure viewers away from their free-TV viewing habits, the stops would have to be pulled out. In the fifties and beyond, any contribution animation or special effects could make to a film became an increasingly "bankable element," in Hollywood terminology; movie budgets would rise accordingly, and pay for a great deal of computer research in the process.

Computer animation would remain too crude for feature films, though, through the decade that began with George Pal's *The Time Machine* and ended soon after Stanley Kubrick's *2001: A Space Odyssey.* Producers and directors of the average large-scale modern film extravaganza are more typically inspirational than instrumental toward the creation of new technology for their films, but Kubrick himself is credited with conceiving the next major special-effects invention: front projection. This is an ingenious way to attain the goal of rear projection, but without the usual resolution loss that older method entails.

Carrying out Kubrick's concept on this and other effects in the film (*2001*) was Douglas Trumbull, who would become known, through such films as *Silent Running* and *Close Encounters of the Third Kind,* as the first great special-effects wizard of the next decade. A multiyear project of Trumbull's in the eighties was Show-Scan, a sort of special effect that takes advantage of better projection machinery to show film at sixty frames per second, for a heightened sense of realism. Trumbull's *Brainstorm,* the first feature meant to show off Show-Scan, failed for other reasons. (Star Natalie Wood died during production, and perhaps the film would not have been successful anyway; presenting an almost physically painful sensation of death, it was strong stuff in a season of kiddie sci-fi competitors.) No prints in the process were released, so the jury is still out on the technique. *Brainstorm* retains interest as a study of the image-making technologist's relationship with society. Show-Scan may retain interest as the last major special-effects technique devised that has nothing necessarily to do with a computer.

Computer effects have not only taken over the terrain of optical effects and animation, they have also stolen some thunder from other kinds of effects. Long Hollywood traditions of make-up and miniature-model effects reached their noncomputerized heights in the seventies. While both traditions will certainly continue for the foreseeable future, they will be ever more often combined with computer realization of equivalent effects.

A.16 Television

The advent of commercial television in the fifties not only meant great change for animation and effects in the movies, it opened up two vast new markets for animation and spurred the development of a new kind of special effects. The new markets were children's cartoons and all sorts of commercials; they opened up almost immediately with the first broadcasters. Analog video effects came on-stream in the middle sixties, first for news and sports programming and later, increasingly in digital form, for all sorts of programs.

Saturday-morning cartoons were first seen as the greatest boon imaginable to animation, and soon came to be seen by animators as the death of animation. Even at its rosy beginning, work done for children's TV shows did not pay as well as the major movie studios' animation departments, but the TV shows represented an ancillary market for the product of those major studios' animation departments, helping to keep employment and output high even as the theatrical market for animated short films began to dry up.

Theatrical markets were being lost to animation because since the forties, when the major studios lost the legal right to own their own theater chains in a Federal antitrust suit, independent distributors and theater owners found it increasingly unprofitable to handle short subjects. In the sixties, as average feature length standardized at just under two hours and audiences didn't mind not seeing a short, shorts (most of which were animated by then) ceased to be seen in theaters, as did another relic of the past, first-run double features.

The ubiquitous Saturday-morning film programs at neighborhood and small-town movie theaters consisted of exactly the sort of films that were becoming less profitable — shorts and "B" double features — even as the new TV broadcasters programmed to children at the same time period. This author's late-fifties childhood was one of the last in America to be punctuated every Saturday morning by twenty-five-cent programs at a movie theater. Increasingly, the major studios' animation departments existed to sell programming to television. Their competition in this business grew, and new animation studios also originated to address this market. The competition grew more quickly than the market, and after beginning with fairly high-quality work, that of the newer studios deteriorated and the older "major" animation studios disbanded. Children's TV was (and is) a ghetto to which adults paid little attention, and as long as sponsors continued to pay the bills with equanimity, programming quality kept deteriorating. By the seventies and eighties, it was as if Winsor McCay, the Fleischers, Walt Disney, Chuck Jones, et al. had never existed; children's-TV animation was generally at the level of the early work of J. R. Bray, and if anything, that's an insult to Bray.

A.17 X-Rated Cartoons

Only one product (thus far) of the purveyors of cheap animation to Saturday morning has managed to advance the art of animation. Ralph Bakshi found himself head of production at a couple of these studios at a very young age, in the middle sixties, and quickly became dissatisfied with the product he had to turn out. Not particularly dedicated to the great animation of two and three decades before, he could see no way to make that sort of product in his own era and could see no way to make it relevant to his time even if it could be made. As happened at the beginning of the century, inspiration came from newsprint comics, this time from the "underground" cartoonists of the sixties counterculture. Bakshi made heavy use of rotoscoping to attain as high quality as he could within a limited budget (and his was far better, technically, than most animation of the time) to produce the first X-rated cartoon, *Fritz The Cat.* In features that followed, like *Heavy Traffic* and *Coonskin,* Bakshi managed to offend practically everyone who had no sense of humor. After the first two features' success, *Coonskin,* Bakshi's strongest social commentary yet, engendered such charges of racism (in this author's and many other opinions, it was one of the more honest statements of its time *against* racism) that it was never fully released. Bakshi retreated to the overblown mythology of *The Lord of the Rings,* followed by sugary children's tales, all worse than the worst of Disney's kitsch. Perhaps this fine creative talent will be emboldened again soon.

A.18 TV Commercials

As much as TV programming might be blamed for a crass commercialism that is responsible for the worst animation of all time, TV commercials have shown some of the best-quality animation of our time. Tex Avery, Chuck Jones, and their peers went from animating Bugs Bunny to the bugs in the Raid commercials, to Charlie the Tuna (always rejected by Star-Kist), and hundreds of other, less often seen characters. Sometimes, as in the above examples, the aesthetics of force and character and just plain fun were part of these ad campaigns, and sometimes just the classic animation technology was drawn upon; but it is surprisingly rare to be able to think back upon really bad animation in TV commercials. Advertising-agency art directors have known the sort of quality they seek, and have often been able to persuade their employers and clients to pay for it. Two whole generations of animators with very high ideals of quality have now grown up to serve those advertising needs, the first devoted to old-fashioned character animation, the second computerized.

A.19 Video Effects

Though video-effects machines started to be used for sports and news programs in the late sixties, not much art worth speaking of was involved until they spread to the few commercials made on video in the early seventies; instant replays and weather maps were the heights of artistic creation in the form. When Lee Harrison's analog Scanimate and Caesar systems came out of Computer Image in Denver, much more creative uses suddenly opened up. Many competitors quickly arose, because the technology was not difficult. Devices such as these distort the video image in a more or less limited number of ways, and came to be widely used by advertising agencies and the producers who made their commercials, for animatics as well as small bits in completed commercials. Video artists (Nam June Paik quickly became the most famous) thought up some seminal tricks, which were soon imitated in relatively uninspired ways for commercial uses.

Digital video-effects devices arose in the middle seventies as a continuation of the need for more versatile tricks. As the available repertory expanded, effects devices came to be used for traditional-style matte-making, as well as newer tricks, in a great many TV programs and music videos. The rise of the music video would have been very different, if not impossible, without these machines. Their availability also served to hasten the coming of many programs produced entirely on video, instead of film. Within ten years it would become rare to find any half-hour of made-on-video programming without any effects by Ultimatte, Dubner CBG, Bosch Fernseh FGS-4000, Chyron, MCI Quantel, etc. In every production company making such programming, animators came to be needed to do more than merely operate the devices — to make something creative out of them. ''Operators'' is, however, what these video-effects designers or animators are most often called and, unfortunately, thought of. That the most creative of all of this video-effects work is most commonly seen on independent productions for cable (like Shelley Duval's ''Fairie Tale Theatre''), or in music videos and low-budget commercials (like Charlex's work; see Chapter 12) continues to say a great deal about the experimental nature of the broadcasting business.

A.20 The Experimentalists

Filmmaking is expensive, whether animation or live action, but the expense of animation can be borne by one independent creator, as it consists chiefly of time and tedious labor. For live action one needs action to film, which has tended to make filmmaking a cooperative, corporate art. At the height of the giant animation studio as epitomized by Disney, it was probably true that anybody with the talent to be an animator could get some sort of job in that highly labor-intensive industry. But not every animator wants to move to Hollywood to work.

Probably the most distinguished animator who never moved to Hollywood has been Norman McLaren, the Canadian pioneer of abstract animated forms both filmed from drawings and drawn directly on film. His wonderful, colorful, jittery, and bouncy images certainly had more in common with the postwar New York school of abstract expressionist painters than with any other animation previous or concurrent.

Besides McLaren and those influenced by him, from the twenties until the sixties, the independent filmmaking tradition followed two schools: the documentarists, who do not concern us, and the surrealists. One gets the feeling, seeing almost any surrealist film from those decades, that the creators would have loved to include special optical effects and animation, if only they could afford them or knew how to make them. One that included limited animation was the more celebrated than cerebrated *Dreams That Money Can Buy,* directed by Hans Richter and made cooperatively with several noted art-world figures.

McLaren was the first prominent representative of various other artistic ideologies to make animation or special-effects experimental film. The very name "experimental film" only came about in the sixties, as experimentalists, structuralists, and artists with varied other ideologies came to make animated or optical effects films. "Experimental" as a catch-all can include those with no guiding ideas, too.

Technology was the greatest spur to all of this. The same portable, inexpensive 16 mm cameras and tape recorders that made possible new live-action film techniques also were the first generation of 16 mm cameras that allowed single-framing, and thus animation. Kits soon became available to customize some of these cameras into optical printers, and computer animation attracted its first, mostly mathematically oriented experimenters in the early sixties, too.

The general affluence of the times was a lesser spur, but not an insignificant one. A college-educated baby boom meant academic support for noncommercial films, and later for video. If only the volume of product churned out of the universities had not been more than matched by the decline of the Hollywood animation industry, this might have turned into a true golden age of animation. As it has turned out, traditional animators working alone or in small groups, typically supported by grants or as part of academic careers, have created a great deal of animation, but not a great deal of high-quality animation. The technical limitations have been large, even where animators have been able to work with adequate equipment: all those drawings, all those drawings . . .

Yet this is where most of the present generation of animators comes from. The best put a "Studios" or "Productions" after their names and support themselves on TV commercials and industrial films while making masterpieces in odd hours.

On the academic special-effects front, there is certainly no way for an individual working with a 16 mm home-made optical printer to do anything to advance the state of technology or practice. Many young experimental filmmakers have, however, been able to prove themselves sufficiently to move into the burgeoning special-effects industry of the seventies and eighties. Also, a few doggedly noncommercial filmmakers have made optical-effects films that have given the world influential new ideas, forms, and images. From the early-sixties beginnings of Stan Brakhage's and Kenneth Anger's films through the seventies and eighties work of James Benning and others, this tradition continues to grow.

The history of computer animation as given in earlier chapters has tended to ignore early artistic experimentation in describing the onward rush of technology, but particularly in universities, artistic exploitation has continued contemporaneously with every technological plateau. Rather than reviewing this work without being able to show much of it, it would seem more efficient to refer those interested to the Bibliography.

A.21 The Myth of Our Medium

Why have either ancient or futuristic myths worked so well with gadget-as-hero movies? Stories about the future certainly seem natural for special effects, so not too much thought has ever been given that match-up, but the ancient past can be visualized with as full realism as modern man can imagine without special effects. The plot-structure and story-element similarities between sagas of the future and sagas of the ancient past, both of which rely on effects or animation for visualization, make one think again about the thematic need for effects in futuristic yarns, too. George Lucas pointed out the similarity between making movies about a proposed ancient past and making movies about the future by setting *Star Wars* "a long time ago . . . " in its opening frame.

Georges Méliès made serials about voyages to the moon and to the ancient past, too. The interchangeability of distant past and future have been associated with special effects from the beginning. In *Computers For Imagemaking* (Pergamon Press, London, 1981), Ken Knowlton of Bell Laboratories, one of the pioneers of computer graphics, contributed an essay titled "Computer Animation As an Aid to Comprehending the Universe." His capsule summary at the beginning seems to promise us an answer: "Computer animation offers the possibility of providing an intellectual framework for understanding the relative magnitudes of time and of space. For every process, whether large or small, fast or slow, there will be an appropriate scale at which to view it, so that its salient features are clear. The chief task in understanding something is often to interrelate these scales, and computer imaging may provide a novel way of facilitating this understanding."

It soon becomes clear from Knowlton's essay, however, that he proposes a sort of comparative time-lapse photography with windows to different time and space scales. This is no solution to our question of why special effects gadgetry goes so well with ancient and supermodern myths, but a scholarly way of falling prey to the same phenomenon! We have a situation here that goes beyond the movie business in its meaning, just as it goes beyond optical effects to computer animation.

Filmmakers have become very conscious of what they are doing by matching gadgets and myth. Lucas has said in interviews that Joseph Campbell's four-volume *Masks of God* series on worldwide mythology was a formative influence in his decision to become a filmmaker at all. Shelley Duval, whose "Fairie Tale Theatre" makes more extensive use of computer video effects than any previous TV series, credits Bruno Bettelheim's *The Uses of Enchantment,* a Freudian analysis of fairy tales, as very influential. Francis Coppola credits Fraser's *The Golden Bough.* Among those makers of movies heavy with special effects who ever study anything besides film, the number one field of study is myth. In their work, then, these filmmakers consciously manipulate mythic themes to better affect audience response.

To find out what this match-up means, it is helpful to look at the movies involved with the same sort of eye for mythic symbolism that Roland Barthes used in his studies of popular culture. What Méliès did unconsciously and these later filmmakers did consciously would not matter so much to an observer like Barthes as the fact that they all do the same thing. Whether the thing is done cynically to make money, or idealistically to entertain millions, or obsessively to depict the products of imagination is all the same. The match-up means something to people, or else people would not use it. What does it mean?

The question itself is as meaningful as any answer can be. "Spectacular Effects!" lobby cards have read for as long as there have been movies. At a time when frontiers of technology have moved on, it is easy to forget that movies were originally a marvelous new technology that captured and presented images of places and things otherwise impossible for the average viewer to ever hope to see. As jaded modern citizens of a time when anybody with a TV can see the whole world, we want a machine to bring us another world. The machines that added to the movies' capabilities to do this were first, optical printers, animation stands, and animated miniature models. Now the machine is the computer, and it has captured popular imagination far more than these other machines, at least partly because movies have been titillating that imagination for decades with fantasies of fancy computers. The computer is the machine, and the only places left for it to take us are the distant past or distant future. Both are equally make-believe, as is the popular conception of the machine. The fantasies combine.

For the noncommercial experimentalists discussed above, a suggestion: animation that explores the medium's own myth-making is worthy of attention. We haven't seen much yet, but expect to.

APPENDIX B

A Guide to the North American Animation Industry

Contents

1. Animation studios
2. Computer-animation schools
3. Suppliers of animation hardware and software systems
4. Industry organizations

B.1. Animation Studios

The industry serves advertising agencies, corporations looking for animated industrial films, and the feature film, teleproduction, and live-action commercial production industries. Total sales of all of these companies might be as much as $300 million in 1986.

Every animator in the continent is not listed here; all of the major studios ought to be. (There might be an omission or two, for which I apologize in advance, if need be.) The guide has been arranged into seven sections, for California, the New York metropolitan area (including New Jersey), the Midwest, the South (including Texas), the Northeast (except for metropolitan New York), the West (except for California and Texas), and Canada.

The companies are listed alphabetically. If a company name begins with its principal's given name, the company is listed under the first initial of the principal's surname. (Thus, Robert Abel is listed under "A".) If the name starts with "the," it is listed according to the second word.

Contact names are typically the people of highest authority at each studio. If no contact name is listed at a studio that goes by an individual's full name, the person in charge is that individual. For most studios, no title is given for the contact name; titles are associated with names for the few studios that are very large.

Not all production facilities with turnkey digital video-effects devices available have been listed. If all such businesses were, the guide would be several times as long. Only those who call animation a significant part of their business are listed.

If no specialties are listed for a company, they may be expected to work in many animation forms, including computerized work. Unless otherwise implied, the companies listed produce work for television commercials, TV station logos, and for insertion within longer films.

California

Robert Abel and Associates
953 N. Highland Ave.
Hollywood, CA 90038
213-462-8100

Howard Anderson
Charles McDonald
1016 N. Cole Ave.
Hollywood, CA 90038
213-463-2336

Tom Anderson Filmworks
6362 Hollywood Blvd., Suite 308
Hollywood, CA 90028
213-464-0386

Animagic
David Fiske
1309 W. Magnolia Blvd.
Burbank, CA 91506
818-848-4429

Animation Filmmakers
Dick Brown
7000 Romaine Street
Hollywood, CA 90038
213-851-5526

Apogee
John Dykstra
6842 Valjean Avenue
Van Nuys, CA 91406
818-989-3156

Apple Productions
Jeff Apple
6240 Afton Place
Hollywood, CA 90028
213-462-0995

Baer Animation Co.
2214 Stanley Hills Drive
West Hollywood, CA 90046
213-656-0976

Saul Bass/Herb Yager and Associates
7039 West Sunset Blvd.
Los Angeles, CA 90028
213-466-9701
programming, miscellaneous design

Blanc Communications
9454 Wilshire Blvd.
Beverly Hills, CA 90212
213-278-2600

Bowers & Eddy
835 N. Martell Street
Los Angeles, CA 90046
213-655-1674

Braverman Productions
Chuck Braverman
6290 West Sunset Blvd.
Los Angeles, CA 90065
213-466-4111

Don Bluth Animation
16134 Hart Street
Van Nuys, CA 91406
818-780-0126
programming

CFI
Tom Ellington
959 N. Seward Street
Hollywood, CA 90038
213-462-3161

California Film, Inc.
Mitchell Bobrowner
8821 Santa Monica Blvd.
Los Angeles, CA 90046
213-656-9900

Cause & EFX
Art Kellner, Henrey Kline, Elrene Cowan
1523 Crossroads of the World
Hollywood, CA 90028
213-466-3939

Celestial Mechanix
612 Hampton Drive
Venice, CA 90291
213-392-8771

Coast Special Effects
Phil Kellison, Harry Walton
4907 Lankershim Blvd.
North Hollywood, CA 91601
213-876-2021

Colossal Pictures
George Merkert, Gary Gutierrez, Drew Takahashi
2800 Third Street
San Francisco, CA 94107
415-550-8872

Calico
Lee Mann
8843 Shirley Ave.
Northridge, CA 91324
818-885-6663

Computer Camera and Disc
Ray Kerns
134 West Verdugo Ave.
Burbank, CA 91502
818-848-9414

Deutsch Design/Quadra Group
Laurence Deutsch
751 N. Highland Ave.
Los Angeles, CA 90038
213-937-3521

Diaquest
Tom Hoppers
1440 San Pablo Ave.
Berkeley, CA 94702
415-526-7073

Digital Productions
John Whitney, Jr., Sherry McKenna
3416 S. La Cienega Blvd.
Los Angeles, CA 90016
213-938-1111

Duck Soup Produckions
Roger Chouinard
1026 Montana Ave.
Santa Monica, CA 90403
213-451-0771

Editel
Jerry Pojawaugall
729 N. Highland Ave.
Hollywood, CA 90038
213-931-1821

Energy Productions
Louis Scwartzberg
2690 Beachwood Drive
Los Angeles, CA 90068
213-462-3310

Fantasy II
Ron Rosenthal
504 S. Varney
Burbank, CA 91502
818-843-1413

Filmation Studios
18107 Sherman Way
Reseda, CA 91335
818-345-7414
programming

Film Effects of Hollywood
Linwood Dunn
1140 N. Citrus Ave.
Hollywood, CA 90038
213-460-2001
opticals, traditional special effects

FilmFair
Gus Jekel
10900 Ventura Blvd.
Studio City, CA 91604
213-766-9441

Flint Productions
Roger Flint
7758 West Sunset Blvd.
Los Angeles, CA 90046
213-851-1060

Harold Friedman Consortium
Rufus Friedman
1426 South Main, Suite D
Venice, CA 90291
213-821-0100

Bo Gehring Associates
13431 Beach Avenue
Venice, CA 90292
213-823-8577
3D computer animation

Hanna-Barbera Productions
Jane Barbera, VP animation production
3400 Cahuenga Blvd.
West Hollywood, CA 90068
213-851-5000
programming

Ed Hansen & Associates
1454 Seward
Los Angeles, CA 90028
213-467-5085

Industrial Light & Music
division of Lucasfilm, Ltd.
Warren Franklin
P.O. Box 2009
San Rafael, CA 94912
415-459-0220
programming

Information International, Inc. (III)
A. Fenauthty
5933 Slauson Ave.
Culver City, CA 90230
213-390-8611

Kurtz and Friends
Bob Kurtz
2312 West Olive Ave.
Burbank, CA 91506
818-841-8188

Las Palmas Productions (Composite Image Systems)
William Barnett
815 N. Cahuenga Blvd.
Hollywood, CA 90038
213-461-5734

Lasermedia
2046 Armacost Avenue
Los Angeles, CA 90025
213-820-3750
laser effects

Linda Jones Enterprises
789 West 20 Street
Costa Mesa, CA 92627
714-548-7793
programming

Lion's Den, Ltd.
Al Lowenstein
6993 Via Valverde
La Jolla, CA 92038
619-459-6649

Mark Kirkland Film/Television
2535 1/2 Beachwood Drive
Hollywood, CA 90068
213-469-3834

Marvel Productions
Lee Gunther, David De Patie, Stan Lee
6007 N. Sepulveda
Van Nuys, CA 91411
818-988-8300
programming

McCall-Coppola/FilmFair
Rod McCall, Frank Coppola, Richard Marshall
Film Fair
10900 Ventura Blvd.
Studio City, CA 91604
818-766-8770

Metavision
Theo Mayer, Peter Inebnit, Peter Chernack
347 S. Ogden Dr., #220
Los Angeles, CA 90036
213-936-8281

Fritz Miller Animation
10806 Ventura Blvd., Suite 3
Studio City, CA 91604
818-985-6074

Modern Film Effects
6824 Melrose Ave.
Hollywood, CA 90038
213-932-1221

Moore Films
John David Moore
953 N. Cole Ave.
Hollywood, CA 90038
213-465-4678

Murakami-Wolf-Swenson Films
Fred Wolf, Chuck Swenson
1463 Tamarind Avenue
Hollywood, CA 90028
213-462-6474

New World Effects
600 S. Main Street
Venice, CA 90291
213-399-9151

Novacom
Jim Gerken
1545 N. Wilcox
Los Angeles, CA 90028
213-461-3688

Omnibus Computer Graphics
J. C. Pennie
5555 Melrose Ave.
Los Angeles, CA 90038
213-468-4620
CGI

Oncore
Larry Chernoff
6344 Fountain Ave.
Hollywood, CA 90028
213-466-7663

One Pass Video
Steve Michelson
One China Basin
San Francisco, CA 94107
415-777-5777
digital video effects

Pacific Data Images
Carl Rosendahl
1111 Karlstad Drive
Sunnyvale, CA 94089
408-745-6755, 213-627-3627
3D computer animation

Pacific Title & Art Studio
Gordon Hubbard
6350 Santa Monica Blvd.
Hollywood, CA 90038
213-464-0121

Pacific Video
809 N. Cahuenga Blvd.
Hollywood, CA 90038
213-462-6260

Pantomime Pictures
Fred Crippen, Jack Hadley
12144 Riverside Drive
North Hollywood, CA 91607
818-980-5555

Praxis Filmworks
Robert Blalack
6918 Tujunga Ave.
North Hollywood, CA 91605
818-508-0402

Quartet Films
Michael Lah
12345 Ventura Blvd. Suite M
Studio City, CA 91604
818-464-9225

R&B Efx
Rocco Damiano
1802 Victory Blvd.
Glendale, CA 91201
818-956-8406

Roto Effects of America
737 N. Seward Street
Hollywood, CA 90038
213-463-2989

Ruby-Spears Enterprises
Joe Ruby, Ken Spears
3255 Cahuenga Blvd.
Hollywood, CA 90068
213-874-5100

San Francisco Production Group
550 Bryant Street
San Francisco, CA 94107
415-495-5595

Spungbuggy
Herb Stott
948 North Fairfax
Los Angeles, CA 90046
213-657-8070

Stokes/Kohne Associates
Linda Stokes
738 Cahuenga Blvd.
Hollywood, CA 90038
213-469-8176

Stop Frame
Robert Hovorka
837 Folsom St.
San Francisco, CA 94107
415-543-5344

Jay Teitzell Film Inc.
5967 West 3 Street
Los Angeles, CA 90036
213-934-3644

Visual Concept Engineering
1157 N. Highland Ave.
Hollywood, CA 90038
213-463-9187

Walt Disney Studios
Tom Whittle, VP, creative development
500 South Buena Vista
Burbank, CA 91521
818-840-1000
programming

New York Metropolitan Area (with New Jersey)

APA Studios
Lee Howard
230 West 10th Street
NY, NY 10014
212-929-9436

Allscope
Sam Wells
P.O. Box 4060
Princeton, NJ 08540
609-799-4200, 212-397-8643

American Animation
Jim Pearson
151 West 28th Street
NY, NY 10001
212-563-5720

American Video Channels
Livingston Hinckley, Yair Trappen, Jack Allalouf
321 West 44 Street
NY, NY 10036
212-765-6324
digital video effects

Ani-Live Film Service
Bernice Steinberg, Sidney Cooper
45 West 45th Street
NY, NY 10036
212-819-0700

Animated Productions
Al Stahl
1600 Broadway, 301
NY, NY 10036
212-265-2942

Animation Services
David Jacobsen, Ray Pierce
221 West 57th Street, 11 fl.
NY, NY 10019
212-333-5656

Animation Stand/Mazin-Wyckoff
36 East 12 Street
NY, NY 10003
212-475-4366

Animus Films
15 West 44 Street
NY, NY 10036
212-391-8716

Atlantic Motion Pictures
162 West 21st Street
NY, NY 10011
212-924-6170

B & O Film Effects
Anthony Bezich
619 West 54th Street
NY, NY 10019
212-246-9390

Broadway Arts
Steve Oakes, Peter Rosenthal
632 Broadway
NY, NY 10012
212-254-5400

Broadway Video
1619 Broadway
NY, NY 10036
212-265-7600
video animator

Buzzco
Buzz Potamkin, Vincent Cafarelli
870 Seventh Ave.
NY, NY 10019
212-586-6333

Elinor Bunin Productions
30 East 60th Street
NY, NY 10022
212-688-0759

Caesar Video Graphics
135 East 25th Street, 2nd fl.
NY, NY 10010
212-684-7673

John Canemaker Productions, Inc.
120 West 70th Street
NY, NY 10023

Celart
Colin Giles
20 East 49th Street
NY, NY 10017
212-751-7515

Charisma Productions
Jim Grau Jr.
32 East 57th Street
NY, NY 10022
212-832-3020

Charlex
Charles Levi, Alex Weil
2 West 45th Street
NY, NY 10036
212-719-4600

Computer Graphics Laboratories
405 Lexington Ave.
NY, NY 10174
212-557-5130

DJM
4 East 46th Street
NY, NY 10017
212-687-0404

Da Silva Animated Films
Ray Da Silva
311 East 85th Street
NY, NY 10028
212-535-5760

Devlin Productions
Sandra Devlin
150 West 55th Street
NY, NY 10019
212-582-5572

Diamond & Diaferia
Fred Diamond, Peter Diaferia
25 West 45th Street
NY, NY 10036
142 Johnson Rd.
Scarsdale, NY 10583
212-986-8500, 914-723-5150

Dolphin Productions
Allan Stanley
140 East 80th Street
NY, NY 10021
212-628-5930

Doros Animation Studio
Doros Evangelides
475 Fifth Avenue
NY, NY 10017
212-684-5043

Dynamic Effects
Bob Pincus
19 West 44th Street
NY, NY 10036
212-221-6020

Editel
Alfie Schloss
222 East 44th Street
NY, NY 10017
212-867-4600

Fandango Productions
Isauro De La Rosa
15 West 38th Street
NY, NY 10018
212-382-1813

Fantastic Animation Machine
Jim Lindner, Suzanne Gavril
12 East 46th Street
NY, NY 10017
212-697-2525

Feigenbaum Productions
Bill, Joyce Feigenbaum, Gerry Cohen
25 West 43rd Street
NY, NY 10036
212-840-3744

Filigree Films
155 Avenue of the Americas
NY, NY 10013
212-627-1770

Harold Friedman Consortium
420 Lexington Ave.
NY, NY 10017
212-697-0858

John Gati Film Effects
881 Seventh Ave.
NY, NY 10019
212-582-9060

Ink Tank
R. O. Blechman, J. J. Sedelmaier
2 West 47th Street
NY, NY 10036
212-869-1630

International Production Center
Steve Swartz
514 West 57th Street
NY, NY 10019
212-582-6530/800-223-0622

KCMP Productions
Phil Kimmelman, Jordan Caldwell, Jimmy Parker
50 West 40th Street
NY, NY 10018
212-944-7766

Gifford Animation
45 West 45th Street
NY, NY 10036
212-719-2530

Synthevision
Bob Robins
110 Greene Street
NY, NY 10012
212-334-1666

Manhattan Design
Pat Gorman
47 West 13th Street
NY, NY 10011
212-620-0506

Modern Telecommunications (MTI)
Mike Saz
885 Second Ave.
NY, NY 10017
212-355-0510

New York Animation
Howard Danelowitz
200 West 79th Street
NY, NY 10023
212-362-6992

Omnibus Computer Graphics
George Heywood
508 West 57th Street
NY, NY 10019
212-975-9050

The Optical House
25 West 45th Street
NY, NY 10036
212-869-5840

Ovation Films
Art Petricone, Julia Whalen
15 West 26th Street
NY, NY 10010
212-686-4540

Perpetual Animation
Hal Silvermintz
17 West 45th Street
NY, NY 10036
212-953-9110

Projection Systems International
Roland Blackway
219 East 44th Street
NY, NY 10017
212-682-0995

R/Greenberg Associates
Richard and Robert Greenberg
350 West 39th Street
NY, NY 10018
212-239-6767

RB/Mavericks Motion Pictures
Nick Mavroson, Ron Bleischer
35 West 45th Street
NY, NY 10036
212-382-2424

Rankin/Bass Productions
Arthur Rankin, Jules Bass
1 East 53rd Street
NY, NY 10022
212-759-7721

Judson Rosebush Co.
1619 Broadway
NY, NY 10019
212-397-5400

SEL Animation
Mick Beck
321 West 44th Street
NY, NY 10038
212-307-7810

Select Effects
14 West 45th Street
NY, NY 10036
212-869-3988

Shadow Light Productions
Marc Chelnick
12 West 27th Street
NY, NY 10001
212-689-7511

Rebecca Singer Studios
264 Lexington Ave.
NY, NY 10016
212-944-0466

Stanart Studios
Stan Popko
1650 Broadway
NY, NY 10019
212-586-0445

Stargate Productions
Steve Corwin, Tony Caronia
231 East 55th Street
NY, NY 10022
212-333-3636

Trilogy Design at JSL
Ray Seti
25 West 45th Street
NY, NY 10036
212-869-0123

Videoworks
Frank Herold, Ken Lorber
24 West 40th Street
NY, NY 10018
212-869-2500

Peter Wallach Enterprises
419 Broome Street
NY, NY 10013
212-966-1970

Mark Zander Productions
Jack and Mark Zander
114 East 25th Street
NY, NY 10010
212-477-3900

Midwest

AGS&R Studios
Aaron Gordon
425 N. Michigan Ave.
Chicago, IL 60611
312-836-4500

Animation Services
Robert Klenner
21501 Harper
St. Claire Shores, MI 48080
313-774-8330

Animation Station
406 West 65th Street
Minneapolis, MN 55423
612-861-3304

Bajus-Jones Film
Don Bajus, Mike Jones
5250 West 74th Street
Edina, MN 55435
612-835-4490

Cinemation & The Optical Center
Richard Laird
6449 Lyndale Ave. South
Minneapolis, MN 55423
612-861-4481

The Cioni Artworks
Ray Cioni
224 West Hubbard Street
Chicago, IL 60610
312-266-0531

Computer Creations
Shaun Reynolds
1657 N. Commerce Drive, Suite 1B
South Bend, IN 46628
219-233-1020

Computer Video Productions
Martha Coleman, Karen West-Reger
1317 Clover Drive South
Minneapolis, MN 55420
612-888-2388

Cranston-Csuri
Charles Csuri, Wayne Carlson
Cranston Center
Columbus, OH 43201
614-421-2000
3D CGI

Crunch Bird Studios
Ted Petok
32969 Hamilton Ct.
Farmington Hills, MI 48024
313-553-4747

Daily Planet
401 N. Michigan Ave.
Chicago, IL 60611
312-670-3766
animatics

Editel
Olita Kins
301 East Erie Street
Chicago, IL 60611
312-440-2360

FilmFair/Chicago
Joanne Bittmann
22 West Hubbard St.
Chicago, IL 60610
312-822-9200

Freese & Friends
Tom Freese
1429 North Wells Street
Chicago, IL 60610
312-642-4475
traditional animation

Goldsholl Design and Film
Kelly Ray
420 Frontage Rd.
Northfield, IL 60093
312-446-8300

Hellman Associates
Mike Grove
P.O. Box 627
Waterloo, Iowa 50704
319-234-7055

Hurwitz Enterprises
Victor Hurwitz
19675 West Ten Mile Road, Suite 305
Southfield, MI 48075
313-357-2000

David Kallaher
602 Main Street
Cincinnati, OH 45202
513-621-6007

Kinetics
George Eastman
444 North Wabash Ave.
Chicago, IL 60611
312-644-2764

Lamb & Co.
Paul Churchill
127 N. 7th St.
Minneapolis, MN 55403
612-333-8666

Magic Lantern Productions
Robert Dyke, James Fox
23705 Industrial Park Drive
Farmington Hills, MI
313-478-4300

Optimus
James Smyth
161 East Grand Ave.
Chicago, IL 60611
312-321-0880

Reelworks
Mark Setterholm
1612 1/2 W. Lake Street
Minneapolis, MN 55408
612-824-8225

Ritter-Waxberg Animation
200 East Ontario Street
Chicago, IL 60611
312-664-3934

Sinnott and Associates
Tom Sinnott
676 N. La Salle Street
Chicago, IL 60610
312-440-1875

Special Effects
1351 West Grand Ave.
Chicago, IL 60622
312-421-2500

Swell Pictures
233 East Wacker Dr.
Chicago, IL 60601
312-649-9000

Tom Roy Graphics
595 South Eton
Birmingham, MI 48008
313-642-6515

South

Acmecartoon Co.
7141 Envoy Ct.
Dallas, TX 75247
214-688-0303
3D computer graphics, opticals, rotoscoping

Audio Visual Specialties
John Schaefer
4220 37th Street NW
Washington, DC 20008
202-362-6191

Candy Apple Productions
2049 W. Broad Street
Richmond, VA 23220
804-358-3852

Capital Video Communications
2121 Wisconsin Ave. NW
Washington, DC 20007
202-965-7800
digital video effects

Cappello Film
Craig Bordlemay
5465 115 Avenue North
Clearwater, FL 33520
813-577-2086

Cinetron Computer Systems
6700 Interstate 85
Norcross, GA 30093
404-448-9463
computer animation, opticals

Computer Art & Animation Studio
10020 Hemphill Ave. NW
Atlanta, GA 30318
404-875-9697

Digital Video
Steve Metheny
4405 Vineland Road, Suite C4
Orlando, FL 32811
305-425-1999

Jack Dyer
1655 Peachtree Street, NE, Suite 1008
Atlanta, GA 30309
404-875-3937
cel, rotoscope, effects

Florida Production Center
150 Riverside Ave.
Jacksonville, FL 32202
904-354-7000
4010 N. Nebraska Ave.
Tampa, FL 33603
904-237-1200
digital video effects

Hallmark Films
Max Brecher
51 New Plant Ct.
Owings Mills, MD 21117
301-363-4500

Hayes Productions
Bill Hayes
710 South Bowie Street
San Antonio, TX 78209
512-224-9565

K & H Productions
Tom Young
4141 Office Parkway
Dallas, TX 75204
214-826-8952

Mirage Film Graphics
Randall Rudd, Dave Hamby
Austin, TX
512-327-4120

Motion Picture Laboratories
Corrine Sousoulas
781 South Main
Memphis, TN 38101
800-238-2636

Screen Presentations
David Gerber
309 Massachusetts Avenue NE
Washington, DC 20002
202-546-8900
video graphics

Third Coast Studios
501 North I.H. 35
Austin, TX 78702
512-476-8905
graphic design, digital video effects

Video Post & Transfer
8036 Aviation Place
Dallas, TX 75235
214-350-2676

Wilming-Reams
Denise Reams
520 N. Medina
San Antonio, TX 78207
512-225-0614

West (Except California, Texas)

Bandelier
Alan Stevens
3815 Oserna NE
Albuquerque, NM 87109
505-345-8021

Coffin & Co.
1506 17 East
Seattle, WA 98112
206-328-2330

Computer Image
Peter Freyschlag, Lee Harrison
12600 West Colfax Ave.
Lakeland, CO 80215
303-235-0077
computer animation, production and hardware

Kinetic Design
Frank Pecora
8201 East Pacific Place
Aurora, CO 80231
303-750-5000

Skaggs Telecommunications
Roger Olson
5181 Amelia Earheart Drive
Salt Lake City, UT 84116
801-537-1427
video effects

Telemation Productions
Glenview, IL, Seattle, WA, Denver, CO, Salt Lake City, UT
303-751-6000, 206-623-5934
video effects

True Vista Productions
Thomas Arndt
1814 S.W. Main
Portland OR 97205
503-220-0527

Z-Axis
Ray Haushel
10800 E. Bethany Dr., Suite 500
Aurora, CO 80014
303-696-9608
CGI

Canada

Atkinson Film-Arts
David Grimes
19 Fairmont Ave.
Ottawa, ON
613-728-3513

Greenlight Productions
70 Richmond St. East
Toronto, ON
416-366-3444

International Rocketship
Marv Newland
1227 Richards
Vancouver, BC
604-681-2716

Light Box Studios
Greg Duffell
345 Adelaide St. West
Toronto, ON M5V 1R5
416-591-1687

Omnibus Computer Graphics
Joe Martin
2180 Younge Street, main floor
Toronto, ON M4S 2B9
416-489-6020
CGI

Rawifilm
Colin Chilvers, Terry Collier, Gilean Proctor, Ousama Rawi
567 Queen Street West
Toronto, ON M5V 2B6
416-366-7881
film effects

Northeast (Except NY Metro Area)

The Animators
Robert Wolcott
247 Fort Pitt Blvd.
Pittsburgh, PA 15222
412-391-2550

Anivision
Rick Catazone
981 Walnut St.
Pittsburgh, PA 15234
412-563-2221
traditional animation

BIP
Milan Slade
99 S. Bedford St.
Burlington, MA 01803
617-272-7310
traditional animation

Centel/Century III Teleproductions
Lee Rubenstein
651 Beacon Street
Boston, MA 02115
617-267-6400
video effects

Center City Video
Jordan Schwartz
1503-05 Walnut St.
Philadelphia, PA 19102
215-568-4134
video effects

Cinemagraphics Film & Video/Video 1
100 Massachusetts Ave.
Boston, MA 02115
617-266-2200
digital video animation

E. J. Stewart
525 Mildred Ave.
Primos, PA 19018
215-626-6500
digital video effects

Kensington Falls Animation
Mike Schwab
1530 Northway Mall
Pittsburgh, PA 15237
412-367-2118

Modern Video Productions
Jean Mason, Dava Jennings
1600 Market Street
Philadelphia, PA 19103
215-569-4100
digital video animation

Penpoint Animation
Peter Toohil
331 Newbury St.
Boston, MA 02116
617-266-1331
traditional animation

Starfleet Animation
John Bahn
R.D. #5, Box 91
Avalon Road
Altoona, PA 16603
814-943-8494

Videosmith
Steven Smith
2006 Chancellor
Philadelphia, PA 19103
215-665-3690
digital video animation

Yellow Ball Workshop
62 Tarbell Ave.
Lexington, MA 02173
617-862-4283
traditional animation

B.2. Schools

The problem with trying to find a good school for computer animation is that the subject matter tends to get shoehorned into unpredictable places. It can fit into art departments, film departments, computer science departments, engineering departments, computer graphics departments, or something else that momentarily escapes my imagination. As a likely course of study one might follow to become an animator, it would seem to make sense to find the right program, wherever it may be, and also to take the best film/video program that can be combined with it.

A word of advice! The film industry is small, and the animation industry is smaller. Television is a big world, yes, but very competitive nonetheless. Some sacrifices in terms of the most convenient school ought to be expected, perhaps even some sacrifice in terms of educational quality, in favor of a place with a reputation for turning out programming executives.

This list does not pretend to include every college or university in North America that teaches some computer graphics courses; such a list would now include almost every institution of higher learning on the continent, as well as all too many institutions of lower learning. Those that are listed have been, or recently have become, notable for teaching full programs of studies in the field. The few schools that have contributed very notably to advancing computer animation art and/or technology have been starred (*).

Many schools that have significant programs in related fields such as CAD, image processing, etc., or in general computer science, or in film production and general film studies have been left out. The emphasis here is on computer animation. (For a list of all colleges with any computer graphics programs, consult the annual survey of *Computer Graphics World* magazine, 1714 Stockton St., San Francisco, CA. It is usually run in their January issue. Perusing recent publications of SIGGRAPH and noticing the affiliations of academic contributors is a good way to find colleges where work is being done that is of particular interest to you. Any major college directory should list colleges with film programs.)

The following list is broken down into the same regions as the one above, except that metropolitan New York has been integrated into the Northeast listings.

Canada

Simon Fraser University
Computing Science Dept.
Burnaby, BC
604-291-4152
Attn: T.W. Calvert

California

Academy of Art College
Graphic Design/Computer Graphics Dept.
San Francisco, CA
415-673-4200
Attn: Carl E. Ballay

*California Institute of the Arts
School of Film and Video
Valencia, CA
805-255-1050
Attn: Ed Emshwiller

California State University, Long Beach
Visual Communication Design Dept.
Long Beach, CA
714-498-4361
Attn: Christa Schubert

California State University, Los Angeles
Art Dept.
Los Angeles, CA
213-224-3521
Attn: Tony Longson

California State University, Northridge
Computer Science Dept.
Northridge, CA
818-885-3398
Attn: Eunice Feder

California State University, Sacramento
Art Dept.
Sacramento, CA
916-454-6166
Attn: Maria Winkler

Orange Coast College
Computer Graphics/Fine Arts Dept.
Costa Mesa, CA
714-432-5629
Attn: Donna Westerman

*Stanford University
Computer Science Dept
Palo Alto, CA
415-497-4097
Attn: Steven Rubin

*University of California, Berkeley
Berkeley Computer Graphics Laboratory
Berkeley, CA
415-642-9838
Attn: Brian Barsky

University of California, Santa Barbara
Computer Science Dept.
Santa Barbara, CA
805-961-4321
Attn: Eric De Jong

West Coast University
Computer Graphics for Artists and Designers
Los Angeles, CA
213-487-4433
Attn: Tony Longson

Midwest

Art Institute of Chicago
Chicago, IL
312-443-3743
Attn: Joan Truckenbrod

Ball State Univ.
Computer Science Dept.
Muncie, IN
317-285-8661
Attn: Roy L. McCormick

Bowling Green State Univ.
Art Dept./Computer Science Dept.
Bowling Green, OH
419-372-2786,2337
Attn: Ronald Coleman (Art), Leland Miller (Com Sci)

Center for Creative Studies
Dept. of Graphic Communication & Industrial Design
Detroit, MI
313-872-3118
Attn: Alan Foxx

Indiana University, Bloomington
Computer Science Dept.
101 Lindley Hall
Bloomington, IN
812-335-6486
Attn: E. Robertson

Kansas City Art Institute
Dept. of Design
Kansas City, MO
816-561-4852
Attn: Roger Funk

Kansas State Univ.
Computer Science Dept.
Manhattan, KS
913-532-6350
Attn: William Hankley

Marycrest College
Davenport, IA
319-326-9512
Attn: Alan Garfield

Minneapolis College of Art and Design
Design Division
Minneapolis, MN
612-870-3161
Attn: Peter Seitz

*Ohio State University
Computer Graphics Research Group
Columbus, OH
614-422-3416
Attn: Thomas Linehan

University of Illinois—Chicago Circle
Electrical Engineering and Computer Science Dept.
Chicago, IL
312-996-5485
Attn: Tom De Fanti

Northeast

Dartmouth College
Mathematics and Computer Science Dept.
Hanover, NH
603-646-3173
Attn: Thomas E. Kurtz

Harvard Univ.
School of Design
Cambridge, MA
617-495-2526
Attn: Allan Schmidt

*Massachusetts Institute of Technology
Visible Language Workshop
Cambridge, MA
617-253-4416
Attn: Muriel Cooper

*New York Institute of Technology
Computer Graphics Laboratory
Old Westbury, NY
516-686-7600
Attn: Louis Schure

*New York University
Computer Science Dept./Tisch School of the Arts
New York, NY
Com Sci: 212-598-1212
Tisch: 212-243-3346
Attn: Oliver McBryan (Com Sci), Darcy Gerbarg (Arts)

Penn State University
Art Dept.
University Park, PA
814-865-1203
Attn: Bill Kinser

Pratt Institute
Computer Science Dept.
Brooklyn, NY
718-636-3623
Attn: Herbert Tesser

Rhode Island College
Art Dept.
Providence, RI
401-456-8054
Attn: Dan Harter

*Rochester Institute of Technology
Computer Science Dept./Dept. of Fine and Applied Arts
Rochester, NY
716-465-6179,2646
Attn: Guy Johnson (Com Sci), James Ver Hague (Arts)

Smith College
Art Dept./Computer Science Dept.
Northampton, MA
413-583-2700
Attn: Gary Niswonger (Art), Tricia Colson (Com. Sci.)

*Syracuse University
Art Media Studies/Computer Science Dept.
Syracuse, NY
315-423-1870
Attn: Edward Zajec

South

University of North Carolina
Computer Science Dept.
Chapel Hill, NC
919-962-5022
Attn: Ralph Mason

West

Brigham Young University
Computer Science Dept.
Provo, UT
801-378-3027

Oregon State University
Computer Science Dept.
Corvallis, OR
503-754-3272
Attn: Fred Tonge

University of Oregon
Fine and Applied Art Dept.
Eugene, OR
503-686-3610
Attn: Ken O'Connell

*University of Utah
Computer Science Dept.
Salt Lake City, UT
801-581-8224
Attn: Richard Riesenfeld

University of Washington
Computer Science Dept.
Seattle, WA
206-543-1695
Attn: Steven Tanimoto

B.3. Vendors of Computer Animation Equipment

As years go by, some of the companies listed below will break out of the pigeonholes in which they have been categorized, but it seems helpful to break a list of vendors down into those who sell broadcast and film-industry equipment, PC-oriented hardware and software, CAD hardware and software, and larger computing equipment that is often utilized for animation. Only those foreign firms are included whose products are actively marketed and supported in the United States. This is a selective list; only those vendors are included whose products seem most pertinent to readers.

I have refrained from listing vendors of useful home video equipment, as their products are quite readily available. Vendors of professional equipment are included under broadcast equipment.

PC Graphics Hardware

AT&T Informations Systems
2002 Wellesley Blvd.
Bloomington, IN 46219
High-resolution PC color graphics and digitizing cards

AVL
56 Park Road
Tinton Falls, NJ 07724

Amtron
2260 De La Cruz Blvd.
Santa Clara, CA 95050
High-resolution color monitors

Artronics/3M
3M Center -225-3N-03
St. Paul, MN 01602
Vector software for PC, turnkey micro system

Autographix
100 Fifth Avenue
Waltham, MA 02154
Paint system based on IBM PC AT

Chorus Data Systems
6 Continental Blvd.
Merrimack, NH 03054
Imigit and PC-Eye PC graphics system, peripherals and software

Color Graphics Systems
5725 Tokay Blvd.
Madison, WI 53719
Turnkey 2D paint system

Cubicomp
3165 Adeline Street
Berkeley, CA 94703
PC-based turnkey 3D animation system

Dunn Instruments
544 Second St.
San Francisco, CA 94107
Film recorder system

Eastman Kodak Co.
Motion Picture and Audiovisual Markets Division
Rochester, NY
Instagraphic Slide Imager system for photographing off CRT

FTG Data Systems
10801 Dale Street, Suite M-2
P.O. Box 615
Scranton, CA 90680
Light pen and graphics terminal emulator for IBM PC

Fairlight Instruments
2945 Westwood Blvd.
Los Angeles, CA 90064
Inexpensive turnkey 2D paint and animation system

Frank Woolley & Co.
529 Franklin Street
Reading, PA 19602
Motionmaster inexpensive video animation stand for shooting off CRT

GTCO
1055 First Street
Rockville, MD 20850
Digipad tablet

Genigraphics
P.O. Box 591
Liverpool, NY 13088
Turnkey slide-making systems

IEV
254 West Fourth South
Suite 280
Salt Lake City, UT 84101
Color graphics cards for IBM PC

Imaging Technology
600 West Cummings Park
Woburn, MA 01801
Video digitizer, image processing, NTSC conversion, software

Intecolor
225 Technology Park
Norcross, GA 30092
Turnkey micro-based 2D digitizing and color graphics system

Kurta
4610 S. 35 Street
Phoenix, AZ 85040
Penmouse input device

Laser Concepts
45 East 20 Street
New York, NY 10003
Marketers of Panasonic OMDR optical memory disk recorder

Madison Computer
1825 Monroe Street
Madison, WI 53711
Light pen

Matrix Instruments
Computer Graphics Products
One Ramland Rd.
Orangeburg, NY 10962
Vector-to-raster adapter for IBM PC, film recorder, software

Matrox Electronic Systems
1055 St-Regis Blvd.
Dorval, Quebec H9P 2T4
Single-board real-time image processor

Monitronix
2971 Silver Dr.
Columbus, OH 43224
High-resolution monitors

Number Nine Computer
691 Concord Ave.
Cambridge, MA 02138
Turnkey micro-based 2D CGI animation

Numonics
418 Pierce St.
Lansdale, PA 19446
Digitizing tablet

Panasonic Industrial Co.
One Panasonic Way
Secaucus, NJ 07094
Optical memory disk recorder, among many other video products

Parallax Graphics
1095 East Duane Avenue
Sunnyvale, CA 94086
Graphics cards for PC

Perspective Technologies
8930 Route 108
Columbia, MD 21045
Turnkey micro-based 3D CGI animation

Photographic Sciences
770 Basket Rd.
P.O. Box 338
Webster, NY 14580
Slide film recording system off CRT

Polaroid
575 Technology Sq.
Cambridge, MA 02139
Palette film recorder for IBM PC, instant slide film

Scriptel
4145 Arlingate Plaza
Columbus, OH 43228
Digitizing tablets

Sigma Designs
San Jose, CA
Color graphics board for PC

Slide Tek
3301 Geary Blvd., Suite 500
San Francisco, CA 94118
Slide and motion-picture film recorders

Sony Corp. of America
Sony Drive
Park Ridge, NJ 07656
Interactive videodisk, graphically oriented micro, etc.

Storage Concepts
3198-G Airport Loop Drive
Costa Mesa, CA 92626
Real-time disk 30 fps storage/retrieval, NTSC resolution

Summagraphics
777 State Street Extension
Fairfield, CT 06430
Digitizing tablet

Vectrix
2606 Branchwood Dr.
Greensboro, NC 27408
Graphics board for IBM PC

Verticom
545 Weddell Dr.
Sunnyvale, CA 94089
Graphics boards, other peripherals, software for IBM PC AT

PC Graphics Software

GIXI
7808 Glenroy Rd., Suite 100
Bloomington, MN 55435
X Paint for IBM PC

Grafpoint
4300 Stevens Creek Blvd.
San Jose, CA 95129
Color graphics terminal emulation software

Interactive Picture Systems
410 South 22 Street
Philadelphia, PA 19146
Movie Maker micro software

Nova Graphics International
1015 Bee Cave Woods
Austin, TX 78746
High-performance IBM PC implementation of Graphical Kernal System for C

Pencept
Waltham, MA
Software for Pencept tablet and IBM PC

Prior Data Sciences
Bell Mews Plaza—Nepean
39 Highway 7
Ottawa, Ontario K2H 8R2
C compiler, GKS implementation software for IBM PC and larger systems

Time Arts
3436 Mendocino Ave.
Santa Rosa, CA 95401
Lumena software and peripherals for IBM PC

Vectrix
2606 Branchwood Dr.
Greensboro, NC 27408
Paint program for IBM PC XT, AT

CAD

AED
440 Potrero
Sunnyvale, CA 94086

Adage
1 Fortune Dr.
Billerica, MA 01821
3D raster graphics workstations, oriented to CAD, usable for animation

Advanced Computer Solutions
2105 Luna Rd.
Carrollton, TX 75006
CAD-oriented graphics adapter for IBM PC

CEL Electronics
Chroma House
Shire Hill
Saffron Walden, Essex CB11 3AQ
England

Calcomp
2411 W. La Palma Ave.
Anaheim, CA 92803

Computervision
201 Burlington Road
Bedford, MA 01730

Cybervision
1280 Main St.
Buffalo, NY 14209
Small turnkey system includes 2D paint package

Dicomed
12000 Portland Ave. South
P.O. Box 246
Minneapolis, MN 55440

Enertronics Research
150 N. Meramec, Suite 207
St. Louis, MO 63105
3D vector display adaptor system for IBM PC

KEL Graphics
400 West Cummings Park
Woburn, MA 01801

New GEA
335 Oser Ave.
Hauppauge, NY 11788
3D vector and raster turnkey systems usable for animation

Raster Technologies
9 Executive Park Dr.
North Billerica, MA 01862
3D raster graphics terminal with ray-tracing software, usable for animation

Silicon Graphics
630 Clyde Ct.
Mountain View, CA 94043
Engineering workstations

TAT Graphics Group
1270 Lawrence Station Rd.
Building E
Sunnyvale, CA 94089
Graphics display system built around IBM PC

Uniras
50 Mall Rd., Suite 212
Burlington, MA 01803
Software for several hardware vendors, many applications

Universal Intergraphix
Ontario, CA
Micro CAD modeling systems

Large-Computer Graphics Systems

AMF Logic Sciences
12343 Hymeadow Dr.
Building 2A
Austin, TX 78750
Vector-to-raster processor

Alias Research
111 Queen Street, 5th Floor
Toronto, Ontario M5C 1S2
Turnkey 2D, 3D system

Artronics
300 Corporate Drive
P.O. Box 408
South Plainfield, NJ 07080

Computer Graphics Laboratories
405 Lexington Avenue
New York, NY 10174
Turnkey 2D and 3D systems

DALIm
Carl-Benz-Strasse 16
D-7608 Willstätt
West Germany
c/o Data Business Vision
3510 Dunhill St., Suite B
San Diego, CA 92121
Turnkey 2D, 3D CGI animation based on Tektronix terminals

Evans & Sutherland
P.O. Box 8700
580 Arapeen Drive
Salt Lake City, UT 84108
3D animation systems

Gould
Imaging & Graphics Division
1870 Lundy Ave.
San Jose, CA 95131
2D, 3D raster graphics and image processing systems

Interactive Machines Inc. (IMI)
Westlake, CA
Superminicomputer often configured for CGI animation

Lucasfilm
P.O. Box 2009
San Rafael, CA 94912
Pixar Image Computer 3D raster graphics system

Megatek
9645 Scranton Road
San Diego, CA 92121
3D solids modeling

Nexus
Bond Building, 3F
3-11, Kanda Nishikicho
Chiyodaku, Tokyo 101
Japan

Ridge Computers
One Greentree Center, Suite 201
Marlton, NJ 08053
Superminicomputer often programmed for animation

Stereographics
Box 2309
San Rafael, CA 94912
3Display paired stereoscopic display

Tektronix
Beaverton, OR
Minicomputer series commonly used for graphics, broadcast video equipment

West End Film
2121 Newport Place NW
Washington, DC 20037
2D and 3D turnkey vector and raster animation systems

Broadcast and Film Equipment

Abekas
319 Lincoln Centre Dr.
Foster City, CA 94404
Turnkey graphics

Adda
Los Gatos, CA
Turnkey 2D digital video graphics

Ampex
401 Broadway
Redwood City, CA 94063
Turnkey graphics and other video equipment

Arriflex
500 Rte. 303
Blauvelt, NY 10913
16 and 35 mm single-framing motion picture cameras

Aurora Systems
San Francisco, CA
Turnkey 2D animation

Barco Industries
2211-B Executive St.
Charlotte, NC 28208
High-resolution monitors

Chroma Digital Systems
2065 Martin Avenue
Santa Clara, CA 95050
Low-cost graphics terminals

Chyron
265 Spagnoli Rd.
Melville, NY 11747
Digital video effects

Dubner Computer Systems
158 Linwood Plaza
Fort Lee, NJ 07024
Turnkey 2D and 3D raster graphics

Eikonix
Bedford, MA
Digital 35 mm motion picture film recorders

Elicon
Brea, CA
Motion control horizontal-track animation systems

Euro Equipment Service
7 Talman Street
Spring Valley, NY 10977
Film and video animation stands and optical printers

Florida Computer Graphics
Lake Mary, FL
Digital video effects

Interactive Motion Control
Culver City, CA
Motion-control computer, computerized traditional animation

Lyon Lamb Animation Systems
4531 Empire Blvd.
Burbank, CA 91505
Still-frame adapter for VCR, complete video animation systems

MCI/Quantel
3290 W. Bayshore Rd.
Palo Alto, CA 94303
Turnkey 2D raster graphics systems

Norpak
10 Hearst Way
Kanata, Ontario K2L 2P4
Canada
Videotex systems

Oxberry
180 Broad Street
Carlstadt, NJ 07072
Optical printers, animation stands, cameras to convert CGI to video and film animation

Robert Bosch, Video Equipment Division
2300 South 2300 West
Salt Lake City, UT 84131
Turnkey 3D raster graphics system

Rosco Laboratories
36 Bush Ave.
Port Chester, NY 10573
Filters

Symtec
15933 West 8 Mile
Detroit, MI 48235
Low-cost graphics terminals

3M Co.
3M Center, Building 223—5S
St. Paul, MN 55144
Turnkey 2D paint and effects systems

Thomson CSF Broadcast
Stamford, CT
2D turnkey graphics generator

Tiffen Manufacturing
90 Oser Ave.
Hauppauge, NY 11788
Filters

Via Video
5155 Old Ironside Dr.
Santa Clara, CA 95054
Turnkey raster graphics and animation systems

Warren R. Smith
P.O. Drawer C
Ocean Gate, NJ 08740
"Analog control" electronic animation stands

B.4 Industry Organizations

Most of these organizations have newsletters, journals, and conventions to enlighten members and nonmembers about ongoing developments in their field. Some work to develop industry standards, and some sponsor large trade shows that are important arenas for the introduction of new products. (Not of incidental importance, the directories to trade shows such as the SMPTE's, SIGGRAPH's, and NCGA's are among the best guides to manufacturers.) These organizations also tend to sponsor or keep tabs on all festivals and competitions in their areas of interest. All exist to help their members meet each other, form contacts, and advance their own careers.

Again, this is a selective list of the groups that ought to interest computer animators most.

Association for Computing Machinery
Special Interest Group on Graphics (ACM-SIGGRAPH)
11 West 42nd Street
New York, NY 10036

Association of Independent Commercial Producers (AICP)
100 East 42nd Street
New York, NY 10017

Association for Multi-Image International
8019 N. Himes Ave., Suite 401
Tampa, FL 33614
The industry organization for producers of slide-tape shows

International Television Association (ITVA)
6311 N. O'Connor Rd. #110
Irving, TX 75039
The industry organization for producers of industrial videotapes

National Computer Graphics Association
2722 Merrilee Drive, Suite 200
Fairfax, VA 22031

Society for Information Display
654 N. Sepulveda Blvd.
Los Angeles, CA 90049

Society of Motion Picture and Television Engineers
862 Scarsdale Ave.
Scarsdale, NY 10583

Glossary

Some sort of glossary seems necessary to keep people from film backgrounds talking with people from computer backgrounds, and to acquaint all concerned with the vocabulary peculiar to animation and especially to terms with usage special to computer animators. Ruthless choices had to be made, however, in selecting words; programming books can best give full glossaries for programming terms, and film books for film terms. Some such works, as well as a good general technology dictionary, are listed in the Bibliography.

aerial imaging: The refilming of an already filmed image by focusing a camera on a projected image. Other flat images may be photographed at the same time, if inserted at the focal plane between projector and camera, thus mixing animated images with whatever was on the original film being projected. Using a traditional animation stand, single frames on an already-filmed motion picture would be projected toward the camera from underneath the table, with the focal planes of projector and camera being located at the plane occupied by a cel.

algorithm: A plan of the precise sequence of steps needed to accomplish any task.

aliasing: Sharply noticeable inaccuracies in the rendering of any line or surface, caused by a too-low sampling rate.

animation: A process in which animate characteristics are given to inanimate objects; usually, sequential still pictures are manipulated to give the illusion of motion.

animation stand or table: The set-up for filming of traditional cel animation; involves a table with a hole cut out for light to shine up through the bottom (for bottom-lit animation) and arms holding flood lamps for top-lit animation. Three levels of either clear or frosted glass surfaces hold cels with images simulating foreground, mid, and background. On a ratcheted and geared assembly overhead a single-framing camera is mounted. Precise calibration for all cels is provided by posts and holes in the table.

array: An ordered list of items, which may be organized in one, two, three, or more dimensions.

aspect ratio: The ratio between vertical and horizontal image measurements.

batch processing: A type of computer operation in which there is no interaction between programmer and machine while the program runs; quantities of information are fed in for processing, and the programmer waits for it all to be processed.

benchmark: A measurement of performance. In computing, various benchmark tests are often established and used for all sorts of software to determine how fast and how well complicated programs will run.

binary: A number in Base 2; an either/or comparison.

bit: The smallest piece of information usable by a computer; one binary off/on switch.

bottom-lit animation: Traditional animation lit from underneath the cels. Also defines a ''look'': bottom-lit images seem to glow, with each colored area emitting its own light.

bottom-up: Working out a project by developing details first, then allowing the larger organization to be decided by what seems to be the best interplay of details.

buffer: A block of memory set aside for temporarily holding data.

byte: Eight bits; the standard amount of information used to define a typographical character.

Cartesian coordinates: Rene Descartes's system for two-dimensional graphic respresentation of numerical phenomena, using a floating point system with positive and negative coordinates extending in four directions on one plane. Also used to describe similar three-dimensional or larger mapping systems.

cel: For ''celluloid,'' a drawing on which is the basic building block of traditional 2D animation.

cel animation: The process of drawing or painting pictures on cels or sheets of acetate, then photographing single frames of motion picture film of successive images to create the illusion of movement; cels showing foreground, midground, and background are layered to create the illusion of three dimensions.

character animation: Animation in which the objects depicted are given their own personal character, often anthropomorphic.

chrominance: Color characteristics, specifically as split into two composite "chroma" measurements in composite television.

compiler: A program that translates the instructions of a high-level language to low-level, machine-understandable language. Compilers translate the whole program at once, when it is complete and just before it is to be run, as opposed to assemblers, which translate the high-level language one line at a time. C is a compiled language, BASIC an assembled language.

composite television: A system of television recording and broadcasting, used throughout the world, in which the color image is broken into three composites: *Y*, or luminance; and *U* and *V*, two chrominance composites of all colors.

computer-aided design (CAD): Any design work that utilizes a computer at any stage of production.

computer-assisted animation: Animation made with the help of a computer, but not CGI; motion control, computer-controlled opticals, digitized images from other sources, etc.

computer-generated imagery (CGI): Images created entirely within computer memory.

data structure: An ordered way to store and access information.

data tree: A data structure with a system of larger-to-smaller branches of data; ever-smaller subsets of sets of data would be accessible along various branches of the program.

debug: To search out and fix any mistakes in a program.

digitize: To sample any natural phenomenon or analog of a natural phenomenon, and make a representation of it coded into digits.

film: A visual communications medium, with images produced by chemical emulsions interacting with light. The emulsions are backed by a layer of celluloid "film." Motion-picture film is a strip of separate frames holding individual photographs on each; each photo shows an image only slightly different from those before and after, with 24 (U.S.) or 25 (Europe) frames per second being standard shooting and projecting speed. An optical illusion, "persistence of vision," allows the continuum of photos to be seen as lifelike moving pictures. Motion-picture film stocks are available in various widths — 8 millimeter, 16 mm, 35 mm, and 70 mm —with 35 mm being the professional standard, 70 (or a 65 mm picture size) being used for wide-screen epics, 16 mm for some professional uses (being generally equivalent in resolution to television), and 8 mm being an amateur medium. Film stocks are also rated in different speeds (in ASA, for American Standards Association, or DIN, in Europe, for the German industry standard), with higher speeds having less resolution but allowing photography with less light. A side-track on the film is used to record sound, either in optical patterns or in electrical impulses on a strip of magnetic tape (see *video*).

firmware: Programs stored in permanent read-only memory within a computer.

floating point system: A system of numbers represented with decimal point at center and extending in positive and negative or multiple and fractional directions. In linear (single) dimension numbers, an example is scientific notation, in which numbers are always represented by one digit to the left of the decimal, then as many fractions as significant, multiplied by an exponent: 2.345×10^5. In two-dimensional graphs, Cartesian coordinates set zero at center and extend in negative and positive directions to infinity.

frame: The outer boundary of an image; the entirety of one static image. Motion-picture film in the U.S. uses 24 static frames per second; U.S. video uses 30 per second.

function: In C, a routine; a complete operation that accomplishes a defined goal.

genlocking: The process of aligning the data rate of a video image with that of a digital device, to digitize the image and enter it into computer memory.

glint: A shiny glow around the edge of an image; a computer graphics visual cliche.

graphic animation: Static graphics given the illusion of motion through any sort of animation technique.

graphics: The rendering of shapes or colors to produce patterns with some signification.

hexadecimal: Base 16, usually signified by a preceding 0x or &H and formed from the standard nine Base-10 digits plus a, b, c, d, e, and f to represent 10, 11, 12, 13, 14, and 15.

high-level language: A machine-transportable computer language; a way of communicating to various computers in a standardized way.

icon: A visual symbol.

library: In computer languages, a group of functions, routines, or full programs that can be called up to perform desired tasks.

low-level language: Machine or assembly languages; communications to a computer that are not machine-transportable, but understandable only to a specific digital device or a small group of digital devices.

luminance: Brightness; one of the three image characteristics coded in composite television, represented by the letter *Y;* may be measured in lux or foot-candles.

macro: A defining statement included at the beginning of a program to set all further conditions within the program to its specifications.

matrix: An array with at least two dimensions — usually just two — with values occupying positions relative to each other in each direction.

matte: A covering; in photography, a 100-percent black patch over an entire frame or over a portion of a frame during exposure; the covered area may be exposed to a different image in a second exposure, allowing one frame to contain a combination of two images. Mattes may be hard-edged for precise line-matching images, or soft-edged for smooth transition between non-critically aligned images. See traveling matte, stationary matte.

motion control: Computer-controlled camera movements and/or computer-controlled movements of objects, to be animated by a single-framing camera; similar to ''numerical control'' of machine instruments in industrial processes.

moving motion animation: Same as stop motion, but involves the object in motion while each single frame is shot. The final image would then present a slightly blurred, dynamic sense of movement, as in very quickly moving live action not quite caught by a camera. Necessitates a precision made possible only by motion control techniques.

octal: A Base 8 number.

optical disk: A recording medium for video or digital information in which a laser records or plays back holographic records of coded information onto successive frames. Vast amounts of data can be stored in this manner. Commonly available optical memories (such as videodisks) are usually ROM, but optical read/write RAM is being used more all the time.

palette: A selection of colors.

pan: Sideways rotation of the camera during live-action filming or videotaping.

pan cel: The bottom cel in traditional animation; a longer cel than the others (horizontally), to be used for backgrounds that may be given the illusion of a live-action pan by moving the cel horizontally between successive single frames.

parallel processing: Processing of more than one task or set of tasks at the same time.

persistence of vision: A phenomenon of sight that allows people to interpret separate, quickly successive images as a moving continuum. Sixteen images per second seems to be the slowest rate to allow for persistence of vision, but movements depicted at this rate still appear somewhat jerky.

pixel: Picture element; a "dot" used as the elemental building block of a picture. One way to measure picture resolution is by the number of pixels used to make up the image.

pixillation: The opposite of animation, made by single-framing of live action, often resulting in motion pictures with sequential jumps between frames that are too great to take advantage of persistence of vision; also may be used to produce certain effects that take advantage of persistence of vision: e.g., by filming only the highest position reached by a actor jumping in the air many times, the final film would seem to show the actor walking on air.

planar: Occupying a single two-dimensional plane.

pointer: In C, a data type that contains another block of memory; "points to," or can be used to immediately access whatever data occupies the contained memory block.

polygon: A many-sided object (at least three sides) existing in two or more dimensions, but usually just two dimensions.

polyhedron: A polygon of at least, and usually only of, three dimensions; usually, a solid body defined totally by planar sides, and of at least four planar sides.

primitive: A basic image or model used as a building block of a more complex image or model.

raster: A television-like projection of numerous electrons emitted as a beam from one or more phosphors (usually three for full color) in predetermined scan lines across the inner front face of a cathode ray tube, completely refreshed with a new image many times per second. Raster graphics program the the raster display with a full-color, full-screen image.

ray tracing: Mapping of programmed positions for simulated light rays as they might illuminate a computer-generated three-dimensional image.

real-time: Computer functions that happen fast enough to keep up with whatever they control or interact with. In animation, this would define instantaneous production of moving images.

reflection: A mirror-like bouncing of light off a surface.

refraction: The changing of the direction of light as it travels through a partially transparent surface.

resolution: The parameters of image quality; can be used in terms of pictoral detailing (most commonly) as relative number of pixel building blocks used to represent a continuous image, and can be measured in the different directions that define a multidimensional image (horizontal resolution, vertical resolution, diagonal resolution, depth resolution); can also refer to other definable qualities such as edge definition between objects depicted in the same frame (edge resolution), number of colors into which the spectrum is broken down (color resolution), etc.

rotoscope: Pseudoanimation made by filming live action, then projecting the film frame by frame onto a drawing table and outlining, then perhaps coloring in the images. The cels thus created would be animated in a traditional way.

saturation: The relative strength of a particular color.

scalar: A factoral quantity used to define the increase, decrease, or other change in a base quantity. Usually a factor in multiplication or division, a scalar can also define the exponential, differential, or other rate of change in a quantity. Often in CGI, matrices are used as scalars to determine changes in original modeled representations of numerical quantities.

slit scan: A traditional animation process, now mostly done with motion control; involves bottom-light shot through a slitted matte, creating a glow in the general shape of the slit.

specular: In imagery, a condition of light; light that changes in reflectivity or refractiveness in contiguous places across a surface or other area.

sprite: In computer graphics, a simple image that can be animated in real time within a larger, static image.

stationary matte: A matte that covers an unmoving position in the frame and may be held in front of the lens for a soft edge, or between lens and film plane for a hard edge.

stop motion: Pixillation or actual animation of solid objects by shooting single frames of successive positions.

storyboard: An outline in images for a film, video, or CGI sequence; may resemble a comic strip, and usually has all action, dialog, sound effects, and camera movements noted.

streak: A slang expression for an animated form often seen in high-tech-style imagery; shiny, streaking surfaces, usually produced with bottom light and slit scan, but possible to emulate with various processes.

tiling: Creating a pattern of pixels that can be used to fill an area or cover a surface.

tilt: An up or down rotational camera movement.

top-down: Developing a project from fully planned generalities first, then working out successively more detailed aspects.

track shot: A camera movement in space through a scene to be filmed, so called because cameras often were, and still sometimes are (especially for motion control) mounted on railroad-type tracks for smoothness and repeatability. Now equivalent to a "dolly shot."

traveling matte: A matte made of a high-contrast negative or positive of any original image, but usually one filmed against a blue screen (thus "blue-screen matting") to isolate precisely the object to be matted. The high-con' matte is then bipacked in a camera or the camera side of an optical printer to obscure a portion of another image. An opposing matte would be made by printing a negative of the first matte, to be used to cover the other portion of the frame in another pass through the printer, while the film is exposed to another image only where it was previously left unexposed by the first matte. The "traveling matte" travels across the frame, because it is a motion picture, like any other "traveling" motion-picture image.

turnkey system: A commercial product of a production system, made to be operable and productive "from the turn of a key"; a computer graphics system made to be usable by unsophisticated users. Contains packaged hardware and software.

variable: An expression that can take any meaning assigned to it. Variables are often divided into classes to facilitate usage; this makes them less variable, to whatever extent they may be typed. Common variable types in computer programming are local (operates only within a defined routine or function); global (takes the same meaning whenever used); static (increments meaning each time it is used).

vector graphics: Graphics made of lines; wire-frame-style line drawings; line drawings programmed by computer to take advantage of lower memory requirements (versus fully drawn images) internally and in display technology.

video: A medium of recording photography in electrical impulses on magnetic tape or disk, or on optical disk. Typically thirty frames per second (U.S.) or 25 fps (countries with 50 Hz electrical standards) are recorded for persistence of vision (see "film"). Video utilizes a sensing device to transfer images to electrical impulses: either a vacuum tube with phosphors (variously, lead oxide, an arsenic-gallium combination, or other chemicals are used), or a digital charge-coupled device (CCD). An image is thus coded into two interlaced fields per frame, each field containing 262 lines of 430 pixels (NTSC, or U.S. standard), with one line used to join the fields. Video may or may not be recorded, and either directly from the camera or from a record it may be broadcasted or carried over wire to a cathode ray tube (CRT) display. This performs the opposite, decoding procedure to a camera tube, using the electronic signal to excite phosphors that shoot out beams in the video line pattern. Video resolution is roughly equivalent to a low-ASA 16 mm film, in terms of pixels, but video allows a latitude of lightest to darkest images of only 30:1, whereas film may allow well over 100:1. Video is a relatively permanent storage medium, however, while film deteriorates (see "film").

videodisk: See optical disk.

videotex: An interactive computer-graphic data base that may be accessed through relatively simple terminals over telephone, cable television, or other lines of mass communication.

viewport: A vantage on a scene; may be an entire terminal screen, or a portion of the screen.

window: An image that is seen through a viewpoint. Used in computer graphics to present scenes from one program, file, memory block, or buffer within a different program, file, etc.

wire frame: See vector.

zoom: A lens movement, or its simulation, that seems to smoothly increment or decrement the relative distance between image and vantage point; a constant increase or decrease in lens focal length.

Bibliography

Rather than a simple list of every book mentioned in this one (and these are all included), this bibliography is meant to be a study guide that will round out any reader's knowledge of the subject matter. For this reason, many scientific papers — useful, indeed groundbreaking, but more esoteric in scope — are specifically *not* included. Such papers may be found in the proceedings of SIGGRAPH, NCGA, and SMPTE (which are included here), or heard at their various conventions.

Unless otherwise noted, all publishers are American.

ACM Transactions on Graphics. New York, quarterly. Vital for keeping up with ground-breaking reseach in computer graphics.

American Cinematographer's Handbook. American Society of Cinematographers, Los Angeles, 1985 (new edition yearly). Handy for depth-of-field charts, color charts, information on film stocks, filters, etc.

Arnold, B. H.: *Intuitive Concepts in Elementary Topology.* Prentice–Hall, 1962. A good beginning idea source for complex mathematical curved surfaces.

Artwick, Bruce A.: *Microcomputer Displays, Graphics, and Animation.* Prentice–Hall, 1985. Concentrates on graphics programming in BASIC.

Broadcast Management/Engineering. New York, monthly trade magazine. Good for staying up to date with the engineering side of the broadcast industry.

Byte, The Small Systems Journal. Peterborough NH, monthly consumer magaine. Often runs articles on graphics.

Canemaker, John: *Winsor McCay.* Abbeville Press, 1987. A biography of the great animator by one of today's better animators.

Cinemagic. Starlog Press, New York, monthly consumer magazine. Tends to concentrate on older forms of special effects, including make-up and stunts.

Clark, David R., Ph.D.: *Computers For Imagemaking.* Pergamon Press, London, 1981. A useful, though somewhat outdated collection of interestingly idiosyncratic approaches to CGI.

Complete Kodak Animation Book. Eastman Kodak, 1985. A good beginning book for traditional animation.

Computer Graphics, Quarterly Report of the Association for Computing Machinery Special Interest Group on Graphics. (ACM SIGGRAPH), New York. A vital publication for keeping up with the field.

Computer Graphics World. Littleton, MA, monthly trade magazine. The best trade book for following commercial developments in computer graphics other than animation.

Computer Pictures. Backstage Publishing, New York, monthly trade magazine. Mostly tracks graphics for TV commercials and programming.

Conference Proceedings, National Computer Graphics Association (NCGA). Fairfax, VA, 1985 (new editions twice yearly). Rarely as ground-breaking as papers introduced at SIGGRAPH, but very worthy nonetheless.

Crafton, Donald: *Before Mickey, The Animated Film 1898–1928.* MIT Press, 1984. Perhaps the best-told early history of animation.

Curtis, David: *Experimental Cinema.* Dell Publishing Co, 1971. An overview of aesthetic trends in noncommercial "art" films, and a good introduction to rarely used animation techniques.

Educational & Industrial Television (EITV). New York, monthly trade magazine.

Eisenstein, Sergei: *Film Form.* Harcourt, Brace & World, 1949. The first and most influential work in film theory.

Encyclopedia of Philosophy. Macmillan, 1967. Many mathematical concepts defined in humanistic terms, which is, in a nongraphical way, just what computer animation can do. The definition of "recursive function" alone is worth the price of admission.

Fielding, Raymond: *Technique of Special Effect Cinematography.* American Society of Cinematographers, Hollywood, CA, 1972. The classic on traditional optical special effects.

Foley, J. D., and Van Dam, A.: *Fundamentals of Interactive Computer Graphics.* Addison–Wesley, 1983. Perfect for designers of interactive systems using Pascal, with many interesting points for animators, too.

Hearn, Donald, and Baker, M. Pauline: *Microcomputer Graphics Techniques & Applications.* Prentice–Hall, 1983. Beginning graphics in BASIC.

Hunt, William James: *The C Toolbox.* Addison–Wesley, 1985. Could be considered a companion volume to this book, for animator–programmers using the IBM PC; supplies all the IBM/C details that wouldn't fit here, along with sound general programming advice.

Jeong, Tung H.: *A Study Guide on Holography.* Lake Forest College, IL, 1976. An excellent, brief introduction to laser holography, perhaps the computer animation output device of the future.

Johnson, S.C.: *LINT, A C Program Checker.* Bell Laboratories, 1981. Explains the C debugging program LINT.

Journal of the American Society of Cinematographers. Hollywood, CA.

Journal of the Society of Motion Picture and Television Engineers. Scarsdale, NY. Neither of the above two journals is essential, but both are useful for keeping up with new technology and practice in their fields.

Kandinsky, Wassily: *Point and Line To Plane.* Dover, 1979. The meanings of images . . . or perhaps not; invaluable nonetheless.

Kelley, Al, and Ira Pohl: *A Book on C.* Benjamin/Cummings, 1984. A good, general C starter text.

Knight, Arthur: *The Liveliest Art.* Mentor, 1959. The classic history of American film.

Kochan, Stephen G.: *Programming in C.* Hayden Book Co., 1983. Another good C starter text.

Lipton, Lenny: *Independent Filmmaking.* Straight Arrow Books, 1972. Almost a classic by now, full of good, straightforward advice on making your own 16 mm films.

Maltin, Leonard: *Of Mice and Magic.* Plume, 1984. A great animation-buff book.

Millimeter Magazine. New York, monthly trade magazine. Frequent coverage of graphics for TV and commercials.

Myers, Roy E.: *Microcomputer Graphics for the IBM PC.* Addison–Wesley, 1983. A good beginning text for PC BASIC.

Newman, William, and Sproull, Robert F.: *Principles of Interactive Computer Graphics.* McGraw-Hill, 1979. A bit outdated by now, and somewhat superseded by Foley and Van Dam's book on the same subject; however, Newman and Sproull have done seminal work, and the book remains a fountain of ideas.

Rubin, Susan: *Animation: The Art and the Industry.* Prentice-Hall, 1985. Some advice on what the industry is like, part beginner's text for traditional animation.

Schachter, Bruce J., editor: *Computer Image Generation.* Wiley-Interscience, 1983. The big-hardware (emphasis on aerospace) origins of computer graphics.

Schustack, Steve: *Variations in C.* Microsoft Press, 1985. Well-written advice for elegant C programming.

Smith, Conrad: *The Early History of Animation.* NY, 1975. As opposed to other histories, this tells the story mostly in the words of those who participated, and is thus all the more interesting.

Smith, Henry Nash: *Popular Culture and Industrialism, 1865–1890.* Doubleday Anchor, 1967. Invaluable to an understanding of animation's roots and place in society.

Trombetta and Trombetta: *Using BASIC on the IBM PC.* Addison-Wesley, 1984. Not much emphasis on graphics, but a very thorough text on PC BASIC.

Wollen, Peter: *Signs and Meaning in the Cinema.* Indiana University Press, 1972. Perhaps the most influential critical book on film since the forties.

Art Credits

Figures 1–7 used by permission of The Fantastic Animation Machine, Inc. Imagery produced by proprietary hardware and software at The Fantastic Animation Machine, Inc., NYC. Figures 8–12 used by permission of Abel Image Research. Figures 13–16 used by permission of Bo Gehring & Associates. Figure 17 used by permission of Colorado Cooler Company. From "Bottle Lift." Directed by Alex Weil and Malcolm McNeill; Produced by Ralph Horan; Paintbox Art by Henry Baker, Page Wood, and Gordon DeWolf; Camera Man: John Kraus; Editors: Bill Weber and Mark Forker; Art Director: Rosalyn Dunham; Copywriter: Charlie Ryant; Producer: Alan Pentaleri; Creative Directors: Rosalyn Dunham and Charlie Ryant. Produced by Charlex, Inc. for Colorado Cooler Company. Figure 18 used by permission of Charlex, Inc. From "Nickelodeon Dinosaur Promo." Designed and Directed by Malcolm McNeill and Charlie Levy; Model Maker: Tony Laudati; Editors: Bill Weber and David Hyland; Paintbox Art: Henry Baker; Produced by Charlex, Inc., for Fred/Alan, Inc. Figure 19 used by permission of USA Network. From "Flapjazz." Designed and Directed by Malcolm McNeill and Charlie Levy; Editors: Bill Weber and Roger Tyrell; Paintbox Art: Martha Kansler. Produced by Charlex, Inc. for USA Network. Figure 20 used by permission of R/Greenberg Associates, Inc. and Silver Pictures, Inc. From "Streets of Fire." Production Company: R/Greenberg Associates, Inc. Client: Universal Studio. Figure 21 used by permission of R/Greenberg Associates, Inc. and Tri-Star Pictures. From "Lifeforce." Production Company: R/Greenberg Associates, Inc. Client: Tri-Star Pictures. Figure 22 used by permission of R/Greenberg Associates, Inc. and Home Box Office, Inc. From "Cinemax Special." Director of Design: Orest Woronewych; Designer: Paul Fuentes. Production Company: R/Greenberg Associates, Inc. Client: Home Box Office. Figure 23 used by permission of R/Greenberg Associates, Inc. and Ketchum Advertising Philadelphia. From "Circles of Light." Art Directors: Joe Caserta and Russ Branscom; Copywriters: Margaret Myers and Charles Tyson, Jr.; Production Company: R/Greenberg Associates, Inc. Agency: Ketchum Advertising. Client: Bell Atlantic Corporation.

Index

Abel, Robert, 231–235, 254
Absolute value of variable in C, 131
A-buffer, 205–207
Advertising design, 242–243
Aerospace companies, graphics use by, 243–244
Algebraic expressions, 1–4, 100, 103, 131, 175–176, 190, 203
Algorithms, 63, 126–129
  bottom-up method of development in C, 127–129
  hidden surface, development of, 203–207
  in-betweening, 193
  scan-line, 205–207
  simulated lighting, 208–211
Aliasing, 15–18, 24
  misrepresentation of curved surfaces, 201
  vector images, 196
  See also Anti-aliasing
American Cinematographer's Manual, 207
Amiga microcomputer, 142
Analytic geometry as animation tool kit, 187
AND in BASIC, 151
Anger, Kenneth, 282
Animatics, 225–226, 243
Anti-aliasing, 16–18, 24, 180
  A-buffer hidden surface technique, 205–207
APAGE in BASIC, 67
Apple Macintosh, 13
Application program, 52
Arcade video games, 216–219, 247–248
Architectural design, 244–245
Arguments, in C, 176
Arrays, 132–137
  structures of, 143–146, 186
  values, assignment of, 175–176
Arithmatic expressions. *See* Mathematical formulas
ASCII code for keyboard input, 183
Assembly-language program, 47
Aspect ratio, 81
Asterisks indicating pointer variables in C, 111
Automatic variables in C, 132
Avery, Tex, 273

Bakshi, Ralph, 279–280
Barrè, Raoul, 269, 270
Barthes, Roland, 284
BASIC, 49–50

BASIC (*continued*)
  alternatives to, 50
  aspect ratio, 81
  background position of PAINT, 83
  BLOAD, 89
  boundary position of PAINT, 83
  BSAVE, 88
  CIRCLE format, aspect in the, 81
  DRAW, 82, 87–88
  ellipse, creation of, 81
  flipping an image, 84
  GET, 88
  motion control, 221–223
  PAINT, 82–83
  PMAP, 86
  POINT, 86
  PUT retrieval of information, 88
  run-length encoding, 194
  STEP, 80–81
  stringing sets of statements, 87–88
  tiling pattern, creation of, 82–83
  track or dolly shots, simulation of, 84–85
  video RAM access, 142
  VIEW, 85–86
  WINDOW, 83–85
  world coordinates, 86
  zoom simulation, 84
Bazin, André, 255
Benchmarks, 149
Ben Hur, 277
Benning, James, 282
Bettelheim, Bruno, 283
Betty Boop, 265, 271–272
Bezier patches, 200–201
Bibliography, 331–334
Birth of a Nation, 266
Bit fields, 160–164
Bit operations, 151, 149–153
Bit pads. *See* Digitizing tablets
Bits, 158, 160–164
  color coding, 165–168
  mapping on IBM PC, 70–72
  optimum bits per pixel, 144
  packing information into, 158–164
  values of pixels, changing bit, 152, 159
Black Maria, 264
Blackton, J. Stuart, 263
BLOAD in BASIC, 89
Bottom-up method of algorithm development, 127–129
Boundary position of PAINT in BASIC, 83
Box drawing
  in BASIC, 79–80
  in C, 179, 185–186
Brakhage, Stan, 282
Brainstorm, 278
Bray, John R., 267, 269, 270
Bright color cliche, 252–253
Briggs, Henry, 99, 103
Bringing Up Baby, 277
Broadcast equipment vendors, list of, 317–318
Brushes, pseudo, 176–177
BSAVE in BASIC, 88
Buffers, 9, 11–12, 19–20, 41–42, 52, 146, 170–172
  edge coherence, 205
  initializing the buffer array, 175–176
  passive block of memory, array as, 169
  scan-line coherence, 205
  video games, 216–219
  See also Window, Refresh buffers
Bugs Bunny, 273
burst in C, 67
Byte values, 10–12, 149. *See also* Bit

CAD vendors, list of, 315–316
California
  schools, list of computer animation, 307–308

studios, list of animation, 290–295
calloc in C, 147–148, 173, 174
Camera
animation stand, development of, 274–275
cinematographe, invention of, 262
invention of, 261–263
resolution of home video, 14
robot devices, connection of, 223
track or dolly shots, simulation of, 84–85
viewpoint, change of, 187–188
Campbell, Joseph, 283
Canada
schools, list of computer animation, 307
studios, list of animation, 304
Canemaker, John, 239
Carlson, Wallace, 268
Carpenter, Loren, 204–207
Cartesian coordinates, grid, 54–55
Cathode ray tube, 23
Catmull, Edwin, 205–207
Cartography, 245–246
Cel animation, 270
Chaplin, Charlie, 267
Character animation, development of, 275
char data type in C. *See* Signed operators
Charlex, 225–228
Charlie the Tuna, 280
Children's TV programs, 256–257
advertisements, 257–258
Saturday morning programs, 256–257
Chrominance. *See* Color characteristics
Cinematographe, invention of, 262
Circles
BASIC, format in, 81
building blocks, 60
Clair, René, 275–276
Clampett, Bob, 273
C, 48–49, 90–125. *See also* specific subheads
Classroom computerization, 246
Close Encounters of the Third Kind, 278
Clown's Little Brother, 271
CLS in BASIC, 75
Cohl, Emile, 264
Colonel Heeza Liar, 270
Color characteristics, 4–6, 10, 12, 161–163
bit fields, coding, 165–168
bright color cliche, 252–253
cycling, 38–39, 105, 184–186
development of Technicolor process, 253
human perception of resolution, 161
labeling system, 139
large palette program vs. small palette program, 168
line-by-line filling-in, 4–6, 79–80
patches of, 165–166
resolution, 25–26, 161
selection of palette, 71, 75, 167–168
temperature, 207–208
variable palette program in C, 106–125
variation perception, 13
vector system, full-color images from, 196
Walt Disney and, 273–274
Columbia Pictures, 272–273
Comics, first appearance of newspaper, 263
Common-sense variable names, 129
compound relational operators in C, 111–113
Computer-assisted imagery, 1
Computer-generated imagery, 1–22. *See also* specific subheads
Conditional compilations in C, building of, 139
constants in C, 95–100

Conversion of hexadecimal to decimal, 69–70
Coons, Steven, 201
Coonskin, 280
Coordinate systems, 54–55
  See also World coordinates
Coppola, Francis, 283
Core graphics system, 47–48
Corporate video, 241–242
Costs, 220–221, 254–255
  hard-disk memories, 181
  motion control systems, 221, 223
  music videos, 258–259
  robot arms, 223
Curved surfaces defined, 201

Data base management systems, use of, 51–52
Data tree or list in C, 102–103
data types in C, 95
DBMS, use of, 51–52
Debevoise, Allen, 235
default indicating input mistake in C, 117–121
#define in C, 139, 174
DeMille, Cecil B., 277
Depth cueing, 202
Descartes, René, 54
Design elegance, 60–61
Dials, 28
Dickson, William K. L., 262
Difference mapping, 19
Digital video-effects devices, advent of, 281
Digitized video input, 172
Digitizing cards, 29
Digitizing tablets, 27, 76, 172, 178
Direct display, 142
Direct view storage tube, 3
Disney, Walt, 272–275
Dolly shots, simulation of, 84–85
DOS interface in BASIC, 141–142
do in C, 105–106
Double-buffering, 41–42
double data type in C. *See* Signed operators
DRAW in BASIC, 82, 87–88
Dreams That Money Can Buy, 282
Duel in the Sun, 278
Dumbo, 275
Duval, Shelley, 281, 283
DVST. *See* Direct view storage tube
Dynamic memory allocation, 146–149

Eastman, George, 262, 276
Edge coherence characteristic, 205
Edge lines, 4
Edge table, 205
Edison, Thomas, 262
Educational institutions, 246
  list of, 306–310
Educational software, 246
Ellipses, uses of, 54–59, 81
#else in C, 139
elseif in C, 106–111, 113–115
Enabling software, 46
#endif in C, 139
English language compared to C, 128
Enoch Arden, 266
Equipment. *See* Hardware
Exclusive OR in BASIC, 152
Experimental film, 282
external variables in C, 132

"Fairie Tale Theatre", 281, 283
Fantasmagorie, 264
Fantastic Animation Machine, 238–239
Filling-in, 4–6, 196–197
Film equipment vendors, list of, 317–318
Filters, 32
Flags in C, 115–117
Flattening the image, 177
Flicker, existence of, 3
Flight simulation, 245, 270

Flipping an image, 84, 105, 177, 188
float in C. *See* Signed operators
Floating point system, 73
Flying spot scanners, 31
for in C, 100–103, 136
FORTRAN, 47
  limitations of, 48
  run-length encoding, 194
Fractals, 3–4
  defined, 6, 201–202
  Mandelbrot, Benoit, 6–8
  ray-tracing, 210
  Richardson, O., 8
  Von Koch, Helge, 7–8
Frame buffer. *See* Buffer
Fleischer, Dave, 270–272
Fleischer, Max, 270–272
free in C, 147–148
Freleng, Isidore "Friz", 273
Friendly software, 247
Friese-Greene, William, 262
Fritz The Cat, 280
Functions in C, 92, 129–132
Fuzzy monitor resolution, 24–25

Gamma measurements, 13
Gance, Abel, 275–276
Gavril, Suzanne, 238–239
Gehring, Bo, 235–238
The General, 266
Genlocking, 29
Gertie the Dinosaur, 267
Giant, 278
Global variables in C, 132
Glossary, 321–329
Graphical Kernel System (GKS), 47–48
Graphics cards, 23, 25, 49–50, 138, 171–172
  IBM PC, 67, 72
  memory locations, specification of, 68
Great Britain, coastline of, 8
The Great Dictator, 273
Greenberg, Richard, 228–231, 255
Greenberg, Robert, 228–231
Griffith, D. W., 265–267

Hardware, 3–6, 23–24
  direct view storage tube, 3
  hidden surface problem, 204
  input components, 27–30, 183, 221–223
  output components, 30–34
  vendors, list of, 317–318
Harman, Hugh, 273
Harmonics, 17
Harrison, Lee, 280
Hays Office, The, 271–272
Headers in C, 140
Hearst, William Randolph, 263
Heavy Traffic, 280
Hermite patches, 200–201
Hexadecimals
  C recognition of, 153–158
  decimal, conversion to, 69–70
  IBM BASIC, 68
Heyl, Henry R., 261–262
Hidden-line problem, 79–80
Hidden-surface problem, 203–207
High-end paint programs, 39
Hitchcock, Alfred, 277
How a Mosquito Operates, 267
Humorous Phases of Funny Faces, 263
Hurd, Earl, 269, 270

IBM PC. *See* specific subheads
#ifdef in C, 139
if in C, 106–111, 113–115
In-betweening program, 191–195
#include in C, 139
Inclusive OR function, 151
increment operator in C, 101
Independent filmmaking, 281–283
Industrial design, 44–45, 243–244
Initializing the buffer array, 175–176

Input, 141–142
  bit pad. *See* digitizing tablets
  joy stick, 28, 172, 217
  keyboard, 27, 183
  light pen, 27–28
  magnetic pen, 27
  mistakes in C, 117–121
  mouse, 28
  robot arm, 221–223
  transformation, 63–65
int in C, 95, 98–101, 132, 149. *See also* Signed operators
Interactive systems, 65
  corporate video, 242
  future of, 251–252
  nonprogrammers' ability to build, 213–216
  pseudocode for video game, 217–218
  real-time, 212–213, 216–217
  ROM, 216–217
  videodisks, 218
Intolerance, 266
Ising, Rudolf, 273
Isotropic memory, 21

Jazz Singer, The, 273
Jones, Chuck, 273
Joy sticks, 28, 172, 217

Kandinsky, Wassily, 76–77
Keaton, Buster, 266
KEY in BASIC, 75
Kinetoscope, development of, 262
Knight, Arthur, 266
Knowlton, Ben, 283
Koko The Clown, 265
Kubrick, Stanley, 85, 278

Lambert, J. H., 208
Lang, Fritz, 233
Large-computer graphics systems vendors, list of, 316–317
Large palette programs, 101–111, 123–125, 168, 180–184, 214
Leprince, Louis, 262
Levi, Charles, 225–228
Libraries of functions, 92, 141–142
Lighting, psychological effects of, 207. *See also* Luminance
Light pens, 27–28
Lindner, Jim, 238–239
Line drawings. *See* Vector graphics
Little Nemo, 263, 267–268
local in C, 132
Logarithms, inventor of, 99
Logical and test in C, 112
logical negation operator in C, 116
logical or test in C, 112
Lois, George, 227–228
Lonedale Operator, The, 266
long in C. *See* Signed operators
Looney Tunes series, 273
Looping statements, 100–105, 133
Lords of the Ring, The, 280
Lucasfilm, 204–207
  motion control, use of, 220
Lucas, George, 283. *See also* Lucasfilm
Luminance, 10–12, 161–163, 252–253

macro in C, 146
main in C, 93–94, 130
malloc in C, 147–148
Mandelbrot, Benoit, 6–8
Man With The Movie Camera, The, 276
Maps, 142, 194–195, 245–246
  difference mapping, 19
  two dimensional mapping, 210–211
Mathematical formulas, 1–4, 97, 186
  conversion from hexadecimal to decimal, 69–70
  edge lines, 4
  input transformation stage, 64
  recursive division, 7
  simulated lighting, 207–211

tool kit, analytic geometry as animation, 187
Matrix (matrices), 134–135, 188
Matte
hard edge, 265–266
in photography, 265–266
soft edge, 265–266
stationary, 207–211
surfaces, reflectance of, 207–211
travelling, 265–266
Mayer, Louis B., 234
McCay, Winsor, 263, 267–269
McLaren, Norman, 281–282
Mechanical movement cliche, 252–253
Méliès, Georges, 264, 266, 283
Memory mapping, 142
Merrie Melodies series, 273
Metro-Goldwyn-Mayer, 272–273
Mickey Mouse, 1–2, 271
Midwest
schools, list of computer animation, 308–309
studios, list of animation, 300–301
Military, graphics use by, 244
Mittleman, Dr. Phillip, 235
Mirror images
simplest sort of image transform, 188
mode in C, 67
Model, creation of image, 54
Modern Times, 273
Monochromatic images, 4
Motion control, 220–223
MS-DOS, 49, 141
Music videos
artistic freedom in, 258–259
color cycling, 105
invention of digital video-effects devices, importance of, 281
Muybridge, Eadweard, 262

Napier, John, 99, 103
NAPLPS, 42
National Computer Graphics Association (NCGA), 244
Nests in C, 107–111
New Jersey animation studios, list of, 295–299
News programming, television, 258, 280–281
New York animation studios, list of, 295–299
Nonmoving window defined, 191
North American Presentation Level Protocol System. *See* NAPLPS
North American Television Standard. *See* NTSC
Northeast
schools, list of computer animation, 309–310
studios, list of animation, 304–305
NTSC, 9–10, 25

Octagons as building blocks, 60
Octals, C recognition of, 153–158
Ones complement in C, 152
Operators in C, 97–98, 115, 139–140, 149–153, 160
Operations on Bits, 149–153
Optical effects, 264–266
Optical memory disk recorder, 33–34
Optical printer, invention of, 264–266
Organizations, list of industry, 319
Out of the Inkwell, 271, 273, 265
Output
C-library I/O functions, 141–142
transformation of, 64–65

Paik, Nam June, 281
Paint systems, 6, 82–83, 169
boundary position of PAINT, 83
image flipping, 177
interactive, 213–216

Paint Systems (*continued*)
  scrolling, 38–39
  versatility of, 37–38
  zooming in or zooming out, 177
PAL, 14
pal-choice, 184–185
Palette programs. *See* Small palette program, Large palette program
Palette, selection of, 71, 75, 167–168. *See also* Color characteristics
Pal, George, 277
PAL M, 14
Pans, 85, 171
Pascal, 48
Pattern assignments, 186
PC-DOS, 49
Pencil, 63
Persistence of vision, 269
Personal computers. *See* specific subheads
Phantasmatrope, development of, 261
Physical movement, caricaturing, 59
Pinocchio, 275
Pixels, 5-6, 132, 150, 181–184
  addressing in BASIC, 74–75
  aliasing problem, 16–18
  assigning color to, 177–180
  changing bit values of, 159
  fractal, use as, 7
  grid character, production of, 183–184
  palette, selection of, 71, 75
  rectangular, 15
  reflections painted pixel-by-pixel, 207
  square, 15
  tiling patterns, 82–83
Planning the program, 53–65
Plotters, 33
PMAP in BASIC, 86
Point-by-point programming, 76–77
Pointers, 86, 121–122, 143–146
  accessing array elements with, 144
  asterisks indicating variables in C, 111
Polygons, 3-4, 60, 199
  algebraic equations, defined by, 186
  meshes, 199–200
Polyhedron, three-dimensional, 199
Portability, 138, 142
Porter, William S., 267
Praxinoscope, development of, 261
Preprocessor commands, 139
Pre-production, four-step model for, 63
Presets in C, 75–76
Primitives
  defined, 54
  design elegance, 60–61
printf in C, 94–95, 98–101, 136
Production schedules, 62–63
PSET in BASIC, 75–76
Psychovisual research, 12, 207
  sensitivity of eye to changes in hue and saturation, 161
Publishing, graphics use in, 44, 243
PUT retrieval of information in BASIC, 88

Radians, arcs and angles defined in, 81
RAM
  BASIC, access in, 142
  buffer building, 170–171
  hidden surfaces, 204
  in-betweening programs, 193
Raster graphics
  data compression, 18–19
  defined, 2–3
  in-betweening program costs, 193
  NTSC, 9–10
  refresh buffers, 9–10
  resolution, 14–15
Ray tracing, 3-4, 6, 207–211

Realism, future of, 250–251
Real-time animation, 3, 6, 26
 game playing, 247–248
 in-betweening, 192
 interactive systems, 212–213, 216–217
Rectangles
 building blocks, as, 60
 pixels, 15
Recursive functions, operations, 7, 100–103
Recursive in C, 101–103
Reflectance, refractance of light, 204, 207–211
Refresh buffers, 9–10
 double-buffered systems, 41–42
 hidden surfaces, 204
 responsibility of, 171
 run-length encoding, 195
Registration, early methods of, 269
Relational operators in C, 97–98
Removal of hidden surfaces or edges, 203–207
"Renders Everything You Ever Saw" system, 207
Resolution, 24, 67
 fuzzy monitor, 24–25
 lower horizontal, 14–15
 NTSC video monitor, 9–10
 publishing, high level used in, 243
 Richardson, O., 8
return in C, 131
REYES imaging system, 207
RGB color system, 12, 196
R/Greenberg Associates, 228–231
Richardson, O., 8
Richter, Hans, 282
Robot arms, 221–223
Robot control, 220–223
Roget, Peter Mark, 261
ROM-BIOS chips, 141–142, 216–217
Rotoscope, invention of, 265, 270–271
Routines. *See* Subroutines
Run-length encoding, 19, 194–195
Running benchmarks, 149

Sampling theory, 6–8, 15, 17, 201–202, 205–207, 210
Saturation, 11, 12, 161
Saturday morning programs
 cinema, 279
 television, 256–257
Scan-line coherence, 205
Schools, list of computer animation, 306–310
Screen aspect ratio, 81
Scrolling found in paint program, 38–39
SECAM, 14
Self-promotion appearances, advent of, 270
Shaded surfaces, 202, 207–211
Shane, 278
Shape table, 206
short in C. *See* Signed operators
SIGGRAPH, 9, 244
 Graphical Kernel System, development of, 47–48
 interactive graphics, model of, 50–51
Signed operators, 95–100, 148–150
Silent Running, 278
Slide show presentations, 242
Small palette program, 108–111, 123–125, 168, 172, 183–185, 214
Snow White and the Seven Dwarfs, 275
South
 schools, list of computer animation, 310
 studios, list of animation, 302–303
Spatial filtering, 17
Special effects, 255
 development of, 263–264
 live-action feature films, 275–278
Splines, 201

Sports programs, 258, 280–281
  videodisks, use of, 10
Sprites, 38, 217, 251
Squares as building blocks, 60
Stacking combinations of arrays and pointers, 144
Standard error file, 141
Standard formats, 6
Stand, development of animation, 274–275
Static variables in C, 132
Stationary iris matte, invention of, 265
stderr in C, 141
stdin in C, 141
stdout in C, 141
Steamboat Willie, 271
STEP in BASIC, 80–81
Still-frame recorders, 30–33
Storyboards, 63, 228, 242–243
  importance of, 62–63
  transformation of idea into equation, 64
Stringing sets of statements in BASIC, 87–88
Structures in C, 91–93, 139–140, 155–158
  of arrays, 143–146, 163–164, 186, 196
Studios, list of animation, 289–305
Surfaces, reflectance of, 207–211
Sweet, Blanche, 266
switch in C, 113–115, 136

Tantalizing Fly, 271
Technology as hero, notion of, 253–254, 257
Teletext systems, 246–247
Television, 9–14
  advent of, 278–279
  children's programming, 256–257
  commercials on, 280
  micro graphics opportunities, 248–249
  news programs, 258, 280–281
  sports programs, 10, 258, 280–281
Ten Commandments, The, 277
Terry, Paul, 268
Textured surfaces, 207–211
3D images. *See* Three-dimensional images.
Three-dimensional arrays, matrices, 98, 134–135, 188–190, 194
Three-dimensional images, 4–5
  complexity of realistic images, 188
  curved surfaces, 201
  depth cueing, 202
  evolution of, 2
  fractals, 201–202
  hidden surface problem, 203–207
  industrial design, 243–244
  lighting, 209
  polygons, 3–4, 60, 186, 199–200
  rotation, 190
  scaling, 188–190
  two images simultaneously, ability to view any, 187–188
  viewpoints, change of camera, 187–188
  See also Vector graphics; specific subheads
Tiling patterns, 82–83, 179–180
The Time Machine, 277
Top-down method of algorithm development in C, 127–129
Track balls, 28
Track shots, simulation of, 84–85
Translation matrix, 188
Trick photography. *See* Special effects
Tron, 2
Trumbull, Douglas, 278
Turing, Alan, 102
2D images. *See* Two-dimensional images
Two-dimensional images, 2, 4–5, 57–59

graphic packages, 45
mapping, 210–211
music videos, 226
realistic lighting in, 210
rotation in, 190
scaling, 188–190
zooming, 85
See also Raster graphics; specific subheads
Twos complement notation, 149
2001: A Space Odyssey, 278

Unary operator, size of, 147–148
Unix operating system, 48–49, 91
Unsigned **int** in C, 149
Unsigned **long** in C, 149

Value-added resellers, 29–30
Variables in C, 95–100
Variable palette program in C, 106–125
Vector graphics, 2–3, 4–6, 79–80
buffer used in assembling, 187
Gehring, Bo, 236
high-tech look of, 195
in-betweening programs, costs of, 193
monochromatic output, 5
refresh buffers, 9–10
run-length encoding, 195
Vertigo, 277
Vertov, Dziga, 276
Video arcades, 216–219, 247–248
Video conferencing, 242
Videodisks, 10, 33–34
corporate videos, 241–242
interactive programs, 216–219
Video-effects machines, 280–281
Video RAM access, 142
Video recorders
editing, 30
resolution, 14
Videotex, 42, 246–247
Viewports, 190–191
VIEW in BASIC, 85-86
View surface, 61–62
Von Koch, Helge, 7-8
vpage in C, 67

Walt Disney Studios, 272–275
Warner Brothers, 272–273
Warping, image, 177
Weather-maps, 44
Weil, Alex, 225–228
West
schools, list of computer animation, 310
studios, list of animation, 303–304
while in C, 103–106
Whitney, John Sr., 201
Window, 19–20, 83–85
defined, 190–191
nonmoving, definition of, 191
paint program, 38
sprite, 40, 217
Wire frame images, 4, 203
Wollen, Peter, 128
Wood, Natalie, 278
World coordinates, 86

X-rated cartoons, 279–280

Yellow journalism, 263

Z-buffer, 205–207
Zoëtrope device, 261
Zoom technique, 177
frame buffers, 171
IBM BASIC, 84